PROPERTY AND HUMAN RIGHTS IN A GLOBAL CONTEXT

Property as a human rights concern is manifested through its incorporation in international instruments and as a subject of the law through property-related cases considered by international human rights organs. Yet, for the most part, the relationship between property and human rights has been discussed in rather superficial terms, lacking a clear substantive connection or common language. That said, the currents of globalisation have witnessed a new era of interrelation between these two areas of the law, including the emergence of international intellectual property law and the recognition of indigenous claims, which, in fundamental ways, speak to an engagement with human rights law.

This collection starts the conversation between human rights lawyers and property lawyers and explores analytical approaches to the increasing relationship between property and human rights in a global context. The chapters engage with key theoretical and policy debates and range across three main themes: The re evaluation of the public/private divide in the law; the tensions between the market and social justice in development and the balance between the rights of individuals and those of communities. The chapters adopt a global, comparative perspective and engage in case studies from countries including India, Philippines, Brazil, the United States, the United Kingdom and includes various regions of Africa and Europe.

Volume 20: Human Rights Law in Perspective

Human Rights Law in Perspective

General Editor: Colin Harvey
Professor of Human Rights Law
School of Law
Queen's University Belfast

The language of human rights figures prominently in legal and political debates at the national, regional and international levels. In the UK the Human Rights Act 1998 has generated considerable interest in the law of human rights. It will continue to provoke much debate in the legal community and the search for original insights and new materials will intensify.

The aim of this series is to provide a forum for scholarly reflection on all aspects of the law of human rights. The series will encourage work which engages with the theoretical, comparative and international dimensions of human rights law. The primary aim is to publish over time books which offer an insight into human rights law in its contextual setting. The objective is to promote an understanding of the nature and impact of human rights law. The series is inclusive, in the sense that all perspectives in legal scholarship are welcome. It will incorporate the work of new and established scholars.

Human Rights Law in Perspective is not confined to consideration of the UK. It will strive to reflect comparative, regional and international perspectives. Work which focuses on human rights law in other states will therefore be included in this series. The intention is to offer an inclusive intellectual home for significant scholarly contributions to human rights law.

Recent titles in this series

Health and Human Rights
Thérèse Murphy

Discrimination, Equality and the Law
Aileen McColgan

Property and Human Rights in a Global Context
Edited by Ting Xu and Jean Allain

Governing (Through) Rights
Bal Sokhi-Bulley

Gender Equality in Law: Uncovering the Legacies of Czech State Socialism
Barbara Havelkova

For the complete list of titles in this series, see 'Human Rights Law in Perspective' link at www.bloomsburyprofessional.com/uk/series/human-rights-law-in-perspective/

Property and Human Rights in a Global Context

Edited by
Ting Xu
and
Jean Allain

•HART•
PUBLISHING
OXFORD AND PORTLAND, OREGON
2018

Hart Publishing
An imprint of Bloomsbury Publishing Plc

Hart Publishing Ltd
Kemp House
Chawley Park
Cumnor Hill
Oxford OX2 9PH
UK

Bloomsbury Publishing Plc
50 Bedford Square
London
WC1B 3DP
UK

www.hartpub.co.uk
www.bloomsbury.com

Published in North America (US and Canada) by
Hart Publishing
c/o International Specialized Book Services
920 NE 58th Avenue, Suite 300
Portland, OR 97213-3786
USA

www.isbs.com

First published in hardback, 2015
Paperback edition, 2018

British Library Cataloguing-in-Publication Data
A catalogue record for this book is available from the British Library.

ISBN: PB: 978-1-50992-115-7
HB: 978-184946-726-1

Library of Congress Cataloging-in-Publication Data

Property and human rights in a global context / edited by Ting Xu and Jean Allain.
pages cm. – (Human rights law in perspective ; volume 20)

Book originated in a panel "The Engagement between Property and Human Rights in a Global Context" at the 26th World Congress of Philosophy of Law and Social Philosophy, held at the Federal University of Minas Gerais (UFMG), Belo Horizonte, Brazil, in July 2013.—ECIP Preface.

Includes bibliographical references and index.
ISBN 978-1-84946-726-1 (hardback : alk. paper) 1. Right of property—Congresses. 2. Human rights—Congresses. I. Xu, Ting, 1982– editor. II. Allain, Jean, 1965– editor.

K721.5.A6P76 2015 343'.023—dc23
2015032034

Typeset by Compuscript Ltd, Shannon

Preface

The book is a collaborative project. We became interested in exploring the relationship between property and human rights while co-teaching the Contemporary Issues in Property Law Module at the School of Law, Queen's University Belfast. The project then started as a panel we organised on 'The Engagement between Property and Human Rights in a Global Context' in the 26th World Congress of Philosophy of Law and Social Philosophy, held at the Federal University of Minas Gerais (UFMG), Belo Horizonte, Brazil, in July 2013. We wish to acknowledge with thanks, Professor Sally Wheeler, Head of the School of Law at Queen's University, for providing funding for our participation in the Congress.

We wish to thank contributors to that panel, Elena Beltrán, Alison Clarke, Jane Dine, Martin Dumas, Wei Gong and Leonardo Machado Pontes, for making ours a successful and fruitful panel. Shortly after the Congress, this book project took shape and developed with more people engaging with the topic: Tom Allen, David Cowan, Belachew Fikre, Fiona Macmillan, Walters Nsoh, Bruce Wardhaugh, and Sally Wheeler. We thank them for this intellectual engagement and support for the project.

Our collaboration continues through ongoing conversations among the authors and editors, and we are pleased to see that this project has opened a conversation between human rights lawyers and property lawyers, through which we are able to explore analytical approaches to an emerging field of study—the engagement between property (from aspects of real property to intellectual property and cultural property) and human rights at the global/transnational level with its theoretical and policy implications.

While working on this edited volume, Ting received an award from the British Academy International Mobility and Partnership Scheme 2014–17 to fund the project 'Diversifying Ownership of Land?: Communal Property in the UK and China'. With the support of the funding, she has established a research network on the study of communal property, which has now expanded from the initial 15 participants from six universities in the UK and four universities in China to 40 scholars worldwide including several contributors to this book. Several chapters in this volume engage with communal property and its interaction with human rights. Ting wishes to thank the British Academy for its support.

We would like to express special thanks to editors at Hart Publishing, Tom Adams, Emily Braggins, Melanie Hamill, Richard Hart, Sinead

Moloney and Rachel Turner, the general editor of the *Human Rights Law in Perspective* Series, Professor Colin Harvey, and the anonymous reviewer of the proposal for their kind help and support with this book project. We also thank Wei Gong for his help in compiling the bibliography of this collection.

TX and JA
Belfast
June 2015

Contents

List of Contributors

Jean Allain holds the Chair in Public International Law at Queen's University, Belfast and is the Director of its Human Rights Centre. He also holds an Extraordinary Professorship with the Centre of Human Right of the Faculty of Law, University of Pretoria. He received his PhD from the Graduate Institute of International Studies (HEI), University of Geneva. As one of the leading legal scholars on issues of slavery and human exploitation, he has published many books including *The Slavery Conventions* (ed) (2008); *The Legal Understanding of Slavery* (2012); *Slavery in International Law* (2013); and *The Law of Slavery* (2015).

Tom Allen is a Professor of Law at the University of Durham and the Master of Grey College, Durham. He has written *The Right to Property in Commonwealth Constitutions* (2000) and *Property and the Human Rights Act 1998* (2005), as well as a number of articles on different aspects of the right to property in constitutional and human rights law.

Elena Beltrán is Professor of Legal Philosophy at the Department of Public Law and Legal Philosophy, Universidad Autonoma de Madrid, where she teaches Legal and Political Philosophy. She is currently researching on property rights in human bodies. She was Visiting Scholar at the Human Rights Direction in the Council of Europe in Strasbourg; New York University School of Law; Boston College; Institut de Theorie du Droit, Paris X; and London School of Economics. She was Vice Dean of the Law School and Chair of the Committee of Equality in the Universidad Autonoma de Madrid.

Alison Clarke is Emeritus Professor of Law in the School of Law at the University of Surrey. She is a property lawyer with a particular interest in property rights regimes governing access to and use of land and other natural resources and how they operate under different social, cultural and economic conditions. She has taught on comparative law courses in China, France and Germany and has written on a variety of property related topics including comparative property law principles, communal and public property rights, indigenous land rights, diversification of property interests and acquisition of property rights by custom and long use.

Dave Cowan is Professor of Law at the University of Bristol. He is a socio-legal scholar who researches in the fields of housing and social security law and policy. He is a fellow of the Academy of Social Sciences and a former vice Chair of the SLSA.

Martin Dumas studied law and social sciences in Quebec, Oxford, Toronto and London. He served as international labour advisor for the Secretariat of the Commission for Labor Cooperation (2002–2005, Washington DC) before obtaining a PhD in law from the London School of Economics and Political Science in 2010. A Commonwealth Fellow, he has been teaching labour law at Laval University since 2009 and pursuing his research on legal theory, the enforcement of protective laws and the transnational development of consumocratic law. He is the holder, since 2015, of the Marcelle-Mallet Research Chair on Law, Philanthropy and Development.

Belachew Fikre is currently engaged as international consultant for the Support to Justice Sector Project in Nigeria at the United Nations Office on Drugs and Crime and lectures at the National Institute for Legislative Studies (NILS) in Nigeria. He has extensively researched, among others, on Ethiopia's rural land rights issues tracing law and policy developments in the context of successive regime changes in the country. He has in the past undertaken consultancy assignments on Ethiopia's land question for various organisations and holds an LLB from Addis Ababa University and graduate degrees from the Royal Institute of Technology, Sweden, University of Essex, King's College London and his PhD from the University of Surrey, United Kingdom.

Wei Gong is a visiting fellow at the School of Law, Queen's University Belfast. He holds a PhD in Law from Renmin University, China. He is an expert in civil law, especially in property law, tort law, contract law and corporate law. He used to work as a Research Fellow at Asia Research Centre, the London School of Economics on an EU FP7 project on urbanisation in China. He has published several papers on land issues in the process of urbanisation in China.

Fiona Macmillan is Professor of Law at Birkbeck, University of London and Visiting Professor of Law at the University of Roma Tre. Her primary research focus, which has been pursued through a number of interdisciplinary collaborations, is on the relationship between intellectual property and cultural property/heritage. She is the Co-director of the International Society for the History and Theory of Intellectual Property (ISHTIP, www.ishtip.org).

Walters Nsoh is a Lecturer in Law at Birmingham Law School, University of Birmingham. Previously he worked as a Lecturer in Law at Anglia Ruskin University Law School and a Postdoctoral Research Assistant at the University of Dundee Law School. In other earlier work, he contributed to the development of standards on land rights, the environment and extractive industries including forestry across Africa; informed development funds allocation under a realistic strategic development plan for the Widikum local authority in Cameroon; and has also worked as an Intern with the World

Trade Organization (WTO) in Geneva. Dr Nsoh's research and teaching interests relate primarily to the intersection between environmental and property (land) law, and the legal and policy challenges to nature conservation and the sustainable management of natural resources in developed and developing countries. He holds a PhD in Law (University of Surrey), an LLM (Distinction) in Environmental Law & Policy (University of Kent), and a BSc (Hons) in Environmental Science (University of Buea, Cameroon).

Leonardo Machado Pontes is a PhD candidate at 'Centre d'Études Internationales de la Propriété Intellectuelle' (CEIPI), Strasbourg University, France and an International Coordinator of the Brazilian Association of Copyright (Associação Brasileira de Direito de Autor). He holds an LLM in European and International Intellectual Property Law from CEIPI. He has been a fellow scholarship researcher at CAPES in Brazil. He was the second place student category winner of the European Communities Trade Mark Association Award (ECTA) (2014). He has written two books *Creative Commons: problemas jurídicos e estruturais* (Arraes, 2013) and *Direito de autor: a teoria da dicotomia entre a idea e a expressão* (Arraes, 2012).

Bruce Wardhaugh is currently Senior Lecturer in Competition Law at the School of Law, Manchester University. Prior to joining Manchester in January 2015, he was a Lecturer at the Law Schools of Queen's University, Belfast (2012–2014) and Newcastle University (2011–2012). His interests are in Competition Law, International Economic Law and Law and Economics. He has published a monograph and articles in these areas. He holds a PhD and a law degree from the University of Toronto, and an LLM from the University of Amsterdam. He was called to the Bar of British Columbia (Canada) in 1998.

Sally Wheeler is a socio-legal scholar who researches in the area of corporate law and contract law. Particular interests are corporate social responsibility, governance of multinational activity and business ethics. She is a member of the Royal Irish Academy and a former chair of the SLSA. She is Head of the School of Law at Queen's University Belfast.

Ting Xu is Senior Lecturer at the School of Law, University of Sheffield. Before joining Sheffield, she was a Lecturer at the School of Law, Queen's University, Belfast (2012–2015) and a Research Fellow at the London School of Economics (2009–2012) on an interdisciplinary and collaborative European Research Council funded project. She holds an LLB from Sun Yat-sen University and an LLM and PhD from the London School of Economics. Her main research interests are in the fields of law, governance and development; property law; property and human rights in a global context; socio-legal studies; political economy; and Chinese law. She has published a monograph and articles in these areas.

Table of Cases

National Cases

Australia

Cameroon

Canada

India

Philippines

South Africa

United Kingdom

United States of America

International Cases

European Court of Human Rights

Inter-American Court of Human Rights

The African Commission on Human and Peoples' Rights

International Court of Justice

International Centre for Settlement of Investment Disputes (ICSID)

World Trade Organization

United Nations Human Rights Committee

Table of Legislation

INTERNATIONAL INSTRUMENTS

International Human Rights Instruments

Bilateral Investment Treaty

International Labour Organisation

United Nations Educational, Scientific, and Cultural Organisation

International Institute for the Unification of Private Law

WTO

International Instruments

NATIONAL INSTRUMENTS

Ancient Roman Law

Australia

Cameroon

Canada, Québec

Ethiopia

France

Germany

India

Kenya

Philippines

South Africa

Spain

Uganda

United Kingdom

United States of America

Introduction: Property and Human Rights in a Global Context

TING XU AND JEAN ALLAIN*

I. ENGAGING PROPERTY WITH HUMAN RIGHTS: A CLASH OF PARADIGMS?

PROPERTY AS A human rights concern is manifested through its incorporation in many international/transnational instruments, including the Universal Declaration of Human Rights (UDHR, 1948), the European Convention on Human Rights (ECHR, 1950), the African Charter on Human and Peoples' Rights (ACHPR, 1981) and the United Nations Declaration on the Rights of Indigenous Peoples (UNDRIP, 2007). Property-related cases have been considered by the European and the Inter-American Court of Human Rights as well as the African Court on Human and People's Rights. Yet, for the most part, engaging the right to property with human rights entails a clash of paradigms: The former concerns 'the self-regarding impulse towards personal appropriation', whereas the latter engages 'an other-regarding vision of the intrinsic merits of strangers'.[1]

Property is mostly governed by domestic law, while human rights law situates in a different, international, territory. Acceptance of the right to property as a human right is controversial, as it is often argued that protection afforded to property does not really concern rights and entitlements based on claims regarding dignity and equality.[2] As Samuel Moyn points out, 'Not surprisingly, it is probably the right of possession that has been the

* We would like to thank Alison Clarke for her helpful comments on this chapter.

[1] K Gray, 'Land Law and Human Rights' in L Tee (ed), *Land Law: Issues, Debates, Policy* (Portland OR, Willan Publishing, 2002) 211.

[2] This may be more true of common law legal systems than of civil law systems where property is enshrined as a constitutional right. See eg, Art 14(2) of the Basic Law of the Federal Republic of Germany ('Property entails obligations. Its use shall also serve the public good'); Art 42(2) of the Italian Constitution 1948 ('Private ownership is recognized and guaranteed by the law, which determines the manner of acquisition and enjoyment as well as its limits, in order to ensure its social function and to make it accessible to all').

most frequently asserted and doggedly fortified right in world history, albeit typically within legal systems that made no real claim to base entitlement on humanity'.[3] Further, compared to other fundamental rights such as the right to life and the right not to be enslaved, the right to property as a human right 'seems less worthy of protection'.[4] The distinction between property and humanity, alongside the dichotomy between domestic and international or between private and public, leads to the disengagement between property and human rights: these two areas lack shared jurisprudential concerns, substantive connections and a common language. For jurisdictions where the 'rule of law' is well developed and property institutions are fully established, such disengagement between property and human rights is not regarded as a major concern. For example, the Law of Property Act 1925 enacted in the UK 'contains little which could be confused with the positive protection or reinforcement of basic concepts of human freedom, dignity and equality'.[5] As a result, the promoting of the engagement between property and human rights is often conceived as a worthwhile enterprise only for underdeveloped countries, in particular those with a colonial past, or for countries emerging from regimes characterised by misuse of state power and abuse of the rule of law.

Yet, in the context of globalisation, human rights law is increasingly engaging with the core fields of private law such as contract, tort and property, and the boundaries between public and private law are shifting.[6] For example, while the English common law has historically protected private rights such as property rights almost on its own,[7] the passing of the Human Rights Act 1998 makes an important step by directly incorporating the ECHR into UK law.[8] While seminal work has been written on some of these developments,[9] there is still a lack of in-depth examination of the

[3] S Moyn, *The Last Utopia: Human Rights in History*, reprint edn (Cambridge MA, Harvard University Press, 2012).

[4] T Allen, *Property and the Human Rights Act 1998* (Oxford, Hart Publishing, 2005) 1.

[5] Gray (n 1) 210.

[6] See eg, D Friedmann and D Barak-Erez, *Human Rights in Private Law* (Oxford, Hart Publishing, 2001); T Barkhuysen and SD Lindenbergh, *Constitutionalisation of Private Law* (Leiden, Brill, 2006); D Oliver and J Fedtke (eds), *Human Rights and the Private Sphere: A Comparative Study* (London, Routledge, 2007); D Hoffman (ed), *The Impact of the UK Human Rights Act on Private Law* (Cambridge, Cambridge University Press, 2011); G Brüggemeier, AC Ciacchi, G Comandé (eds), *Fundamental Rights and Private Law in the European Union, Vol I A Comparative Overview* (Cambridge, Cambridge University Press, 2010); RP Malloy and M Diamond (eds), *The Public Nature of Private Property* (Surrey, Ashgate Publishing, 2011).

[7] See M Hunt, 'Constitutionalism and the Contractualisation of Government in the United Kingdom' in M Taggart (ed), *The Province of Administrative Law* (Oxford, Hart Publishing, 1997) 21–39.

[8] B Dickson, *Human Right and the UK Supreme Court* (Oxford, Oxford University Press, 2013) 692.

[9] See eg, Allen (n 4); D Rook, *Property Law and Human Rights* (London, Blackstone, 2001); D Cowan, L Fox O'Mahony and N Cobb, *Great Debates in Property Law* (Basingstoke, Palgrave Macmillan, 2012), in particular the chapter on 'Human Rights and Property Law';

relationship between property (especially beyond the traditional forms of property that are tied up with the image of land) and human rights in different social, cultural and political contexts and at the global/transnational level.[10]

The term 'globalisation' refers to 'an aggregate of multifaceted, uneven, often contradictory economic, political, social and cultural processes'.[11] These processes have been galvanised by the rise of new networks of political and economic actors, such as transnational corporations, supranational organisations and non-governmental organisations, bringing about the emergence of a new global culture and, at the same time, the marginalisation of many local cultures.[12] And each of these transformations has been associated with new, newly applied, or newly revised, laws—local, national, transnational and international. As a result, the traditional distinctions between domestic and international and between private and public are no longer sufficient to capture the complexity of a multiplicity of norms emerging in globalisation, cutting across the boundaries of the nation states. More recently, attention has extended to the study of 'global governance', in particular contemporary shifts of power and decision making from nation states to regional, international or transnational sites of governance.[13] These various 'sites' provide potential arenas for both conflict and engagement between property and human rights.

In this collection, we do not propose that the human rights paradigm is the ideal approach to property questions, nor do we focus on the question usually raised in the studies of the interplay of these two fields: 'Are human right and property rights compatible?' Indeed, as Fiona Macmillan argues, 'if everything that seems a good or fair or morally defensible thing automatically becomes a "human right" then every so-called human right is reduced to the symbolic and legal significance of the most banal and the very idea of "human rights" as the unsurpassable moral high ground, the trumps of trumps, disappears'.[14] Instead, we look at the ways in which the process of globalisation has altered the scope or the 'reach capacity' of both fields, transcending some of the entrenched territorial and normative

Dickson, ibid, in particular ch 12 'Property, Education, Elections'; TRG van Banning, *The Human Right to Property* (Antwerp, Intersentia, 2002) and AR Çoban, *Protection of Property Rights within the European Convention on Human Rights* (Surrey, Ashgate, 2004); Gray (n 1).

[10] Some works have examined the interface of intangible property and human rights. eg, T Cottier, J Pauwelyn and EB Bonanomi (eds), *Human Rights and International Trade* (Oxford, Oxford University Press, 2005); CB Graber and M Burri-Nenova (eds), *Intellectual Property and Traditional Cultural Expressions in a Digital Environment* (Cheltenham, Edward Elgar, 2008), in particular Pt 2 'Intellectual Property and Human Rights'.

[11] F Snyder, *Global Economic Networks and Global Legal Pluralism* (Florence, European University Institute, 1999).

[12] ibid, 7–8.

[13] F Snyder, *The EU, the WTO and China: Legal Pluralism and International Trade Regulation* (Oxford, Hart Publishing, 2010).

[14] F Macmillan, 'Human Rights, Cultural property and Intellectual Property: Three Concepts in Search of A Relationship' in Graber and Burri-Nenova (n 10) 73.

boundaries such as local versus global, private versus public, legal versus illegal/extralegal, as well as the shifts in the power relationship between different actors (for example, property owners and non-property owners). These transformations have given new impetus to the emergence of alternative normative frameworks within each area and hybrid normative frameworks that straddle both areas. Indeed, 'dichotomising human and property rights is misleading' (Wardhaugh in chapter 8), for globalisation has galvanised a new era of interface between the two areas, in particular with the emergence of international intellectual property law,[15] the growth of the global market and international trade,[16] and the movements for recognition and protection of indigenous land and resource rights and indigenous culture and customs at the national, transnational and international levels.[17] Developments in these areas point to a need to re-evaluate the engagement between property and human rights beyond the current studies that focus on the national and European contexts.

II. THE CONCEPTS OF PROPERTY

There are different understandings of the concept of property. It could refer to things, relations, or the relations between persons with respect to things.[18] The orthodox view of property speaks to the most cited, classical, liberal concept of private property defined by William Blackstone, as 'the sole and despotic dominion which one man claims and exercises over the external things of the world, in total exclusion of the right of any other individual in the universe'.[19] Such a perception of property as 'exclusive rights of possession, use, and disposition'[20] has been strengthened by the economic analysis of law, which argues that property rights must be 'strong and clear' in order to preserve a well-functioning market and thereby promote economic growth.[21] In such an analysis, the scope of property is reduced to wealth or 'assets'. Accordingly, the purpose of property is limited to promote 'the predictability and certainty of protecting the individual owner's rights of

[15] eg, W Grosheide (ed), *Intellectual Property and Human Rights: A Paradox* (Cheltenham, Edward Elgar, 2010); LR Helfer and GW Austin, *Human Rights and Intellectual Property: Mapping the Global Interface* (Cambridge, Cambridge University Press, 2011).

[16] eg, Cottier, Pauwelyn and Bonanomi (n 10); Graber and Burri-Nenova (n 10).

[17] eg, F Lenzerini, *The Culturalization of Human Rights Law* (Oxford, Oxford University Press, 2014).

[18] SR Munzer, *A Theory of Property* (Cambridge, Cambridge University Press, 1990) 16.

[19] W Blackstone, *Commentaries on the Laws of England, Volume I, Of the Rights of Persons* (Oxford, Clarendon Press, 1766) 2.

[20] R Epstein, *Takings: Private Property and the Power of Eminent Domain* (Cambridge MA, Harvard University Press, 1985) 220.

[21] Ronald Coase is most cited for this proposition. See eg, 'The Problem of Social Cost' (1960) 3 *Journal of Law and Economics* 1.

exclusion and alienation primarily for wealth-maximization purposes'.[22] As a result, other forms of property holding such as communal property, public and open access property have been largely ignored, and common-pool, public and open access resources are increasingly being enclosed by both the market and the state and being transformed into commodities.[23] Property lawyers who endorse this approach are primarily concerned with sustaining a market which allows for the transfer of property, setting aside issues concerning the morality of such a market. In their view, the concept and value of property is tied up with this market. In this way, as Beltrán argues in chapter 5, they conflate two different issues: Acknowledging humans' entitlements to some forms of property or proprietary interests is one thing; allowing the free transfer of some kinds of property on the market is something quite different. That said, the liberal conception of property remains influential in theoretical analysis[24] and has been deeply embedded in many development projects promoted by the World Bank and International Monetary Fund.[25] Furthermore, the liberal conception of property enshrines 'efficiency' but largely ignores 'equality' in the use and allocation of property rights.[26] In so doing, it overlooks the question of who wins and who loses in the process of appropriation and development and the necessity of looking for alternative property regimes and paths of development.

A more sophisticated framework to understand the meaning of property is through the 'bundle of incidents' proposed by Anthony Honoré (see further considerations of this framework in Allain's and Beltrán's chapter in this collection).[27] It should be noted that Honoré's analytical framework is of 'ownership', not of 'property' in the broad sense. As Honoré himself admits, the subject of his analysis is still within the ambit of 'the "liberal" concept of "full" individual ownership',[28] but at the same time, he emphasises that 'the thesis of this essay [must not] be confused with the claim that

[22] KA Carpenter, S Katyal and AR Riley, 'In Defense of Property' (2009) 118 *Yale Law Journal* 1027.

[23] Public property (eg public access to the highway) is not the same as the state property and also different from public ownership. See also Clarke's discussion in s II of ch 1.

[24] See eg, Epstein (n 20); H De Soto, *The Mystery of Capital: Why Capitalism Triumphs in the West and Fails Everywhere Else* (London, Black Swan, 2001); T Bethell, *The Noblest Triumph: Property and Prosperity through the Ages* (New York, St Martin's Press, 1998).

[25] For criticism on this approach, see eg, D Kennedy, 'Some Caution about Property Rights as a Recipe for Economic Development' (2011) 1 *Accounting, Economics, and Law* 1. Available at: www.bepress.com/ael/vol11/iss1/3; R Dyal-Chand, 'Exporting the Ownership Society: A Case Study on the Economic Impact of Property Rights' (2007) 39 *Rutgers Law Journal* 59; M Heller, *The Gridlock Economy: How Too Much Ownership Wrecks Markets, Stops Innovation, and Costs Lives* (New York, Basic Books, 2008).

[26] See eg, Allen's chapter in this volume on the tensions arising from the constitutionalisation of property rights which have fundamental impact on the redistribution of wealth and social justice in India and Philippines.

[27] AM Honoré, 'Ownership' in AG Guest (ed), *Oxford Essays in Jurisprudence (First Series)* (Oxford, Clarendon Press, 1961) 107–47.

[28] ibid, 107.

all systems attach an equal importance to ownership in the full, liberal sense or regard the same things as capable of being owned'.[29] Stephen Munzer contends that the idea of property along the lines proposed by Honoré is not attached to any 'particular economic or cultural data', based on any specific societies, and therefore it allows for variation in terms of 'who may own property, which incidents comprise ownership or other property interests, and which things can be owned'.[30] By focusing on property encompassing relations among people with respect to things, Honoré's analytical framework enables us to observe and describe what kinds of claim-rights, powers, liberties and immunities are involved in these relations.[31] Honoré's conception of ownership is flexible and inclusive, and may be applied to different social settings in a global context.

Honoré's ownership paradigm is particularly useful when dealing with some of the paradoxes concerning what may constitute property and the identities of its owner(s). With the rapid development of science and technology, it is no longer clear what constitutes 'things' and where to draw a line between 'persons' and 'things'.[32] The controversy surrounding property in human bodies is an epitome of such blurred distinctions. Likewise, ambiguity may arise as to who—whether individuals, groups or mankind—may own property. Here, we can employ a distinction drawn by Honoré between 'having a right to' and merely 'having'.[33] This distinction implies that property could mean both rights and interests attached to 'the thing' and 'the thing' in its material form; focusing on the former may help us circumvent the impossible task of exhausting the list of things that may constitute property. Exploring rights and interests extended over the thing also helps to distinguish 'full ownership' from 'limited property rights'.[34] Put another way, having a collection of rights in the 'bundle' over a thing may constitute property, but it does not necessarily amount to full ownership. This is, as Beltrán discusses in this collection, helpful in deciphering the complexity of recognising property in human bodies. Notice, also, that Honoré's approach implies that various persons can have a collection of incidents, and therefore 'it breeds error to assume that some one person has to be *the* owner, then to launch a search for *that* person, and finally to announce the consequences of his or her *ownership*'.[35]

[29] ibid.

[30] Munzer (n 18) 26.

[31] ibid, 27.

[32] See eg, A Pottage and M Mundy (eds), *Law, Anthropology, and the Constitution of the Social: Making Persons and Things* (Cambridge, New York, Cambridge University Press, 2004).

[33] Honoré (n 27) 114.

[34] Munzer (n 18) 23.

[35] ibid, Munzer's comments on Honoré by citing JW Singer, 'The Reliance Interest in Property' (1988) 40 *Stanford Law Review* 611, 637–41.

Honoré's framework allows various persons, who are not necessarily *the* owner, to claim proprietary rights or interests over a thing. This may potentially help to recognise claims made by 'non-property owners', such as indigenous peoples who hold no formal title over their land and cultural resources. Even without formal title, indigenous peoples may nevertheless carry out a duty of care, that is, 'non-owners' fiduciary obligations', toward land and cultural resources, which may be considered as 'a stewardship model of property'.[36] Joseph Singer and others develop Honoré's concept of property, seeing property as social relations, encompassing entitlements and obligations.[37] This view 'honors the legitimate interests of both owners and *nonowners*, in furtherance of various *human and social values*, potentially including nonmarket values' (emphasis added).[38] Such an expansion of the scope of property opens up possibilities of engaging property with humanity.

Honoré's approach to property is not without criticism. For example, James Penner argues that the notion of property as a 'bundle of rights' is 'a kind of deficient concept, whose persistence in the language is to some extent inexplicable'.[39] Penner's concern lies in the fact that it is not clear which of these incidents/rights are essential and can constitute property when grouped together, although Honoré's framework entails that a collection of a certain number of these incidents may amount to property. However, Honoré does rank these incidents and regards the right to possess, that is, 'to have exclusive physical control of a thing', as 'the foundation on which the whole superstructure of ownership rests'.[40] Other incidents such as the right to exclude others, the right to use, the power of alienating, and an immunity from expropriation are considered as 'cardinal features of ownership'.[41] That said, it is not easy to pin down the power to exclude and the power to transfer in property relations concerning resources that are shared or collectively-owned, or resources that are closely linked to personhood or group identity. Indeed, Honoré's conception of property is still closely attached to a model of individual ownership, and it needs to be modified to reinterpret the meaning of 'possession' and to encompass other rights such as the right to access or the right not to be excluded.[42]

[36] Carpenter, Katyal and Riley (n 22). See also Macmillan's chapter in this volume.

[37] JW Singer, *Entitlement: The Paradoxes of Property* (New Haven, Yale University Press, 2000) 61; SR Munzer, 'Property as Social Relations' in SR Munzer (ed), *New Essays in the Legal and Political Theory of Property* (Cambridge, Cambridge University Press, 2001) 36–37.

[38] Carpenter, Katyal and Riley (n 22) 1027.

[39] JE Penner, *The Idea of Property in Law* (Oxford, Clarendon Press, 1997) 1.

[40] Honoré (n 27) 113.

[41] ibid.

[42] See eg, CB Macpherson's famous tensions between property as a right to exclude and property as a right of access. CB Macpherson, 'Capitalism and the Changing Concept of Property' in E Kamenka and RS Neale (eds), *Feudalism, Capitalism and beyond* (London, Edward Arnold, 1975) 105–24.

With modifications, Honoré's framework may be applied to a full spectrum of property—private, communal, state and public. The introduction focuses on communal property, as it has an uneasy relationship with human rights law (see section IV below; see also chapters 1, 2, 10, 11 and 12).

'The commons' is often used interchangeably with 'communal property',[43] and is often seen as a system opposite to private property,[44] and can be defined as 'a diversity of resources or facilities as well as property institutions that involve some aspects of joint owners or access'.[45] The commons links to the question of the manner in which a resource can best be managed. For some people, the commons is often regarded as open to many users without regulation. As a result, each individual exploits the resources to maximise his or her own benefits without thinking about any adverse long-term impact on the resources. Such overuse of resources leads to what Garrett Hardin calls 'the tragedy of the commons' (for some discussions on 'the tragedy of the commons', see Pontes in chapter 6), for 'freedom in a commons brings ruin to all'.[46] To overcome the tragedy of the commons, some solutions are offered, either to reduce the resources to private ownership, or to transfer them into state ownership. However, these solutions neglect the role of cooperation or communal rules in managing shared resources. Furthermore, if the solution is privatisation, and if it goes too far, resources can be underused, leading to what Michael Heller calls, 'the tragedy of the anticommons'.[47] In this situation, too many owners block each other, and diminish possibilities that can lead to innovation.[48]

The term 'the commons' is ambiguous between two types of meaning: The resource itself and the ways in which people utilise the resource. Its meaning also depends on the context. In intellectual property discourse—for example, in 'the digital commons'—it usually refers to open access resources, or open access resource use; whereas in land and environmental discourse, it usually refers to limited access resources, or limited access resource use.[49] The ambiguity of the term 'the commons' is manifested in Hardin's analysis, as he conflates two distinct categories of the commons.

[43] 'Communal property' is a better concept, as it encompasses three important aspects: The resource which is used communally or collectively; the institution of governing the resource; and communal property rights or communal property holdings, when we refer to the rights held by the community.

[44] JB Holder and T Flessas, 'Emerging Commons' (2008) 17 *Social & Legal Studies* 299, 300.

[45] T Dietz et al, 'The Drama of the Commons' in E Ostrom et al (eds), *The Drama of the Commons* (Washington DC, National Academy Press, 2002) 18.

[46] G Hardin, 'The Tragedy of the Commons' (1968) 162 *Science* 1243, 1244.

[47] MA Heller, 'The Tragedy of the Anticommons: Property in the Transition from Marx to Markets' (1998) 111 *Harvard Law Review* (1998) 621.

[48] MA Heller and RS Eisenberg, 'Can Patents Deter Innovation? The Anticommons in Biomedical Research' (1998) 280 *Science* 698; Heller (n 25).

[49] Thanks to Professor Alison Clarke for raising this point.

The first is '*open access* common property', 'where everyone in the world has a right to use the resource, in the sense of a right not to be excluded from it'.[50] Examples given by Hardin—including an unregulated public right of access to Yellowstone Park and an unregulated right for herders to breed in a pasture 'open to all'—can fit into this category and reinforce a link to tragedy. However, Hardin overlooks the second type of commons—'*group access* common property'[51] or '*limited access* common property',[52] where a group of commoners can exclude outsiders but cannot exclude each other within that group. Group access commons can have effective rules of managing resources (see some examples discussed by Clarke, Fikre, Macmillan, Nsoh, and Xu and Gong in this volume), as Elinor Ostrom demonstrates in her work, these common property rules are usually based on trust and mutual reciprocity.[53] The extent to which property may effectively engage with human rights largely depends on the 'reach capacity' of property and whether it is open to embrace diverse forms of property beyond simple private ownership.

III. THE REACH OF PROPERTY

By the early twentieth century, the reach of property and the scope of appropriation were rather limited: The concept of property was tied up with the image of land; the international flow of capital was relatively infrequent; and issues pertinent to property were considered in a domestic context. However, since the second half of the twentieth century, the scope of property has dramatically expanded from land to intangible assets and from the local to the global. As a result, a plethora of treaties, customary norms, arbitral and judicial decisions and soft law instruments have emerged to constitute a new body of law—'international property law', as Sprankling calls it.[54] That said, the expansion of property is circumscribed, as Allen points out in chapter 3, by 'the international convergence on a liberal right to property', which has been largely driven by 'the increased flow of international capital into land'.[55] As such, when the liberal model of property is imposed on the local context, it often leads to the expulsion of non-property owners, who do not hold formal title and rely on customary property rights (see some

[50] A Clarke, 'Creating New Commons: Recognition of Communal Land Rights within a Private Property Framework' (2006) 59 *Current Legal Problems* 319, 322.

[51] Heller (n 25) 34.

[52] Clarke (n 50) 322.

[53] See eg, E Ostrom, *Governing the Commons: The Evolution of Institutions for Collective Action* (Cambridge, Cambridge University Press, 1991).

[54] JG Sprankling, *The International Law of Property* (Oxford, Oxford University Press, 2014).

[55] The flow of finance capital is less visible, as finance capital has no physical locus. See more discussion in ch 9.

examples given by Fibre, Nosh, Xu and Gong in this volume). To tackle this problem, formalising these 'extralegal' or informal property rights may not be the best solution, if—as is generally the case—it is assumed that 'formalising' must mean replacing with individual private property rights. For example, Fikre in chapter 11 examines Ethiopia's decade-old formalisation process that has led to the issuance of holding certificates for over 10 million households. Although the process may enhance tenure security, it may lead to an adjudicatory exercise, acknowledging what already exists on the ground and regularising existing inequities especially in gender relations, rather than correcting them. As a result, the formalisation process may further exacerbate problems of landlessness and inequalities in asset distributions.

Beyond the liberal model of ownership, we need to rethink a number of intricate and complex questions: what (for example, human bodies with strong links to personhood and cultural objects which embody group identity) can constitute property? Who can be property owners? How can property rights be exercised? And to what extent can the property paradigm be stretched? If the narrow, liberal, absolute ownership model remains unchallenged and unchanged in this globalised world, and if privatisation goes too far, global dispossession will become a major problem that threatens human rights.[56] It should be noted that the property paradigm can be employed to tackle dispossession. For example, Allain's chapter engages with the definition of slavery established in international law by utilising a property paradigm, and therefore gives the definition substance, which helps to hold individuals criminally responsible for this extreme manifestation of human exploitation, and affords human rights protection to its victims. However, we need to distinguish the broad conception of property from simple private ownership, and global dispossession is often associated with an individualist and exclusive model of property, as is the case with the unfettered expansion of intellectual property rights. For example, Macmillan argues in chapter 2 that 'it is clear that indigenous peoples and other communities in the global south have been victims of the unauthorised appropriation of their intangible cultural property by private interests through the use of intellectual property rights'.

It is time to rethink the relationship between property, the market and human and social values. The fact that some 'things' may constitute property does not mean that they can be transferred freely on the market; new mechanisms are needed to govern the market to avoid the situation that monopoly power is handed over to a few powerful individuals and companies. Seeking these mechanisms requires us to re-evaluate the concept of property. For example, we often think of property as (consumer) goods transferred on

[56] See S Andreasson, 'Stand and Deliver: Private Property and the Politics of Global Dispossession' (2006) 54 *Political Studies* 3.

the market, but rarely question the processes through which these goods are made and the societal value of these goods. To elaborate on this point, Dumas in chapter 7 gives an example: the sale of a stolen carpet might be tainted with illegality, whereas the sale of a carpet manufactured under illegal working conditions would not normally raise any issues concerning illegality, whether or not the buyer is aware of the manufacturing conditions. As a result, goods produced under conditions that violate the workers' 'fundamental rights' can be offered and sold legally on end markets. Dumas argues that consumer goods embody social meanings and responsibilities, and the societal attributes of goods have important implications for the 'legality' of purchase of goods. He proposes the use of 'consumocratic law', as a new mode of governance and an effective mechanism to tackle violations of labour rights (for example, the use of forced labour or child labour in making goods). In his proposal, production and consumption processes are linked together in ways that rehabilitate morality in the operation of markets.

Alternative concepts of property are proposed in this volume. For example, Macmillan's chapter focuses on the question of whether we need a concept of 'cultural property' in order to ensure the protection of culture and cultural heritage, including the cultural heritage of indigenous peoples. It starts from the proposition that cultural heritage must be conceptualised as implicating community rights, transcending the public/private boundaries. It then argues that the community interests in cultural heritage are, by their nature, under threat from the forms of private property that are considered by law to be rivalrous individual rights.[57] To tackle this threat, the chapter analyses the utility of proposals for a stewardship form of property rights[58] and for community property rights; the concept of property needs to be separated from the traditional, narrow model and to embrace the idea of 'membership'. Because indigenous cultural heritage is associated with group identity, the idea of membership requires the inclusion of the right of access, or at least the right not to be excluded, in a broad and flexible bundle of interests. In terms of property in human bodies, as Beltrán argues in chapter 5, recognising property in the human body does not contradict dignity and human rights; rather, it strengthens the autonomy of people and their control over their own bodies, which are crucial elements constituting dignity and human rights. Pontes, in chapter 6, also gives a similar argument that property permits self-preservation and sustains human flourishing; by engaging property with humanity, appropriation becomes part of humanisation.

[57] See also F Macmillan, 'The Protection of Cultural Heritage: Common Heritage of Humankind, National Cultural 'Patrimony' or Private Property?' (2013) 64 *Northern Ireland Legal Quarterly* 351; see also Macmillan (n 14).

[58] See, eg, Carpenter, Katyal and Riley (n 22).

Apart from the inclusion of human and social values in the conception of property, the role of the natural environment has been increasingly recognised in valuation of land that has been expropriated. Nsoh in chapter 12 argues that the natural environment provides vital ecosystem services, which helps to re-evaluate the question as to what amounts to 'just and equitable' compensation that has given rise to litigation under the ECHR. He challenges the current Cameroonian position by which, he says, the existing set of interests and values considered in the payment of compensation do not reflect the true value of the land expropriated. He argues that although not recognised as legal rights under the expropriation regime, customary rights remain part of the land tenure system in Cameroon. The concept of ecosystem services may provide a basis of getting beyond the narrow and artificially created set of 'commercial' interests and market values attributed to only a few of the uses and interest in land. It may also help to recognise the different interests that contribute to the value of the land to the customary owners.

Our discussion in this section echoes our suggestion made above that Honoré's bundle of rights needs to be broadened so as to encompass diverse interests and values—human, social, and environmental—beyond narrow commercial interests and market values. An effective engagement between property and human rights depends on the re-conception of property, for in this globalised world, 'true freedom ... is born of sharing, not possessing. One can't really be free if one is unable to share, empathize with, and embrace others'.[59]

IV. THE REACH OF HUMAN RIGHTS

The right to property was perceived as a natural right in the seventeenth and eighteenth centuries by Hugo Grotius, John Locke and others in Europe, asserting 'the theory that universal property rights could arise independently of the state'.[60] This view persisted into the formulations of the right to property in the American Declaration of Independence (1776, Paragraph 2) and the French Declaration of the Rights of Man and of the Citizen (1789, Article 2), in which the right is vested with private owners against state expropriation.[61] Whilst in the period leading up to the twentieth century regulation of property was dominated by domestic laws,[62] the natural right to property was 'revived in the post-World War II era as a part of the

[59] J Rifkin, *The Age of Access: The New Culture of Hypercapitalism, Where All of Life is a Paid-for Experience*, (New York, JP Tarcher/Putnam, 2000) 264.
[60] Sprankling (n 54) 6.
[61] ibid, 6–7.
[62] ibid, 8.

international human rights movement'[63] and the increase in the number and variety of countries adopting constitutional rights to property.

Globalisation has galvanised the international reach of human rights especially when considering issues concerning the protection of the right to property in expropriation, which is no longer an issue that may only be considered at the domestic level. Non-state actors not only increasingly become the victims of expropriation, but also beneficiaries that are exercising the power to expropriate property. The rise of 'hidden expropriation' (see Xu and Gong in chapter 10) involves different interests, tensions and conflicts whether at the local, regional or global levels. The lack of a level playing field between competing claimants calls for strengthening the role of the international community and involving non-state actors in establishing global standards and rules to redress those imbalances, taking into account marginalised groups such as minorities and indigenous peoples.[64] Employing the human rights approach has been such an endeavour. Yet in contrast to the recognition of individual property rights in international human rights instruments, treating communal property rights as an actual fundamental human right is highly contentious. Xu and Gong in chapter 10 survey the emerging human rights protection of communal property rights and re-evaluate the content and scope of property rights, powers to expropriate, the legitimacy of expropriation, the state obligations toward property owners, compensation standards, and so on. The global reach of human rights also enables non-state actors—including transnational corporations, other business enterprises and foreign investors—to have a responsibility to respect human rights and legitimate tenure rights (see chapter 9). That said, the reach of the international human rights regime to responsibilise transnational corporations and other business enterprises may be limited, as the motivations of corporate actors to adopt responsibilities posed by the human rights regimes, such as the UN Principles for Responsible Investment and the Guiding Principles on Human Rights, are largely driven by external factors, like establishing a 'business case' for making greater profits (chapter 9).

An emphasis on the global reach of human rights does not mean that we should ignore multi-cultural 'relativism'[65] or the local contexts. Instead, the global reach of human rights interacts with the local context and may empower proprietary claims made by local actors. Human rights protection of communal property rights has already been extended to communities

[63] ibid, 8. See also Xu and Gong in ch 10.

[64] See T Xu, 'Hidden Expropriation in Globalisation and Soft Law Protection of Communal Property Rights' in B Hoops, E Marais, L Verstappen, H Mostert and J Sluysmans (eds), *Rethinking Expropriation Law: The Context, Criteria and Consequences of Expropriation Law* (The Hague NL, Boom/Eleven; Cape Town, RSA, Juta, 2015 forthcoming).

[65] See eg, Lenzerini (n 17).

which embody racial, ethnic or cultural identity such as indigenous peoples. Clarke in chapter 1 argues that such protection should also be extended to unincorporated communities defined solely by locality, that is, to protect customary use of local resources by local communities even where the community has no separate racial, ethnic or cultural identity. This argument speaks to the need to protect 'group access common property', discussed above, as a regime where a group of users manage resources collectively. Such a property regime is both exclusive and inclusive in the sense that it excludes outsiders, but at the same time, embraces insiders of that group so that each member of the community regards himself/herself as entitled to use the resource in certain ways in association with other members of the community. Clarke argues that communal resource use of this kind should be the subject of human rights protection of the same kind as that afforded to resource use by private individuals, so that whenever a local community has a customary relationship with the resources it utilises, the state recognises that relationship as proprietary and gives it the same level of protection as private property rights. A human right of this kind, Clarke concludes, would oblige the state to recognise that in certain conditions, norms of collective resource use evolved by communities give rise to legally enforceable property rights held by the community itself in its own right, distinct from and in addition to the individual right that each member of the community acquires to use the resource in common with the other members of the community.

Yet the global reach of human rights should not be overstated, as it can be restricted by the narrow, liberal 'absolute ownership' model. Cowan and Wheeler point out the limits of the UN Guiding Principles on Business and Human Rights: they may well regulate the flow of productive capital and hold extraction and garment industries responsible for activities of overexploiting natural resources, but they are less powerful when dealing with the flow of finance capital. The shifts in the role of the neo-liberal state and political economy further strengthen the role of finance capital, which has begun to change the identify of (local) UK social housing as providing affordable accommodation to households in need. As a result, security of tenure has been weakened, and exclusions from social housing have been generated. More perplexing examples can also be found in regimes of protecting cultural property or cultural heritage that 'the power of the intellectual property system to trump community rights to cultural property is often advanced and, when necessary defended, as an exercise of human rights' (Macmillan in chapter 2). To effectively engage human rights with the right to property, human rights protection for property ought to extend beyond what is categorised as 'property' in the liberal, absolute ownership model.

V. STRUCTURE OF THE BOOK

This collection of essays provides a timely opportunity for examining important theoretical debates and policy issues in an emerging field of study—the engagement between property (from aspects of real property to intellectual property and cultural property) and human rights at the global/transnational level. It starts the conversation between human rights lawyers and property lawyers and explores analytical approaches to the increasing interaction between the two fields. The chapters range across three main themes which also highlight the key theoretical and policy debates in the studies of the engagement between property and human rights: the re-evaluation of the public/private distinction in the law; the tensions between equality (social justice and human values) and efficiency (the market approach) in economic and social development; and the balance between the rights of individuals and of communities. In so doing, the studies adopt a global and comparative perspective by looking at case studies that highlight the most recent development in the engagement between property and human rights in a wide range of countries including India, Philippines, the United States, the United Kingdom and in regions of Africa and Europe.

Part One

Shifts in the Public–Private Divide

1

Property, Human Rights and Communities

ALISON CLARKE

I. INTRODUCTION

HUMAN RIGHTS LAW has an uneasy relationship with property. The protection of property rights against the state can be seen as fundamental to the freedom of the individual and the maintenance of the rule of law. From another view it reinforces the grip on power and privilege held by the property-haves over the property-have-nots. Modern human rights law, at both the international and the national constitutional level, struggles to reconcile these opposing views.[1] This chapter is concerned with a complicating factor in achieving this reconciliation, which is that property rights holders are not necessarily private individuals. Whilst humans sometimes utilise resources individually for their own private benefit, at other times they organise themselves into communities to utilise them collectively, either for their collective benefit or for the better realisation of benefit for their members. How far should human rights protection extend beyond the relationships humans have on an individual basis with the resources they use? Should it also extend to the relationships they have as communities with the resources they use collectively?

II. RESOURCES COLLECTIVELY USED BY COMMUNITIES

We are concerned here with land and other natural resources,[2] and with unincorporated communities defined by their locality. Once a community

[1] See generally T Allen, 'Compensation for Property under the European Convention on Human Rights' (2006–2007) 28 *Michigan Journal of International Law* 287; TRG van Banning, *The Human Right to Property* (Oxford, Intersentia, 2002); H Mostert, *The Constitutional Protection and Regulation of Property and its Influence on the Reform of Private Law and Landownership in South Africa and Germany* (Berlin, Springer, 2002).

[2] Primarily land and water resources, whether in their natural state or as adapted by human intervention.

becomes incorporated it becomes a legal person and, as we see later, different human rights considerations arise. Also, we are concerned only with communal resource use which is exclusive of outsiders, in the sense that each member of the community regards herself as entitled to use the resource in a particular way[3] in common with other members of the group and to prevent non-members from doing so. This exclusivity is important: it is what distinguishes communal resource rights from public resource rights such as public rights of way or the *allemansrätt* access rights recognised in much of Europe and Scandinavia.[4] As far as exclusive communal resource use is concerned, the exclusive use by the community may be explicitly protected by the state, in which case the community can be said (relatively uncontroversially) to have a communal property right in the resource. Alternatively, but equally significantly from a human rights perspective, exclusive communal use may be customary but not, or not yet, regarded by the state as proprietary.

III. COMMUNITIES DEFINED BY LOCALITY

Some of these resource sharing communities also have a common racial, ethnic or cultural identity, or a system of shared values, which sets them apart from their neighbours. We are primarily although not exclusively concerned with those which do not, but which do have an identity defined by reference to locality in the sense considered below. The object of this exercise is to consider whether these local communities should have human rights protection in respect of the resources they utilise collectively *simply by virtue of their local identity*, and not by virtue of any special consideration that should be given to them because of the indigenous or minority status of the community, or because their resource use is integral to the cultural identity of the community.

The justifications for protecting the communal property rights of communities who have a cultural identity that separates them from their neighbours, or from the dominant ethnic and cultural groups within a state, are primarily based on ideas of protecting cultural identity, removing racial and ethnic

3 The use might be so extensive as to amount to full ownership or it may be more limited, for example drawing water from a particular source for personal or agricultural use.

4 The Swedish *allemansrätt* is a right for any person 'to use the property of others, land and water, primarily by travelling over it, at least by foot, and to stay there for a short time' but subject to responsibilities to the landowner and the environment encapsulated in the phrase 'Don't disturb—don't destroy': see further A Sténs and C Sandström, 'Divergent Interests and Ideas around Property Rights: The Case of Berry Harvesting in Sweden' (2012) *Forest Policy and Economics* 56, where it is discussed in relation to foraging rights. For an appraisal of similar rights in England and Wales, see J Lee and S Garikipati, 'Negotiating the Non-negotiable: British Foraging Law in Theory and Practice' (2011) *Journal of Environmental Law* 415. Public access and resource rights such as these may also need to be brought within the human rights equation, but again they raise different issues and are not considered here.

discrimination, and/or reversing the effects of past and present injustices to minority, disadvantaged or oppressed communities. If we separate off those justifications, are we left with additional justifications that depend solely on ideas of protecting local community resource use for its own sake, either as an independent good in its own right or in order to achieve fairness of treatment between different patterns of resource use?

There are a number of situations in which this question assumes importance. First, it must be appreciated that there are local communities who utilise resources collectively who have no cultural identity separating them from their neighbours. Arguments based on preservation of distinctive culture are irrelevant for these groups: What is at issue is protection of their resource use in its own right. A clear case would be the local inhabitants who hold town and village green recreational rights in England and Wales, an example we return to later. On the other hand there are other local resource-sharing communities who do have a distinct cultural identity but do not fall within any of the recognised categories of peoples who currently attract human rights protection. For example, the international law protection for property rights of communities provided by the United Nations Declaration on the Rights of Indigenous Peoples (UNDRIP)[5] protects indigenous peoples only. It is disputed whether 'indigenous' for these purposes extends beyond peoples whose cultures predated invasion or colonialism[6] to all self-identifying groups with a distinctive culture who have experienced 'subjugation, marginalisation, dispossession, exclusion or discrimination'.[7] Nevertheless on any definition there are arguably many culturally distinct groups with strong claims to protection of their land rights which fall outside this definition.[8] In any event it is not obvious that the kind of protection that UNDRIP provides for indigenous peoples should necessarily be extended in full to all of them, even if there was the political will to do so. Not all cultures are necessarily deserving of human rights protection: Consider the example provided by James Griffin of the Boers in apartheid South

[5] Declaration on the Rights of Indigenous Peoples, GA Res 61/295, UN Doc A/RES/47/1 (2007).

[6] The only groups covered by the often quoted definition provided by UN Special Rapporteur M Cobo, *Study of the Problem of Discrimination Against Indigenous Populations* E/CN.4/Sub.2/1886/7/Add.4, para 375.

[7] C Baldwin and C Morel, 'Rights of Indigenous Peoples in Litigation' in S Allen and A Xanthaki (eds), *Reflections on the UN Declaration on the Rights of Indigenous Peoples* (Oxford, Hart Publishing, 2011) 132–38.

[8] eg, the inhabitants of the Chagos Islands evicted by the UK government from their lands between 1967 and 1973 so that the islands could be used for defence purposes by the United States government: *Chagos Islanders v United Kingdom* (35622/04) (2013) 56 EHRR SE15 and S Allen, 'Looking Beyond the *Bancoult* Cases: International Law and the Prospect of Resettling the Chagos Islands' (2007) 7 *Human Rights Law Review* 441, 469–475. See also the Latin American examples given by TT Ankersen and TK Ruppert, 'Defending the Polygon: the Emerging Human Right to Communal Property' (2006) 59 *Oklahoma Law Review* 681.

Africa.[9] Equally, the full range of protection given to indigenous peoples is not necessarily appropriate for all disadvantaged groups. People living in 'illegal' settlements all over the world do not necessarily want protection and preservation of any distinctive culture they may have evolved to enable them to exist in intolerable conditions. They do, however, want their usage of local resources to be respected and protected by law, whether the usage is on an individual basis or a collective basis.[10]

Finally, there are collective resource users who might be able to claim protection for their resource usage on the basis that it is integral to their culture, but might also want to claim that the resource use itself is of a kind that merits protection in its own right, regardless of the identity of the rights-holder. Pastoralist resource use provides an important example. In some regions of the world pastoralists are fundamentally culturally different from sedentarists, but in others the cultural difference subsists in, or arises out of, no more than their approach to resource use. The question of human rights protection for pastoralists' collective resource use is therefore important not just because of its relevance to the protection of the cultural identity of distinct pastoralist communities. Its prime significance is for the argument that pastoralism and sedentarism present equally viable approaches to resource use and, where both are practised, legal systems should not favour one over the other.[11]

IV. COLLECTIVE RESOURCE USE BY COMMUNITIES

This leads on to one more clarification that needs to be made here. Most resource utilising communities, whether or not culturally distinct, use only some of their resources collectively. The rest of their resources may be loosely regarded as community assets but will be allocated to individuals or individual families on a more or less private property basis, perhaps subject only to a prohibition against alienation out of the community. *Mabo v Queensland (No 2)*[12] which established the recognition and protection of native title for indigenous peoples in Australia, concerned this kind of resource use, and some (but not all) pastoralists groups use their resources in this way. Alternatively, resources which are not used collectively may not be regarded as community assets at all. In other words, the community as such may have no proprietorial role or function in relation to any of its members' resources beyond those that are used collectively. This is

[9] J Griffin, *On Human Rights* (Oxford, Oxford University Press, 2008) 267.

[10] For other reasons not to extend indigenous rights protection to other minority groups see W Kymlicka, 'Beyond the Indigenous/Minority Dichotomy?' in Allen and Xanthaki (n 7).

[11] J Gilbert, 'Nomadic Territories: A Human Rights Approach to Nomadic Peoples' Land Rights' (2007) 7 *Human Rights Law Review* 681, 695.

[12] *Mabo v Queensland (No 2)* [1992] HCA 23.

characteristic of some other pastoralist or semi-pastoralist groups, and of many of the recreational and agricultural commons and collective irrigation systems referred to below. Those who use, for example, a grazing common collectively, whether nomadically or sedentarily, may nevertheless each privately own their own homes or farms and the animals they pasture on the common. At the international and national level, human rights protection for resource use by culturally distinct indigenous, minority or disadvantaged communities usually encompasses all aspects of the resource use patterns adhered to by the community and its members, whether they are collective or individual.

The terms 'communal property' or 'communal tenure' are sometimes, confusingly, used as blanket terms to cover the whole of that mix of communal and individual resource use adopted by a local community and its members.[13] 'Communal property' in that sense is not the area of concern here.[14] The question at issue is the narrower, or at least different, one of whether the collective resource use of a local community should be given the same human rights protection as individual resource use by an individual human being, regardless of any cultural distinctiveness or disadvantaged status of the community.

V. INDETERMINATE AND DETERMINATE COMMUNITIES

Our focus then is on local resource-sharing communities who do not have a distinct cultural identity, or whose cultural identity is irrelevant for present purposes, and we are concerned only with their collective resource use, in other words with the resources the community uses collectively, not with the resources which members of the community may use on an individual basis.

These resource-sharing communities can usefully be put into two categories. In the first, membership of the community is loosely defined by reference to locality or neighbourhood, so anyone 'of' or 'belonging' to that locality/neighbourhood is entitled to use the resource. These communities may be called 'indeterminate' communities. The indeterminacy relates to the membership rather than to the nature of the use, which is often highly specific. Membership of such a community is usually fluctuating and in the

[13] Ankersen and Ruppert (n 8) use 'communal property' in this way. They say: 'Our use of the term "communal property" simply means that the Western legal system's recognition of a title or property right is not specific to an individual but to a defined group of individuals. The property rights assigned by those within the group may run the gamut from systems that assign extensive land rights to individuals over specific parcels (virtually making the individual the "owner" of the parcel) to systems in which individuals have little or no rights to a specific land area' (ibid fn 78 at 698). The question they address is therefore different from the one at issue here.

[14] And the term is not used here in that sense, but as meaning the collective resource use of a community.

normal course of events no-one would be concerned to draw up a definitive list or be concerned with borderline cases. The resources used tend to be of a nature that can tolerate fluctuations in the level of use by the community, some degree of use by non-members and a low level of regulation. A good example is the use of land for recreational purposes by a local community, such as the town and village green rights in England and Wales already noted. These rights are ancient communal proprietary rights of inhabitants of a locality to use land designated as a town or village green for 'lawful sports and pastimes', recently reaffirmed by statute.[15] The community of resource users is characteristic of one of the types of resource-sharing community noted above, in that the members of the community share nothing in common other than the shared resource and a local identity. There are other examples of such communities. A local community may have a right to use a local water source such as a well or stream, for example. Inhabitants of the locality may be happy that anyone loosely 'belonging' to or even visiting the neighbourhood draws water from it, but would feel that their rights were being infringed if, say, a tanker arrived to draw water to take it to supply a nearby city or a water bottling plant.

In the second category, in what may be called 'determinate' communities, membership is more strictly limited to specific categories of local people so that precise identification of the members at any one time is possible. This kind of resource use tends to involve extraction from a rivalrous resource, and the obvious examples are communal grazing lands or fishing grounds or irrigation systems. In small and isolated communities anyone 'belonging' to the locality of neighbourhood may be entitled to graze their animals, to fish or to irrigate their land. In other cases, where pressure on the resource is greater and there is a greater need to distinguish members from non-members, membership may be confined to those who own or inhabit or cultivate specified neighbouring land, or to tightly circumscribed ethnic, family or kinship groups. The communities whose enduring communal resource use is recorded on the Common Pool Resource database set up by Elinor Ostrom[16] mostly come within this category. Other well documented examples cover a wide range of geographic locations and land usages: alpine

[15] The Commons Registration Act 1965 and the Commons Act 2006. The mechanism for recognition of this statutory right is that inhabitants of a locality or neighbourhood who have used any land, whether publicly or privately owned, for 'lawful sports and pastimes' for at least 20 years can apply to have the land registered as a 'town or village green'. Registration of the land as a town or village green gives the local inhabitants the right to use it indefinitely for any recreational purposes: see further A Clarke, 'Land Titling and Communal Property' in W Barr (ed), *Modern Studies in Property Law: Volume 8* (Oxford, Hart Publishing, 2015) 215–31.

[16] Now held by the University of Arizona's Centre for the Study of Institutional Diversity. For further details see M Cox, G Arnold and SV Tomás, 'A Review of Design Principles for Community-based Natural Resource Management' (2010) 15 *Ecology and Society* 38, and A Clarke, 'How Property Works: The Complex World View' (2013) *Nottingham Law Journal* 143, 14950.

commons in Austria and Switzerland,[17] irrigation communities in South India,[18] *iriae* commons in Japan,[19] agricultural commons in England and Wales,[20] and residential communities all over the world who share communal areas in residential developments.[21]

The difference between the two categories therefore lies in the degree of exclusivity and the degree of elasticity in the membership. Partly because of the high level of elasticity and indeterminacy in their membership, indeterminate communities are less likely to evolve management structures in advance of a threat to the resource use, and the management structures they do develop are less likely to involve active participation by all members. Determinate communities, on the other hand, usually need to evolve complex resource sharing arrangements between themselves in order to survive at all, and these will tend to include decision-making processes. This has implications for the ease with which the community is able to engage with the outside world.

One common factor shared by these two categories is however locality. Both categories of community are 'local' in the sense that the members of the community live or work in or have some other strong link with a particular locality and they utilise resources collectively, usually but not necessarily resources in the same locality.[22]

VI. SCOPE OF HUMAN RIGHTS TO PROPERTY

The question at issue is therefore whether local communities of these kinds should have human rights protection in respect of their collective resource use. This raises two preliminary issues. First, a distinction needs to be made between rights of the community as such, and rights of the individual members of the community. There is no great difficulty in ascribing human rights to individuals in respect of the resources which the individual uses in

[17] H van Gils, G Siegl and RM Bennett, 'The Living Commons of West Tyrol, Austria: Lessons for Land Policy and Land Administration' (2014) 38 *Land Use Policy* 16; GG Stevenson, *Common Property Economics: A General Theory and Land Use Applications* (Cambridge, Cambridge University Press, 1991), a case study on Swiss Alpine meadows.

[18] P Pardhan, 'Irrigation and Cooperation: An Empirical Analysis of 48 Irrigation Communities in South India' (2000) 48 *Economic Development and Cultural Change* 847.

[19] T Suzuki, 'Custom and Legal Theory of *Iriai* in Japan' in T Murota and K Takeshita (eds), *Local Commons and Democratic Environmental Governance* (Tokyo, United Nations University Press, 2013); MA McKean, 'Management of Traditional Common Lands (*Iriaichi*) in Japan' in DW Bromley (ed), *Making the Commons Work: Theory, Practice, and Policy* (San Francisco, Institute for Contemporary Studies, 1992).

[20] Also now regulated by the Commons Registration Act 1965 and the Commons Act 2006: Clarke (n 15).

[21] S Blandy, 'Collective Property: Owning and Sharing Residential Space' in N Hopkins (ed), *Modern Studies in Property Law: Volume 7* (Oxford, Hart Publishing, 2013).

[22] Local fishing communities, for example, may communally utilise fishing grounds elsewhere but still legitimately be regarded as local resource-sharing communities.

common with others, and indeed this is expressly provided by Article 17(1) of the Universal Declaration of Human Rights adopted in 1948: 'Everyone has the right to own property alone *as well as in association with others*.'[23] The matter for concern here is whether the community as such has rights in the resources it uses collectively which are greater than, or different from, the sum of the rights of its individual members. These would be collective rights on the lines of the rights of *peoples* to self-determination and to freedom from deprivation of means of subsistence enshrined in Articles 1 of the International Covenant on Civil and Political Rights and the International Covenant on Economic, Social and Cultural Rights.[24] We return to this point later.

Second, as far as human rights to property are concerned, three types of human rights protection may be distinguished for present purposes. A human right to property may consist of a right to be protected by the state against violation of recognised property rights. This is the kind of human rights protection afforded by Article 1 Protocol 1 of the European Convention on Human Rights and Freedoms. Many constitutional human rights provisions such as Article 14(1) of the German Constitution (the *Grundgesetz*), the Takings Clause of the United States Federal Constitution[25] and section 25(1) of the Constitution of South Africa[26] provide similar protection.

A second type of human right to property may consist of just that—a human right that the state should provide the rights-holder with the resources it needs to flourish, mandating a form of distributive justice. The human right to water recognised by UN Resolution 64/292 2010[27] encompasses such a right. It 'entitles everyone to sufficient, safe, acceptable, physically accessible and affordable water for personal and domestic uses.'[28]

[23] See also Art 27 of the International Covenant on Civil and Political Rights adopted by the United Nations General Assembly on 16 December 1966, and in force from 23 March 1976: 'In those States in which ethnic, religious or linguistic minorities exist, *persons belonging to such minorities shall not be denied the right, in community with the other members of their group*, to enjoy their own culture, to profess and practise their own religion, or to use their own language' (emphasis added). It is accepted that this confers only an individual right, not a right for the community as such: see D Misiedjan and J Gupta, 'Indigenous Communities: Analyzing Their Right to Water under Different International Legal Regimes' (2014) 10 *Utrecht Law Review* 77, 81.

[24] Whilst these are clearly collective rights, the complaints procedure under ICCPR is available only to individuals: see further Misiedjan and Gupta, ibid 80.

[25] Clause 7 of the Fifth Amendment to the United States Constitution, illuminatingly compared with the German constitutional provision in GS Alexander, 'Property as a Fundamental Constitutional Right? The German Example' (2003) 88 *Cornell Law Review* 733.

[26] Mostert (n 1).

[27] Resolution on Human Right to Water and Sanitation (UN General Assembly Resolution A/64/292, 28 July 2010), available on www.un.org/News/Press/docs/2010/ga10967.doc.htm. See generally Misiedjan and Gupta (n 23) and IT Winkler, *The Human Right to Water: Significance, Legal Status and Implications for Water Allocation* (Oxford, Hart Publishing, 2012).

[28] Para 2 of General Comment No 15 (2002) E/C.12/2002/11, 20 January 2003, which describes the normative content of the right.

This includes 'freedoms', which are essentially human rights of the first kind, consisting of 'the right to *maintain* access to existing water supplies necessary for the right to water, and the right to be free from interference, such as the right to be free from arbitrary disconnections or contamination of water supplies' (emphasis added).[29] However, the distinctive feature of the human right to water is the 'entitlements.' These are positive distributive rights: 'the right *to* a system of water supply and management that provides equality of opportunity for people to enjoy the right to water' (emphasis added).[30] States are obliged not only to respect and protect pre-existing access to water but also to fulfil the right by providing access to water where no adequate access exists.[31] Although human rights to property of this second type are highly relevant to communities' resource use they raise separate issues because of their strong distributive element and they are not considered here.

The third type of human right to property is, however, central. This is a right that, whenever there is a customary relationship between people and the resources they utilise, the state respects and protects that relationship as proprietary and accords it the same level of protection as formally created property rights. This kind of human right is conferred on indigenous peoples by UNDRIP.[32] A human right of this third kind for all local communities would impose two obligations on states. The first would be to recognise that norms of collective resource use evolved by communities give rise to legally enforceable property rights, even where the pattern of resource use does not resemble conventional property rights recognised by the state,[33] and even where those resources are subject to pre-existing property rights held by others. The second would be to put these distinctive property rights (both to collective resource use and to interdependent individual resource use) on the same footing as other property rights recognised by the state. National laws in many states do, in effect, give proprietary effect to customary collective resource rights in these ways. It may be done to achieve one or more of a range of objectives, including the recognition of the customary resource rights of their indigenous peoples, or the reversal of the effects of past racially discriminatory laws and policies, or the preservation of the cultural identity of any culturally distinct group, whether indigenous or not. It may also be done to preserve historically important or environmentally

[29] ibid, para 10.
[30] ibid.
[31] ibid Pt III.
[32] Declaration on the Rights of Indigenous Peoples (2007), in particular Art 26 but see also Arts 8(b), 10, 20, 27–29 and 32.
[33] In other words, the legal system may not refuse to categorise the rights claimed by the community as proprietary on *numerus clausus* grounds, ie on the basis that the rights claimed do not have the proprietary characteristics normally required under that system (eg certainty of physical extent, clear excludability or alienability). Until the recognition of native title, this was a barrier to the recognition of indigenous land rights in Australia: *Milirrpum v Nabalco Property Ltd* [1971] 17 FLR 141.

successful resource use patterns.[34] The questions at issue here are whether communities have a human right to *require* the state to recognise and protect their customary collective resource use in this way, and if they do, whether the human right extends to all communities defined by reference to the common locality of their members, not just communities which are culturally distinct and indigenous or disadvantaged.

The notion of a community holding a collective human right to property of the first or third kind is problematic in many respects. The first concerns the political acceptability of communal property rights. Traditionally there have been doubts as to the viability of communal property rights at all, on social, economic and practical grounds. These are addressed briefly in Section G, where the particular relationship between communal property rights and customary use is also explored. Second, equally strong doubts have been expressed over whether it is coherent or morally justifiable to recognise communities as rights-holders at all, and (a quite different question) whether they can properly be regarded as holders of human rights. These issues, which are considered in Section VIII, lead into the central issue of whether communities do or should have human rights to property, as opposed to other human rights. It is argued in Section IX that even if there are difficulties in recognising communities as holders of all kinds of human rights, it is nevertheless justifiable to confer on local communities human rights to property of the first and third kind, and that these justifications extend to all local communities, not only those whose relationship with the resources they use is intrinsic to the culture identity of the community. Finally Section X briefly sketches out the obligations that would have to be imposed on a state to ensure that it adequately respects and protects local communities' human rights to property of the first and third kind.

VII. COMMUNAL PROPERTY RIGHTS AND CUSTOMARY USE

The common law and most other legal systems have always recognised communal property in at least some resources during at least some periods in their history. However, modern states which are or aspire to be market economies often exhibit reluctance to accommodate communal property rights within their property rights systems. Communal property rights do not fit well into a property rights system centred on marketable private property rights. This is partly a matter of logistics. Markets demand communication and negotiation between participants, and in these respects communities can make poor participants. Indeterminate communities in particular may have agency problems: who speaks for the community? Who has the legitimacy to act on its behalf? Even when there is a clear answer to these questions

[34] For example, those referred to in nn 12–14 and 16 above.

and it is readable by outsiders,[35] it may be painfully slow for the community to acquire and process the information necessary for it to make and act on decisions and to reach a consensus on strategies to adopt and action to be taken. In indeterminate communities decision making may be particularly difficult because of difficulties in ascertaining the extent of the land over which the rights are exercisable and in determining who is and who is not a member, especially if the locality requirement for members is not defined with precision, for example by reference to any recognised administrative unit such as a unit of local government or postcode.[36]

So, even when communities have the capacity to participate in resource markets they may not be equipped to do it well. Often however they do not even have the capacity. The individual members of the community and the community itself may all hold recognised property rights in the shared resource yet may have no power to alienate their rights. This may be because governing legislation expressly prohibits or severely restricts alienation.[37] Inability to alienate may also arise by necessary implication. When states formally recognise customary property rights of culturally distinct communities, continued recognition often depends on the community continuing to use the resource within its pre-existing cultural norms.[38] And even when the question of cultural identity does not arise, purported dealings with the community's resources by the members for the time being may not effectively free the resource from claims by future members.

These characteristics of communal property holding are only a problem to the extent that the community wants to participate in resource markets. If, as may well be the case, the object of the communal property holding is to conserve and manage the resources for the benefit of the community or for environmental reasons, the community's slow participative processes,

[35] For an illustration of the problems of readability see eg M Demian, '"Land Doesn't Come From Your Mother, She Didn't Make it with Her Hands:" Challenging Matriliny in Papua New Guinea' in H Lim and A Bottomley (eds), *Feminist Perspectives on Land Law* (Abingdon, Routledge-Cavendish, 2007) 155.

[36] Compare those entitled to make recreational use of town and village greens in England and Wales ('the inhabitants of [the] locality, or of [the] neighbourhood[s] within [the] locality' s15(2)(a) Commons Act 2006) with the very precise definition of the local inhabitants entitled to acquire community ownership of land in Scotland through the Community Right to Buy introduced by the Land Reform (Scotland) Act 2003, for further details of which see M Hoffmann, 'Why Community Ownership? Understanding Land Reform in Scotland' (2013) 31 *Land Use Policy* 289. On indeterminacy of boundaries and membership in a quite different context see eg C Filer, 'Local Custom and the Art of Land Group Boundary Maintenance in Papua New Guinea' in JF Weiner and K Glaskin (eds), *Customary Land Tenure and Registration in Australia and Papua New Guinea: Anthropological Perspectives* (Canberra, ANU E Press, 2007).

[37] As under the Australian Native Titles Act 1993.

[38] Also the case under the Australian Native Titles Act 1993; and see the seminal discussion of the issue in the Supreme Court of Canada in *Delgamuukw v British Columbia* [1997] 3 SCR 1010.

lack of transactional skills and inability to alienate its interest may be a positive advantage.[39]

Nevertheless, because of these characteristics communal property holdings are particularly vulnerable in societies where they must compete for the same resources with private and state holdings, regardless of whether the community itself is disadvantaged because of cultural difference. Indeterminate communities in particular may not have mechanisms to alert them to threats to their resource use emanating from the state or from developers, their rights may be overlooked or overridden because not recorded nor easily discoverable or quantifiable, and the communities might not have readily available finance or the administrative resources necessary to enable them to establish and protect their claims effectively against experienced and well organised market participants.

States may have political and/or policy reasons for disliking communal property and for seeking to replace it with private property holdings or state ownership. This is not the place to explore these land tenure issues, nor to repeat arguments on the one hand about the economic efficiency of private property and on the other about the social, economic and environmental gains achievable by local communities collectively controlling and managing their own resources. However, the reality is that some communities do choose to utilise some of their resources collectively. When they do so habitually, it seems perverse, to put it at its mildest, for the state to ignore this reality and refuse to recognise communal property as a legitimate form of property holding. It is one thing for a state to try to eradicate communal resource use in order to replace it with private or state ownership. It is quite another for a legal system to recognise some patterns of resource use observed by its citizens and ignore others. The relationship that people habitually develop with the natural resources they use is not sacrosanct, but the degree of recognition and protection accorded to it by the legal system should not depend on the particular form of the relationship. Indeed, if there is an obligation on states to give legal recognition to all patterns of resource use observed by its citizens it is arguably even stronger in relation to communal property because of the inherent vulnerability of communal property holdings already noted.

The argument can be taken further. It is a characteristic of communal resource use that it often originates in custom. Because of the logistical difficulties sketched above, it is much easier for communities to acquire a relationship with their resources through long use rather than by express

[39] The reality may be more complex. For the difficulties and possibilities where, for example, the community wants to conserve its territorial and resource-utilising rights but also wants or is required to negotiate with outsiders to allow activities such as commercial extraction of minerals, see L Goldman, 'Incorporating Huli: Lessons from the Hides Licence Area' in Weiner and Glaskin (n 36).

grant or bargain. This contributes towards the unpopularity of communal property rights amongst legislators and policy makers. Rights acquired by custom or long use remain inchoate until requirements for formalisation have been satisfied and until then they cannot be captured on property registers or otherwise subjected to formal publicity requirements. For this reason they can be a trap for prospective purchasers of private rights unless apparent on inspection of the land. An obvious additional difficulty is that they will invariably be acquired over land which is already owned by someone else: The recognition of customary resource rights necessarily involves violation of pre-existing property rights. However, this is a universal problem faced by all property rights systems (and all human rights systems), and rules on the acquisition of rights by custom, through the equivalents of prescription, adverse possession etc, are designed precisely to strike a balance between these competing rights.

Arguably, the very difficulties faced by communities in acquiring communal resource rights by bargain justify a greater readiness to recognise their customary resource uses as proprietary. There are other justifications. In England and Wales property rights can in general be acquired by long use only if the use has been *nec vi, nec clam* and *nec precario*, which is taken to mean open and without either protest or permission from the landowner.[40] This applies to communal property rights as well as to private property rights.[41] The significance is that the owner of the land which the community has been using must have tolerated the community's resource use for a number of years when it could have stepped in at any time to stop it. This suggests either that the landowner had no use for the land throughout that period (or for the foreseeable future) or that, over time, landowner and local community had evolved mutually compatible shared resource use patterns. The latter is not fanciful, as the history of the land in dispute in *R (on the application of Lewis) v Redcar and Cleveland Borough Council*[42] demonstrates. *Lewis v Redcar*, one of several recent UK Supreme Court decisions on town and village greens, concerned land owned by the borough council let to a golf club which had used it as a golf course for more than 80 years. Throughout that period local inhabitants had also habitually used the golf course for recreational purposes—walking, picnicking, taking dogs

[40] The literal translation is 'not by force, nor secretly nor by licence of the owner'; the gloss given in the text here is derived from the remarks of Lord Rodger in *R (on the application of Lewis) v Redcar and Cleveland Borough Council* [2010] UKSC 11 noted below (n 42) at paras 87–93.

[41] The tests differ depending eg on whether the interest to be acquired is private ownership (in which case adverse possession rules apply) or a right acquired under a fiction of presumed grant, or under statutory provisions such as s 15 Commons Act 2006 (which do not have a basis of presumed grant): see Lord Hoffmann in *R v Oxfordshire County Council, ex parte Sunningwell Parish Council* [2000] 1 AC 335, 349D–351H. For the present purpose, however, the differences are immaterial.

[42] *R (on the application of Lewis) v Redcar and Cleveland Borough Council* (n 40).

for walks, playing with children etc—and they now claimed to have the land registered as a town or village green so that their right to use it in that way would be formalised. Evidence established that relations between golfers and local users had always been 'generally cordial' until the dispute arose. The recreational users

> would avoid the playing areas when play was in progress, waiting until play had passed or until they were waved across by the golfers. Where local people inadvertently impeded play, a shout of 'fore' would be enough to warn them to keep clear.[43]

In other words, golfers and locals had established norms of shared use: The locals went out of their way not to interfere with the golf, and the golfers made no attempt to interfere with the activities of the locals except where necessary to avoid interrupting the game (or injuring the locals). If this consensus had not evolved, the dual use could not have lasted for 80 years. What the customary communal users (the locals) were seeking was legitimisation of a successful shared resource system, albeit one no longer desired by the landowner.

Another way of looking at the relationship between landowner and customary communal resource user is that the customary resource user has evolved over time a system of resource use at the local level which is specifically adapted to the particular nature of that resource and the circumstances of those who are using it, and which has demonstrated its success by its longevity. There are strong arguments, most notably those of Elinor Ostrom,[44] in support of the proposition that this probably provides the best solution to the sustainable management of that resource. Indeed there is increasing evidence that management of complex ecosystems will be effective only if it incorporates and legitimises local communities' customary use of the resources making up the ecosystem.[45]

For all these reasons, it is argued, states ought not only to protect and respect formally granted communal property rights; they ought also to recognise long standing customary resource use by communities as giving rise to communal property rights.

[43] ibid, para 11.

[44] E Ostrom, *Governing the Commons: The Evolution of Institutions for Collective Action* (Cambridge, Cambridge University Press, 1990); E Ostrom, T Dietz, N Dolšak, PC Stern, S Stonich and EU Weber (eds), *The Drama of the Commons* (Washington DC, National Academy Press, 2002).

[45] See for example L Cotula and J Mayers, *Tenure in REDD—Start-point or Afterthought?* (2009) International Institute for Environment and Development Natural Resource Issues No 15 and G Wright, 'Indigenous People and Customary Land Ownership Under Domestic REDD+ Frameworks: A Case Study of Indonesia' (2011) *Law, Environment and Development Journal* 117 available at www.lead-journal.org/content/11117.pdf.

VIII. COMMUNITIES AS RIGHT-HOLDERS

The proposition that communities have property rights in the resources they use collectively presupposes that communities are capable of holding rights. This is by no means universally accepted, but for present purposes the relevant controversy is over what it means to say that a community holds rights. As noted in the previous section, as a matter of historic and present legal fact communities have held and do hold property rights in many jurisdictions. But does this mean that the community holds property rights in a resource in its own right, or is it just short-hand for the aggregate of the rights held in the resource by each individual member of the community?

If collective rights are conceptualised as no more than what Michael McDonald describes as 'class action rights',[46] in other words as aggregative of or reducible to the rights of individual members,[47] this seems to cause at least three problems for communities' collective resource use.

First, the class action approach fails to capture the intergenerational nature of collective resource use and the limited interest in the resource held by each member. There is no conceptual difficulty in regarding a community as an entity holding resource rights for the benefit of present and future members. If however the community's rights in the resource are reducible to those of its members, this can only mean the members for the time being: where then are the interests of future members located? Do they operate as a limitation on the rights of present members in their dealings with the resource, and if so, precisely how? As a matter of practicalities the community may not be able to interact effectively with the rest of the world unless members for the time being are given rights to bind future members in specified ways, but this does not mean that each member holds its individual resource right absolutely subject only to the absolute rights of other current members. This conjuring away of the interests of future members seems particularly inappropriate in the case of the local communities under consideration here, where membership is defined by reference to the retention of a local connection.

Another problem with the class-action approach is *locus standi*: it may not always be possible to locate an individual member who is eligible to bring a claim. This was one of the problems that defeated the Chagos Islanders when they sought to bring their case before the European Court of Human Rights in 2013.[48] They argued that the UK Government violated their

[46] M McDonald, 'Should Communities Have Rights? Reflections on Liberal Individualism' (1991) 4 *Canadian Journal of Law & Jurisprudence* 215, 218.

[47] Griffin (n 9) 256–76 prefers 'reducible to'; see also W Kymlicka's more nuanced model of 'group-differentiated' rights held by members of a community: W Kymlicka, *Multicultural Citizenship* (Oxford, Clarendon, 1995) 35. The distinctions are significant, but not for present purposes.

[48] *Chagos Islanders v United Kingdom* (n 8), where the substance of their claim is outlined.

Convention rights by evicting them from their lands and the subsequent failing to allow them to return or provide adequate compensation. Their claims failed because, amongst other reasons, they could not establish the victim status required under Article 34 of the ECHR (European Convention on Human Rights), which allows the Court to receive applications from 'any person, non-governmental organisation or group of individuals' claiming to be the victim of a violation. The applications were made on behalf of 1786 natives of, or descendants of natives of, the Chagos Islands. However, it was found that none of them could establish that they had victim status: one group consisted of those who had accepted, or were treated as being bound by, an admittedly inadequate money settlement some years earlier; another group was now resident in the Seychelles and was found not to have exhausted all their domestic remedies; all the rest were disqualified because they were born after the eviction of the Islanders.[49] So, whilst communities of Chagos Islanders continued to exist and indisputably were still suffering from the aftermath of the eviction, no individual member could bring an action.

The third problem for communities if the class-action approach is adopted is the difficulty in ensuring that all goods which accrue to the community from its communal resource use are fully recognised and appropriately quantified. One difficulty arises if there is a quick turnover of members, so that each member enjoys the resource use only briefly. Is the benefit to the community of the resource use really properly reflected by aggregating only the short term benefit to each of the current members? Another arises over the identification and quantification of collective goods. It is not seriously disputed that communities generate collective goods which would not accrue if their activities were carried out separately by their constituent members. Some of these are participatory goods, where the good is the product of the participation of the members and could not be produced by or for one individual only. The classic example, first provided by Jeremy Waldron, is conviviality of a party.[50] An example closer to home here is the social cohesion resulting from neighbours meeting each other on walks and their children playing together. Other collective goods can be described as knock-on and spill-over effects of community cohesion, some felt by outsiders as well as by members: the enhancement of the reputation of the neighbourhood as a desirable place to live, lower crime rates, increased social support, more conviviality etc. Even if it is possible to individuate these

[49] ibid at paras 77–81.

[50] J Waldron, 'Can Communal Goods be Human Rights?' in *Liberal Rights: Collected Papers 1981–1991* (Cambridge, Cambridge University Press, 1993); see also Réaume's notion of 'participatory goods,' D Réaume, 'Individuals, Groups, and Rights to Public Goods' (1988) 38 *University of Toronto Law Journal* 1, and the illuminating discussion of both in DW Newman, *Community and Collective Rights: A Theoretical Framework for Rights Held by Groups* (Oxford, Hart Publishing, 2011).

goods it is extremely difficult to quantify them accurately on an individual basis, particularly if the interests of future members are to be taken into account.

In any event, in important ways we do recognise the community as an entity in itself, distinct from its members. For example, in order to establish customary use of a resource by a community, we do not require proof that any given individual member has habitually regarded herself as bound by the customs of usage over a sufficient period of time; we ask whether, if we look at the community as a whole over a sufficiently long period, we find that all (or most or many) of the members for the time being have regarded themselves as bound by the customary pattern of usage. Similarly, to take again the England and Wales village green example, when we ask whether local inhabitants have used the land for recreational purposes for at least 20 years, we do not require proof that each or even any present or past member of the community has used it as such for at least 20 years. What is required is proof that, at all times during at least the last 20 years, each (or most or many) of the then inhabitants were using it for recreational purposes. In both examples the customary use would be established even if it could be proved that no one individual had ever been a member of the community for more than, say, two years.

In these respects at least a community making collective use of a resource is properly regarded as an entity in its own right, different from the aggregate of its members. Once we accept this, is there anything to debar us from saying that, if there is a *right* to make this collective use of the resource, it inheres not only in each member of the community but also, and in a different way, in the community itself? Moral and practical arguments about a community's lack of agency do not seem sufficient to deny the legitimacy of communal rights-holding,[51] nor to justify individualisation of those rights. This is particularly so when they are balanced against the difficulties noted above that communities face when asserting and quantifying their property rights (as opposed to other rights) if the class-action approach is adopted. Other stronger moral and philosophical arguments against the recognition of group rights in general are less easy to dismiss,[52] but they are largely founded on arguments about the moral and political justifications for protecting cultural identity, irrelevant here, and on rights other than property rights. For this reason, it is argued, they too should not be taken to outweigh our real concerns that communal property rights are not adequately protected unless the community itself is regarded as the rights-holder. This is not a matter of moral or political entitlement, as it is when groups claim the

[51] In any event convincingly dismissed by Griffin (n 9) 256–58.

[52] By Griffin (n 9) and Kymlicka (n 47); compare eg Newman (n 50) and L Green, 'Two Views of Collective Rights' (1991) 4 *Canadian Journal of Law & Jurisprudence* 329.

status of rights-holder by virtue of cultural distinctiveness or minority status or disadvantage, but a matter of effective protection of legally recognised property rights.

IX. HUMAN RIGHTS TO PROPERTY FOR COMMUNITIES

Once this is accepted, the question of whether communities have human rights to property can be more shortly addressed. Broadly, the argument is this. It is difficult to see how a human right to property of the second kind—a right to be provided with adequate resources—could be justified for the kind of local community under consideration here. 'Adequate resources' can only mean in this context adequate for the survival or flourishing of the community, and not all communities equally deserve to survive or flourish. A community can therefore claim the human right to property of the second kind, that is the right to adequate resources to survive or flourish, only if it can show that it *does* deserve to do so. It is accepted that indigenous people can do this, and arguably so too can minorities and historically disadvantaged groups. The local communities under consideration here, however, cannot. That is not to say that their members do not have human rights of the second kind—they have them by virtue of being humans—but these individual rights can be vindicated only on a class-action basis, not by the community asserting the right in its own right.

Human rights of the first and third kind—the right of a community to respect and protection for its property holdings, and the right to have its customary collective resource use recognised as proprietary—are a different matter. If these human rights to property are justifiable at all, on what basis could they be justifiable when humans utilise resources individually, under a private property regime, but not when they utilise them collectively under a communal property regime? Private property is just one form of property institution along a spectrum of property forms, as Hanoch Dagan and others have argued.[53] We should be wary of an international human rights system that attaches human rights protection only to private property, and not to any other form of property holding practised by humans. A failure to give human rights protection to one particular form of property holding is not neutral. Property rights are rivalrous in the sense that a disregard of the property rights in a resource which are held by one rights-holder necessarily enlarges the property rights in that resource held by others. So if human rights protection of any kind is to attach to any form of property right it must be extended to all types unless good reasons can be found for excluding a particular type.

[53] H Dagan, *Property: Values and Institutions* (Oxford, Oxford University Press, 2011) especially ch 3.

The reason for questioning whether communities can have a human right to property is that human rights are for humans and communities are not humans. This is the basis for the compelling arguments raised against the justifiability of recognising corporations as holders of human rights.[54] However, they are less compelling when applied to the local resource-sharing communities under consideration here. Corporations have a complex set of relationships with the humans whose interests are bound up with those of the abstract entity which is the company. Their constituent humans include not only or even primarily their shareholders but also their managers and non-managerial employees, and in the case of some corporations such as regulated utility companies, even their customers. This gives them an existence which is, in substance and not just in legal form, wholly separate from, and often floating free from, that of their members. Communities of the kind we are considering, on the other hand, have a simple and direct relationship with their members: it is much easier to see them as embodying the shared human vulnerability of their members (albeit future as well as present ones) in which, Grear argues, human rights are grounded.[55]

Communities, therefore, do not seem sufficiently detached from their constituent humans to justify withdrawing human rights protection from their property holdings, even if that would be justifiable in the case of corporate property holdings.

X. IMPLEMENTING THE COMMUNITY'S HUMAN RIGHTS TO PROPERTY

It has been argued here that human rights to property of the first and third kind—rights to respect and protection for their collective property holdings, and for recognition of their customary collective resource use as proprietary—should extend to local communities irrespective of any special claims they may be able to make on the grounds of cultural distinctiveness or disadvantaged status. If this is correct it has significant implications for the ways in which legal systems deal with communal property rights. We conclude by sketching these out, drawing on the conclusions reached so far.

Human rights to property for communities would seem to entail, as a minimum:

(i) Providing the community as such with access to human rights tribunals, so that it can speak for its future members and bring into proper

[54] See in particular A Grear, 'Challenging Corporate "Humanity": Legal Disembodiment, Embodiment and Human Rights' (2007) 7 *Human Rights Law Review* 511 and A Scolnicov, 'Lifelike and Lifeless in Law: Do Corporations Have Human Rights?' *University of Cambridge Legal Studies Research Paper No 13*, 2013.

[55] Grear, ibid 540.

account its interest in its collective goods. This would be additional to the access afforded to members of the community claiming protection of their individual rights in respect of the collectively used assets.

(ii) Providing remedies that properly take into account and quantify any loss to the community as such as well as loss to individual members.

(iii) Recognition that communal property rights are of equal status to private, public or state property rights and cannot be trumped by them. This would require, for example, at the very least a re-casting of the arguments of the Supreme Court in *R (on the application of Barkas) v North Yorkshire County Council*[56] where it was held that local inhabitants could not acquire town and village green rights over land made available for public recreation.

(iv) Recognition that the interest of that community in its resources is not the same as the interest that the community at large may have, nor the same as the public interest, and that general community interest and public interest should no more (and no less) easily defeat communal property holdings than they do private property. The failure to distinguish community interest in general from the interest of a particular resource-utilising community is a perennial problem in English law. Democratically elected local government institutions in England and Wales operate the planning system and also provide and maintain land and facilities for the benefit of the wider community. There is a running thread of argument in government policy papers that town and village green rights must be kept under tight control because they subvert the democratic process by allowing local inhabitants to take over local land for their own recreational purposes when the local authority has already earmarked it for other purposes.[57] On the basis that the local community has a communal property right protectable as a human right, such objections are misconceived.

(v) Provision by the state of machinery for the recognition, protection and vindication of communal property rights which is appropriate for local communities, including indeterminate communities. The machinery must take account of the logistical difficulties noted above that communities have in participating in bureaucratic processes and must be sensitive to the ways in which these put them at a competitive disadvantage. This applies with particular force to communities trying to prove long-standing customary use, especially where the community has to provide evidence of the nature and extent of customary use at a distant point in time and of the continuity of the custom up to the present time. The crippling difficulties faced by indigenous peoples

[56] *R (on the application of Barkas) v North Yorkshire County Council* [2014] UKSC 31.

[57] See eg House of Commons Research Paper 12/61 25 October 2012 on the Growth and Infrastructure Bill, para 2.10.

in establishing their claims where this is required are well known and well documented, but it should be appreciated that similar difficulties, perhaps on a smaller scale, face local communities all over the world trying to establish customary collective use of resources.

(vi) Recognition of the specific communal resource use patterns in use as part of the state's property rights system. Most legal systems have a *numerus clausus* of property interests, a fixed list of the kinds of resource interests that they recognise as property rights. It has been a historical problem that communities may customarily make collective use of resources in ways which do not correspond to the state's *numerus clausus*. The Australian decision in *Mabo v Queensland (No 2)*[58] can be taken as establishing as a matter of soft international law that if that is the case in relation to resource use by indigenous peoples, the state must expand its *numerus clausus* to include appropriate new rights. The same should apply to the collective resource use patterns of all local communities. Communal resource use may amount to exclusive possession and exercise of full ownership-type rights by the community, but it does not always do so. Legitimising customary resource use should not involve either diminishing or enlarging it. Apart from anything else, it is a waste of resources to 'reward' communities making a particular use of resources with full ownership or effectively full possession of the land, and gives rise to unnecessary conflicts between them and the owners they have displaced, as well as between them and potential exploiters of other natural resources in the same geographical area. States do not necessarily have to decide whether, for example, minerals should be exploited commercially or whether communal land rights should be respected: often they can do both.[59]

Many states and national and international tribunals have already started to devise strategies to achieve these objectives with respect to indigenous people's resource rights. Recognition of human rights to property for communities as advocated here may be what is needed to persuade states to develop similar strategies in the aid of all local resource-sharing communities of all kinds.

[58] *Mabo v Queensland (No 2)* (n 12).

[59] See eg Weiner and Glaskin (n 36).

2

Cultural Property and Community Rights to Cultural Heritage

FIONA MACMILLAN

I. INTRODUCTION: CULTURAL HERITAGE IN INTERNATIONAL LAW

DISPUTES ABOUT THE ownership of cultural stuff mark the recorded history of humanity. It is, therefore, unsurprising that the philosophical and legal concept of cultural heritage-property can be traced back to antiquity.[1] Then, as now, it is clear that these disputes were primarily generated by the unattractive human propensity to plunder, loot, steal, pillage and (mis)appropriate. Under these circumstances, there is a certain inevitability in the fact that cultural heritage first became a recognised concept in international law at the time of the Vienna Treaty of 1815,[2] which was imposed by the British victors after the conclusion of the Napoleonic Wars. The precise motivations for the British insistence that France return the movable artefacts looted by Napoleon during his campaigns might reasonably be regarded as being obscured by the passage of time. However, given the context, it seems reasonable to assert that the relevant clause was punitive. More interesting for present purposes, it is likely that it was influenced by the concurrent rise of a discourse that linked people, territory and cultural objects.[3] That this was an entirely Eurocentric and imperial discourse is hardly a great surprise: at the same time as Britain was championing the return of European cultural artefacts[4] it continued

[1] See MM Miles, *Art as Plunder: The Ancient Origins of Debate about Cultural Property* (New York, Cambridge University Press, 2010).

[2] AF Vrdoljak, *International Law, Museums and the Return of Cultural Objects* (Cambridge, Cambridge University Press, 2008) 23–29.

[3] ibid, Pt 1.

[4] Even if the championing tended to be more rhetorical than anything else: see F Macmillan, 'The Protection of Cultural Heritage: Common Heritage of Humankind, National Cultural "Patrimony" or Private Property?' (2013) 64 *Northern Ireland Legal Quarterly* 351, 356–57.

to plunder the cultural artefacts of its colonies with impunity.[5] By the end of the Second World War, however, this colonial free-for-all was coming to an end. Britain had been replaced by America as the dominant world power, the regimes of international law were being remade, and the period of decolonisation was commencing.[6] Even though the current international law regime for the protection of cultural heritage was born out of the rupture that marked the end of the British period of world dominance and inaugurated the American one, it is nevertheless marked by both its historical antecedents[7] and by contemporaneous movements in the geo-political order.

Of these contemporaneous geo-political movements, three are particularly important to the argument in this chapter. First of all, there is the very process of decolonisation itself and the political aspirations that accompanied it. At the international law level, this process was managed in a rather ex post facto fashion by something that eventually became the Vienna Convention on the Succession of States in Respect of State Property, Archives and Debts of 1983. In the current context there are two key (low) points of this treaty. The first of these is its failure to recognise the distinctive position of indigenous peoples within former colonial subject states. This, of course, is a serious problem with which the international law system continues to struggle. In part, it was a consequence of the strongly state-based thinking that characterised the development of international law in the post-war period. This explanation (the inadequacy and injustice of which needs no elaboration), however, cannot serve to explain the second important aspect of the Vienna Convention, which is the absence of any rules on restitution of works of art or artefacts to the former colonial states. Instead, the question of the return of works of art and artefacts was to be governed by bilateral negotiations under the auspices of a UNESCO Committee, the operation of which has continued up until to the present period.[8] A significant part of the current political concern with the question of the protection of cultural artefacts is a consequence of the failure of international law properly to address the wrongs of the colonial period.[9]

The second important political current in the post-colonial period was the re-institutionalisation of the concept of free trade. The concept

[5] Special Rapporteur, Mohammed Bedjaoui, who was responsible for the preparation the work that eventually lead to the conclusion of the Vienna Convention on Succession of States in respect of State Property, Archives and Debts (1983) found that the removal of cultural objects during the colonial period was generally not 'in accordance with the canons of justice, morality and law': UN Doc.A/CN.4/292, quoted in Vrdoljak (n 2) 202.

[6] G Arrighi, *The Long Twentieth Century: Money, Power and the Origins of Our Times* (London, Verso, 1994) 47–74 and ch 3.

[7] See also, eg, Miles (n 1) 1–12.

[8] For a critical assessment of the work of this committee, see Vrdoljak (n 2) 211–17.

[9] For an argument on the significance of this failure in relation to identity and sovereignty, see Macmillan (n 4).

of international free trade had been floating around in international law since the Treaty of Westphalia of 1648.[10] While the economic freedoms of Westphalia were not observed during the Napoleonic Wars, they were restored in the Settlement of Vienna of 1815 and the Congress of Aix-la-Chapelle of 1818.[11] And then these freedoms were restored again, after the cataclysms of the First and Second World Wars, at Bretton Woods, starting the international legal system(s) on a process that led eventually to the World Trade Organization (WTO).[12] The strength of this discourse, and the political and economic baggage that it has dragged in its wake, has had a particular effect on the way in which the public/private distinction has played out in relation to cultural artefacts. Rhetorically, there seems to have always been some types of public claims to certain types of cultural artefacts, but the nature of these claims are rather vague. Sometimes they manifest themselves in forms of state ownership, but they also often take the form of attempts to limit the rights that would otherwise be associated with private ownership. In the latter situation, the rather inchoate nature of the non-private rights that are pitted against the very well developed concept of private property rights, on which the international free trade system depends, has tended to undermine their effectiveness.

Third, the post-colonial period has also witnessed the development of the international law regime for the protection of human rights. This regime, which grew out of the Dumbarton Oaks negotiations, also at the end of the Second World War, and is managed under the auspices of the United Nations, is a bedfellow of the UNESCO regime for the protection of 'culture'. It is clear, therefore, that there is a historical and institutional relationship between these two bodies of international law. The extent of the legal, political and philosophical relationship between them is open to more conjecture. Certainly, twenty-first century UNESCO conventions make rather florid claims to some type of association,[13] but the extent to which the UNESCO conventions can be regarded as a direct expression of international human rights law is unclear. The provisions of international human rights law that are usually cited in support of this claim[14] are probably

[10] Arrighi (n 6) 43–44.

[11] ibid, 52.

[12] See further F Macmillan, 'The World Trade Organization and the Turbulent Legacy of International Economic Law-making in the Long Twentieth Century' in J Faundez and C Tan (eds), *International Law, Economic Globalization and Developing Countries* (Cheltenham, Edward Elgar, 2010).

[13] See Convention for the Safeguarding of Intangible Cultural Heritage, Recitals 1–2; and Convention on the Protection and Promotion of Cultural Diversity, Recitals 1–5 and Arts 2.1 and 5.1.

[14] Universal Declaration of Human Rights, Art 27; United Nations Charter Covenant on Civil and Political Rights, Arts 1, 19 and 27; United Nations Charter Covenant on Economic, Social and Cultural Rights, Art 15.

most convincingly construed as a right to cultural self-determination.[15] Under these circumstances, perhaps the most that can be said for the claim that human rights law is the well-spring of the UNESCO regime is that a right to cultural self-determination suggests the valorisation of the sort of concepts, such as cultural heritage, cultural property and cultural diversity, with which the UNESCO regime is concerned. However, it is also apposite to note that this same body of international human rights law is often argued as providing the normative justification for the system of intellectual property rights.[16] If, as this chapter argues, the intellectual property system as a system of private rights poses a threat to community rights in cultural property, then it might be concluded that not all that much is gained by attempts to invoke human rights rhetoric—let alone human rights law itself—in support of claims for stronger cultural property rights.

So far as the UNESCO conventions themselves are concerned, they started off with a concern for the protection of cultural property during armed conflict (UNESCO Convention on the Protection of Cultural Property in the Event of Armed Conflict (Hague Convention, 1954)),[17] moved on to a concern for restitution to states of movable cultural property (UNESCO Convention on the Means of Prohibiting and Preventing the Illicit, Import, Export and Transfer of Ownership of Cultural Property (1970)), and then to the preservation of immovable cultural heritage (UNESCO Convention Concerning the Protection of the World Cultural and Natural Heritage (1972)). In this century, while the rate of international law-making with respect to the protection of culture and cultural heritage has increased, the focus of protection has moved to a concern for underwater cultural heritage (UNESCO Convention on the Protection of the Underwater Cultural Heritage (2001)), intangible cultural heritage (UNESCO Convention for the Safeguarding of the Intangible Cultural Heritage (2003)) and the concept of 'cultural diversity' (UNESCO Convention for the Protection and Promotion of the Diversity of Cultural Expressions (2005)).

As already suggested, the trajectory and content of the UNESCO Conventions has been affected by the contemporaneous political, economic and legal developments in two principal ways. First, despite using the language of the cultural heritage of mankind/humanity, the regime is intensely statist, which is also (obviously) a consequence of its location in the system of international law. This, of course, reflects the strongly statist

[15] See F Macmillan, 'The UNESCO Convention as a New Incentive to Protect Cultural Diversity' in H Schneider and P van den Bossche (eds), *Protection of Cultural Diversity from a European and International Perspective* (Mortsel, Intersentia, 2008).

[16] This is the case with respect to the Universal Declaration of Human Rights, Art 27.2 and UN Charter Covenant on Economic, Social and Cultural Rights, Art 15.1.

[17] Which locates itself within the context of the 1907 Hague Regulations on Law & Customs of War: See UNESCO Convention on the Protection of Cultural Property in the Event of Armed Conflict 1954, Preamble, para 4.

ideology that characterised the period of decolonisation. There are now some small breaches in this discourse as witnessed at the general level of public international law, for example, in the United Nations Declaration on the Rights of Indigenous Peoples (UNDRIP) of 2007 and reflected in the UNESCO Intangible Cultural Heritage Convention[18] and the Cultural Diversity Convention.[19] Second, at the same time, and arguably running counter to this strongly statist approach, the ambit of the UNESCO regime is circumscribed by the dominance of free trade ideology and the associated importance of private ownership rights. One classic example of this is the UNESCO Convention on the Means of Prohibiting and Preventing the Illicit, Import, Export and Transfer of Ownership of Cultural Property, which makes its provisions on the return of movable cultural property subject to ensuring compensation for 'innocent' purchasers and persons 'who have valid titles' to the relevant artefacts.[20] The Cultural Diversity Convention is also marked by the dominance of free trade ideology. In one way, its very existence can be considered a reaction to the international legal implementation of that ideology in the WTO agreements because one of the primary motivations of the Convention's promoters was to compensate for the absence of a general cultural exception in the WTO agreements.[21] However, it might also be regarded as accommodating aspects of the ideology underpinning the WTO through its uncritical acceptance of the role of private property rights, in the form of intellectual property rights, in sustaining the type of cultural creativity that it regards as essential to the flourishing of cultural diversity.[22] A similar uncritical acceptance characterises the Convention for the Safeguarding of the Intangible Cultural Heritage.[23] Given the historical intertwining of the trade regime and the UNESCO regime, it is probably not surprising that UNESCO's increasing concern with the protection of intangibles has been matched by an enormous growth in the

[18] Which recognises in recital 6 'that communities, in particular indigenous communities, groups and, in some cases, individuals, play an important role in the production, safeguarding, maintenance and recreation of the intangible cultural heritage'; and also recognises the role of communities and groups in Art 2.1.

[19] Which makes repeated references to 'traditional cultural expressions' and notes in its recital 15 'the importance of the vitality of cultures, including for persons belonging to minorities & indigenous peoples, as manifested in their freedom to create, disseminate & distribute their traditional cultural expressions & to have access thereto, so as to benefit them for their own development'.

[20] UNESCO Convention on the Means of Prohibiting & Preventing the Illicit, Import, Export and Transfer of Ownership of Cultural Property (1970), Art 7(b)(ii).

[21] See further CB Graber, 'The New UNESCO Convention on Cultural Diversity: A Counterbalance to the WTO?' (2006) 9 *Journal of International Economic Law* 553.

[22] According to recital 17, the Convention recognises 'the importance of intellectual property rights in sustaining those involved in cultural creativity'; and see Art 20. For a further analysis, see Macmillan (n 15).

[23] See Art 3(b).

scope and application of intellectual property rights—classically private proprietary rights over intangibles—which are now part of the WTO package in the form of its Agreement on Trade-Related Aspects of Intellectual Property (TRIPs Agreement). What might be considered more surprising is the fact that the power of the intellectual property system to trump community rights to cultural property is often advanced and, when necessary defended, as an exercise of human rights. At least in this sense it might be said that UNESCO's embrace, at the same time, of both human rights and intellectual property rights—in the Intangible Cultural Heritage Convention and the Cultural Diversity Convention—is not internally inconsistent.

The foregoing serves to provide the background against which this chapter considers the interplay of public and private interests in cultural stuff. Specifically, the objective of the chapter will be to consider whether the concept of property is open to re-conception as a form of community right, bearing in mind that the early use of the expression 'cultural property', in the Hague Convention and in the Convention on the Means of Prohibiting and Preventing the Illicit, Import, Export and Transfer of Ownership of Cultural Property, as a description of their objects of protection was subsequently abandoned. The significance of this is open to speculation, but it may have been partly on the basis of its association with traditional concepts of rivalrous property rights[24] and partly on the basis that it made reference to a form of property that is not generally recognised in Western legal systems. Whatever the explanation for this change, it now seems clear that understanding what cultural property is, or could be, depends on understanding its relationship to the concept of cultural heritage, which replaced that of cultural property and with which the UNESCO regime now concerns itself. Using the UNESCO conventions as a starting point, Part II of this chapter seeks to unpick the nature of cultural heritage. Part III considers whether a new change in discourse from cultural heritage back to cultural property would be effective, as a legal or a political strategy, in the process of recognising and protecting community interests in cultural artefacts. Part IV considers the systemic conflict between cultural property and forms of intellectual property. It is premised on the argument that community interests in cultural property are, by their nature, under threat from such forms of private property, which are considered by law to be rivalrous individual rights.[25]

[24] See J Blake, 'On Defining Cultural Heritage' (2000) 49 *International & Comparative Law Quarterly* 61, 65–67.

[25] See Macmillan (n 4); F Macmillan, 'Human Rights, Cultural Property and Intellectual Property: Three Concepts in Search of a Relationship' in C Graber and M Nenova (eds), *Intellectual Property and Traditional Cultural Expressions in a Digital Environment* (Cheltenham, Edward Elgar, 2008).

II. THE CONCEPT OF CULTURAL HERITAGE

Attempting to understand the concept of cultural heritage through the lens of the UNESCO conventions presents some difficulties. Viewed as a whole the conventions tend to organise their objects of protection in accordance with the traditional way in which legal systems categorise property. That is, the conventions are divided between those concerned with tangible property, which is further split between movables[26] and immovables,[27] and those concerned with intangible property.[28] Certainly, there are conventions that stand in some respects outside this classification,[29] but overall the influence of Western legal concepts of property is strong. The question of what types of tangible or intangible property constitute cultural heritage is not consistently addressed at a general level. The conventions do not define their object of protection by reference to an overarching concept but rather by closed or open lists of specific objects to which the relevant convention intends to extend protection. An example of a closed list is provided by the Convention Concerning the Protection of the World Cultural and Natural Heritage (1972) (the World Heritage Convention), the first UNESCO Convention to employ the expression 'cultural heritage' to describe its object of protection. This Convention provides in Article 1 that for its purposes 'cultural heritage' is:

> monuments: architectural works, works of monumental sculpture and painting, elements or structures of an archaeological nature, inscriptions, cave dwellings and combinations of features, which are of outstanding universal value from the point of view of history, art or science;
> groups of buildings: groups of separate or connected buildings which, because of their architecture, their homogeneity or their place in the landscape, are of outstanding universal value from the point of view of history, art or science;
> sites: works of man or the combined works of nature and man, and areas including archaeological sites which are of outstanding universal value from the historical, aesthetic, ethnological or anthropological point of view.

The concept that appears to link these different classes of immovables together is that of 'outstanding universal value', although the type of outstanding universal value in question undergoes a subtle shift in relation to the protection of 'sites'.

[26] UNESCO Convention on the Means of Prohibiting and Preventing the Illicit, Import, Export and Transfer of Ownership of Cultural Property (1970).

[27] Convention Concerning the Protection of the World Cultural and Natural Heritage (1972).

[28] Intangible Cultural Heritage Convention (2003) and perhaps the Cultural Diversity Convention (2005).

[29] Convention for the Protection of Cultural Property in the event of Armed Conflict (1954), which does however refer to 'movable or immovable property' (Art 1(a)); Convention for the Protection of the Underwater Cultural Heritage (2001).

Reflecting perhaps millennial uncertainties about everything, the Intangible Cultural Heritage Convention employs a more open-ended list prefaced by an attempt to arrive at a wider concept. According to Article 2.1 'intangible cultural heritage' means:

> the practices, representations, expressions, knowledge, skills—as well as the instruments, objects, artefacts and cultural spaces associated therewith—that communities, groups and, in some cases, individuals recognize as part of their cultural heritage. This intangible cultural heritage, transmitted from generation to generation, is constantly recreated by communities and groups in response to their environment, their interaction with nature and their history, and provides them with a sense of identity and continuity, thus promoting respect for cultural diversity and human creativity.

Article 2.2 provides:

> The 'intangible cultural heritage', as defined in paragraph 1 above, is manifested inter alia in the following domains:
>
> (a) oral traditions and expressions, including language as the vehicle of the intangible cultural heritage;
> (b) performing arts;
> (c) social practices, rituals and festive events;
> (d) knowledge and practices concerning nature and the universe;
> (e) traditional craftsmanship.

The open-ended listing approach has also found its way into other semi-official descriptions of the nature of cultural heritage. A good example is provided by the recent European Union *Heritage Plus* funding call, the first footnote of which observes that:

> Cultural heritage exists in tangible, intangible and digital forms. Tangible heritage includes artefacts (for example, objects, paintings, archaeological finds etc), buildings, structures, landscapes, cities, and towns including industrial, underwater and archaeological sites. It includes their location, relationship to the natural environment and the materials from which all these are made, from prehistoric rock to cutting edge plastics and electronic products. Intangible heritage includes the practices, representations, expressions, memories, knowledge and skills that communities, groups and individuals construct, use and transmit from generation to generation. Digital heritage includes texts, databases, still and moving images, audio, graphics, software and web pages. Some of this digital heritage is created from the scanning or converting of physical objects that already exist and some is created digitally, or 'born digital'.[30]

While this list clearly owes something to those populating the UNESCO conventions, it categorises cultural heritage differently, introducing a third

[30] *Cultural Heritage: A Challenge for Europe* (JPI Cultural Heritage and Global Change—Heritage Plus Call, 2014).

class of digital cultural heritage. No attempt is made here to understand the relationship between intangible and digital heritage nor the origin of the concept of digital heritage.[31] Rather, the focus for present purposes is on the apparently rather random nature of the list, covering a vast range of subject matter and introducing concepts like digital heritage without any clear explanation of their origin. Since it seems reasonably clear that not every instantiation of the contents of this list would be regarded as cultural heritage, there is a need for some overarching concept of cultural heritage that provides some basis for distinguishing between, for example, buildings and structures that constitute cultural heritage and those that do not, or between databases that contain or constitute digital heritage and those that do not.

Strangely, such an overarching concept is difficult to pin down.[32] Looking to the UNESCO conventions for inspiration suggests a number of related possibilities. One would be, as the World Heritage Convention suggests, to focus on stuff that is of 'outstanding universal value' historically, artistically, scientifically, ethnologically or anthropologically. There is an obvious problem here of working out who decides what is of relevant 'outstanding universal value' according to a range of disciplines that have a strong whiff of European enlightenment thought and thus might be regarded as, in any case, suspect in the context of the 'universal'. The Convention on the Means of Prohibiting and Preventing the Illicit, Import, Export and Transfer of Ownership of Cultural Property, which deals with the protection of tangible movables and employs similar concepts to those in the World Heritage Convention, presents a possible solution to this problem. Article 1 provides that the subject matter of protection is 'property which, on religious or secular grounds, is specifically designated by each State as being of importance for archaeology, prehistory, history, literature, art or science' and which belongs to a closed list of categories. Despite the certainty that flows from designation by a state, it is suggested that this manifestation of statist thinking is an unsuitable solution in a world where not all peoples and communities enjoy the benefit of statehood.[33]

A second possibility, suggested by the UNESCO conventions, for a broad concept of cultural heritage would be to generalise the statement in Article 2.1 of the Intangible Cultural Heritage Convention. This would

[31] Although I strongly suspect that it owes something to the now well-established Digital Humanities movement.

[32] See also T Flessas, 'Cultural Property Defined and Redefined as Nietzschean Aphorism' (2003) 24 *Cardozo Law Review* 1067.

[33] This seems to have been recognised in the UNIDROIT Convention on Stolen or Illegally Exported Cultural Objects (1995), which seeks to give private international law architecture to the UNESCO Convention. The definition in the UNIDROIT Convention, Art 2, of the subject matter of protection is almost identical to that in the UNESCO Convention except that it refers to cultural objects, rather than property, and it leaves out the requirement for state designation.

produce something to the effect that cultural heritage is what is transmitted from generation to generation by communities and groups in response to their environment, their interaction with nature and their history, thus providing them with a sense of identity and continuity. The more up to date language of this second approach[34] has clearly influenced twenty-first century commentators (including me) who have proposed an overarching concept of cultural heritage as being expressions of creativity (movable and immovable, tangible and intangible) that a community or people considers worth handing on to the future.[35] There is, of course, an obvious political element in identifying what is considered to be worth handing on to the future[36] and this carries with it a degree of malleability and slipperiness. Thus, what we understand to be cultural heritage based on this type of overarching concept reflects current political concerns.

Despite, or perhaps because of, the vagueness of the concept of cultural heritage in law, it has become a potent rhetorical moving feast in cultural and political discourse. This potency owes a substantial debt to the strong relationship between community and/or national identity and cultural heritage.[37] Perhaps because the question of identity has become so important in our rapidly globalising and homogenising world, claims to cultural heritage are imbricated with the politics of identity. Depending on how the world is understood, there are various ways of expressing this relationship. Not all cultures express it as a claim to ownership, but in an international political and legal context that is dominated by occidental ways of seeing the world, this is a frequent claim. Whether it is always a claim to some type of property in the heritage itself is not clear. What is, however, much clearer is that the claim is one made by a community.[38] At least, it is clearer until one reads the UNESCO conventions closely. There are at least two reasons why the community nature of cultural heritage claims is obscured in the UNESCO conventions. One is their constant references to the cultural heritage of (hu)mankind. While this can be taken as a claim to some sort of universal community ownership, which in its abundant inclusiveness tends to exclude any specific or workable idea of community, it is probably better understood as a justification for protecting cultural heritage.[39] Second, the pervasive influence of state-based thinking in the early UNESCO conventions

[34] See also the Cultural Diversity Convention (2005), Art 4.1–4.3.

[35] F Macmillan, 'Arts Festivals as Cultural Heritage in a Copyright Saturated World' in H Porsdam (ed), *Copyrighting Creativity: Creative Values, Cultural Heritage Institutions and Systems of Intellectual Property* (Farnham, Ashgate, 2015) 95–115 citing Blake (n 24) 68–69.

[36] Blake, ibid 68.

[37] See further Macmillan (n 4) 352–56. See also, eg, E Hobsbawm, *Fractured Times: Culture and Society in the Twentieth Century* (London, Little Brown, 2013) ch 12, esp at 148ff.

[38] See, eg, UN Declaration of the Rights of Indigenous Peoples, Arts 11.1, 12.1, 13.1 and 31.1.

[39] Macmillan (n 4).

tends to obscure the concept of community,[40] although it is possible to understand the conventions as referring to a community that is co-extensive with the nation state.[41] The recent conventions, on the other hand, more readily accept the relationship between community and cultural heritage. The Intangible Cultural Heritage Convention, for example, recognises 'that communities, in particular indigenous communities, groups and, in some cases, individuals, play an important role in the production, safeguarding, maintenance and recreation of the intangible cultural heritage'.[42] It is notable, however, that this Convention does not talk about the claims or rights of such communities to their cultural heritage.

The constant movement, and not only in the UNESCO conventions,[43] in the discourse of cultural heritage between the cultural heritage of humanity, nation states, peoples and communities complicates the question of the interplay of traditional concepts of public and private in this context. This is especially the case if one associates the concept of the public with that of the state. On the other hand, if we move towards a discourse of cultural property, there may be some advantages in drawing a distinction between private and non-private (where non-private is capable of representing not only state interests but also non-individual interests other than those claimed by or on behalf of the nation state.) The traditional concept of (private) property is not only heavily loaded with an elevation of the private over the public good, it is also part of the process by which all values become subject to the logic of the market.[44] In these circumstances, hanging on to the distinction between public and private, or at least non-private and private, may be a way to retain social and political values that rise above those of the market.[45] However, it seems clear that only a concept of property that

[40] See, eg, UNESCO Convention on the Means of Prohibiting and Preventing the Illicit, Import, Export and Transfer of Ownership of Cultural Property (1970), Recitals 3-5: '**Considering** that cultural property constitutes one of the basic elements of civilization and national culture ... **Considering** that it is incumbent upon every State to protect the cultural property existing within its territory ... **Considering** that ... it is essential for every state to become increasingly alive to the moral obligations respecting its own cultural heritage and that of all nations'.

[41] UNIDROIT Convention on Stolen or Illegally Exported Cultural Objects (1995), which is based upon the UNESCO Convention on the Means of Prohibiting and Preventing the Illicit, Import, Export and Transfer of Ownership of Cultural Property (1970) (see n 33 above), recital 3 makes reference to 'the cultural heritage of national, tribal, indigenous or other communities'.

[42] Intangible Cultural Heritage Convention (2003), recital 6. See also Cultural Diversity Convention, recitals 7 and 8, referring to respectively 'peoples and societies' and 'indigenous peoples'.

[43] Hobsbawm (n 37) ch 12.

[44] E Christodoulidis, 'On the Politics of the Public/Private Distinction: What Does it Mean to Sustain the Politics of A Lost Distinction?' *ESRC Seminar Series: The Public Life of Private Law* (Kent Law School, 18 January 2013), http://backdoorbroadcasting.net/2013/01/emilios-christodoulidis-on-the-politics-of-the-publicprivate-law-distinction-what-does-it-mean-to-sustain-the-politics-of-a-lost-distinction/.

[45] See also ibid.

explodes the traditional values of private property is capable of pulling off this trick. In the light of these observations, this chapter now turns to consider what it means, politically and legally, to talk about cultural property instead of cultural heritage.

III. FROM CULTURAL HERITAGE TO CULTURAL PROPERTY

The first thing that should be conceded here is that legally, at least in a positivist sense, it doesn't mean much in common law systems to talk about cultural property,[46] except perhaps in the specific context of the international conventions, and implementing legislation, using this language. Some civil law countries recognise a concept that is translatable into English as cultural property, but in general this is a fairly limited legal category that is not broad enough to cover what is currently considered by the UNESCO conventions to be cultural heritage,[47] let alone any wider concept. On the other hand, it is notable that outside positivist legal scholarship the expression is widely used.[48] So this section is concerned with two different questions. First, what is the theoretical and political significance of such a change in discourse? And, second, what is its potential legal significance?

There are a number of good arguments that can be advanced against the use of the expression cultural property. A pervasive argument to this effect is that the use of the word 'property' is problematic precisely because it has a clear legal, political and economic significance that is at odds with its use in conjunction with the qualifier 'cultural'.[49] There are various aspects to this argument that merit further enquiry. First, there is the problem that the

[46] See LV Prott and PJ O'Keefe, '"Cultural Heritage" or "Cultural Property"' (1992) 1 *International Journal of Cultural Property* 307, 312–18.

[47] ibid, 312, making reference to the French concept of *biens culturels* and the Italian concept of *beni culturali.*

[48] See, eg, in what could be a very long list: MF Brown, 'Heritage Trouble: Recent Work on The Protection of Intangible Cultural Property' (2005) 12 *International Journal of Cultural Property* 40; KA Carpenter, S Katyal and A Riley, 'In Defense of Property' (2009) 118 *Yale Journal of Law* 1022; Flessas (n 32); R Handler, 'Who Owns the Past? History, Cultural Property & the Logic of Possessive Individualism' in B Williams (ed), *The Politics of Culture* (Washington, Smithsonian Institution Press, 1991); JR Slaughter, 'Form & Informality: An Unliterary Look at World Literature' in R Warhol, *The Work of Genre: Selected Essays from the English Institute* (English Institute in Collaboration with the American Council of Learned Societies, 2011), http://quod.lib.umich.edu/cgi/t/text/text-idx?c=acls;idno=heb90055. To which list should be added the influential *International Journal of Cultural Property* itself. *cf* Prott and O'Keefe (n 46) 319, who claim that the expression 'cultural heritage' is 'well recognized and universally used by historians, archaeologists, anthropologists and other researchers of human life both past and present'.

[49] See, eg, Prott and O'Keefe (n 46) 309: 'While "cultural heritage" is a relatively new term and has far less ideological baggage in tow, "property" has acquired a wide range of emotive and value-laden nuances from the arguments of John Locke to the challenge of Communism in the first two-thirds of this century'. See also Blake (n 24) 65–66.

legal concept of property is not sufficiently broad to cover everything that is intended to be encompassed in the concept of cultural property.[50] For instance, the property concept does not extend to a wide range of intangibles, such as spiritual beliefs[51] or values that bind together and regulate the relationship between persons, communities and tangibles.[52] This is, of course, also a consequence of the fact that when we talk about property in a legal sense we, here at the self-declared centre of the world,[53] are generally talking about a Western concept that embodies Western values. Apart from its scope, perhaps the Western value that is most bothersome in the context of cultural property is the concept of rivalrous ownership and possession that is Western property's special bedfellow.[54] It is not clear that ownership and possession are always appropriate concepts in this context. This is partly because they may not reflect the way that all cultures think about their cultural property.[55] But also because, even in the Western context, they trail in their wake other values and practices that might be thought to be undesirable. Rivalrous property rights are at the centre of a market-based thinking that has shown itself to be capable in the neo-liberal period of eclipsing any notion of public (as in non-private) good.[56] In the specific context of tangible cultural property, the results of this are evident in the thriving private international market for the sale of cultural artefacts.[57] It also seems to be

[50] Prott and O'Keefe (n 46) 311–12; Blake (n 24) 66; Flessas (n 32) 1068.

[51] See, eg, M Blakeney, 'Protecting the Spiritual Beliefs of Indigenous Peoples—Australian Case Studies' (2013) 22 *Pacific Rim Law & Policy Journal* 391.

[52] See, eg, RJ Coombe, 'The Properties of Culture & the Possession of Identity: Postcolonial Struggle & the Legal Imagination' in B Ziff and PV Rao (eds), *Borrowed Power: Essays on Cultural Appropriation* (New Jersey, Rutgers University Press, 1997); Prott and O'Keefe (n 46) 308–09 and 311–12; M Strathern, *Property, Substance & Effect: Anthropological Essays on Persons & Things* (London, Athlone Press, 1999).

[53] See Slaughter (n 48) 196.

[54] See also N Mezey, 'The Paradoxes of Cultural Property' (2007) 107 *Columbia Law Review* 2004.

[55] See, eg, Coombe (n 52); Strathern (n 52); MF Brown, *Who Owns Native Culture?* (Cambridge, Harvard University Press, 2003). See also Prott and O'Keefe (n 46) 310 citing *Milirrpum v Nabalco Pty Ltd* (1971) 17 FLR 141, in which the Federal Court of Australia found that the Yolngu people (the traditional owners of the Gove Peninsula in Arnhem Land) 'rather than believing that the land belonged to them ... believed that they belonged to the land: that it had been entrusted to them by their spirit ancestors and that they had certain duties towards it and rituals to perform on it.' (The decision in this case denying native title was subsequently overruled in *Mabo v Queensland (No 2)* (1992) 175 CLR 1, but without disturbing this finding). On the relationship of Australian Indigenous peoples to land, see J Gibson, 'Community and the Exhaustion of Culture: Creative Territories in Traditional Cultural Expressions' in F Macmillan and K Bowrey (eds), *New Directions in Copyright Law: Volume 3* (Cheltenham, Edward Elgar, 2006).

[56] Christodoulidis (n 44).

[57] Prott and O'Keefe (n 46) 311; Carpenter, Katyal and Riley (n 48) 1039–40, critiquing the defence of private property rights and market freedoms in relation to cultural property in EA Posner, 'The International Protection of Cultural Property: Some Skeptical Observations' (2007) 8 *Chicago Journal of International Law* 213.

implicated in the practices of museums that claim possessive property rights in their exhibits, which have limited or even prevented return of sensitive cultural objects.[58]

In the face of these arguments, it is clear that if we want to employ a concept of cultural property then it has to be one that is somehow divorced, or at least separated, from these traditional Western property notions. One way of doing this might be to conceive property in this context not as a relation of ownership but rather one of membership.[59] This conception of property reinforces the idea of cultural stuff as being intrinsically connected to identity. In fact, referring to property rather than heritage may avoid 'the privileging of preservation',[60] which has been at the heart of Western concepts of heritage,[61] at the expense of a dynamic relationship with identity.[62] This type of re-conception also moves us away from a strict division in ownership between public (as in state) and private property, which both operate to exclude community interests in ways which vary depending upon the community in question.[63] At the same time, the use of the word has an important political significance retaining the ideas of 'embattled space'[64] and that property itself is productive of community.[65] Using the word property here, instead of heritage, makes the conflict between cultural property and other types of property evident and unavoidable, both politically and legally. Further, it allows us to think about whether property concepts themselves, so well-known to the law, can be used to produce a liberatory tool that can be fitted into or recognised by the law.[66]

[58] See T Flessas, 'The Ends of the Museum' *Law Society & Economy Working Papers* 14/2013 (London, London School of Economics, 2013). In this context, it should be noted that civil law concepts of cultural property have also played a significant role in impeding return: see G Serino, *The Bilateral Disputes between Museums & States of Origin for the Recovery of Cultural Objects, Artistic Creations & Indigenous Heritage* (Ph D thesis, Università Roma Tre, 2014), s 5.5 on the dispute over Australian Indigenous cultural property held by the Museo Nazionale Preistorico Etnografico Luigi Pigorini.

[59] S Keenan, 'Holding Up Subversive Property', *ESRC Seminar Series: The Public Life of Private Law* (Kent Law School, 18 January 2013), http://backdoorbroadcasting.net/2013/01/sarah-keenan-holding-up-subversive-property/. This idea of property is part of many non-Western systems: see, eg, Gibson (n 55) esp 32–36, for a discussion of the difference between 'This land is mine ... This land is me' in the film *One Night the Moon* (2001, dir R Perkins).

[60] Flessas (n 32) 1091.

[61] See, eg, Flessas (n 32); Flessas (n 58); Macmillan (n 4) 354–55; MD Simpson, *Making Representations: Museums in the Post-Colonial Era* (London, Routledge, 2001); P Yu, 'Cultural Relics, Intellectual Property and Intangible Heritage' (2008) 81 *Temple Law Review* 433 at 471–73.

[62] *cf* Prott and O'Keefe (n 46) esp 311.

[63] On this point generally, see Keenan (n 59). On its specific application in the context of cultural artefacts, see Prott and O'Keefe (n 46) 315ff.

[64] Flessas (n 32) 1085.

[65] Keenan (n 59); Gibson (n 55).

[66] As Prott and O'Keefe (n 46) 312, citing R Crewdson, 'Cultural Property—A Fourth Estate?' (1984) 18 *Law Society Gazette* 126, make clear the idea of recognising cultural property as a further class of common law property (in addition to real property, personal property and intellectual property) has been around for some time.

The idea that property, or property concepts, might have liberatory or even subversive[67] power has seductive power, even if (like all subversive ideas in their early stages) it requires careful articulation and constant defence.[68] Any attempt to use, or even propose, property devices in the context of cultural protection appear to fly in the face of a vast movement, scholarly and political, that lauds free access to culture and tends to be suspicious of any attempts at what it regards as propertisation of cultural artefacts, especially intangible cultural artefacts. The much debated idea of the cultural commons or public domain[69] is primarily located in a concern to safeguard community interests in cultural stuff.[70] The method by which this safeguarding takes place is by using the cultural commons or public domain as a defence against private appropriation. One of the limitations of this concept, however, is that it raises more difficult questions about how to protect communities from other forms of inappropriate uses of their cultural property. The problem is that the unregulated commons or public domain provides no legal architecture for the vindication of specific community interests in cultural property.[71] This makes the unprotected exposure of cultural property in the commons problematic. As a result, the discourse of the commons has been cogently criticised on the ground that it has the capacity to amount to what is effectively a second, post-colonial misappropriation of the culture of indigenous peoples.[72] While this particular addition of insult to injury requires specific recognition, the likelihood that the issue has a wider application should be recognised.[73] In response, it is—at the very least—clear that the concept of cultural property, residing outside the scope of traditional private property rights, requires legal architecture.

Such a form of architecture has been proposed by Carpenter, Katyal and Riley.[74] Their proposal for a stewardship model of property in order to vindicate the cultural property claims of indigenous peoples seeks to find

[67] See Keenan (n 59).

[68] See, eg, Flessas (n 32) 1092.

[69] There is a vast literature on this theme, including: J Boyle, *The Public Domain: Enclosing the Commons of the Mind* (New Haven, Yale University Press, 2008); Brown (n 55); E Hemmungs Wirtén, *Terms of Use: Negotiating the Jungle of the Intellectual Commons* (Toronto, University of Toronto Press, 2008); JB Holder and T Flessas, 'Emerging Commons' (2008) 17 *Social & Legal Studies* 299; Mezey (n 54).

[70] There is also a strand of cosmopolitan thought that takes a similar position, see KA Appiah, *Cosmopolitanism: Ethics in a World of Strangers* (London, Penguin, 2006) 115–35.

[71] F Macmillan, 'Many Analogies, Some Metaphors, Little Imagination: The Public Domain in Intellectual Space' (2010) *Pòlemos* 25.

[72] K Bowrey and J Anderson, 'The Politics of Global Information Sharing: Whose Cultural Agendas are Being Advanced?' (2009) 18 *Social & Legal Studies* 479. *cf* Mezey (n 54).

[73] See further F Macmillan, 'Arts Festivals: Property, Heritage or More?' in K Bowrey and M Handler (eds), *Law and Creativity in the Age of the Entertainment Franchise* (Cambridge, Cambridge University Press, 2014).

[74] n 48 above.

a liberatory model for the use of the property paradigm that transcends its current narrow legal focus on private rights and on the distinction between private property and some form of publicly held property. According to this model, indigenous peoples become the custodians or trustees of their cultural property with responsibilities to ensure the appropriate use of the property and its transmission to subsequent generations. Effectively, this stewardship model uses the property paradigm without replicating those aspects of traditional property law that have already been identified as problematic in the context of cultural stuff. Theoretically, the model is located in Radin's work on the relationship between property and personhood:[75]

> Radin's account of personhood captures precisely the meaning that cultural property may carry for indigenous people: that some properties are so constitutive of one's identity that they demand treatment that transcends—and surpasses—that of an ordinary market transaction. It is quite legitimate in Radin's view, to make exceptions to the prevailing 'universal commodification' standard for property that is nonfungible, incommensurable, and inalienable, as some indigenous cultural properties surely are.[76]

To use Radin's work in this way, however, requires a transition from her emphasis on the relationship between individual personhood and property to a concern with the relationship between peoplehood and property that is implicated in the idea of a group claim. In laying the groundwork for this development of the argument, Carpenter, Katyal and Riley do not neglect the possibility that some indigenous claims to property maybe be located in personhood rather than peoplehood.[77] However, their emphasis is on community rights. As they are fully aware, arguments about community rights often appear to be teetering on the edge of the type of essentialism that suggests cultural (and political) closure. In the context of cultural stuff, this is the type of closure that provokes anxiety because it appears to fly in the face of traditions of cultural and creative interchange that have made the world (for better or worse) what it is today[78] and is also capable of generating forms of political closure often associated with the extreme political right.[79] A notion of community rights that is capable of resting on more than one level of identity, and therefore moves away from an essentialist position, is

[75] See, in particular, MJ Radin, 'Property & Personhood' (1982) 34 *Stanford Law Review* 957.

[76] Carpenter, Katyal and Riley (n 48) 1022, referring to and quoting MJ Radin, *Contested Commodities* (Cambridge, Harvard University Press, 1996) 8–15.

[77] Carpenter, Katyal and Riley (n 48) 1022–23: 'Following Radin, we observe that some indigenous cultural property claims may well fall into these categories of property that are critical for personal development, either because the property forms the context for human individuation or because individual rights are exercised in a collective setting' (footnotes omitted).

[78] This is a concept embedded in the UNESCO Convention on Cultural Diversity, Art 1.

[79] See, eg Macmillan (n 4) 352–55, on claims to cultural heritage by the Danish Peoples Party.

better adapted to responding to these concerns. In relation to indigenous peoples this type of multilevel identity is often present and is increasingly legally embedded.[80] Not only does this make it easier, from a legal point of view, to identify the various levels of identity, it also suggests some basis for passing between what the UNESCO conventions would describe as the heritage of (hu)mankind to the particular interests of peoples and groups.

Whether the elegant and persuasive use of the property concept embedded in the stewardship model, which is intended to address the situation of indigenous peoples, can function as well outside the context of indigenous cultural property claims is open to question. The fact that the identity and claims of indigenous peoples as a community are recognisable within the legal environment of many states in which indigenous communities live is, ironically, a reaction to the dispossession and loss of political autonomy visited upon them in the colonial and post-colonial periods. However, it is this very environment of legally recognised identity, in the context of multi-layered identities, that may make the stewardship model functional. Further, the suggestion that the use of the property paradigm may be a specific response to the massive land dispossession suffered by indigenous peoples everywhere[81] may be interpreted as providing only very limited support for a paradigm of cultural property outside the context of indigenous cultural property. Finally, the particular treatment of indigenous peoples in the post-colonial period, especially the denial of political autonomy, may be a ground for arguing that models designed to protect their cultural property are not, in any case, necessarily appropriate for all communities or groups.

IV. CULTURAL PROPERTY VERSUS INTELLECTUAL PROPERTY

The question of the protection of the cultural property of indigenous peoples is addressed by the UNDRIP, which also proposes a model for the use of property rights in the specific context of indigenous peoples' claims. The Declaration's main assertion with respect to cultural heritage is in Article 31.1:

> Indigenous peoples have the right to maintain, control, protect and develop their cultural heritage, traditional knowledge and traditional cultural expressions, as well as the manifestations of their sciences, technologies and cultures, including human and genetic resources, seeds, medicines, knowledge of the properties of fauna and flora, oral traditions, literatures, designs, sports and traditional games and visual and performing arts. They also have the right to maintain, control, protect and develop their intellectual property over such cultural heritage, traditional knowledge, and traditional cultural expressions.

[80] See, in relation to the US, Carpenter, Katyal and Riley (n 48) 1056–59.
[81] Carpenter, Katyal and Riley (n 48) 1060.

The model, thus, envisages an intellectual property rights model as a mode of protecting the cultural property rights of indigenous peoples. Apart from circumstances in which the cultural property of indigenous peoples is properly understood as being privately owned,[82] this claim to elide cultural property with intellectual property is problematic. If one of the stronger arguments in favour of using 'property' rather than 'heritage' is that it makes the normative conflict between cultural property and other forms of property clear and unavoidable, then this elision takes us back into the murky waters of confusion.

A central reason for recognising community rights to cultural property is to defend that property from privatisation. While it is clear that indigenous peoples and other communities in the global south have been victims of the unauthorised appropriation of their intangible cultural property by private interests through the use of intellectual property rights,[83] it is at least worth pausing to consider the consequences of using the sword as a shield. The argument that underlies claims of the sort contained in Article 31.1 is that the best defence to the cultural threat posed by private intellectual property rights encroaching on those cultural rights it to turn those cultural rights into private rights. This argument has an intrinsic appeal. Moreover, the post-colonial political context of these claims is not easy to ignore. At the same time, it is perhaps this very context that is responsible for the fact that attempts to use intellectual property rights in this way have been problematic because of the difficulty in using a private right to vindicate a community right. That is to say that there is a significant lack of political interest in changing intellectual property law in order to recognise the claims of indigenous peoples as communities.[84] Further, while noting the inherent injustice in the failure to recognise the particular position of indigenous peoples, the idea of turning cultural property into intellectual property may not be optimal from the point of view of the integrity of the cultural property itself. One result of turning of cultural property into intellectual property is that the cultural property has to be corralled into the shape of Western intellectual property law.[85] If the item of cultural property is a story, music or artwork then it has to be fitted into copyright law; designs and symbols must fit into the netherworld of the relationship between copyright, designs and trademarks; knowledge about local flora and fauna must be fitted somewhere into patent law, plant breeders' rights and geographical indications.

[82] See n 77 above.

[83] See Slaughter (n 48); Macmillan (n 4); Carpenter, Katyal and Riley (n 48).

[84] See, eg, M Blakeney, 'Protecting Traditional Cultural Expressions: The International Dimension' in F Macmillan and K Bowrey (eds), *New Directions in Copyright Law: Volume 3* (Cheltenham, Edward Elgar, 2006).

[85] See M Blakeney, 'The Protection of Traditional Knowledge Under Intellectual Property Law' (2000) 22 *European Intellectual Property Law Review* 251.

This will mean that different levels of protection will apply to different types of indigenous cultural property. In short, the end result is that occidental intellectual property law comes to constitute indigenous (and other non-Western) cultural property.[86] In so doing, it may change the shape of that property in ways that are not necessarily the consequence of the reflexive cultural practice that constitutes it. This seems to be inimical to the very purpose of protecting cultural property.

The tendency to elide intellectual property rights and cultural property rights, which has been remarkably persistent, owes at least something to the confusion provoked by their competing invocations of intangibility. Intellectual property rights, unlike cultural property rights, are never claims to tangible property but rather claims to intangible rights (albeit claims that often implicate tangible objects).[87] Cultural property, on the other hand, has an awkward relationship with the distinction between the tangible and the intangible. While it applies to both, it is possible to exaggerate the significance of the distinction precisely because what makes a tangible thing into cultural property is its intangible or symbolic association.[88] Even though their ideas of intangibility are different, the disorientation of the intangible realm seems to augment the dangers of confusing, eliding and overlapping cultural property and intellectual property. One possible consequence of this becomes evident if we turn our attention from the question of the protection of non-Western cultural property to that of Western cultural property. In this context, rather strangely, instead of arguing that we should turn cultural property into intellectual property, it would be tempting to argue that we should turn intellectual property (back) into cultural property.

Slaughter argues that the relationship between intellectual property and cultural property can be mapped onto global geo-political relations, with the result that we think of the West as having intellectual property and the rest as having cultural property.[89] By this he means to suggest, not a difference in the subjects of these property rights, but rather a difference in their treatment:

> In the Western tradition, cultural property may be what becomes of some literary texts and their creators after copyrights run out (for example, when

[86] P Fitzpatrick and R Joyce, 'Copying Right: Cultural Property and the Limits of (Occidental) Law' in F Macmillan (ed), *New Directions in Copyright Law: Volume 4* (Cheltenham, Edward Elgar, 2007) 171.

[87] In fact the relationship between intellectual property and tangible objects is often problematic. The most obvious example of this relates to the intellectual property protection of works of visual art: see F Macmillan, 'Is Copyright Blind to the Visual?' (2008) 7 *Visual Communication* 97.

[88] See Blake (n 24) 67–69; Macmillan (n 4) 361–62.

[89] This characterisation might well be regarded as reinforced by the contents of the Representative List of the Intangible Cultural Heritage of Humanity, established under the UNESCO Intangible Cultural Heritage Convention, Art 16, which is overwhelmingly populated by contributions from the global south.

Proust becomes French, Goethe German, Joyce Irish, Dickens British, Melville American); but historically the distinction between cultural and intellectual property has generally (once again) been mapped onto the divide between the developing and developed world, trailing behind it a long series of old familiar orientalist oppositions: individual versus collective, personal property vs group commons, formal versus informal knowledge, and so forth. Accordingly, we in the West produce spontaneous original intellectual property; they in the rest of the world have a rich (though probably burdensome) collective legacy of cultural heritage and traditional knowledge that is, so the logic goes, part of what keeps their societies underdeveloped.[90]

As Slaughter goes on to argue, the 'power and prestige' of the formal system of property relations which governs intellectual property overwhelms the informal and 'traditional' system of cultural property protection.[91] Despite some rather simple formalisation as a result of the requirement that to have protection under the UNESCO Intangible Cultural Heritage Convention intangible cultural heritage must be listed,[92] it seems relatively clear that intellectual property has the upper hand since it is a formalised technique of private appropriation of intangible cultural property.[93] While the idea that all non-Western cultural property is open to private appropriation is unjust and outrageous, it might also be noted that the notion that the West lacks intangible cultural property is socially (and culturally) impoverishing.[94] Hence, at least in the Western context, the idea of rolling back intellectual property protection in favour of the recognition of communal rights in cultural property is attractive.

V. CONCLUSION: RESISTING THE PRIVATISATION OF EVERYTHING

There are two particular attractions of the concept of cultural 'property' over that of 'heritage'. First, it draws attention to a conflict that exists as a matter of fact, between community rights and other forms of property, but is neither addressed nor resolved in law. Apart from the lack of political will in the face of this problem, it is also affected by a 'category' problem in a positivist legal sense. The organisation of law as a discipline depends on a distinction between public (as in non-private) and private rights, which tend to be considered in discrete categories. This way of thinking about law creates difficulties in resolving conflicts across these notional boundaries. Historically, and consistently with the requirements of capitalist relations, this has

[90] Slaughter (n 48) 198–99 (footnote omitted).
[91] ibid, 200.
[92] Intangible Cultural Heritage Convention, Arts 16 and 17.
[93] See Slaughter (n 48); Macmillan (n 4).
[94] See further Macmillan (n 73).

led to the legal sacralisation of private property rights. In the late twentieth century this unquestioning devotion to the sanctity of private rights and private property started to come under some pressure, not the least as a result of the rise of a strong human rights discourse. However, the power balance between the discourse of private property and that of non-private property rights, such as human rights, is always perched on a knife edge. Cultural heritage rights, which derive their normative impact from the human rights regime, have certainly not been immune from this conflict. Further complicating this picture in the present context is that fact that public (non-private) rights in law do not necessarily comprehend rights of communities forming less than the public as a whole.

The second attraction of the cultural property concept is that by employing the strength of the property construct it would seem to provide a better bulwark against the creeping privatisation of everything. While it is possible to come up with a list of things that might constitute cultural heritage in certain circumstances, it is much harder to find an overarching concept that defines cultural heritage. Even if we say that we don't know much about cultural heritage, but we know it when we see it, it is still the case that the positive rights in relation to cultural heritage in international law are weak and expressly unable to resist the incursions of private property. Stronger rights exist in some national systems with respect to particular types of cultural heritage,[95] but there is not much in the way of general consensus. Bearing in mind the fairly uniform understanding of the power of private property rights in most legal systems, the fact that there is little consensus on what it means to have cultural heritage rights makes those rights largely impotent when it comes to resisting the privatisation of everything. On the other hand, the fact that the concept of cultural heritage exists in international law should not be cast too lightly aside. Perhaps, in relation to the unknown quantity that is reflected in the concept of cultural property, there is a political or strategic advantage in the use of the cultural heritage concept. But if this is so, it needs to be radicalised, and the obvious path of radicalisation seems to lead towards the idea of cultural property.

If the concept of cultural property as a bulwark against privatisation is to have any value, however, it must be more than just a vague notion defined by the absence of positive property rights, whether private or public. It needs to provide safeguards against the unauthorised appropriation and use of cultural property. It needs to transcend outdated thinking that divides property rights between public (as in state) and private rights holders, by recognising community interests. It also needs to recognise that people often have more

[95] This is particularly so in relation to the return of human remains, but is also the case with respect to civil law jurisdictions that confer rights on the state in relation to particular types of cultural artefacts: see text acc n 47 above.

than one community identity. At the same time, as if all this was not difficult enough, it needs to safeguard against the dangers of the type of exclusivity that is oppressive and constrains cultural interchange and development. In other words, if cultural heritage requires radicalisation through the use of the property construct, then the ensuing concept of cultural property must be based on a radicalisation of the very concept of property. Proposals exist for this type of subversive approach to cultural property. The stewardship model suggested by Carpenter, Katyal and Riley is one of them. The extent to which this might work well outside the context of indigenous cultural property needs further examination. There is also the question of the liberatory potential of a regulated commons.[96] That is, one that has at least the following types of characteristics: first, a notion of the difference between what is subject to community ownership in intellectual space and what is unowned and thus ripe for appropriation; second, an associated recognition that some things can never be owned, at least privately, because of their cultural significance; third, development of the concept of group and communal rights, belonging to less than the public as a whole, bounded by property on the outside, but inside promoting freedom and space for creativity, innovation, invention and cultural conservation.[97] Excellent work has started to emerge on this front.[98] Its development requires legal and political commitment. Perhaps the time frames for seeing in the changes are longer than might be imagined by those who think that the 'impact' of academic work can be measured out in a handful of years, but that is of little relative importance against the social and cultural wealth that a developed concept of cultural property is capable of bestowing. The challenge is to find a way of recognising in law rights that should belong to us all. It is, therefore, worth reflecting on how we might 'read reality in different legal terms'[99] and on whether existing legal instruments might be re-imagined in order to perform this task.

[96] As Hemmungs Wirtén (n 69) shows, the real property commons was always regulated.

[97] On each of these points, see further F Macmillan, 'Altering the Contours of the Public Domain' in C Waelde and H MacQueen (eds), *Intellectual Property: The Many Faces of the Public Domain* (Cheltenham, Edward Elgar, 2007).

[98] See, eg, MR Marella (ed), *Oltre il pubblico e il privato. Per un diritto dei beni comuni* (Verona, Ombre Corte, 2012); A Ciervo, *I beni comuni* (Rome, Ediesse, 2013); M Bruncevic, *Fixing the Shadows: Access to Art and the Legal Concept of Cultural Commons* (Ph D Thesis, University of Gothenberg, 2014).

[99] '[L]eggere in termi giuridici diversi la realtà': Ciervo, ibid 190 (my translation).

3

Constitutional Law, Social Justice and the Redistribution of Land

TOM ALLEN

I. INTRODUCTION

THIS CHAPTER EXAMINES the interplay between human rights, constitutional law, the compulsory redistribution of land and the forces of globalisation. Rural poverty and gross inequality seem to compel state intervention in land ownership, and yet a strong right to property can entrench the very interests that governments wish to challenge. This is especially acute in the developing world, where a right to full compensation for land taken for redistribution can make it financially impossible for governments to take significant action. This chapter therefore concentrates on two states—India and the Philippines—where politicians and judges have frequently dealt with the tension between the egalitarianism and relief of poverty, on one side, and the right to property on the other. In both countries, promises of redistribution and agrarian reform have been part of political life since World War II, if not before. At one time, such promises were very much the norm for post-colonial nations.[1] Many hoped that implementing promises of 'land to the tiller' would address both inequality and poverty, and that compulsion would be necessary for meaningful action. However, in recent decades, most states have moved away from redistribution. In the Philippines, the national programme of land acquisition that was initiated in 1987 is drawing to a close; in India, there is even less activity. Yet, in both countries, the level of inequality in the distribution of land remains high and success has been only partial, at best.

In these countries, land reform has featured in constitutional law, both in specific provisions and as a key consideration in the framing of rights to

[1] See generally, M Lipton, *Land Reform in Developing Countries: Property Rights and Property Wrongs* (Oxford, Routledge, 2009); P Krugman, 'Inequality and Redistribution' in N Serra and JE Stiglitz (eds), *The Washington Consensus Reconsidered: Towards a New Global Governance* (Oxford, Oxford University Press, 2008).

property. The courts in both countries have produced rich jurisprudence on the interpretation of relevant constitutional clauses. From independence, the highest courts in India and the Philippines maintained a requirement of full compensation for land taken for redistribution (and other purposes). There have been interludes where the courts allowed greater flexibility but, as this chapter demonstrates, the general trend is for full compensation. The impact on the cost of redistribution has made it more difficult to implement reform, and helps to explain why the achievement is less than anticipated. Indeed, the Indian and Philippine record on redistribution contrasts sharply with that of Japan, Taiwan and South Korea.[2] These countries carried out the most comprehensive post-World War II programmes for land reform and redistribution in Asia (leaving aside the socialist nations). Moreover, as in India and the Philippines, land redistribution was implemented through the use of legal powers of compulsory acquisition, rather than consensual, market-led reform or the confiscatory methods of the socialist governments. However, the cost of compensation was significantly lower: in Japan, Taiwan and South Korea, compensation was based on the value of rents or crop yields, and generally fell well below market values. As explained below, proposals for such compensation standards were brought forward in India and the Philippines. However, they were either dismissed before they could be implemented, or they were subject to constitutional challenges that restored the market standard. Arguably, these constitutional differences had the effect of making extensive land redistribution far more difficult to achieve.

Of course, factors other than compensation have been important. External forces have played a crucial role: it is worth noting, for example, that the United States supported redistribution in Japan, Taiwan and South Korea.[3] Both the American and the national governments were fearful that, without land reform, the peasants would support communist insurgencies. In India, the United States had less influence, and in any case the communist threat was much weaker. However, in the Philippines, where American influence has been greater, the focus has been on military action, rather than social

[2] See generally J Putzel, *A Captive Land: The Politics of Agrarian Reform in the Philippines* (London, Catholic Institute for International Relations, 1992) 101–05; J-S You, 'Inequality and Corruption: The Role of Land Reform in Korea, Taiwan, and the Philippines' Annual Conference of the *Association for Asian Studies*, Atlanta, Georgia, 3–6 April 2008; H-C Tai, *Land Reform and Politics: A Comparative Analysis* (London, University of California Press, 1974); on each country, see NL Nathanson, 'Constitutional Adjudication in Japan' (1958) 7 *American Journal of Comparative Law* 195; A YC Koo, *The Role of Land Reform in Economic Development: A Cast Study of Taiwan* (New York, Praeger, 1968); Y-D Jeon and Y-Y Kim, 'Land Reform, Income Redistribution, and Agricultural Production in Korea' (2000) 48 *Economic Development and Cultural Change* 253, 254–58.

[3] Putzel, ibid 96–99, 127–37, 283–303 (Putzel also discusses the World Bank's brief period of support for more radical reforms: ibid, 287–90); SM Borras Jr, D Carranza Jr, C Franco and MA Manahan, *Anti-Land Reform Land Policy?: The World Bank's Development Assistance to Agrarian Reform in the Philippines*, focusweb.org/sites/www.focusweb.org/files/WORLDBANK-Boras-Carranza-Franco-Manahan.pdf, 9–12.

measures aimed at winning over the rural peasantry. More recently, the World Bank urged the Philippine government to abandon its programme of compulsory redistribution in favour of market-led, voluntary transfers.[4]

Whilst external forces are undoubtedly important, this chapter concentrates on the internal forces of globalisation, and in particular on the tendency of judges to frame their reasons for supporting full compensation by reference to comparative law. The chapter demonstrates that, so far as the judges are concerned, comparative law has almost invariably pointed them in the direction of the liberal model of state power and property. By this view, the right to property is an integral element of personal liberty: the rights of property describe a part of individual autonomy that deserves the same level of protection as (for example) rights to freedom of expression and conscience.[5] This is not to say that property is immune from expropriation in the public interest. However, where this does occur, the owner has no obligation to shoulder a greater part of the burden of serving the public interest than any other citizen. In constitutional and human rights law, this is expressed through provisions that guarantee full compensation for the compulsory acquisition of property. This ensures that the owner suffers no economic loss beyond the additional tax burden in funding compensation that falls on all citizens.

This has had two main doctrinal implications. First, the courts of India and the Philippines have generally interpreted constitutional property clauses as requiring full compensation for taking, even where there is some doubt that the plain language or original intention would justify such a reading. Second, in cases related to property, the courts have given little to no weight to constitutional provisions on social justice, egalitarianism and land reform. In the Philippines, the result is that redistribution cannot proceed unless the landowners are paid full compensation for their land. In effect, the option of providing below-market compensation, as in Taiwan, Japan and South Korea, has not been available. The situation in India is more complex: the right to property normally requires full compensation, but it does allow exceptions. Moreover, there are recognised mechanisms by which the legislature may narrow the scope of judicial review. Nevertheless, the ideology of property remains liberal.

[4] Borras et al, ibid. An extensive literature examines the relationships between the national laws on the protection of property and international capital flows: see eg DS Law and M Versteeg, 'The Evolution and Ideology of Global Constitutionalism' (2011) 99 *California Law Review* 1163; DS Law, 'Globalization and the Future of Constitutional Rights' (2007) 102 *Northwestern University Law Review* 1277; DA Farber, 'Rights as Signals' (2002) 31 *Journal of Legal Studies* 83; M Tushnet, 'The Inevitable Globalization of Constitutional Law' (2009) 49 *Virginia Journal of International Law* 985; R Dixon and EA Posner, 'The Limits of Constitutional Convergence' (2010–2011) 11 *Chicago Journal of International Law* 399; T Moustafa, 'Law versus the State: The Judicialization of Politics in Egypt' (2003) 28 *Law & Social Inquiry* 883, 885.

[5] See RA Epstein, *Takings: Private Property and the Power of Eminent Domain* (Cambridge MA, Harvard University Press, 1985).

The chapter begins by considering the framing of constitutional rights to property in each country at independence, and the subsequent rise of the liberal interpretation of compensation guarantees. It then follows the weakening of the liberal position through the 1970s and 1980s before considering the revival of the liberal model in more recent years. Throughout, it shows how comparative law has been utilised to justify support for the liberal model. It closes with an examination of the comparative methodology of the courts, by asking whether it is a form of judicial learning from comparator models, a type of signalling (and if so, the intended audience), or a means of legitimating socially conservative judgments intended to support a landed elite.

As this collection concentrates on human rights and property, it may appear that a chapter on constitutional law is out of place. However, the judicial analysis of the right to property under international human rights law, especially that of the European Convention on Human Rights, is very similar to that of constitutional law in these countries. In practical terms, the rights to property in the constitutional law of India and the Philippines provide a similar constraint on state power as the right contained in Article 1 of the First Protocol to the Convention. Indeed, the Indian Supreme Court has increasingly referred to the judgments of the European Court of Human Rights on the European right to property in its constitutional jurisprudence.[6] It is not surprising that this is the case: in Europe, India and the Philippines, the rights to property—constitutional or international—are treated as safeguards of individual freedom and human dignity in the face of state power. Hence, for this collection, it makes sense to concentrate on the national jurisprudence of constitutional property rights when seeking to identify global trends on human rights and property.

II. LIBERAL, SOCIALIST AND SOCIAL DEMOCRAT CONSTITUTIONAL THEORIES AT INDEPENDENCE

Liberal views on land ownership had a strong influence on the framing of the colonial constitutions of both India and the Philippines. In India, as in England itself, questions were frequently raised over the legitimacy of land laws that allowed and sustained the concentration of holdings.[7] In much of India, these patterns of concentrated ownership were created by the British.[8]

[6] See eg *KT Plantation Pvt Ltd v State of Karnataka* [2011] 13 (ADDL) SCR 636 [85].

[7] See generally I Packer and L George, *Liberalism and the Land: The Land Issue and Party Politics in England, 1906–1914* (London, Royal Historical Society Studies in History New Series, 2001); A Offer, *Property and Politics, 1870–1914: Landownership, Law, Ideology, and Urban Development in England* (Cambridge, Cambridge University Press, 1981).

[8] PK Agrawal, *Land Reforms in India: Constitutional and Legal Approach (with Special Reference to Uttar Pradesh)* (New Delhi, MD Publications, 1993) 1–18; HCL Merillat, *Land and the Constitution in India* (New York, Columbia University Press, 1970) ch 1.

In the late eighteenth century, the British East India Company sought to create a landholding system that would secure it a satisfactory level of income and, ideally, provide incentives for the further development of agriculture. Their solution lay in the creation of a near-feudal system of tenure, under which a group of tax collectors and administrators were allocated territory over which they had the right to set and collect rents from tenants. In exchange, they were required to make a fixed annual payment to the Company. This arrangement, known as the Permanent Settlement of 1793, effectively transformed the tax collectors, or '*zamindars*', into private owners of extensive tracts of land. The system did not apply throughout the country, and by the early nineteenth century the British had decided not to extend it to the remaining parts of India under their jurisdiction. It became increasingly unpopular through the twentieth century, with growing demands for tenancy reform or outright abolition of the system. However, the *zamindars* supported British rule, and hence the British were reluctant to embark on reforms that would diminish their property rights. This was demonstrated in 1934: the Parliamentary Joint Committee on Indian Constitutional Reform rejected Indian demands for a bill of rights whilst recommending a right to property 'in order to quiet doubts which have been aroused in recent years by certain Indian utterances'.[9] These proposals were incorporated in the Government of India Act, 1935.[10] By expressing the constitutional issue in terms of property, rather than political or social power, a special status was reserved for a group of landowners whose claim to ownership and influence was coming under attack.

The use of constitutional law to support a landed elite was also found in the Philippines. The United States took over the Philippines from Spain under the Treaty of Paris (1898), but without the intention of making it a colony on a permanent basis. It became a Commonwealth in 1935 and fully independent in 1946. When the United States took power, the Catholic Church owned most of the private land, with tenant farmers in a position of servitude.[11] The territorial government intended to redistribute land, and

[9] The Joint Committee on Indian Constitutional Reform, *Report of the Joint Committee on Indian Constitutional Reform* (1934), Vol 1, Pt 1, para 366. See also Merillat, ibid, and T Allen, *The Right to Property in Commonwealth Constitutions* (Cambridge, Cambridge University Press, 2000) 43–46.

[10] Government of India Act, 1935, s 299. The key provisions required legislation to state the principles on which compensation would be determined (s 299(2)), and also required prior sanction of the Governor General or Governor for the introduction of such legislation in the legislature (s 299(3)).

[11] See Putzel (n 2) 43–66 and WG Wolters, 'The Development of Property Rights to Land in the Philippines, 1850–1930' in T van Meijl and F von Benda-Beckmann (eds), *Property Rights and Economic Development: Land and Resources in Southeast Asia and Oceania* (London and New York, Kegan Paul International, 1999) 110, 113–38 for the history of land ownership under the territorial government and before; see also JM Riedinger, *Agrarian Reform in the Philippines: Democratic Transitions and Redistributive Reform* (Stanford, Stanford University Press, 1995); TM Hanstad, 'Philippine Land Reform: The Just Compensation Issue' (1988) 63 *Washington Law Review* 417; ALA Martin, 'Philippine Land Reform Cycles: Perpetuating US Colonial Policy' (1999) 47 *Philippine Studies* 181.

indeed it acquired lands held by the Church for this purpose. However, to cover the cost of acquisition, it offered the land for resale at prices that most tenant farmers could not afford. Consequently, the concentration of holdings remained, although with a different group of owners. The United States then made it very difficult for Philippine governments to give serious consideration to further acquisitions for redistribution, as it entrenched property rights in the constitution of the territory. Section 5 of the Philippines Bill of 1902,[12] which set up the territorial government, included the due process guarantee of the Fifth Amendment of the United States Constitution: 'no law shall be enacted in said Islands which shall deprive any person of life, liberty, or property without due process of law, or deny to any person therein the equal protection of the laws'. The Fifth Amendment also incorporates the 'takings clause', which adds the provision 'nor shall private property be taken for public use, without just compensation' to the due process clause. Under American law, the due process clause only provides protection in respect of the procedural aspects of an interference with property. The takings clause guarantees 'just compensation'. Crucially, this only applies to 'takings'; in broad terms, an American 'taking' is equivalent to a compulsory acquisition of property under British law.

At first glance, the omission of the takings clause from the Philippines Bill would appear to be a significant matter. However, section 63 of the Bill delegated the power of eminent domain to the Government of the Philippines (under American law, the power to compulsorily acquire property is known as the power of eminent domain). Section 74 then provided that the Government could further delegate the power of eminent domain, but only subject to the condition 'That no private property shall be taken for any purpose under this section without just compensation paid or tendered therefor'. Subsequently, the Philippine Autonomy Act of 1916 repeated the property provisions of the 1902 Bill, and added a takings clause based on the corresponding clause of the Fifth Amendment.[13] All the subsequent constitutions (1935, 1973 and 1987, excluding the Japanese occupation) include both due process and takings clauses.[14]

The colonial constitutions of both countries therefore ensured that the dependent legislatures had the power to acquire and redistribute land, whilst providing constitutional protection for the special status of a small class of landowners. Independence therefore provided an opportunity to reconsider the constitutional position of property in both jurisdictions, especially in relation to compensation on expropriation. However, this only occurred

[12] See generally EM Fernando, 'An Asian Perspective on the American Constitutional Influence in Asia: Its Impact on the Philippine Legal System' (1976) 18 *Malaya Law Review* 281.

[13] Section 3; s 28 included the clause regarding delegation of the power of eminent domain.

[14] Constitution of the Republic of the Philippines, 1935, Art III, s 1.1 and 1.2; Constitution of the Republic of the Philippines, 1973, Art IV, s 1, s 2; Constitution of the Republic of the Philippines, 1987, Art III, s 1, s 9.

in India. In the Philippines, the process for achieving independence was set up by the Philippine Independence Act of 1934.[15] The Act authorised a convention to draft a proposed constitution for approval by the President of the United States. Approval would not be given unless the Act included a bill of rights.[16] Not only did the Convention's proposal include the due process and takings clauses, but it added a new section 4: 'The Congress may authorize, upon payment of just compensation, the expropriation of lands to be subdivided into small lots and conveyed at cost to individuals'. The proposed text was certified by President Roosevelt on 23 March 1935.

The new Constitution came into effect at a crucial point in American history. The legislative programme of President Roosevelt's New Deal was in progress, but many aspects were subject to constitutional challenge. In a line of cases including the famous *Lochner v New York* (1905), the Supreme Court of the United States invoked the Bill of Rights, including the Fifth Amendment, to strike down social legislation as an interference with liberty.[17] The New Deal reflected the social democrat belief that human dignity was at stake in periods of economic crisis, and that the protection of human rights could require active intervention in markets.[18] Plainly, this challenged narrower characterisation of individual freedom and liberalism in the form expressed in *Lochner.* In the Philippines, President Quezon also sought to enact legislation in pursuit of social justice, not unlike President Roosevelt.[19] However, the constitutional concerns were similar: in *People v Pomar*, the Philippine Supreme Court followed *Lochner* and related cases.[20] In both countries, the majority of cases concerned labour laws and the contracts clause of the Bill of Rights, rather than the right to property. Nevertheless, the *Lochner* jurisprudence came to be regarded, both within the United States and internationally, as an illustration of the potential impact of the constitutional protection of property on legislative programmes for social and economic change.[21] The liberal doctrines of the *Lochner* line of cases were coming under challenge when the 1935 Constitution was approved, but would not be reversed until *West Coast Hotel Co v Parrish* (1937)[22] and *United States v Carolene Products* (1938).[23] Given the potential obstacle of the *Lochner/Pomar* doctrines, the framers of the 1935 Constitution added

[15] Public Law 73–127 (1934; US); see generally Fernando (n 12).

[16] Public Law 73–127, s 3.

[17] *Lochner v New York* (1905) 198 US 45; S Choudhry, 'The Lochner Era and Comparative Constitutionalism' (2004) 2 *International Journal of Constitutional Law* 1.

[18] See S Berman, *The Primacy of Politics: Social Democracy and the Making of Europe's Twentieth Century* (Cambridge, Cambridge University Press, 2006).

[19] Putzel (n 2) 57–59.

[20] *People v Pomar* (1924) GR No L-22008: the Philippine Supreme Court applied American cases on due process to strike down legislation on maternity leave.

[21] Choudhry (n 17).

[22] *West Coast Hotel Co v Parrish* (1979) 300 US 379.

[23] *United States v Carolene Products* (1938) 304 US 144.

a 'Declaration of Principles' on social justice. Section 5 provided that 'The promotion of social justice to insure the well-being and economic security of all the people should be the concern of the State'.

Plainly, the Constitution of the United States has no provision corresponding to section 5, and it was uncertain how it would be received by the Philippine Supreme Court. Oddly, section 5 first arose as an argument for the continuation of the *Lochner* doctrine. In *Calalang v Williams* (1940),[24] the petitioner argued that a restriction on use of animal-drawn carts in Manila was unconstitutional because it affected his economic well-being and therefore it did not promote social justice. Laurel J rejected the argument, stating that social justice reflects 'the fundamental and paramount objective of the state of promoting the health, comfort, and quiet of all persons, and of bringing about "the greatest good to the greatest number"'.[25] In other cases of that period on the relationship between constitutional law and economic policy, the Court did not even raise section 5, but preferred to rely on the American jurisprudence.[26]

At this time, alternatives to the liberal ideology were being put forward in the Indian debates on property and land reform. The Constituent Assembly convened on 9 December 1946; the Constitution was agreed on 26 November 1949 and took effect on 26 January 1950.[27] The Indian National Congress ('Congress'), which held the majority of seats, had traditionally emphasised liberal ideas of individual liberty and equality. As early as 1928, in the report of the Committee Appointed by the All Parties' Conference ('Nehru Report'), Congress put forward constitutional principles for self-government, with a declaration of fundamental rights.[28] The declaration included a right to property: Recommendation 4(ii) provided that 'No person shall be deprived of his liberty nor shall his dwelling or property be entered, sequestered or confiscated, save in accordance with law.' Other aspects of the Report also reflected the interests of the *zamindars*, as it rejected the inclusion of tenancy rights.[29] In addition, it reassured investors that 'It is inconceivable that there can be any discriminating legislation against any community doing business lawfully in India'.[30] Overall, it appeared that Congress would do little to challenge the landed interests.

[24] *Calalang v Williams* (1940) 70 Phil 726, GR No 47800.

[25] ibid, 734.

[26] See *Leyte Land Transportation Company, Inc v Leyte Farmer's and Laborer's Union* (1948) GR No L-1377; *Antamok Goldfields Mining Company v Court of Industrial Relations* (1940) GR No L-46892.

[27] G Austin, *The Indian Constitution: Cornerstone of a Nation* (Oxford, Oxford University Press, 1966) 84–99; G Austin, *Working a Democratic Constitution: A History of the Indian Experience* (Oxford, Oxford University Press, 2003); Merillat (n 8); HCL Merillat, 'The Indian Constitution: Property Rights and Social Reform' (1960) 21 *Ohio State Law Journal* 616.

[28] Committee Appointed by the All Parties' Conference 1928, The Nehru Report: An Anti-Separatist Manifesto (New Delhi, Michiko & Panjathan, 1928 reprinted 1975).

[29] ibid, 90.

[30] ibid, 11.

The situation changed within a short period. By the 1930s, it was obvious that Congress would not win popular support unless it took a stronger line on land reform. On the left, communist and radical movements were gathering support; on the right, the rural poor were being drawn into religious or caste conflicts, often provoked by the landed elite as a way of suggesting that the solution to rural poverty lay anywhere but in tenure reform.[31] Jawarharlal Nehru, a rising figure in the Party, expressed his disappointment with the Nehru Report's recommendations on property.[32] Under his influence, the Party swung to the left and secured a dominant position in Indian politics following independence.

These tensions between social change and stability continued to the convening of the Constituent Assembly, and after.[33] Ultimately, the Indian Assembly expressed the economic and social aspirations of the newly independent nation in Part IV of the Constitution, entitled the 'Directive Principles of State Policy'. There are clear parallels with section 5 of the 1935 Philippine Constitution, although there is no evidence that the Indian framers were aware of the Philippine provision. The Directive Principles require the State to secure a 'social order in which justice, social, economic and political, shall inform all the institutions of the national life'.[34] The State was also charged to 'strive to minimize the inequalities in income, and endeavour to eliminate inequalities in status, facilities and opportunities, not only amongst individuals but also amongst groups of people residing in different areas or engaged in different vocations.' The Directive Principles did not specifically require land reform or redistribution; however, they required the State to ensure 'that the ownership and control of the material resources of the community are so distributed as best to subserve the common good'[35] and that the 'operation of the economic system does not result in the concentration of wealth and means of production to the common detriment'.[36] Many state governments had already begun to move on land reform, which immediately raised questions regarding the desirability of incorporating a right to property in the Constitution's chapter on fundamental rights.

The central issue in the Assembly concerned the amount of compensation (if any) to be provided for *zamindars*. As in the Philippines, the large landowners employed liberal arguments to protect their position. After lengthy debate, the Indian Assembly settled on a right to property that would

[31] DA Low, 'Congress and Mass Contacts, 1936–37: Ideology, Interests, and Conflict over the Basis of Party Representation' in R Sisson and S Wolpert (eds), *Congress and Indian Nationalism: The Pre-Independence Phase* (Berkeley, University of California Press, 1988) 134.

[32] S Bhattacharya, 'Swaraj and the Kamgar: The India National Congress and the Bombay Working Class, 1919–1931' in Sisson and Wolpert, ibid, 223, 237.

[33] Austin, *Indian Constitution* (n 27); Merillat (n 8).

[34] Constitution of India, Art 38(1).

[35] Constitution of India, Art 39(b).

[36] Constitution of India, Art 39(c).

leave the legislature the freedom to determine compensation. As originally enacted, Article 31 of the Constitution provided as follows:

(1) No person shall be deprived of his property save by authority of law.
(2) No property, movable or immovable, including any interest in, or in any company owning, any commercial or industrial undertaking, shall be taken possession of or acquired for public purposes under any law authorising the taking of such possession or such acquisition, unless the law provides for compensation for the property taken possession of or acquired and either fixes the amount of the compensation, or specifies the principle on which, and the manner in which, the compensation is to be determined and given.

These provisions were very similar to those of the Government of India Act, 1935. Ironically, provisions that were originally intended to protect the landowners were now employed to protect legislative power.[37] However, in the independence Constitution, it would be the President, acting on the advice of the Prime Minister, who would give assent to legislation. Under the Government of India Act 1935, the Governor General was not responsible to the Indian provincial legislatures, and it was expected that he would exercise his discretion in favour of the landowners. In the independence Constitution, the combination of Article 31 and responsible government meant that the provisions were seen as sufficiently open to allow state legislatures to pursue land reform without full compensation. Nehru stated that 'Eminent lawyers have told us that on a proper construction of this clause, normally speaking, the Judiciary should not and does not come in'.[38] The courts would become involved only where 'there has been a gross abuse of the law, where, in fact, there has been a fraud on the Constitution'.[39]

In summary, the constitutional position on property in India differed greatly from that in the Philippines.[40] Politically, the rural peasantry were better able to command attention in India. Moreover, the educated urban classes that dominated the Congress Party leadership were relatively independent: their power did not depend on the landed elite, the former colonial power or foreign investors. Moreover, the Party itself was not ideologically bound to a specific position on economics and property. The liberal values of individual autonomy and equality were certainly important, especially as they challenged the systems of colonial and caste privilege that had held back many Congress members. However, social democracy and socialism were also attractive: a strong public sector, run by Indians, offered prospects for advancement that had not been available during the colonial period. By contrast, in the Philippines, the United States, as colonial power, held a

[37] See Government of India Act, s 299(1) and (2); Art 31(3) was similar to s 299(3), except that the President held the power of approval previously held by the Governor General.

[38] Constituent Assembly Debates, vol IX, p 31, 10 Sept 1949.

[39] ibid.

[40] See Austin, *Indian Constitution* (n 27), for a general review.

veto over constitutional proposals; whilst it allowed the introduction of section 5, it also insisted on the retention of the takings clause.[41] In any case, the peasantry lacked the organisation and influence to counterbalance the power of the landed elite over national politics. Consequently, property was not subject to the same kind of challenge as seen in India.

Despite these differences, there was an important common feature. Neither group of framers found a way to integrate social justice with a right to property. In India, the initial solution was, in essence, to take questions relating to both social justice and property away from the courts, as neither the Directive Principles nor compensation were justiciable. In the Philippines, the opposite route was taken: both compensation and social justice were justiciable. In essence, the framers of both constitutions were aware of, and drew on, the international debates on liberalism, social democracy and socialism, as well as their own national values. However, as subsequent events would show, they struggled in their effort to pull them together in a coherent structure.

III. JUDICIAL INTERPRETATION OF THE PROPERTY CLAUSES AFTER INDEPENDENCE

After achieving independence, both countries pursued land reform and redistribution, with varying degrees of commitment and success. The territorial government did attempt to break up concentrations of land ownership; however, it worked on the principle of full compensation, and the cost soon put the programme beyond the government's financial capacity.[42] The possibility of reducing compensation was then put beyond reach by the Supreme Court: in 1915, in *Manila Railroad Company v Velasquez, Allarey and Maligalig*, the Court held that 'There is no question but that the compensation to which a defendant owner is entitled is the market value of the condemned property'.[43] Arguably, the addition of section 5 in the 1935 Constitution, with its emphasis on the promotion of social justice, invited a re-examination of the meaning of 'just' compensation in cases of land reform. This was tested after World War II, in relation to Commonwealth Act No 539 (1940), which allowed the President to acquire large estates for subdivision and transfer to tenants. In line with the takings clause, full compensation was paid to the owners. However, in a post-War case on

[41] Putzel (n 2) 43–66; Wolters (n 11); Riedinger (n 11).

[42] Putzel, ibid, 83–101; Riedinger, ibid 91–98.

[43] *Manila Railroad Company v Velasquez, Allarey and Maligalig* (1915) GR No L-10278 (the case is concerned with a statutory requirement for 'just compensation', but has been taken as valid interpretation of the constitutional standard: see eg *Province of Tayabas v Perez* (1938) 66 Phil 467, GR No 44778 (1938).

Act No 539, *Republic of the Philippines v Gonzales*,[44] the Supreme Court suggested that 'just' compensation may require *more* than full compensation in redistribution cases, because the purpose was primarily private. Unlike a taking for a public amenity, the owner would not benefit from the subsequent use of the land. There was no re-examination in the light of section 5 and no consideration of the intended social impact of the legislation. Not surprisingly, the Act had very little impact on land distribution.[45] The Court may have left behind some of the *Lochner* era doctrine, but not the commitment to property nor the requirement for full compensation. It seemed that the constitutional provisions on social justice would have no impact on the rights of landlords.

This was confirmed with subsequent programmes. The Land Reform Act of 1955 only applied to only a small proportion of agricultural land, with less than 0.4 per cent of farmland redistributed in the six years following its enactment.[46] Another attempt at redistribution was launched with the Agricultural Land Reform Code of 1963, but it also suffered from limited scope and ineffective implementation.[47] The Supreme Court avoided political controversy: as noted above, *Republic of the Philippines v Gonzales* favoured the landowners, but the lack of political will over redistribution was more important in practice. Indeed, the peasant movements gained strength in the post-World War II period but, crucially, police and military action became more important than land reform in suppressing rebellion. This was supported by the United States, which was now turning away from the policy of encouragement that it pursued in Japan, Taiwan and South Korea.[48]

In India, as the states began to abolish the *zamindar* system, the constitutional structure of property and social justice came under judicial examination. Some state courts held that the Constitution did not allow the amount of compensation to be scaled to the size or nature of the holding, as land reform legislation in Japan, Taiwan and South Korea had done.[49] Parliament then enacted the First Amendment to the Constitution, which insulated land reform legislation from review under the provisions guaranteeing fundamental rights.[50] This should have resolved the controversy, but

[44] *Republic of the Philippines v Gonzales* (1954) GR No L-4918.

[45] Riedinger (n 11) 96–97.

[46] Putzel (n 2) 83–101; Riedinger, ibid 87–91.

[47] Putzel, ibid 114–18; Riedinger, ibid 91–98.

[48] EB Kapstein, 'Land and Rebellion: Lessons for Counter-insurgency' (2014) 56 *Survival: Global Politics and Strategy* 109.

[49] *Maharahadhiraja Sir Kameshwar Singh Darghanga v State of Bihar*, AIR 1951 Patna 91; *State of Bihar v Maharahadhiraja Sir Kameshwar Singh Darghanga*, (1952) 1975 AIR 1083 the Supreme Court allowed an appeal (in part) on the basis that the First Amendment excluded review (the Supreme Court judgment was not reported until 1975, although decided in 1952).

[50] Constitution (First Amendment) Act, 1951, ss 4, 5. The First Amendment added Art 31A to protect land reform legislation from review. Art 31B added the Ninth Schedule to the Constitution; the Schedule constituted a list of enactments that were specifically excluded from judicial review for violations of fundamental rights.

the Court held, in *State of West Bengal v Bela Banerjee*, that Article 31(2) sets a 'basic requirement of full indemnification of the expropriated owner'.[51] Legislation 'must ensure that what is determined as payable must be compensation, that is, a just equivalent of what the owner has been deprived of'.[52] Separately, it indicated that the exclusions granted by the First Amendment would be narrowly construed.[53] Parliament then sought to reverse *Bela Banerjee* by the Fourth Amendment (1955), which altered Article 31.[54] However, the Supreme Court interpreted the amended provisions so as to reinstate the guarantee of full compensation.[55] Further amendments followed; in each case, the Supreme Court would reinstate the compensation guarantee through increasingly strained interpretation of the amended provisions.[56]

The conflicting views between Parliament and the Supreme Court over the compensation issue became increasingly important in political life. In the 1971 election campaign, Indira Gandhi and her Congress Party blamed the Court for the lack of progress on land reform.[57] However, it is difficult to judge the real impact of the Court's defence of property on redistribution. The exclusions of the First Amendment allowed the abolition of the *zamindar* system to proceed, and it was largely complete by 1960.[58] However, a second phase of reform was intended to impose ceilings on holdings and redistribute the surplus to tenants. Very little progress was made from this point, but it seems that political forces were more important than judicial decisions in thwarting land redistribution. Landowners had become more adept at exerting influence through local political institutions. As Chibber puts it:

> The very institutions that were supposed to implement government policy—the Congress party machine and the local state organizations—were thoroughly penetrated by groups hostile to agrarian policy. Even the halting attempts at reform tried by Nehru foundered against their resistance.[59]

[51] *State of West Bengal v Bela Banerjee* 1954 SCR 558, 563 (the legislation authorised land expropriation, but lay outside the exclusion of the First Amendment).

[52] ibid, 563.

[53] *State of Bihar v Maharahadhiraja Sir Kameshwar Singh Darghanga* (n 49).

[54] Constitution (Fourth Amendment) Act, 1955, s 2.

[55] *Vajravelu Mudaliar v Special Deputy Collector*, West Madras 1965 SCR (1) 614; *Karimbil Kunhikoman v State of Kerala* 1962 SCR Supl (1) 829; *Rustom Cavasjee Cooper v Union of India* 1970 SCR (3) 530.

[56] Constitution (Seventeenth Amendment) Act, 1964, ss 2, 3; Constitution (Twenty-Fifth Amendment) Act, 1971, s 3.

[57] Austin, *Working a Democratic Constitution* (n 27) 232–33; WH Morris-Jones, 'India Elects for Change -- and Stability' (1971) 11 *Asian Survey* 719, 728–29.

[58] Tai (n 2) 214–18.

[59] V Chibber, 'Organized Interests, Development Strategies, and Social Policies' in R Nagaraj (ed), *Growth, Inequality and Social Development in India: Is Inclusive Growth Possible?* (Basingstoke, Palgrave Macmillan, 2012) 170; see also A Kohli, 'State and Redistributive Development in India' in R Nagaraj (ed), *Growth, Inequality and Social Development in India:*

Against this background, the immediate effect of the Supreme Court's judgments may have been marginal. At most, the Court merely provided another mechanism for the landed elite to protect its interests.

As the highest courts began to develop their jurisprudence on property, a common trend emerged. In both countries, the early post-independence judgments were characterised by lack of engagement with social justice and indeed with local conditions. Comparative law was part of this. In the Philippines, the Supreme Court treated American law as though it were binding. Consequently, there was no room to bring section 5 into the interpretation of 'just compensation', or indeed any other cases, as it had no American counterpart. In India, the leading cases reveal very little interest in local conditions and the reasons for land reform. In some of the leading cases, such as *Dwarkadas Shrinivas of Bombay v The Sholapur Spinning and Weaving Co*, American authorities were cited on almost every point by all of the judges.[60] In the early cases, the judges did not seek to place the right to property within a specifically Indian context.[61] Indeed, in both countries, the highest courts situated the constitutional protection of property within an international context that transcended national politics. Why the judges did so is unclear: it may have been that the international, comparative approach provided a kind of credibility or legitimacy to politically contentious decisions in favour of landowners. There was no reference to international sources that might have led the judges to allow land reform programmes to proceed. Social democrat ideas seemed to have little influence on the courts, whether in the form of the social justice provisions of each constitution or in the broader international conceptions of human rights that underpinned those provisions. Arguably, there was a kind of globalism in evidence, but more in the form of an internal body looking to global values (and only one set of values) to bolster its domestic position.

IV. THE (TEMPORARY) DECLINE OF LIBERALISM

If the 1950s and 1960s were the high point of the liberal ideology of the property in the courts, the 1970s and 1980s represent its weakest point.

Is Inclusive Growth Possible? (Basingstoke, Palgrave Macmillan, 2012); Tai (n 2) 93–97; J Harriss, 'Politics and Redistribution in India' in A Kohli and P Singh (eds), *Routledge Handbook of Indian Politics* (London, Routledge, 2013).

[60] *Shrinivas of Bombay v The Sholapur Spinning and Weaving Co* 1954 SCR 674; U Baxi, 'The Constitutional Quicksands of Kesavananda Bharati and the Twenty-Fifth Amendment' (1974) 1 *Supreme Court Cases* (Jour) 45.

[61] In some cases, the reasoning is based entirely on the 'plain meaning' of Art 31. In *Bela Banerjee*, above n 51, the Court relied entirely on a brief analysis of the language of Art 31. There was no citation of comparative law, but equally there was no discussion of local conditions.

By the 1970s, the liberal model of constitutions and property had become increasingly out of touch with changing international developments. The rise of the non-aligned movement and the adoption of the New International Economic Order were the global movements of importance, and this was reflected in the national debate on property. In India, the Janata Government brought the Forty-Fourth Amendment through Parliament in 1978. It was intended to resolve issues over compensation, as it deleted the right to property from the list of fundamental rights. A new right to property was enacted as Article 300A.[62] However, as it stated only that 'No person shall be deprived of his property save by authority of law',[63] it appeared that there was no guarantee of compensation; more generally, there seemed to be no scope for judicial review of legislation that authorised takings. Instead, it seemed that property owners were only protected from unlawful administrative action.[64]

After the Forty-Fourth Amendment, the Supreme Court retreated from its earlier dogmatism on compensation. For example, in a case on the old right to property, Iyer J stated that 'short of paying a "farthing for a fortune" the question of compensation is out of bounds for the court to investigate'.[65] Property could be taken 'not for a return, but for almost free, if the justice of the situation commended itself to the legislation to take it that way.'[66] He dismissed a separate argument based on the right to equality (that is, that the owner of extensive landholdings should be compensated at the same rate per acre as a smallholder), asking 'Which is more basic? Eradication of die-hard, deadly and pervasive penury degrading all human rights or upholding of the legal luxury of perfect symmetry and absolute equality attractively presented to preserve the status quo ante?'[67] Iyer J came close to ridiculing the Court's earlier position for ignoring the realities of Indian life. Moreover, by casting human rights in terms of human dignity in the face of poverty and economic uncertainty, he challenged the Court's earlier liberal tendency to narrow the focus of justice on the specific harm to the owner, without consideration of the broader social context of ownership.

In the Philippines, the Supreme Court also retreated from its earlier position. After declaring martial law in 1972, Ferdinand Marcos adopted

[62] Arts 30(1A) and 30A (1) remained in place; they contain guarantees for religious property and certain smallholders.

[63] Constitution (Forty-Fourth Amendment) Act, 1978, s 34.

[64] See the explanation of the Law Minister in the Rajya Sabha, 28 Aug 1978, col 54 (the Rajya Sabha is the upper house of India's Parliament). Moreover, Art 300A was not enacted as a fundamental right, but merely as a 'legal' or 'constitutional' right. As such, petitioners would not have direct access to the Court for redress. Art 32 of the Constitution gives petitioners a right of direct access to the Supreme Court for their vindication of their fundamental rights.

[65] *Bhim Singh v Union of India* 1985 SCR Supl (1) 862, 881 (the claim arose before the Forty Fourth Amendment came into effect; hence, the Court decided it against the prior law).

[66] ibid, 883.

[67] ibid, 890.

populist policies on land reform. Presidential Decree No 27 imposed an upper ceiling on land ownership and declared that tenants would be deemed to own the land that they cultivated. Landlords would be compensated at a rate of two-and-a-half times the value of the average annual yield. This formula was borrowed from the Taiwan land reform programme of the post-War period.[68] It would not have withstood scrutiny under the interpretation of the takings clause seen in cases such as *Manila Railroad Company v Velasquez, Allarey and Maligalig* and *Republic of the Philippines v Gonzales*. However, along with the due process and takings clauses, the 1973 Constitution also included a declaration that all decrees issued by the President were valid law.[69] Implicitly, the doctrine on full compensation was no longer good law, at least in respect of takings under Presidential Decree No 27. The Constitution also added to the provisions on social justice, with the following:

> The State shall promote social justice to ensure the dignity, welfare, and security of all the people. Towards this end, the State shall regulate the acquisition, ownership, use, enjoyment, and disposition of private property, and equitably diffuse property ownership and profits. *And*

> The State shall formulate and implement an agrarian reform program aimed at emancipating the tenant from the bondage of the soil and achieving the goals enunciated in this Constitution.[70]

In *Chavez v Zobel*,[71] the Court upheld the provisions of Presidential Decree No 27 deeming the tenants to be owners and in *Association of Rice and Corn Producers v National Land Reform Council*, it upheld the principle that 'just compensation' did not necessarily equate with full market value compensation.[72] The case did not turn on the 1973 provisions, but Fernando J remarked of section 5 of the 1935 Constitution that '[i]ts philosophy is a repudiation of laissez-faire'.[73]

In both India and the Philippines, constitutional law of the 1970s and 1980s followed the international trend of the 1960s and 1970s in favour of greater state control over natural resources in the developing nations. Whilst the international statements such as the New International Economic Order (NIEO) were aimed more at foreign ownership of resources than internal concentrations of property, they did challenge the principle of full compensation for all takings. Indeed, scepticism over the value of entrenching the judicial protection of property rights was also seen outside the developing

[68] See Putzel (n 2) 123–27 on the formulation of the programme.
[69] Constitution of the Republic of the Philippines, 1973, Art XVII, s 3, para (2).
[70] Constitution of the Republic of the Philippines, 1973, Art XIV, s 12.
[71] *Chavez v Zobel* (1974) GR No L-28609.
[72] *Association of Rice and Corn Producers v National Land Reform Council* (1982) GR No L-29007.
[73] ibid [2].

world. For example, in the early 1980s, Canada rejected economic and property rights in the Canadian Charter of Rights and Freedoms. In Europe, the European Court of Human Rights had not yet begun its expansion of the right to property that would continue to the present day,[74] and there were no signs that the socialist nations of Eastern Europe, the Soviet Union and Asia would move toward market economies. Hence, to some extent, the judicial relaxation of the constitutional standards in India and the Philippines in the 1980s was consistent with global developments. However, by the time the courts in India and the Philippines had accepted the shift away from the guarantees of full compensation, the liberal 'Washington Consensus' was gaining force externally and their governments had largely abandoned any commitment to internal land reforms. By the end of the decade, the international trend would shift back to bring pressure on governments to incorporate compensation guarantees at national level.

V. REVIVAL OF THE LIBERAL RIGHT TO PROPERTY

The weakening of the right to property did not last long in either country; moreover, it did not contribute to greater progress on redistribution. In the Philippines, Presidential Decree No 27 did not have a significant impact. This was partly due to its limited scope, as it only applied to rice and corn lands, thereby omitting the large sugar plantations. In any case, implementation was marred by extensive corruption, as Marcos often targeted the land of his political opponents for expropriation and redistribution.[75] By the 1986 revolution, dissatisfaction over land reform helped to bring together the rural poor and the landed elite in a loose anti-Marcos alliance. For the poor, the Marcos regime represented a failure to honour promises of redistribution; for the landowners, Presidential Decree No 27 was part of a general breakdown of a constitutional order that had protected their interests. Both groups had an interest in finding a new constitutional settlement on land reform.[76]

As the negotiations went forward, it became clear that the liberal vision of property would be restored. At an early stage, the Committee on Social Justice proposed 'a fair and progressive system of compensation', with payment of a lower proportion of market value for larger estates. The Constitutional Commission, dominated by the landed interests, overruled the Committee and made the land reform provisions subject to the 'just compensation'

[74] See T Allen, 'Liberalism, Social Democracy and the Value of Property under the European Convention on Human Rights' (2010) 59 *International and Comparative Law Quarterly* 1055.

[75] Putzel (n 2) 137–43; Riedinger (n 11).

[76] Hanstad (n 11).

standard of the takings clause.[77] As explained above, the Supreme Court had interpreted the clause so as to allow below-market compensation in *Association of Rice and Corn Producers v National Land Reform Council*. However, following the revolution, it restored the market standard as the measure of 'just compensation', even in respect of Presidential Decree No 27. In *Association of Small Landowners in the Philippines v Hon Secretary of Agrarian Reform*[78] the Court stated that

> Just compensation is defined as the full and fair equivalent of the property taken from its owner by the expropriator. It has been repeatedly stressed by this Court that the measure is not the taker's gain but the owner's loss. The word 'just' is used to intensify the meaning of the word 'compensation' to convey the idea that the equivalent to be rendered for the property to be taken shall be real, substantial, full, ample.[79]

The Supreme Court not only restored the earlier doctrine, but also the emphasis on American law. This passage is taken from a 1915 authority, *City of Manila v Estrada and Estrada*, which in turn takes it from *Virginia and Truckee R R Co v Henry*, a nineteenth century Nevada state court judgment.[80] *City of Manila v Estrada and Estrada* and *Virginia and Truckee R R Co v Henry* concerned takings by private railway companies under delegated powers of eminent domain. The Court in *Philippines v Hon Secretary of Agrarian Reform* did not consider whether such cases provide a useful guide to land redistribution. Indeed, the Court made numerous approving references to social justice and land reform, but none to the potential impact of full compensation on the cost and prospects for implementation.

The 1986 Constitution also included new provisions on social justice. Section 6 of Article XII, 'National Economy and Patrimony', included a provision on the social conception of ownership:

> The use of property bears a social function, and all economic agents shall contribute to the common good. Individuals and private groups, including corporations, cooperatives, and similar collective organizations, shall have the right to own, establish, and operate economic enterprises, subject to the duty of the State to promote distributive justice and to intervene when the common good so demands.

Section 1 of Article XIII, on 'Social Justice and Human Rights', directs Congress to

> give highest priority to the enactment of measures that protect and enhance the right of all the people to human dignity, reduce social, economic, and political

[77] Putzel (n 2).

[78] *Association of Small Landowners in the Philippines v Hon Secretary of Agrarian Reform* (1989) 256 Phil 777 (1989); recently affirmed in *Land Bank of the Philippines v Honeycomb Farm* (2012) GR No 169903.

[79] *Ass'n of Small Landowners*, ibid, 812.

[80] *City of Manila v Estrada* (1913) 25 Phil 208; the Nevada source is *Virginia and Truckee R R Co v Henry* (1873) 8 Nev 165, 165 (1873) (the Nevada case was not cited on this point in *Estrada*).

> inequalities, and remove cultural inequities by equitably diffusing wealth and political power for the common good.

Sections 4 to 10 lay out detailed principles on agrarian and urban land reform, including a specific right 'of farmers and regular farmworkers who are landless, to own directly or collectively the lands they till'.

These provisions are stronger than the provisions of the 1973 Constitution that the Court relied on in *Association of Rice and Corn Producers v National Land Reform Council*, where it held that social justice could allow for a departure from a strict reading of 'just compensation' standard.[81] However, the post-revolutionary conception of social justice turned back to liberal, individualist conceptions of justice. The following statement by Mr Justice Isagani Cruz, made as a member of the 1986 Constitution Commission, has been quoted in a number of cases:

> [S]ocial justice—or any justice for that matter—is for the deserving, whether he be a millionaire in his mansion or a pauper in his hovel. It is true that, in case of reasonable doubt, we are called upon to tilt the balance in favor of the poor, to whom the Constitution fittingly extends its sympathy and compassion. But never is it justified to prefer the poor simply because they are poor, or to reject the rich simply because they are rich, for justice must always be served, for poor and rich alike, according to the mandate of the law.[82]

Following this approach, the Court has rejected the argument that the nature and importance of agrarian reform, and its separate treatment in the Constitution, justifies an exceptional approach.[83] In *Apo Fruits Corporation and Hijo Plantation, Inc v Land Bank of the Philippines*, it stated that 'nothing is inherently contradictory in the public purpose of land reform and the right of landowners to receive just compensation for the expropriation by the State of their properties'.[84] Any tension between the rights of property and the rights of the tenants must be resolved in favour of the landowner: 'That the petitioners are corporations that used to own large tracts of land should not be taken against them'.[85]

[81] Above (n 73).

[82] The statement appears in the Record of the Constitutional Commission, Volume III, 7 August 1986, 17, and has been repeated by Justice Cruz in his judicial capacity (see eg *Gelos v Court of Appeals and Alzona* (1992) GR No 86186.

[83] For the contrary argument, see Hanstad (n 11) and Fr JG Bernas, *The 1987 Constitution of the Philippines, A Commentary*, 2003 edn (Manila, Rex Book Store, 2003) 1203:

> In trying to determine just compensation for purposes of agrarian reform, we must remember that we have to look at this in the context of the Article where it is. It is in the Article on Social Justice, and the thrust of this Article is precisely to make it easier for the disadvantaged to be able to obtain land.

[84] *Apo Fruits Corporation and Hijo Plantation, Inc v Land Bank of the Philippines* (2011) GR No 164195.

[85] ibid.

Apo Fruits examined the Comprehensive Agrarian Reform Program,[86] which was enacted in 1988. As *Apo Fruits*, *Association of Small Landowners v Secretary of Agrarian Reform* and *Land Bank of the Philippines v Honeycomb Farm* confirm, the guarantee of full compensation to all owners lies at its core. The land is bought by a government agency for resale to tenants at an affordable price, with the State expected to absorb the difference (as well as all other costs). In this respect, there is no change from the previous land redistribution schemes, as the cost of the programme quickly exceeded the capacity of the public treasury. It is worth noting, however, that section 17 of the legislation states that 'just compensation' should include consideration of 'The social and economic benefits contributed by the farmers and the farmworkers'. However, the administrative agency charged with implementing the law has set a valuation formula that does not appear to take this into account,[87] and the Supreme Court has upheld its approach.[88]

A further point concerns control over the large estates. Section 4, Article XIII of the Constitution requires the State to 'undertake an agrarian reform program founded on the right of farmers and regular farmworkers who are landless, to own directly or collectively the lands they till'. Section 31 of the Comprehensive Agrarian Reform Program then stated that landowners could transfer their estates to corporations, which would then distribute stock to farm workers. This, it was argued, would satisfy the Constitution, although the workers would own shares rather than the land itself. Moreover, the law allows the holding company to limit the workers' aggregate share in the company to the proportion of agricultural land held by the company.[89] Hence, in the case of *Hacienda Luisita, Inc v Presidential Agrarian Reform Council*,[90] the company argued that the agricultural land only constituted about one-third of the value of its assets, with the result that the tenants collectively would not have a controlling share in the company. The Supreme Court upheld this arrangement, although it appears contrary to the principle of direct peasant ownership. Together, the enactment of the 1987

[86] Republic Act No 6657. For assessments of its implementation, see T Adamopoulos and D Restuccia, 'Land Reform and Productivity: A Quantitative Analysis with Micro Data', Working Paper 509, University of Toronto Department of Economics, 04 April 2014; J Adam, 'Land Reform, Dispossession and New Elites: A Case Study on Coconut Plantations in Davao Oriental, Philippines' (2013) 54 *Asia Pacific Viewpoint* 232; RV Fabella, 'Comprehensive Agrarian Reform Program (CARP): Time to Let Go' Discussion Paper No 2014-02, University of the Philippines School of Economics.

[87] DAR in Administrative Order No 6, Series of 1992, as amended by DAR Administrative Order No 11, Series of 1994: LV= (CNI x 0.6) + (CS x 0.3) + (MV x 0.1), where LV = Land Value; CNI = Capitalised Net Income; CS = Comparable Sales; MV = Market Value (as declared by the owner for other purposes).

[88] *Land Bank of the Philippines v Banal and Arenas-Banal* (2004) GR No 143276; *Land Bank of the Philippines v Celada* (2006) GR No 164876; *Land Bank of the Philippines v Lim and Cabochan* (2007) GR No 171941.

[89] See A Sawchenko, 'Choosing a Mechanism for Land Redistribution in the Philippines' (2000) 9 *Pacific Rim Law & Policy Journal* 681, 703.

[90] *Hacienda Luisita, Inc v Presidential Agrarian Reform Council* (2011) GR No 171101.

Constitution and its interpretation by the Supreme Court has reinstated the liberal compensation guarantees of the earlier period. Once again, the social justice provisions have been given very little real significance. Moreover, as it did in the pre-Marcos era, the Court has justified its position by reference to the American constitutional law. Indeed, American cases are cited as though there is no distinction between American and Philippine law. Not only does this apply to compensation, but in the leading case on regulatory takings, the Supreme Court cited more American cases than Philippine cases (and the Philippine cases that were cited themselves relied on American authorities).[91]

In India, the conflict over compensation and property subsided after the Forty-Fourth Amendment. This was largely due to the declining importance of land redistribution in Indian politics: unlike the Philippines, no significant programmes for redistribution were announced in the 1980s or after. This is not to say that redistribution did not continue in some States: indeed, cases are still reaching the Supreme Court on the scope and application of land reform legislation that was first enacted in the 1960s or 1970s.[92] Moreover, by the mid-1990s, the Supreme Court began to revive the constitutional standards of the earlier period. It first focused on the guarantee in Article 14 against arbitrary state action. In *State of Tamil Nadu v Ananthi Ammal*, on the acquisition of land for Harijan housing sites, the Court held that statutory provisions for the payment of compensation by instalment were contrary to Article 14 because they were 'unreasonable' (no further explanation was offered).[93] Subsequently, the Court developed a right to compensation under Article 300A. As explained above, Article 300A appears to provide only procedural safeguards in respect of takings. However, in the leading case *KT Plantation Pvt Ltd v State of Karnataka*, the Court stated that although Article 300A 'enables the State to put restrictions on the right to property by law', it was also the case that a 'limitation or restriction [on property] should not be arbitrary or excessive or what is beyond what is required in public interest. The limitation or restriction must not be disproportionate to the situation or excessive'.[94] In practice, a taking of property is 'arbitrary', 'excessive', or 'disproportionate' if compensation is not paid.

The Supreme Court of India has therefore followed a similar path to its Philippine counterpart, in reinstating a right to compensation. However, in *KT Plantation*, the Court stated that the legislature has some flexibility to

[91] *City of Manila v Laguio and Malate Tourist Development Corporation* (2005) GR 118127.

[92] *IR Coelho v State of Tamil Nadu*, judis.nic.in/supremecourt/imgs1.aspx?filename=28469; *Glanrock Estate Ltd v The State of Tamil Nadu*, 9 Sept 2010, judis.nic.in/supremecourt/imgst.aspx?filename=36827.

[93] *State of Tamil Nadu v Ananthi Ammal* 1995 AIR 2114 [17].

[94] *KT Plantation Pvt Ltd v State of Karnataka* (n 6) [122].

adapt compensation standards to the context. The Court did not elaborate, except to say that:

> Measures designed to achieve greater social justice, may call for lesser compensation and such a limitation by itself will not make legislation invalid or unconstitutional or confiscatory … in each case, the scheme of the impugned Act, its object, purpose as also the question whether payment of nil compensation or nominal compensation would make the impugned law unjust, unfair or unreasonable in terms of other provisions of the Constitution as indicated above.[95]

Although the Indian law allows greater latitude to the legislature than in the Philippines, there is another significant point of similarity. In *KT Plantation,* the Court again returned to comparative law to justify its position, just as the Supreme Court of the Philippines did in *Association of Small Landowners in the Philippines v Hon Secretary of Agrarian Reform.* However, the Indian Court began to look to other comparative sources. In particular, it borrowed from the doctrine on the right to property contained in the First Protocol to the European Convention on Human Rights. As drafted, the Protocol did not guarantee compensation; however, the European Court of Human Rights has interpreted it so as to require compensation in most cases. In the leading cases *Sporrong and Lönnroth v Sweden,*[96] *James v United Kingdom*[97] and *Lithgow v United Kingdom,*[98] the Court of Human Rights held that the Protocol requires States to strike a 'fair balance' between private and public interests. From this, it concluded that 'the taking of property without payment of an amount reasonably related to its value would normally constitute a disproportionate interference which could not be considered justifiable' under the Protocol.[99] There is some flexibility in cases of social or economic justice: in *James v UK*, the Court held that legislation giving residential tenants on long leases the right to buy the freehold at below-market rates did not violate the Convention, on the basis that

> [l]egitimate objectives of 'public interest', such as pursued in measures of economic reform or measures designed to achieve greater social justice, may call for less than reimbursement of the full market value.[100]

In *KT Plantation*, the Supreme Court briefly referred to the European right to property, although not specifically in relation to the standard for compensation.[101] However, the language employed by the Supreme Court is so close to that of *James v UK* that it seems likely that it borrowed directly from the European judgments. The Court also referred to constitutional

[95] ibid [121], [122].
[96] *Sporrong and Lönnroth v Sweden* Series A No 52 (1983) 5 EHRR 35.
[97] *James v United Kingdom* Series A No 98 (1986) 8 EHRR 123.
[98] *Lithgow v United Kingdom* Series A No 102 (1986) 8 EHRR 329.
[99] *James v UK* (n 97), [54]; *Lithgow v UK*, ibid [121].
[100] *James v UK*, ibid [54].
[101] *KT Plantation Pvt Ltd v State of Karnataka* (n 6) [87].

principles from the United States, Germany, Australia, Canada, and the United Kingdom, as well as the historic writers Grotius, Pufendorf, Locke, Rousseau and Blackstone, to demonstrate that some form of compensation requirement is universal amongst the nations that adhere to the rule of law.[102]

In terms of the rhetoric, the Court has restored the post-independence approach. In terms of doctrine, there are some differences. In particular, it seems that Indian law now accommodates the flexibility of some European constitutions and European human rights law. However, it is worth noting that the European Court of Human Rights has itself begun to restrict legislative discretion in areas of social justice.[103] The Court is settling on the liberal view that the burden for alleviating poverty and achieving social justice is borne solely by the State. In principle, this view allows exceptions to the general rule of full compensation, but increasingly the exceptions arise only where there are specific concerns over the conduct of the owner in acquiring property.[104] This is much narrower than a general conception of social obligation, and significantly closer to the liberal vision of property and the constitution. Whether the Supreme Court in *KT Plantation* was aware of this trend is not clear, but it does suggest that the Indian law will retain its liberal focus.

VI. GLOBALISM, COMPARATIVE LAW AND THE RIGHT TO PROPERTY

Judgments on property and compensation in the Philippines and India are regularly justified by reference to American and European authorities. It is easy to understand why the courts did so in their early periods, especially in the Philippines: American judges sat on its Supreme Court, and interpreted clauses taken from the Bill of Rights of the United States. However, by now, one might have expected the Philippine Court to have developed its own jurisprudence on property and the constitution. One might have expected that, if American cases are cited, there would be a clear sense of the purpose for doing so, the weight to be given to them, and how they help (or hinder) the understanding of the issues. This has not been the case, however.

The situation in India is similar. Whilst the use of comparative law by the Supreme Court across all cases has declined since independence,[105] it remains important in property cases. The Supreme Court has been more

[102] *KT Plantation Pvt Ltd v State of Karnataka*, ibid [84]–[91].

[103] Allen (n 74).

[104] ibid; compare *Jahn v Germany* ECHR 2005-VI (GC); *Kozacioğlu v Turkey* (App No 2334/03) (2009).

[105] AM Smith, 'Making Itself a Home—Understanding Foreign Law in Domestic Jurisprudence: The Indian Case' (2006) 24 *Berkeley Journal of International Law* 218, 239–41.

willing to look beyond American authorities, but there is very little discussion of comparative methodology. Neither court considers the relevance of the broader context of comparative analysis. American sources are frequently cited, and yet none of the American states have engaged in land redistribution on anything like the scale attempted in India or the Philippines. The provisions on social justice in the constitutions of India and the Philippines have no counterpart in the United States, yet it seems that the courts in India and the Philippines see no need to examine national differences or the context in which takings occur and constitutional principles evolve. Constitutional models that integrate ideas of social obligation, public power and individual autonomy within a right to property are rarely cited; even when they are cited, as in *KT Plantation*, there is no discussion of the differences in approach.[106] In *KT Plantation*, the Court even acknowledged that the constitutional systems of Canada and the United Kingdom do not provide a justiciable right to property, but without explaining how its consideration of these systems affected its analysis of Indian law.[107]

The superficiality of the analysis leads to the question: What purpose does comparative law serve? An earlier generation of comparativists argued that comparative law provides an opportunity to improve domestic law, on the basis that the analysis of laws of different systems on a specific issue helps to identify the best solution to a legal problem.[108] However, whatever the merits and limitations of this approach may be, especially in the judicial context, it has not been the purpose of using comparative law in either country. At best, the use of comparative law is observational rather than analytical, as the Philippine and Indian courts do little more than offer brief summaries of the law in other jurisdictions. No function for law is identified, and there is no discussion of the operation of the law within the host system or its practical impact in serving that function. Indeed, where there are different approaches across the comparators, there is no attempt to determine a 'best solution' from amongst them.[109]

An alternative view is held by those who argue that comparative law has little impact on legal change.[110] Change in law, and specifically the

[106] Indeed, in *KT Plantation*, the Court incorrectly stated that the German Basic Law bars uncompensated takings: above (n 6), [84] and compare to *Jahn v Germany*, above (n 104).

[107] *KT Plantation*, ibid.

[108] See Dixon and Posner (n 4) 411–14. Ernst Rabel's work on the codification of the law on international sales of goods is an example (although it was aimed at perfecting national law rather than drafting a uniform law): see E Rabel, 'A Draft of an International Law of Sales' (1937–1938) 5 *University of Chicago Law Review* 543, 563–65 and E Rabel, 'The Hague Conference on the Unification of Sales Law' (1952) 1 *American Journal of Comparative Law* 58, 67–68. On Rabel's comparativism, see DJ Gerber, 'Sculpting the Agenda of Comparative Law: Ernst Rabel and the Facade of Language' in A Riles (ed), *Rethinking the Masters of Comparative Law* (Oxford and Portland, Hart Publishing, 2000) 190.

[109] See eg *KT Plantation Pvt Ltd v State of Karnataka* (n 6).

[110] See Dixon and Posner (n 4) 408–11.

convergence of law, is driven by structural forces that are beyond the control of lawmakers. For example, the prominence of land reform is likely to be affected by population movements and markets for labour and land. In recent years, it could be argued that the international convergence on a liberal right to property has been driven less by judicial borrowing than by global factors such as the decline of socialism and the increased flow of international capital into land. Internally, the framing and interpretation of a right to property may have involved a comparative analysis of different models, but it would be a mistake to treat the comparative analyses as the cause for the adoption of a right to property or indeed of a liberal right to property. Hence, in India and the Philippines, one might argue that the judicial discussion of comparative law shows that the courts have favoured the liberal model of a right to property, but it does not explain why they do so.

Although these two models suggest that comparative law is either significant or irrelevant to legal change, the lack of any real functional analysis suggests that the conclusion is the same: comparative analysis has not been a driver for change. Comparative law in the courts is, at most, evidence of choices made for other reasons. However, as Daniel Farber has shown, it may serve an important function in signalling those choices to relevant audiences.[111] Indeed, the practice of citing without analysis suggests that comparative law does serve this function. To the courts, it seems that it is enough to show that a right to property is found in the constitutional systems of developed states. By itself, this does not seem especially compelling, but, as Adam M Smith points out, it appeals to specific aspirations in India:

> Foreign law and precedent come into judgments in the form of culturally persuasive (even if not legally relevant) support for a change that coheres with the judges' views of the type of culture to which their state aspires.[112]

In India, this may explain why many of the discussions of comparative law in the leading cases on property are more observational than analytical. As he notes, Indians have 'desperately wished to join' the international, developed community.[113] Hence, there is receptiveness to measures that help to place India within the international community of states that respect individual rights. Indeed, this has been a central aspiration of Indian national leaders from the drafting of the Nehru Report in 1928.[114] Accordingly, if a right to property is found in the constitutions of liberal states that respect human rights, a similar right should be 'found' within the Indian system, if at all possible. This is certainly evident in *KT Plantation*: the purpose, language

[111] Farber (n 4).
[112] Smith (n 105) 265.
[113] ibid.
[114] US Mehta, 'Constitutionalism' in NG Jayal and PB Mehta (eds), *The Oxford Companion to Politics in India* (Oxford, Oxford University Press, 2010) 16: debates in the Constituent Assembly were characterised by an 'intense concern with India's standing in the world'.

and intention underlying Article 300A do not provide room for the kind of guarantee constructed by the Court, unless one assumes that the compensation guarantees simply must exist somewhere within the Constitution.

If comparative law is used as a form of signalling, who is the audience? Eyal Benvenisti has argued that, in some cases, it may be aimed at other national courts, as a means of co-ordinating responses to certain forces of globalisation.[115] One example is environmental law: some national courts have challenged the failure of governments to control pollution, especially by powerful multinational actors. However, for this to work effectively, some degree of co-ordination between national courts is essential to avoid a 'race to the bottom'. The citation of comparative law can be helpful in this regard:

> Courts that wish to signal readiness to cooperate [with courts of other countries] will tend to use the language that other courts understand: comparative law (primarily comparative constitutional law) and international law.[116]

Benvenisti argues that this can be seen in Indian environmental cases.[117] However, there is little evidence that has happened with the right to property. Indeed, as Part III shows, the weakest point in both countries for the protection of property came during the 1970s and early 1980s, when co-operation between governments in the developing world on the nationalisation of property was at its high point. The national courts in India and the Philippines in this period did not act as a counterbalance to their governments; rather, by weakening the protection of property, they tracked government policy. More recently, there has been a considerable level of concern over land grabs.[118] National and local governments have often acquiesced in the displacement of vulnerable people. Arguably, there is room for transnational co-operation between courts along the lines suggested by Benvenisti, but it has not occurred in the property cases.

Arguably, any signalling through comparative law is aimed more at investors than the courts of other countries. Indeed, there is an extensive literature on the role of constitutional law in attracting investment. There is evidence that judges in both countries cite comparative law to assure investors that national standards are similar to international standards, and hence that there is no greater political risk to capital than elsewhere.[119] In *KT*

[115] E Benvenisti, 'Reclaiming Democracy: The Strategic Uses of Foreign and International Law by National Courts' (2008) 102 *American Journal of International Law* 241.

[116] ibid, 251.

[117] ibid, 258–62.

[118] See Borras et al (n 3); J Baka, 'Biofuels and Wasteland Grabbing: How India's Biofuel Policy is Facilitating Land Grabs in Tamil Nadu, India', Paper presented at the International Conference on Global Land Grabbing 6–8 April 2011, Institute of Development Studies, University of Sussex; O De Schutter, 'The Green Rush: The Global Race for Farmland and the Rights of Land Users' (2011) 52 *Harvard International Law Journal* 503.

[119] See the material cited above n 4.

Plantation, the Indian Supreme Court not only cited numerous comparative examples, but explicitly acknowledged the importance of building investor confidence in its legal system.[120] The choice of comparators also provides some evidence of this. The Philippine Supreme Court relies more on American legal authority than its Indian counterpart; arguably, this reflects the historic dependence of the Philippines on American investment and support. Moreover, neither court engages in any discussion of the law of other developing nations, or of nations that do not guarantee compensation for expropriation. Such comparators could provide more potential for judicial learning, but would not send the same signal to investors.

Finally, at least some of the cases raise the suspicion that comparative law provides a claim for legitimacy for socially conservative policies. In particular, the language of liberal right to property, within a broader scheme of internationally recognised human rights, gives a privileged minority a credible case for maintaining their position. Comparative law in the courts almost invariably supports a liberal theory of property; one of the key features of the liberal theory that emerges from comparative law is its abstraction from the local context. For example, cases from both jurisdictions demonstrate that the courts have resisted arguments that land reform requires a different approach to compensation. It is, of course, difficult to judge how far the courts participate in constitutional clientelism, as judges are unlikely to say that their decisions are guided by class loyalties rather than legal principle.[121]

Of the two courts, it seems more likely that this is the case in the Philippines. Not only has constitutional interpretation favoured landed interests, but the statutory interpretation of the Comprehensive Agrarian Reform Program legislation has done so as well. At no point has it challenged the legislature in the ways seen in India. Hence, the citation of American constitutional law provides a convenient rhetoric to justify the limits on land reform, for audiences at home and abroad. The global aspect of comparative law lacks the local or even historical context that the opponents of agrarian reform do not wish to acknowledge. Indeed, it seems that that is its attraction: it shifts the focus outward and away from local conditions, and by doing so, it undermines the case for reform. In India, the picture is more complex because the Supreme Court accepted the constitutionality of the amendments that excluded judicial review from most land reform legislation. Nevertheless, the use of comparative law has allowed the Court to maintain the separation of the right to property from social justice, as it treats the ownership of land as a matter of private law. In effect, comparative law has restricted

[120] Above (n 6), [142].

[121] See NG Quimpo, 'The Limits of Post-Plunder Reform in the Philippines' Oligarchic Democracy' in ESK Fung and S Drakeley (eds), *Democracy in Eastern Asia: Issues, Problems and Challenges in a Region of Diversity* (Abingdon, Routledge, 2013) on constitutional clientelism in the Philippines.

the vocabulary for debating agrarian reform, and the global, transnational nature of liberal property has indirectly legitimated the demands of the elite for constitutional protection.

VII. CONCLUSION

Governments in both India and the Philippines have made grand promises about agrarian reform and land redistribution at various points in their history. Both countries have achieved some success, but the general picture is one of a series of failed plans. This chapter has highlighted the judicial role in these successes and failures, especially in terms of the globalising aspect of the use of comparative law. With the exception of a brief period in the 1970s and 1980s, the highest courts have taken a liberal position on redistribution and compensation. To be sure, there are differences between them: currently, the Indian Supreme Court is more flexible in terms of the standard for compensation and in the recognition of specific exclusions of judicial review than the Philippine court. The Indian court has also come into conflict with Parliament over constitutional interpretation and amendment, whereas the Philippine court's relationship with governments and the legislature has been comparatively calm. Nevertheless, there is a striking similarity in their use of comparative law and its relationship with the liberal model of property.

Part Two

The Market versus Social Justice

4

Property in Persons: Prohibiting Contemporary Slavery as a Human Right

JEAN ALLAIN

WHILE THE FOCUS regarding property and human rights has been, in the main, on issues of intellectual property and indigenous rights, a more fundamental synergy between these two areas has developed, and in so doing gives slavery contemporary relevance. Vital to breathing legal life into slavery beyond abolition has been the use of property law in providing content to a norm which is applicable both to slavery in law, but also slavery in fact. In other words, property law has provided the theoretical foundation allowing for the application of slavery both de jure—though legal ownership of another person that is predominantly a vestige of the past—and de facto—where a person is held in fact, though not in law, in a condition of slavery. Thus, property law has been fundamental to giving slavery the life which had escaped it during the last three-quarters of the twentieth century, and provided the breakthrough which now sees the application of this fundamental human right for the first time.

The international norms regarding the prohibition of slavery and lesser servitudes, including debt bondage, forced labour, serfdom, servile marriage and sham adoption, evolved from the 1926 Slavery Convention onwards have been, until recently, a regime in disarray. The most significant 'moments in time' of the evolution of this norm will be mapped out in this chapter so as to demonstrate the tangled web in which the regime prohibiting 'modern slavery' (ie: the overall framework of slavery and lesser servitudes) found itself at the dawn of the twenty-first century.[1] That done, consideration will turn to property law so as to demonstrate how its theoretical foundations allowed for the removal of the various threads which had reduced the legal applicability of slavery to near naught. Having brushed away these

[1] For an overall consideration of the regime of slavery see J Allain, *Slavery in International Law: Of Human Exploitation and Trafficking* (Leiden, Martinus Nijhoff, 2013).

cobwebs, the development of the *Bellagio-Harvard Guidelines on the Legal Parameters of Slavery* are considered. These are the product of cooperation among leading property lawyers, including Antony Honoré, Robin Hickey and James Penner; in collaboration with slavery experts such as Kevin Bales, Seymour Drescher, Stanley Engerman and Orlando Patterson. The results are *not the breathing of new life* into the prohibition against slavery, rather *breathing life itself* into the legal concept, as prior to the *Guidelines* the norms, as legal rights, were for all intents and purposes dead.

I. MOMENTS IN TIME

One would think, and expect, that one of a handful of fundamental human rights, which has been on the international agenda for more than 200 years, would have a settled core content. Yet this was not so: as the argument went, slavery was about owning another person, and as one could no longer have a legal claim of ownership over another human being vindicated in a court of law, slavery no longer existed. However, this logic raises doubts when considered against the prohibition against torture. Would we accept that because states have outlawed torture that it no longer exists? Clearly the answer is no. The end of de jure torture did not bring about the end of de facto torture. And yet, this analogy cannot be considered as being exact, as slavery is fundamentally about ownership … or is it? As Rebecca Scott and Allison Gorsuch have demonstrated in *The Legal Understanding of Slavery* a person did not necessarily have to be legally owned to be regarded as a slave.[2] This was brought to the public consciousness most evidently through the 2013 film that won the Oscar award for Best Picture, *12 Years a Slave*, which was adapted from the 1853 narrative of Solomon Northup who was kidnapped and brought to work on a plantation of the Southern United States, despite the fact that nobody actually had a claim of ownership over him. While the law did not recognise his status as a slave, Mr Northup was held in the conditions of slavery, that is: he was de facto, a slave.

How was it then that by the end of the twentieth century, it was considered that slavery could only exist de jure and as a result, the human right which prohibited slavery was, for all intents and purposes, dead-letter law, little more than an historical relic? It is to a number of these moments in time that I now turn to demonstrate how the regime prohibiting slavery had fallen into a quagmire and how ultimately, a lifeline was thrown by property

[2] See AM Gorsuch, 'To Indent Oneself: Ownership, Contracts, and Consent in Antebellum Illinois' and RJ Scott, 'Under Color of Law: Siliadin v France and the Dynamics of Enslavement in Historical Perspective' in J Allain (ed), *The Legal Understanding of Slavery: From the Historical to the Contemporary* (Oxford, Oxford University Press, 2012) 135 and 152.

law, thus saving slavery from the annals of history by giving it content and contemporary application. I will first consider those moments in time which fundamentally altered the regime, causing its legal value to be stillborn and its content to be dismissed, as no longer being relevant in a post-abolition era. Fundamental to writing history is the principle that the construction of a narrative lies on an understanding which is either based on continuity or change. Those 'moments in time' to be considered are those instances when the fundamental currents (the meta-narrative, if you wish) of twentieth century history weighed upon the regime prohibiting slavery, forcing continuity to give way to change.

The first of these fundamental currents transpired during the League of Nations era; an era dominated by colonialism, with the League institutionalising much of the dominance of colonial powers. Where slavery is concerned, this colonial dominance is best demonstrated by the 1922 proposal put forward by the United Kingdom, that Ethiopia—an independent State—should be, in effect, colonised, by being placed under a Mandate to be shared by France, Italy and the UK, or directly under the control of the League of Nations.[3] The basis for this proposal was the perceived inability of Ethiopia to suppress the slave trade. It was at this moment and time, in considering this question, that the machinery of the League was engaged; the ultimate outcome being a movement away from a focus on Ethiopia towards a more general approach to slavery and the slave trade, the result of which was the drafting of the 1926 Slavery Convention. That Convention, for its part, defines slavery and the slave trade, and sets out obligations to penalise these, while requiring State Parties to 'take all necessary measures to prevent compulsory or forced labour from developing into conditions analogous to slavery'.[4] Despite the fact that the legal definitions of slavery and the slave trade had been set out, as had the obligations for States to suppress these within their own territory and to provide assistance where requested, the *Zeitgeist*—colonialism—would mean that such legal obligations would be side-lined when, in the lead-up to the 1936 occupation and annexation of Ethiopia by Italy. The diplomatic cover for this Italian venture was framed by the Mussolini Government as a colonial civilising mission justified in terms of supressing the slave trade, despite Ethiopia having become a member of the League of Nations and undertaking the obligations of the 1926 Convention to bring an end to the slave trade on its territory.[5]

During the first half of the twentieth century—that is during the League of Nations era—only two African States were deemed independent: Ethiopia

[3] See J Allain, 'Slavery and the League of Nations: Ethiopia as a Civilised Nation' (2006) 8 *Journal of the History of International Law* 213, 219–20.

[4] Art 5, Slavery Convention, 1926.

[5] See Allain (n 3) 237–39.

and Liberia. Just as the slave trade had been utilised for political ends in Ethiopia, so too would it be used in Liberia. Here an International Commission of Inquiry was established in collaboration with the League of Nations, in 1930, to consider 'whether slavery as defined in the anti-slavery convention in fact exists in the Republic'.[6] Through its Report, we witness a further moment in time, as the Commission failed to find slavery, though much forced labour, and sought to redefine its mandate noting that the 'definition of slavery as formulated by the anti-slavery convention ... leaves little room for distinguishing between degrees of restrictive freedom'.[7] The Commission then interpreted (as I will argue shortly—misinterpreted) elements of the negotiation of the 1926 Slavery Convention so as to read into the definition of slavery a wider understanding, more in line with the political outcome it sought rather than a legal interpretation of the Convention provisions. In so doing the Commission, while acknowledging that 'classic slavery ... no longer exists in the Republic of Liberia' stated that 'forced labour has been made use of in Liberia'.[8] The Commission had implicated high-ranking officials; the fall-out was such that it forced the resignation of both the President and Vice President of Liberia, much to the relief of both the United States of America and the US-based Firestone Natural Rubber Company which held a 99 year lease over 1 million Liberian acres of plantation land.[9]

A dominant strand of history during the first half of the twentieth century was colonialism. Although a legal framework to address slavery, the slave trade and forced labour was established in 1926, the emerging regime was mobilised against the two independent States of Africa—Ethiopia and Liberia. During the League of Nations era, the evolving regime prohibiting slavery was thus utilised instrumentally at the expense of establishing and developing those legal norms set out in the 1926 Slavery Convention. Yet, the most far-reaching moment in time with regard to setting a course whereby the regime prohibiting slavery would, by the end of the century, be deemed, for all intents and purposes, dead, was the interpretation of the definition of slavery set out in the just noted 1930 Report of the International Commission of Inquiry into the Existence of Slavery and Forced Labour in the Republic of Liberia.

In 1926, Members of the League of Nations finalised the Slavery Convention which established, inter alia, the definition of slavery. Although placed

[6] See *Report of the International Commission of Inquiry into the Existence of Slavery and Forced Labour in the Republic of Liberia*, 8 September 1930, 13.

[7] ibid, 14.

[8] ibid, 133.

[9] J Allain, 'The Legal Definition of Slavery into the Twenty-First Century' in Allain (n 2) 205–06; See *Report of the International Commission of Inquiry into the Existence of Slavery and Forced Labour in the Republic of Liberia*, 8 September 1930; and WEB DuBois, 'Liberia, the League and the United States' *Foreign Affairs* July 1931.

on the table again during the negotiations of the 1956 Supplementary Convention and again in 1998 during the deliberations of what would become the Statute of the International Criminal Court, the 1926 definition is accepted as being *the* established definition in international law. That definition, which is far from being elegant or vivid in conjuring up an image of slavery, nevertheless has now found its legal place despite having been waylaid during the twentieth century. That definition reads:

> Slavery is the status or condition of a person over whom any or all of the powers attaching to the right of ownership are exercised.

When the International Commission of Inquiry produced its Report in 1930, it provided an expansive reading of the 1926 definition of slavery which continued to be utilised within the United Nations (UN) system as late as the year 2000. However, that understanding by the Commission was based on a mis-reading of the negotiation history of the 1926 Slavery Convention. To demonstrate this mis-reading would be rather technical, as a result, I would point the reader elsewhere.[10] That said, the approach taken by the Commission was to state that since the Convention spoke about 'bring about ... as soon as possible the complete abolition of slavery in all its forms' and 'to take all necessary measures to prevent compulsory and forced labour from developing into conditions analogous to slavery', that the 1926 definition should be understood as applying not only to cases of slavery, but also to lesser servitudes including debt-bondage and forced labour.[11] This interpretation of the definition of slavery, that it was seen as an umbrella term consisting of slavery itself and lesser servitudes, would persist throughout the twentieth century. For instance, in their 2000 Report on Contemporary Forms of Slavery produced within the United Nations, David Weissbrodt and Anti-Slavery International continued this stream of interpretation, stated that:

> By referring to '*any* or all of the powers of ownership' in its definition of slavery, and setting forth as its stated purpose the 'abolition of slavery in *all* its forms' the Slavery Convention covered not only domestic slavery but also the other forms of slavery listed in the Report of the [1924] Temporary Slavery Commission [re: debt bondage, serfdom, servile marriage, etc].[12]

This interpretation, however, cannot be sustained. It is clear that States, in negotiating the content of the 1926 Convention, did *not* intend to widen the scope of 'slavery' by subsuming within the definition lesser servitudes which

[10] Allain, ibid 204.
[11] ibid, 205.
[12] See United Nations Sub-Commission on the Promotion and Protection of Human Right, *Contemporary Forms of Slavery: Updated Review of the Implementation of and Follow-up to the Conventions on Slavery*, Working Paper prepared by D Weissbrodt and Anti-Slavery International, UN Doc E/CN.4/Sub.2/2000/3, 26 May 2000, 5.

did not meet the threshold of the 'status or condition of a person over whom any or all of the powers attaching to the right of ownership are exercised'. The *travaux préparatoires* bear this out, as the Union of South Africa, in commenting on the 1925 League of Nations Draft Convention, noted that the 'Convention as drafted goes somewhat further than seems necessary for the abolition of slavery and the slave trade'. Where an early draft of the Convention introduced the concept of 'domestic slavery and similar conditions' beside slavery, the Union of South Africa protested saying that either a person was a slave as defined by the proposed Convention or they were not:

> If ... they have become domestic slaves or persons in similar conditions in the manner indicated, that can only be because others have acquired a right of property in them, and they are therefore slaves as defined in Article 1.[13]

When the 1926 Slavery Convention was presented to the Assembly of the League of Nations for signature, the Report which accompanies it recognised that: 'these last practices do not come under the definition of slavery as it is given in Article 1'.[14] As a result the provision 'domestic slavery and similar conditions' had been deleted from the final provisions of the 1926 Slavery Convention. The outcome of those 1925–1926 deliberations was that slavery existed, no matter the so-called 'form' of slavery, only when the definitions threshold was met. That is to say that slavery only existed where the 'status or condition of a person over whom any or all of the powers attaching to the right of ownership are exercised'. Best if we stop here with regard to interpreting the definition of slavery and return to further consider its parameters in the next section when attention turns to property law.

In the meantime, it should be understood that just as the meta-current of history—colonialism—would come to influence the regime prohibiting slavery during the League of Nations era, so too would the meta-current which dominated the historical reading of the second half of the twentieth century—the decolonisation process—play a significant role in steering the regime prohibiting slavery into a situation where the legal elements were lost, deemed no longer relevant nor applicable. While the decolonisation process would start in earnest in the late 1950s, colonial powers were able to pass one last piece of colonial legislation: the 1956 Supplementary Convention.

[13] League of Nations, Draft Convention on Slavery, Replies of Governments, Reply from the Government of the Union of South Africa, A.10(a).1926.VI, 22 July 1926, 5; as found in League of Nations, Publications of the League of Nations, VI.B.Slavery.1926, VI. B. 3.

[14] League of Nations, Slavery Convention: Report presented to the Assembly by the Sixth Committee, LofN Doc. A.104.1926.VI, as found in League of Nations, Publications of the League of Nations, VI.B.Slavery.1926, VI. B. 5, 24 September 1926, 1–2.

In 1956 the United Nations established an instrument to supplement the 1926 Slavery Convention. As I have shown elsewhere, that treaty was meant to cover those servitudes which had been identified as far back as during first deliberation on the 1926 Slavery Convention by the League of Nations.[15] Yet, during the negotiation process which transpired in 1956, it emerged that there was a conflict between those States who wanted to include in the supplementary convention the same obligations which existed in the 1926 Convention—to end these servitudes 'progressively and as soon as possible'—and those States which pointed to the 1948 Universal Declaration of Human Rights which called upon States to abolish slavery and servitude forthwith. Not wishing to be seen as going against the Universal Declaration, the negotiators of the 1956 Supplementary Convention, while opting to seek to end four types of servitudes—debt bondage, serfdom, servile marriage and child exploitation—'progressively and as soon as possible', found a diplomatic compromise. They simply erased any trace of the term 'servitude' from the substance of their instrument, which in draft form had been termed the 'Draft Supplementary Convention on Slavery and *Servitude*'; but would emerge from the negotiation conference as the 1956 'Supplementary Convention on the Abolition of Slavery, the Slave Trade, and *Institutions and Practices Similar to Slavery*'.[16] As a result, from this moment in time onwards much confusion would be carried into the regime prohibiting slavery as the term 'servitude' would persist in being used in human rights instruments such as the 1966 UN Covenant on Civil and Political Rights, while the four conventional servitudes set out in the 1956 Supplementary Convention would be all but forgotten, neglected through their labelling as 'practices similar to slavery'. That said, the confusion caused by the drafting of the 1956 Supplementary Convention would be compounded 10 years later as the decolonisation process reached a critical mass within the United Nations, as newly independent States constituted a majority and thus could set the agenda throughout most of the United Nations system.

In 1966, the Soviet Union, showing its anti-imperial credentials, stated that the 'main factors upholding and encouraging slavery at the present time are colonialism, *apartheid* and racism'.[17] This was followed by an attempt to equate colonialism and apartheid with slavery lead by Mr Waldo Waldron-Ramsey, the Representative of the United Republic of Tanzania. Clearly speaking in legal terms, referencing both slavery and practices similar to slavery, Mr Waldron-Ramsey noted that the 'policy of apartheid' applied in various Southern African countries 'were flagrant examples of slavery', while 'the methods traditionally used by the colonialist must be regarded as

[15] See J Allain, 'On the Curious Disappearance of Human Servitude from General International Law' (2009) 11 *Journal of the History of International Law* 303.

[16] ibid.

[17] United Nations, Mohamed Awad, *Report on Slavery*, UN Doc E/4168/Rev.1, 1966, 285.

practices similar to slavery'.[18] When seeking to introduce such notions into a resolution of the UN Economic and Social Council, it came up against a challenge by the Greek representative who argued that if there was a desire to change the definition of slavery or add new instances of practice similar to slavery then a negotiation conference of plenipotentiaries would have to be convened.[19] Here the penny dropped, as the creation of international law by way of such diplomatic conferences requires two-thirds majority, a majority which the newly independent States lacked. As a result, the resolution which followed replaced the legal terms 'slavery' and 'practices similar to slavery' with a term of art: 'slavery-like practices' as in the 'slavery-like practices of apartheid and colonialism'.[20]

This nomenclature would move the confusion established by the disastrous 1956 negotiations of the Supplementary Convention to a wholesale abandonment of regime prohibiting slavery, as being too opaque to be of any value beyond the rhetorical. Thus, even the United Nations Secretary-General could not weave his way through the confusion thus far visited upon the regime, as he would invoke the term 'slavery-like practices' when speaking of the 1956 Convention.[21] The confusion created by the term of art 'slavery-like practices' at the expense of the legal regime, coupled with both the interpretation given to the definition of slavery by the 1930 International Commission dealing with Liberia and the creation of the 1956 Supplementary Convention, which replaced servitude with the notion of 'practices similar to slavery', would be enough to sound an echo of the death knell of the regime prohibiting slavery by the mid-1960s. The United Nations would find it very hard to recover. By the 1990s, the regime prohibiting slavery had lost any semblance of the legal, instead 'slavery' itself was used for its rhetorical value. Under the heading of 'contemporary forms of slavery', a UN Working Group would consider items rather far removed from the legal parameters of slavery including: Child pornography, children in armed conflict (1990); child soldiers (1991); removal of organs (1992); incest (1993); migrant workers, sex tourism (1994); illegal adoption (1996); early marriages, detained juveniles (1997).

[18] United Nations, Economic and Social Council, Social Committee, Summary Record of the Five Hundred and Thirty-Sixth Meeting, 7 July 1966, UN Doc E/AC.7/SR.536, 14 December 1966, 5.

[19] United Nations, Economic and Social Council, Social Committee, Summary Record of the Five Hundred and Thirty-Eight Meeting, 11 July 1966, UN Doc E/AC.7/SR.538, 14 December 1966, 4.

[20] United Nations, Economic and Social Council, Social Committee, Slavery, Algeria, Gabon, Cameroon, Iran, Iraq, Morocco and the United Republic of Tanzania: draft resolution, UN Doc E/AC.7/L.492, 14 July 1966.

[21] United Nations, Economic and Social Council, Commission on Human Rights, Sub-Commission on Prevention of Discrimination and Protection of Minorities, *Apartheid as a Collective Form of Slavery, Report of the Secretary-General*, UN Doc UN Doc E/CN.4/Sub.2/449, 18 July 1980, 5.

II. SLAVERY IN INTERNATIONAL HUMAN RIGHTS LAW

The legal regime prohibiting slavery emerges in public international law, not human rights law. As late as the 1956 Supplementary Convention negotiations, there was no guarantee that international human rights law would emerge, the French Representative at the diplomatic conference having intimated that there was no appetite at this time for human rights *law* within the United Nations system.[22] This despite the 1948 Universal Declaration of Human Rights, a non-binding instrument which, at Article 4 reads: 'No one shall be held in slavery or servitude; slavery and the slave trade shall be prohibited in all their forms'. Yet, despite the ability of East and West to maintain a freeze on much of the work of the United Nations during this juncture of the Cold War, international human rights law would find the light of day, a result of the decolonisation process and the Non-Aligned Movement of newly independent States putting forward, in 1966, the UN Convention on the Elimination of Racial Discrimination. This Convention broke the logjam which then allowed the two international covenants to become law. Where slavery specifically is concerned, it entered the corpus of international human rights law in 1966, with the adoption of the International Covenant on Civil and Political Rights (ICCPR) which reads in part at Article 8(1): 'No one shall be held in slavery; slavery and the slave-trade in all their forms shall be prohibited'.[23]

Beyond this, it might be noted that the norm prohibiting slavery has also been included in more recent international criminal law instruments, including the 1998 Statute of the International Criminal Court and the 2000 Palermo Protocol related to trafficking as well as the 2005 European Convention on Action against the Trafficking in Human Beings. They are of relevance as these instruments have aided in hoisting the issue of contemporary slavery onto the international agenda and precipitating a need to consider what constitutes slavery today, in the context of bringing individuals to trial for crimes which include slavery.

Returning to international human rights law, it should be emphasised that in the main, the United Nations system has been quiet in developing jurisprudence around the prohibition against slavery. Here I am thinking of the Human Rights Committee, the supervisory body of the ICCPR, which

[22] United Nations, Economic and Social Council, United Nations Conference of Plenipotentiaries on a Supplementary Convention on the Abolition of Slavery, the Slave Trade and Institutions and Practices Similar to Slavery, Summary Record of the Fourth Meeting, 15 August 1956, UN Doc E/CONF.24/SR.4, 11 November 1958, 9. See the discussion in Allain (n 1) 147.

[23] Note that at the regional level, we have also seen the inclusion of the norm prohibiting slavery into human rights legislation within the 1950 European Human Rights Convention, the 1969 Inter-American Convention of Human Rights and the 1981 African Charter on Human and Peoples' Rights.

can consider petitions from individuals claiming violations of the Covenant, as well as providing General Comments—authoritative pronouncements which seek to add substance to the provisions of the Covenant. To date no such petitions have been considered, nor has a General Comment been promulgated with respect to Article 8 of the ICCPR, which covers slavery, servitude and forced labour. This should come as no surprise, if one takes into consideration the historical evolution of the legal regime prohibiting slavery set out in the previous section of this chapter.

Likewise, the jurisprudence of the regional human rights courts has been unable to provide any firm guidance as to the substance of what the prohibition of slavery might constitute. For the Inter-American Court of Human Rights, while evidence was led in the 2006 *Case of Montero-Aranguren et al (Detention Center of Catia) v Venezuela* that slavery was taking place within the Detention Center of Catia—as laid out below—the Court made no determination on the issue:

> Inside Detention Center of Catia 'the strongest dominated the weakest'. This was condoned by prison officers. In addition, this type of dominance was represented graphically by branding inmates who served as slaves. There were two types of slavery: labor slavery and sexual slavery. Labor slaves were branded with a burner, like cattle brands, which identified who owned the slave, ie who was the head prisoner of the hall. If they were branded on the buttocks, they were sexual slaves.[24]

Elsewhere, the European Court of Human Rights has, in its limited jurisprudence, failed to provide a coherent narrative as to the substance of its provisions related to slavery, servitude and forced labour. As late as 1999, the authors of a text of the leading cases of the European Court of Human Rights could write, taking in the jurisprudence of the first 50 years of the European Convention of Human Rights, that the provisions dealing with slavery, servitude and forced labour, had conclude that 'the leading case on Article 4 is *Van der Mussele*, in which a lawyer complained about the obligation to provide free legal assistance to poor clients'.[25] In 2005, the European Court of Human Rights dealt for the first time with the substance of Article 4 of the European Convention, in the *Siliadin v France* case related to a Togolese child exploited as a domestic labourer in a private home in France. The Court found in this case that there was a breach of the provisions of Article 4 touching on forced labour and servitude, but found no violation with regard to slavery. The approach of the Court was to consider slavery, servitude and forced labour set out in Article 4 as gradations

[24] *Case of Montero-Aranguren et al (Detention Center of Catia) v Venezuela*, Judgment (Preliminary Objection, Merits, Reparations and Costs), Inter-American Court of Human Rights, 5 July 2006, 23.

[25] RA Lawson and HG Schermers, *Leading Cases of the European Court of Human Rights* (Nijmegen, Ars Aequi Libri, 1997) xx.

of exploitation. While the Court found violations of servitude and forced labour; it noted with regard to slavery and its 1926 Convention definition that:

> this definition corresponds to the 'classic' meaning of slavery as it was practiced for centuries. Although the applicant was, in the instant case, clearly deprived of her personal autonomy, the evidence does not suggest that she was held in slavery in the proper sense, in other words that Mr and Mrs B exercised a genuine right of legal ownership over her, thus reducing her to the status of an 'object'.[26]

Thus, in 2005, the Court determined that short of the State passing legislation allowing for the enslavement of people, the Court did not have jurisdiction to deal with slavery. Thus, the Court sought the prohibition against slavery as regards de jure rather than de facto.

That said, in 2010, the European Court of Human Rights reversed course on this pronouncement, but in so doing, it muddied the waters further. The 2010 case *Rantsev v Cyprus and Russia*, related to the death of Oxana Rantseva, a young woman who had been caught up in the sex tourism industry in Cyprus against her will. The Court for its part noted that it 'is not regularly called upon to consider the application of Article 4', despite its reiteration that Article 4 along with the provisions regarding the right to life and the prohibition against torture enshrine 'the basic values of the democratic societies making up the Council of Europe'. Despite Article 4 being silent with regard to trafficking in human beings, the Court in *Rantsev* determined that it is 'unnecessary to identify whether the treatment about which the applicant complains constitutes "slavery", "servitude" or "forced and compulsory labour"'.[27] Instead, the Court conflated trafficking with slavery.[28] Despite the Court having reproduced the definition of trafficking in human beings, it equated trafficking with slavery—at the expense of other types of exploitation noted in that trafficking definition. The Court determined that it 'considers that trafficking in human beings, by its very nature and aim of exploitation, is based on the exercise of powers attaching to the right of ownership'.[29]

[26] *Siliadin v France* App no 73316/01 (ECtHR, 26 July 2005) para 122.

[27] *Rantsev v Cyprus and Russia* App no 25965/04 (ECtHR, 7 January 2010) para 282.

[28] See J Allain, '*Rantsev v Cyprus and Russia*: The European Court of Human Rights and Trafficking as Slavery' (2010) 10 *Human Rights Law Review* 546.

[29] *Rantsev v Cyprus and Russia* (n 24) para 281. The definition of trafficking in human beings which is reproduced in substance in the 2000 United Nations and the 2005 Council of Europe trafficking conventions reads:

> 'Trafficking in human beings' shall mean the recruitment, transportation, transfer, harbouring or receipt of persons, by means of the threat or use of force or other forms of coercion, of abduction, of fraud, of deception, of the abuse of power or of a position of vulnerability or of the giving or receiving of payments or benefits to achieve the consent of a person having control over another person, for the purpose of exploitation. Exploitation shall include, at a minimum, the exploitation of the prostitution of others or other forms of sexual exploitation, forced labour or services, slavery or practices similar to slavery, servitude or the removal of organs.'

While the Court has been unable to provide a coherent narrative with regard to the substance of slavery, servitude or forced labour, it has done well to set out the obligations which States have in ensuring respect for the human right set out in Article 4. In the 2013 *CN v The United Kingdom* case, the European Court of Human Rights sought to some extent to backtrack on its pronouncement in *Rantsev* which assimilated trafficking to slavery, by noting that in the case at hand, the Court was concerned by the 'heavy focus' of the investigating officers on the offence of trafficking for forced labour, rather than on the stand-alone offense of forced labour.[30] That said, the importance of that case—which dealt with a case of a Ugandan national working in the United Kingdom in an apparent case of domestic servitude—to our considerations are the positive obligations noted by the European Court when dealing with issues of slavery, servitude and forced labour.

The Court confirmed obligations first noted in the *Siliadin* case, that 'Article 4 entails a specific positive obligation on member States to penalise and prosecute effectively any act aimed at maintaining a person in a situation of slavery, servitude or forced or compulsory labour'. The Court also noted that Article 4

> may, in certain circumstances, require a State to take operational measures to protect victims, or potential victims [where] the State authorities were aware, or ought to have been aware that an identified individual had been, or was at real and immediate risk of being subjected to [treatment falling under the preview of Article 4].

The European Court noted that positive obligations flowing from Article 4 also entail procedural obligations tied to investigation. This relates to obligations of means not results, in that investigations are to be independent, that they should be carried out *proprio motu*, and that there is a 'requirement of promptness and reasonable expedition' in carrying out such investigations.[31] As a result, the European Court of Human Rights found the United Kingdom in violation of Article 4 of the European Convention, deciding that 'the investigation into the applicant's complaints of domestic servitude was ineffective due to the absence of specific legislation criminalising such treatment'.[32] Here then is the fullest elaboration of positive obligations set out by the regional human rights system of Europe.

See Art 3(a), 2001 United Nations Protocol to Prevent, Suppress and Punish Trafficking in Persons, especially Women and Children and Art 4(a), 2005 Council of Europe Convention on Action against Trafficking in Human Beings. Note that the Palermo Protocol speaks of 'trafficking in persons' not 'trafficking in human beings'.

[30] *CN v The United Kingdom*, App no 4239/08 (ECtHR, 13 February 2013) para 80.

[31] ibid, paras 66, 67 and 69.

[32] ibid, para 81.

As for those human rights obligations more generally, that all States are bound by with regard to the legal regime of governing the prohibition of slavery, Article 2 of the ICCPR states that each 'State Party to the present Covenant undertakes to respect and to ensure to all individuals within its territory and subject to its jurisdiction the rights recognized in the present Covenant'. The Covenant requires that States 'adopt such laws or other measures as may be necessary to give effect to the rights recognized in the present Covenant'. The ICCPR further requires that States provide for a remedy where a violation has transpired and have possible breaches of rights determined by the competent authorities, and the requirement to 'develop the possibilities of judicial remedy'.[33] Such fundamental obligations chime nicely with the mantra of the United Nations human rights system that 'States assume obligations and duties under international law to respect, to protect and to fulfil human rights'. Where the legal regime prohibiting slavery is concerned, the duty to respect the human right prohibiting slavery, servitude or forced labour to a large extent is moot, as such an obligation requires the State not to interfere with the exercise of that right—that is, a negative obligation—not to enslave, to utilise servile labour or forced labour. Where 'protect' is concerned, this turns on the positive obligations, requiring the State to protect the right bearer from third parties who would seek to infringe on those human rights established by the legal regime prohibiting slavery. Finally, where 'fulfil' is concerned, this speaks to the requirement of States to take legislative, administrative, budgetary, judicial and other actions towards the full realisation of the right in question.

III. PROPERTY LAW AT THE SERVICE OF A HUMAN RIGHT

Recognising the various moments in time which have led to the regime prohibiting slavery falling into disuse as a result of the confusion created by such nomenclature as 'practices similar to slavery' and 'slavery-like practice', along with the near disappearance of 'servitude' as a normative concept, is but one element in seeking to bring to life this regime prohibiting slavery as a legal tool. More fundamental was a requirement for the law to take back the concept of slavery from a United Nations system which saw its worth as little more than rhetorical. This task was taken on in earnest in 2004 when, for the first time, the League of Nations Archives and the United Nations Library in Geneva were visited to consider the work undertaken by these two organisations with regard to the overall regime, that is, in the domain of slavery and lesser servitudes. A fundamental building block for understanding the legal elements of the regime prohibiting slavery was produced in 2008 with the publication of *The Slavery Conventions*, which

[33] Art 2, International Covenant on Civil and Political Rights, 1966.

sets out the legislative history of the 1926 and 1956 slavery conventions.[34] *The Slavery Conventions* is fundamental to understanding the overall legal regime prohibiting slavery, but more so, specifically with regard to what constitutes 'slavery' in international law. This is so, as in a situation where a provision of a treaty is ambiguous, obscure, manifestly absurd, or unreasonable; then recourse may be had, by the principles of international law, to the so-called *travaux préparatoires*, that is the preparatory works or legislative history, as a supplementary means of treaty interpretation.[35]

In pre-production, *The Slavery Conventions* were utilised as a basis of an intervention by the Australian Human Rights and Equal Opportunity Commission in the 2008 *Tang* case before the High Court of Australia.[36] The outcome of that case was that the highest court in the land accepted the contemporary application of the 1926 definition and started to unpack the wording of the definition of slavery. Recalling that the definition speaks of the 'status or condition of a person over whom any or all of the powers attaching to the right of ownership are exercised', the High Court first considered the phrase 'status or condition'. Referencing a 2007 paper that I had presented at the International Criminal Court, the High Court of Australia stated that its criminal law refers only to '"condition", not "status or condition" [as] legal ownership of a person is impossible'. Thus, the Court adjudged that 'status' relates to *de jure* ownership, while condition 'is concerned with *de facto* slavery'.[37]

The Court went on to consider the second element of the definition, that is: 'any or all of the powers attaching to the right of ownership', and cited a 1953 Memorandum of the Secretary-General of the United Nations—which had been rescued from the archives—that listed six such powers.[38] The High

[34] J Allain, *The Slavery Conventions: The Travaux Préparatoires of the 1926 League of Nations Convention and the 1956 United Nations Convention* (Leiden, Martinus Nijhoff, 2008).

[35] Art 32, Vienna Convention on the Law of Treaties, 1969.

[36] See Human Rights and Equal Opportunity Commission, *Submissions in Support of Application for Leave to Intervene and Submissions on the Appeal in the Case the Commonwealth Director of Public Prosecutions v Wei Tang*, 5 May 2008.

[37] *The Queen v Tang* [2008] HCA 39, 28 August 2008, para 23. The High Court of Australia went on to explain the essence of such de facto slavery:

> 'the reference to powers attaching to the right of ownership, which are exercised over a person in a condition described as slavery, is a reference to powers of such a nature and extent that they are attributes of effective (although not legal, for that is impossible) ownership.'

The High Court cites Jean Allain, 'The Definition of "Slavery" in General International Law and the Crime of Enslavement within the Rome Statute', paper delivered at the International Criminal Court, *Guest Lecture Series of the Office of the Prosecutor*, 26 April 2007.

[38] See United Nations Economic and Social Council, Slavery, the Slave Trade, and other forms of Servitude (Report of the Secretary-General), UN Doc E/2357, 27 January 1953, 28, which sets out six powers attaching to the right of ownership:

1. the individual of servile status may be made the object of a purchase;
2. the master may use the individual of servile status, and in particular his capacity to work, in an absolute manner, without any restriction other than that which might be expressly provided by law;

Court satisfied itself that the five Thai women had been held in a condition of slavery in a brothel in Melbourne, by reference to some, but not all of the powers attaching to the right of ownership to which the United Nations Secretary-General had pointed.

Here then, with regard to the powers attaching to the right of ownership, do we see the need to bring into the discussions of the contemporary law of slavery the principles and basic tenets of property law? For his part, the UN Secretary-General noted that:

> In the absence of such an indication, it may reasonably be assumed that the basic concept which they [the negotiators] had in mind was that of the authority of the master over the slave in Roman law, the '*dominica potestas*'. This authority was of an absolute nature, comparable to the rights of ownership, which included the right to acquire, to use, or to dispose of a thing or of an animal or of its fruits or offspring.[39]

As the Court did not go beyond what was required in making its finding in the *Tang* case, it was left to a group of property law scholars and experts of slavery both past and present, to give voice to what should be understood as the exercise of the powers attaching to the right of ownership where human beings are concerned.[40]

Having met at both the Rockefeller Foundation's Bellagio Conference Centre and at Harvard University in 2010 and 2011 respectively, this network produced both the 2012 edited collection titled *The Legal Understanding of Slavery*, and the 2012 *Bellagio-Harvard Guidelines on the Legal Parameters of Slavery*. The latter brings to bear the foundations of property law so as to provide a coherent reading of the definition of slavery.[41] Not surprising, for those versed in property law, is that the starting point for engaging with the topic is Anthony Honoré's work in developing the standard incidents of ownership.[42] As Robin Hickey has shown, those

3. the products of labour of the individual of servile status become the property of the master without any compensation commensurate to the value of the labour;
4. the ownership of the individual of servile status can be transferred to another person;
5. the servile status is permanent, that is to say, it cannot be terminated by the will of the individual subject to it;
6. the servile status is transmitted *ipso facto* to descendants of the individual having such status.

[39] ibid, 27.

[40] The member of this group, known as the Research Network on the Legal Parameters of Slavery, are noted, along with Bellagio-Harvard Guidelines on the Legal Parameters of Slavery, in the Appendix to this chapter.

[41] See more generally J Allain and R Hickey, 'Property Law and the Definition of Slavery' (2012) 61 *International and Comparative Law Quarterly* 915.

[42] AM Honoré, 'Ownership' in AG Guest (ed), *Oxford Essays in Jurisprudence* (Oxford, Oxford University Press, 1961) 105. See also LC Becker, *Property Rights: Philosophical Foundations* (Boston, Routledge and Kegan Paul, 1983) 7 and 18; J Waldron, *The Right to Private Property* (Oxford, Clarendon Press, 1990) 27, 28 and 49; SR Munzer, *A Theory of Property* (Cambridge, Cambridge University Press, 1990) 22–27; JE Penner, 'The Bundle of Rights Picture of Property' (1995–96) 43 *UCLA Law Review* 711; L Katz, 'Exclusion and Exclusivity

powers attaching to the right of ownership should be understood as being synonymous with Honoré's standard incidents of ownership.[43]

Before delving into those powers attaching to the right of ownership, it might be worthwhile to start from the most fundamental: what is ownership? What may come as a surprise to those who have more of an interest in human rights issues, is that ownership—a fundamental tenet of liberal legalism and the basis of the capitalist economic order—has no set definition. Ownership has no fixed meaning, rather it is an elusive concept. A social construct, it is typically understood as a priorital right over something. As Honoré puts it, 'those legal rights, duties and other incidents which apply, in the ordinary case, to the person who has the greatest interest in a thing admitted by a mature legal system'.[44] That 'greatest interest' thus does not mean that an individual has a sovereign or absolute right over a thing but, rather, the ability to enjoy and dispose of the thing 'provided that one abstains from any use forbidden by statute or subordinate legislation'.[45] Thus ownership entails rights, but those rights are often termed not as absolute but as rights vis-à-vis others, where one holds the best claim to a thing. Moving beyond the common characterisation of ownership as constituting a 'bundle of rights', Honoré lists what he calls the 11 'standard incidents' of ownership, of which the majority are rights, but some are also obligations. These incidents include the right to possess, to use, to manage, to the income of the thing, to its capital, to its transmissibility, and the right of security; along with prohibition of harmful use and liability in instances of insolvency.

The 2012 *Bellagio-Harvard Guidelines on the Legal Parameters of Slavery* set out a general understanding of what constitutes slavery through the exercise of those powers attaching to the right of ownership by highlighting in its Guideline 2, that is: 'control over a person in such a way as to significantly deprive that person of his or her individual liberty, with the intent of exploitation through the use, management, profit, transfer or disposal of that person'. Thus, in seeking to understand what constitutes contemporary slavery—cases of de facto slavery—we must ultimately recognise that enslavement is about control. Once control is established over a person, only then can they be exploited. The property paradigm utilised results from the nexus which is to be found between 'ownership' and slavery; that nexus is between *possession* in property law and *control* in cases of contemporary slavery.

in Property Law' (2008) 58 *University of Toronto Law Journal* 275; and JW Harris, *Property and Justice* (Oxford, Clarendon Press, 1996) 125–30.

43 R Hickey, 'Seeking to Understand the Definition of Slavery', but also in the same collection JE Penner 'The Concept of Property and the Concept of Slavery' in Allain (n 2).

44 Honoré (n 38) 105.

45 ibid.

For Honoré, the very sub-structure upon which ownership rests is possession. The notion of possession in property law is a background relationship of control between the person and the thing owned. In property law, to own something is to have exclusive control over it. In such terms, it is not difficult to make the leap from property law to the human right prohibiting slavery. That contemporary slavery—where legal ownership is no long allowed—*de facto* ownership can be recognised where a person has exclusive control over another. The Guidelines go into some detail with regard to possession, as establishing that control is at play will be fundamental to determining in law a case of slavery. In the language of the Guidelines, we are speaking of 'control tantamount to possession'; that is controlling a person as one would possess a thing they own. Where one can demonstrate that a person controls another in the same manner as they would in possessing a thing, then we are speaking of a contemporary manifestation of slavery. What would such control look like? As already noted, such control would significantly deprive that person of his or her individual liberty, allowing for that person's exploitation through various means (use, management, profit, transfer or disposal of a person).

Where contemporary slavery is concerned, those incidents of ownership, those 'powers attaching to the right of ownership', start and end with possession—with control tantamount to possession. This is so, as possession allows for the exercise of the other powers attaching to the right of ownership. Yet, without possession—that control which significantly deprives that person of his or her individual liberty—slavery cannot in law exist.

Beyond possession, the powers attaching to the right of ownership set out in the Bellagio-Harvard Guidelines are: a) Buying, Selling or Transferring of a Person; b) Using a Person; c) Managing the Use of a Person; d) Profiting from the Use of a Person; e) Transferring a Person to an Heir or Successor; and f) Disposal, Mistreatment or Neglect of a Person. Let us unpack the first of these so as to understand the manner in which the Guidelines capture the essence of modern day slavery. In speaking of buying, selling or transferring of a person, Guideline 4(a) makes plain that such buying, selling or transferring might well provide evidence of slavery. But this is not enough. Consider the case where a professional athlete is traded from one club to another—she is transferred, it may even be said that she has been 'sold' to another club or 'bought' by it. One would be hard placed to call this slavery. Why? What is missing is the underlying element of possession. Without the exercises of control tantamount to possession, such buying, selling or transferring will not meet the threshold of slavery. Our professional athlete need not accept the transfer, she can take on other employment, but ultimately she will not be forced to take the field against her will—her personal liberty has not be reduced to such an extent. More is needed—only when control tantamount to possession is brought into the equation can we speak of slavery. Thus, while the buying, selling or transferring of a person *may* provide evidence of slavery, only in cases where control tantamount to possession are at play can we then speak of slavery. Guideline 4(a) speaks in such terms: 'Buying, selling or otherwise transferring a person may provide evidence of slavery. Having established control tantamount to possession; the act of buying, selling or transferring that person will be an act of slavery'.

Beyond buying, selling or transferring of a person, the Guidelines speak to the *use of a person*, which is straightforward. The actual use of a person is not enough to constitute slavery, only when, having first established control over a person tantamount to possession, can we speak of slavery in law. The managing the use of a person provides a good example of why the underlying need to establish control tantamount to possession is necessary. In any labour relationship, the employee will be managed. In base terms, an employee will be told where to work and the hours they will have to labour. But it would overcook the proposition to say such management constitutes enslavement. Here then we recognise that the background relationship of control tantamount to possession is needed to constitute slavery. It is not enough in law to say that the power of managing the use of a person amounts to slavery. Such managing of the use of a person will, in the first instance, help to identify a possible case of slavery, however, in and of itself, it is not enough to constitute enslavement. The background relationship known in property law of possession will slide a banal act of managing the use of a person from being not only permissible and fundamental to any working relationship; to being a case of enslavement if control in such that if it were exercised against a thing, we would recognise it as possession.

Without going into detail as to the other powers attaching to the right of ownership set out in the Guidelines, reference might be made to one further power which has not yet been mentioned; that of expropriation as against Honoré's incident of ownership known as the 'right of security'. In property law, it is recognised that the State may take your property for public purposes while providing compensation. Thus, the State has an obligation to uphold your right of security of ownership. Yet, as the State no longer recognises nor supports a property right in persons, such 'expropriation'—the taking of such human 'property' away from its 'owner'—is not only permissive, but is required. In human rights law, a fundamental distinction exists between negative obligations on the State—not to infringe a human right: in this case not to enslave—and positive obligations—the requirement of the State to protect a human right from being violated by a third party.

The emphasis of the 2012 *Bellagio-Harvard Guidelines on the Legal Parameters of Slavery* is to back away from considering the *form* of a relationship—that is, whether a person is in a situation which we might call 'child soldiering', 'debt bondage', 'forced marriage', 'forced labour', or 'trafficking'; but instead look to the *substance* of the relationship which has been created by the parties involved. Thus, in looking at the particular circumstances of a given situation, one must ask oneself whether the 'powers attaching to the right of ownership' are being exercised and if so, can it be demonstrated that during such exercise that control tantamount to possession was at play. By such means of determination, it then becomes possible to consider the distinctions in law between slavery and those practices similar to slavery as set out in the 1956 Supplementary Conventions. Thus, with debt bondage, serfdom, servile marriage and child exploitation, the distinction will be made vis-à-vis slavery, where in substance, the exercise of the powers attaching to the right of ownership are at play. Short of that, the case will not amount to slavery and thus attention would have to be given to consider whether the particular circumstances of the exploitation meet the prescription established by the definition of such a 'practices similar to slavery'.

IV. CONCLUSION

Property law has been fundamental in bringing to life what has become a fundamental human right, though it lay dormant for more than 75 years. The prohibition against slavery, it should be emphasised, is not just any right, but is one which the European Court of Human Rights considers to be comparable in importance to the right to life or the prohibition against torture.[46] The basic tenets of property law have been fundamental to a project which has not only succeeded in giving legal clarity to the concept of slavery in a contemporary setting where, in the main, de facto rather than de jure slavery exists. More so, the *Bellagio-Harvard Guidelines on the Legal Parameters of Slavery* have managed to capture the essence of the lived experience of those caught up in the condition of modern day slavery.[47]

While the regime prohibiting slavery was in complete disarray by the end of the twentieth century, a concerted effort has taken place to think of slavery through a property paradigm and provide it with legal certainty. Honoré's incidents of ownership provide the basis for unpacking those 'powers attaching to the right of ownership' which form the basis of the definition of slavery as first set out in the 1926 Slavery Convention. While a number of 'moments in time' during the twentieth century conspired to bring much confusion to the regime prohibiting slavery, rendering it, for all intent and purpose, dead-letter; a fundamental engagement both with its drafting history and with property law has been able to bring it to life. In so doing, this effort has shed much light on the content of the various norms which make up that regime, including slavery itself, but also those conventional servitudes—those practices similar to slavery—set out in the 1956 Supplementary Convention. So too does this spadework provide insights into

[46] *CN v The United Kingdom* (n 27) para 65.

[47] These Guidelines are included in the Appendix at p 113.

'enslavement', as a crime within the Statute of the International Criminal Court, and to various types of exploitation set out in the common definition of trafficking set out in both the United Nations and Council of Europe conventions related to human trafficking.

One should not hesitate to acknowledge a great debt which human rights law owes to property law. Property law has acted in the service of human rights by providing normative content and clarity to definition of slavery. It is now time for the various international human rights fora, be they within the United Nations or as part of regional systems, to reciprocate by engaging with issues of slavery and lesser servitudes. Courts and treaty-monitoring bodies of these international organisations risk becoming irrelevant to the recently emerged anti-slavery and anti-trafficking movements by their failure to take up and lead in developing the regime prohibiting slavery. That said, it should be emphasised that no matter the extent to which international human rights law engages with the regime prohibiting slavery, that the very engagement with slavery could only transpire through the paradigm of property law.

APPENDIX

BELLAGIO-HARVARD GUIDELINES ON THE LEGAL PARAMETERS OF SLAVERY

We, the Members of the Research Network on the Legal Parameters of Slavery,

Recognizing that there has been a lack of legal clarity with regard to the interpretation of the definition of slavery in international law;

Conscious that the starting point for understanding that definition is Article 1(1) of the 1926 Slavery Convention which reads: '*Slavery is the status or condition of a person over whom any or all of the powers attaching to the right of ownership are exercised*';

Recalling that this definition is reproduced in substance in Article 7(a) of the 1956 Supplementary Convention on the Abolition of Slavery, the Slave Trade, and Institutions and Practices Similar to Slavery;

Also noting that the 1926 definition of slavery is once again reproduced in substance in the definition of enslavement found in Article 7(2)(c) of the 1998 Statute of the International Criminal Court and developed in more detail in the secondary legislation of the Court, in its Elements of Crimes;

Bearing in mind the provisions in international human rights law regarding slavery within the 1948 Universal Declaration and 1966 International Covenant on Civil and Political Rights; as well as the provisions regarding slavery in regional human rights conventions of the African, European, and Inter-American systems;

Considering the inclusion of slavery as an enumerated type of human exploitation in both the 2000 United Nations Palermo Protocol on Trafficking in Persons and the 2005 Council of Europe Convention on Action against Trafficking in Human Beings;

Mindful of the pronouncements and case-law related to slavery of international, regional and domestic courts;

Having met to consider the issue at the 2010 symposium entitled: 'The Parameters of Slavery' at the Rockefeller Foundation's Bellagio Conference Centre in Bellagio, Italy; having further deliberated in 2011 at a meeting under the auspices of the Harriet Tubman Institute for Research on the Global Migrations of African Peoples, York University, Canada; and came together once more at a 2011 symposium entitled: '**The Legal Parameters of Slavery: Historical to the Contemporary**' at Harvard University, under the auspices of the Charles Hamilton Houston Institute for Race and Justice, Harvard Law School; the Harvard Sociology Department; the W.E.B. DuBois Institute;

Recommend the following Guidelines related to the legal parameters of slavery:

Guideline 1—The Legal Definition

The legal definition of slavery in international law is found at Article 1(1) of the 1926 Slavery Convention, which reads: 'Slavery is the status or condition of a person over whom any or all of the powers attaching to the right of ownership are exercised'.

Guideline 2—The Exercise of the Powers Attaching to the Right of Ownership

In cases of slavery, the exercise of 'the powers attaching to the right of ownership' should be understood as constituting control over a person in such a way as to significantly deprive that person of his or her individual liberty, with the intent of exploitation through the use, management, profit, transfer or disposal of that person. Usually this exercise will be supported by and obtained through means such as violent force, deception and/or coercion.

Guideline 3—Possession is Foundational to Slavery

Where there is a right of ownership in respect of a thing, ownership implies a background relation of control. That control is the power attaching to the right of ownership known as possession.

Possession is foundational to an understanding of the legal definition of slavery, even when the State does not support a property right in respect of persons. To determine, in law, a case of slavery, one must look for possession.

While the exact form of possession might vary, in essence it supposes control over a person by another such as a person might control a thing. Such control may be physical, but physical constraints will not always be necessary to the maintenance of effective control over a person. More abstract manifestations of control of a person may be evident in attempts to withhold identity documents; or to otherwise restrict free movement or access to state authorities or legal processes; or equally in attempts to forge a new identity through compelling a new religion, language, place of residence, or forcing marriage.

Fundamentally, where such control operates, it will significantly deprive that person of his or her individual liberty for a period of time which is, for that person, indeterminate.

Cases of slavery are to be distinguished from those where, though there has been control exercised, it does not constitute control tantamount to possession, such as where employers make legitimate decisions about the management of workers.

Possession is foundational in that, not only is it a power attaching to the right of ownership, it also creates the factual conditions for the exercise of any or all of other powers attaching to the right of ownership, such as those set out in *Guideline 4*.

Guideline 4—Further Examples of Powers Attaching to the Right of Ownership

Where a person controls another such as he or she would control a thing owned, such possession makes possible the exercise of any or all of the powers attaching to the right of ownership.

Correlatively, the exercise of any or all of the powers attaching to the right of ownership may serve to indicate the presence of control of a person tantamount to possession, and so provide evidence of slavery.

The following are further examples of powers attaching to the right of ownership:

a) Buying, Selling or Transferring a Person

Buying, selling or otherwise transferring a person may provide evidence of slavery. Having established control tantamount to possession; the act of buying, selling or transferring that person will be an act of slavery.

Evidence of slavery may also be found in similar transactions, such as bartering, exchanging, or giving or receiving a person as a gift, where control tantamount to possession has been established.

b) Using a Person

Using a person may provide evidence of slavery. Having established control tantamount to possession; the act of using that person will be an act of slavery.

Evidence of such use of a person may include the derived benefit from the services or labour of that person. In such cases, a person might be used by working for little or no pay, utilised for sexual gratification, or used by providing a service.

c) Managing the Use of a Person

Managing the use of a person may provide evidence of slavery. Having established control tantamount to possession; the act of managing that person will be an act of slavery.

Evidence of such management of the use of a person may include indirect management such as a brothel owner delegating power to a day manager in a situation of slavery in the context of sex work.

d) Profiting from the Use of a Person

Profiting from the use of a person may provide evidence of slavery. Having established control tantamount to possession; the act of profiting from the use of that person will be an act of slavery.

Evidence of profiting from the use of a person may include cases where a person is mortgaged, lent for profit, or used as collateral.

Evidence of profiting from the use of a person may also include making money or deriving any other kind of income or benefit from the use of the person. Such as the use of an agricultural worker in a situation of slavery, where the profit from the picking of a crop is taken or received by another whether in the form of wages or of the harvest.

e) Transferring a Person to an Heir or Successor

Transferring a person to an heir or successor may provide evidence of slavery. Having established control over a person tantamount to possession; the act of willing that person to a child or other heir or successor will be an act of slavery.

Evidence of such transferring of a person may include a case of inheritance where a woman, on the death of her husband, is deemed to be inherited by another person.

Evidence of such a transferring of a person may also include the conveying of a status or condition of a person to that of a successive generation, such as from mother to daughter.

f) Disposal, Mistreatment or Neglect of a Person

Disposing of a person following his or her exploitation may provide evidence of slavery. Having established control over a person tantamount to possession; the act of disposing of a person will be an act of slavery.

Mistreatment or neglect of a person may provide evidence of slavery. Having established control tantamount to possession, such disregard may lead to the physical or psychological exhaustion of a person, and ultimately to his or her destruction; accordingly the act of bringing about such exhaustion will be an act of slavery.

Evidence of such mistreatment or neglect may include sustained physical and psychological abuse, whether calculated or indiscriminate; or the imposition of physical demands that severely curtail the capacity of the human body to sustain itself or function effectively.

Guideline 5—Making a Determination as to Whether Slavery Exists

The exercise of any or all of the powers attaching to the right of ownership just considered shall provide evidence of slavery, insofar as they demonstrate control over a person tantamount to possession.

Accordingly, in determining whether slavery exists in a given case, it is necessary to examine the particular circumstances, asking whether '*powers attaching to the right of ownership*' are being exercised, so as to demonstrate control of a person tantamount to their possession.

In evaluating the particular circumstances to determine whether slavery exists, reference should be made to the substance and not simply to the form of the relationship in question.

The substance of the relationship should be determined by investigating whether in fact there has been an exercise of one or more of the powers attaching to the right of ownership. This will include a determination as to whether control tantamount to possession is present.

Guideline 6—Expropriation

Ordinarily exclusion from expropriation or 'security of holding' would be deemed a power attaching to the right of ownership. However, as the State generally does not support a property right in persons, a negative obligation against the State generally no longer exists.

However, the State has *at minimum* the positive obligation to bring about the end of either the status or condition of a person over whom any or all of the powers attaching to the right of ownership are exercised.

The State may have further positive obligations with regard to the prohibition against slavery on the basis of domestic law as well as regional or international instruments.

Guideline 7—Terminology

The term 'slavery' has often been utilised to describe circumstances that go beyond the legal definition as established by the 1926 Slavery Convention.

In law, only 'slavery' and 'institutions and practices similar to slavery', which is often abbreviated to 'practices similar to slavery' have standing and are defined in international law via the 1926 Slavery Convention and the 1956 Supplementary Convention.

Guideline 8—Distinction between Slavery and Forced Labour

The 1926 Slavery Convention recognises that forced labour can develop 'into conditions analogous to slavery'.

Although forced or compulsory labour is defined by the 1930 Forced Labour Convention as 'all work or service which is exacted from any person under the menace of any penalty and for which the said person has not offered himself voluntarily'; forced labour will only amount to slavery when, in substance, there is the exercise of the powers attaching to the right of ownership.

Slavery will not be present in cases of forced labour where the control over a person tantamount to possession is not present.

Guideline 9—Distinction between Slavery and 'Institutions and Practices Similar to Slavery'

Article 1 of the 1956 Supplementary Convention recognises that the 'institutions and practices similar to slavery', that is: debt bondage, serfdom, servile marriages, or child exploitation; may be 'covered by the definition of slavery contained in article 1 of the Slavery Convention of 1926'.

The distinction between these servile statuses as defined by the 1956 Supplementary Convention in the following terms and slavery is that slavery is present where in substance there is the exercise of the powers attaching to the right of ownership.

It should be emphasised that slavery will only be present in cases of such 'institutions and practices similar to slavery' where control over a person tantamount to possession is present.

The following are the conventional servitudes set out in the 1956 Supplementary Convention on the Abolition of Slavery, the Slave Trade, and Institutions and Practices Similar to Slavery:

(a) Debt bondage, that is to say, the status or condition arising from a pledge by a debtor of his personal services or of those of a person under his control as security for a debt, if the value of those services as reasonably assessed is not applied towards the liquidation of the debt or the length and nature of those services are not respectively limited and defined;

(b) Serfdom, that is to say, the condition or status of a tenant who is by law, custom or agreement bound to live and labour on land belonging to another person and to render some determinate service to such other person, whether for reward or not, and is not free to change his status;

(c) Any institution or practice whereby:

  (i) A woman, without the right to refuse, is promised or given in marriage on payment of a consideration in money or in kind to her parents, guardian, family or any other person or group; or

  (ii) The husband of a woman, his family, or his clan, has the right to transfer her to another person for value received or otherwise; or

  (iii) A woman on the death of her husband is liable to be inherited by another person;

(d) Any institution or practice whereby a child or young person under the age of 18 years is delivered by either or both of his natural parents or by his guardian to another person, whether for reward or not, with a view to the exploitation of the child or young person or of his labour.

Guideline 10—When Slavery and Lesser Servitudes are Present

Accepting that both slavery and lesser servitudes such as forced labour or 'institutions and practices similar to slavery' may be found in substance in a particular circumstance; the manner to proceed is by making reference to that substance and not simply to the form, and first ask whether there has been an exercise of the powers attaching to the right of ownership. If so, then the more serious offence of slavery is present.

If not, reference should be made to the legal definition of the lesser servitude which corresponds in substance to the particular circumstance in question.

Adopted on this day, 3 March 2012, by the Members of the Research Network on the Legal Parameters of Slavery.

Jean Allain, Queen's University, Belfast
Kevin Bales, Free the Slaves
Annie Bunting, York University
John Cairns, University of Edinburgh
William M. Carter Jr., Temple University
Holly Cullen, University of Western Australia
Seymour Drescher, University of Pittsburgh
Stanley Engerman, University of Rochester
Paul Finkelman, Albany Law School
Bernard Freamon, Seton Hall University
Allison Gorsuch, Yale University
Robin Hickey, Durham University
Richard Helmholz, University of Chicago
Antony Honoré, University of Oxford
Aidan McQuade, Anti-Slavery International
Orlando Patterson, Harvard University
James Penner, University College, London
Joel Quirk, University of Witwatersrand
Jody Sarich, Free the Slaves
Rebecca Scott, University of Michigan

5

Property in Human Bodies, Self-Preservation and Human Rights

ELENA BELTRÁN*

I. INTRODUCTION

ADVANCES IN MEDICAL biotechnology demonstrate that the human body has become the source of materials which are deemed essential for scientific development. Such material is often utilised, without qualms or query, as the property of laboratories and companies from the very moment when it leaves the human body. These laboratories and companies may obtain huge profit from their research activities, as Holland argues, 'we are witnessing nothing less than a new kind of gold rush and the territory is the body'.[1] While 'a person is not, in most systems, regarded as owning his body, reputation, skill, honour or dignity',[2] the question to be considered in this chapter is whether the person whose body the material is extracted from should have some sort of property rights over that material.

In order to consider this *problematique* some considerations on the relationships between human body, dignity and human rights will need to be undertaken, with a series of cases examined to enlighten the debate on whether some idea of property in the human body should be recognised. Issues and debates raised in these cases have led to an evaluation of the

* This article was developed on my research during my stay in the London School of Economics funded by the Mobility Program within the framework of the Plan for Scientific and Technical Research and Innovation of Spanish Government. I would like to thank Professor A Phillips for the opportunity of the stay. I am very grateful to the reviewers for their insightful comments and helpful suggestions on earlier drafts of this paper and I would like to emphasise my gratitude for the tremendous help provided by the Editors.

[1] S Holland, 'Contested Commodities at both Ends of Life: Buying and Selling Gametes, Embryos, and Body Tissues' (2001) 11 *Kennedy Institute of Ethics Journal* 263, 261.

[2] AM Honoré, 'Ownership' in AG Guest (ed), *Oxford Essays in Jurisprudence (First Series)* (Oxford, Clarendon Press, 1961) 130.

classic philosophical justifications of property which are frequently utilised to defend the recognition of property in the human body. Having undertaken this consideration, an analysis of different concepts of property will be considered with a focus on the incidents of ownership set out by Honoré as a means of understanding the idea of property. Finally, a review of different approaches to the idea of self-ownership and the need to make distinctions between personal rights and property rights, as well as between strong property rights and weak property rights, will be undertaken. With this in mind, one will be better placed to argue that property in the human body should be recognised.[3] Adopting such a position will strengthen the links between the human body, property and human rights, as property itself derives from the basic human rights of self-preservation, which in turn allows humans to flourish.

II. HUMAN BODY, DIGNITY AND HUMAN RIGHTS

The origin of human rights is linked to the historical moments in which the idea of human dignity was consolidated; an idea that is inseparable from the development of the concept of human beings as moral agents.[4] In the foundation of human rights we find the principle of autonomy implying a human being with the capacity to be one's own person, to be governed only by its own principles and laws.[5] Thus, it is not by chance that great enlightened revolutions arose while the conception of human rights was being forged.[6] The proclamation of universal rights appears in declarations of revolutionary rights, even though this 'universality' happened to leave out a great part of humanity, such as women, servants and slaves.[7] These exclusions were born mainly from criteria that authors such as Kant articulated with care; one of these is the criterion of dependency, resulting from exclusion of ownership of property.[8]

We should not forget that in the declarations of rights, property plays an important role; in fact these declarations are the manifestation of the power

[3] For criticism on this proposition, see eg, A Phillips, *Our Bodies, Whose Property?* (Princeton NJ, Princeton University Press, 2013).

[4] A Gewirth, *Human Rights: Essays on Justification and Applications* (Chicago, University of Chicago Press, 1982).

[5] I Kant, *Groundwork of the Metaphysic of Morals* in *Practical Philosophy* (MJ Gregor trans, Cambridge, Cambridge University Press, 1996[1785]); *Critique of Practical Reason* in *Practical Philosophy* (MJ Gregor trans, Cambridge, Cambridge University Press, 1996 [1787]) 5: 33.

[6] L Hunt, *Inventing Human Rights: A History* (New York, WW Norton and Company, 2008) esp 27–30.

[7] J Locke, *Two Treatises of Government* (P Laslett ed, Cambridge, Cambridge University Press, 1988).

[8] I Kant, *The Metaphysics of Morals*, M Gregor (ed), introduction by RJ Sullivan (Cambridge, Cambridge University Press, 1996) para 46, 6:314.

of the ascendant bourgeoisie in face of the *ancien régime*.[9] To be the owner of property is a manifestation of such power; those excluded from the ownership of property became second-class citizens, who were not recognised as the real holders of the human rights which were being so loudly proclaimed, as was the case of women and servants. Or, as in the case of slaves, they were simply not recognised as holders of any right whatsoever.

All non-owners share the feature of being dependant, either on a master, a father, an employer or a husband, but they also had something else in common: the lack of control or decision over their own bodies; this was manifested in different ways, to different degrees and in different circumstances. This was frequently justified as being natural in the case of women, but also, on occasion, in the case of slaves.[10] Regarding servants, some authors establish a connection between the body that performs the tasks and work, and the possibility of ownership of that fruit yield resulting therefrom (that would be allotted to the master, not to the servant whose body produces them).[11] Generally speaking, non-owners lack the possibility of controlling the use, care and fruits yielded by their own body.

For many authors, speaking of ownership of the human body or its parts goes against the idea of human dignity. This would lead us to question our conception of dignity which underlies the idea of human rights. The concept of dignity that makes its way hand in glove with the development of human rights is an idea understood as inherent in being a person; an idea of dignity that is not lost, even in the case of acting immorally, as it is a trait of all beings.[12]

Therefore the acceptance of this concept of human dignity cannot be seen to contrast with the defense of a certain type of property rights related to the body.[13] On the contrary, a concept of human rights that is born from the idea of humans as moral agents; autonomous beings capable of making decisions concerning their life, seems, at present, to expect these people to be able to choose how best to use their body. This despite the most com-

[9] Declaration of Rights of Man and the Citizen 1789, Art 17: 'Property being an inviolable and sacred right, no one may be deprived of it except when public necessity, certified by law, obviously requires it, and of the condition of just compensation in advance', quoted in Hunt (n 6) 222.

[10] See J-J Rousseau, *Emile or on Education* (ed, Trans, and notes A Bloom, New York, Basic Books, 1979).

[11] See below, Section III.

[12] 'Kant's use of the idea of dignity rests on an innovative reaction to predecessors in the history of political theory. One identifies dignity with honor. Under an ethic of honor, only some persons have dignity': S Munzer, 'An Uneasy Case against Property Rights in Body Parts' in EF Paul, FD Miller and J Paul (eds), *Property Rights* (New York, Cambridge University Press, 1994) 267; see also C Taylor, *Sources of the Self: The Making of Modern Identity* (Cambridge, Cambridge University Press, 1989) esp 12.

[13] See Munzer, ibid; C Foster, 'Dignity and the Use of Body Parts' (2014) 40 *Journal of Medical Ethics* 44.

monly held view that autonomy and control can be exercised on the basis of different legal constructions.[14] The protection of rights over the human body can be supported by the principle of bodily integrity and the rights which flow from it: Freedom, security, privacy. However, scientific research and technological advances have led us to question whether these mechanisms are sufficient when we speak of protecting human rights. If we are willing to accept that 'property is power', then it will be the weak, the passive and the historically dependant citizens, who will need stronger mechanisms to defend the right to control their own bodies, not only in the face of husbands, fathers and employers, but also against powerful entities such as corporations.[15] The golden thread of this chapter is the idea of property in relation to the human body as the means by which each person can control its use and preserve its integrity in the face of external pressures.

The cases below further illustrate the kinds of problems and difficulties that can arise when people claim various control over the elements originating from their body. The decisions and verdicts regarding the cases can leave us feeling unsatisfied, and, at times, even bewildered; making it necessary to explore alternatives and the possible advantages of some type of recognition of property rights over human body parts and materials.

An old and infamous case that made it back to the front page of the *New York Times* is the case of Henrietta Lacks, a poor, 31 year old African woman, who in 1951 suffered from an extremely aggressive type of cervical cancer.[16] From the tissues extracted without her knowledge, a Baltimore hospital derived a cell line: HeLa. The importance of this cell line cannot be overestimated, as to its contribution to the scientific progress in the developing of the polio vaccine, drugs for treating herpes, leukaemia, Parkinson's and many other diseases.[17] The results, aside from achieving scientific advances, have been the yielding of enormous amounts of money. Neither Ms Lacks nor her family had any insurance coverage and she, as well as some of her descendants, died without having access to basic medical care. Up to 1973, her family had no knowledge of what had transpired.[18] The story suddenly changed in 2013, when scientists sequenced its genome and made it public, once again, without family authorisation, in clear violation of Ms Lacks's privacy. It is only recently, more than half a century after

[14] See I Goold, K Greasley, J Herring and L Skene, 'Conclusion' in I Goold, K Greasley, J Herring and L Skene (eds), *Persons, Parts and Property. How Should We Regulate Human Tissue in the 21st Century* (Oxford, Hart Publishing, 2014) 281–99.

[15] See D Dickenson, 'Alternatives to a Corporate Commons: Biobanks, Genetics and Property in the Body' in Goold, Herring, Greasley and Skene (n 14) 177–95.

[16] C Zimmer, 'A Family Consents to a Medical Gift, 62 Years Later' *New York Times* (New York, 7 August 2013) www.nytimes.com/2013/08/08/science/after-decades-of-research-henrietta-lacks-family-is-asked-for-consent.html.

[17] See R Skoot, *The Immortal Life of Henrietta Lacks* (New York, Crown Publishers, 2010).

[18] ibid, esp pt III.

Ms Lacks's death, that the National Institute of Health has invited two members of her family to participate in the HeLa Genome Data Access Workgroup that is in charge of evaluating its applications; but the family has not been granted any right to potential profits from any future products derived from the HeLa Genome.

Another case which is similar in nature is set out in *Moore v the Regents of the University of California* (1988).[19] John Moore was being treated for leukaemia in UCLA Hospital (University of California, Los Angeles) in the late 1960s and was frequently called in for tests that involved the extraction of blood, bone marrow, hair and semen. He was collaborating without his knowledge, in the elaboration of a cell line later to be called the Mo Cell-line. The University obtained a patent and negotiated a substantial contract with a biotechnology company. When Moore became suspicious of the doctors' activities and discovered the truth, he brought forward a claim. The California Court of Appeal held that Moore ultimately had no property rights in his tissues and determined that to admit the notion of property in the body would be an obstacle for research, since with the obligation of having to share the benefits, the incentives for companies and laboratories to carry out research might well vanish. The Court of Appeal denied Moore the ownership of his tissues and elements extracted from his body, and yet recognised the rights of UCLA, leaving open the possibility in the case of the latter, to appear as the victim in court if the extracted substances were to be stolen. The primary argument for the recognition of UCLA's rights was the lack of value assignable to the tissues without the level of value-added knowledge and work invested in these by the scientists in the UCLA labs.[20]

Despite the majority opinion in the *Moore* case, we find a vindication of some capacity of control over elements of the human body, which has been further argued by a group of patients, in the case of *Washington University v Dr W Catalona et al.*[21] In this case Dr Catalona, an urologist, had compiled tissue samples collected from his patients for two decades. When he left Washington University, he asked his patients for their consent to take with him the tissue bank he had collected. Most of them gave their consent. However, Washington University went to court to reclaim its property in the samples. Donors could not recover them, even though their consent theoretically allowed them to take these samples back at any time. In this case, the Court did not insist on the work and expertise of researchers, for it was Dr Catalona and his team who worked on the samples. The University

[19] *Moore v the Regents of the University of California* 249 Cal Rptr 494, 497, 172 (1988 Court of Appeals).

[20] *Moore v the Regents of the University of California* (1990) 51 Cal 3d 120 (Sup Ct Cal); 793 P 2d 479, 146, 168.

[21] *Washington University v Dr W Catalona et al* United States Court of Appeals, Eighth Circuit. Nos 062286, 06-2301. Decided: 20 June 2007.

simply stored them. But the Court gave priority to the University's possession of the samples, and determined in favour of the University.

Such cases allow us to contemplate an alternative approach to property in the body in the context of increasingly frequent advances in biotechnological research. It should be noted that the recognition of some kind of property in the human body and its parts may lead to the *commodification* of the body. Yet, to admit the idea of property does not, in and of itself, forcefully imply the next step: A market in which there is free circulation of organs, ovules, tissues, corneas or any parts of the body. To think about humans as beings entitled to some kind of property in their body is one thing; to think that human bodies or their parts are on offer in the market is another thing. Many of the disputes regarding this matter result from shifting perspectives of the notion of property in the body as towards the supposition of commodification with no restrictions.[22]

III. THE JUSTIFICATION OF PROPERTY IN HUMAN BODIES IN CLASSICS

A. John Locke on Self-Preservation and Self-Ownership

Contemporary libertarians emphasise that all human beings are self-owners; they own their self and everything that constitutes that self, including the body with all its products, whether they be organs, tissues or capacities and talents. In consequence, each person is the owner of everything he or she creates or builds as from this original self-ownership. Libertarian authors trace the origin of this conception of property back to John Locke's *The Second Treatise of Civil Government* which is considered by some scholars as, fundamentally, a work on property.[23] However, we cannot forget that in this text, the word *property* is polysemic.[24] In some parts of the *Second Treatise* the term property is discussed in a very broad sense, involving life and liberties; while in other places it is used with a more restricted meaning, close to the most common use, as ownership over material goods.[25] Some of Locke's statements regarding property even appear contradictory. For example, he states on occasion that all men are self-owners; other times that human beings are the work of God and that we are *His* property, the reason for which suicide or voluntary slavery are not allowed.[26] It would be

[22] See M Radin, *Contested Commodities* (Cambridge, Harvard University Press, 2001).

[23] See R Nozick, *Anarchy, State and Utopia* (Oxford, Blackwell, 1977); P Laslett (ed), *Two Treatises on Government* (Boston, Cambridge University Press, 1989) 115–18.

[24] See K Olivecrona, 'Locke's Theory of Appropriation' (1974) 24 *Philosophical Quarterly* 220, 224. For Olivecrona it would be necessary to take into account the very relevant notion of 'suum' understood as that which belongs to a person present in all the natural law of the XVIII Century.

[25] Locke, *Second Treatise of Government* (n 7) paras 25, 26, 27 and 87, 123, 124.

[26] ibid, paras 6, 23, 135; *First Treatise* (n 7) para 39.

helpful to distinguish in Locke between human relations and the relations of humans with God: in the former instance, each person has a series of rights that allows him or her to exclude others from that body; in the latter instance, the human body should belong to God.

Some of Locke's affirmations must be understood in a particular context. For example, Locke attempts to refute Robert Filmer and his support for the power of parents over their children. Instead Locke argues that humans have no power over other humans because they are not their creators, and thus nobody has the same type of power as a creator over his body and the body of others.[27] What Locke is also interested in, aside from contradicting Filmer, is to defend the idea of property as control over one's own body. Being 'master' of yourself, you are 'proprietor of your own person'.[28] In Paragraph 27 of *The Second Treatise* he states that 'every man has a Property in his own Person: this nobody has any right to but himself. The Labour of his Body, and the Work of his Hands, we may say, are properly his'.[29] The ultimate legitimation of this type of appropriation derives from the fact that everyone has property in their own body that transfers to the property in the work done and from this, to the product obtained or derived, as something deserved resulting from the effort made.[30] Locke's idea of self-ownership is closely linked with the notion of personal freedom.

Conditions to legitimise the appropriation of material goods derive from respect for a Supreme Law of Creation that orders above all else, the preservation of human beings. This idea entails that human beings have the natural right as well as a duty to God to preserve themselves. At the beginning Locke wrote of a common property regime that would allow all people, depending on their needs, to gain access to the goods that can satisfy them with the goal of preserving their lives.[31] Earth was given to all humans, so they need to take possession of some products. The right criterion to proceed with appropriation is the taking of the part of the land that is used to work on; labour determining what a person can take. People mix with their labour to do things more useful for themselves. We have thus, a first condition (*Lockean proviso*) of appropriation, the *labour theory* of appropriation.[32] Further, something can become private property only if there is an amount and quality available for the rest of human beings to enjoy; here we find another condition of legitimation of appropriation.

[27] ibid, *First Treaties*, ch VI.

[28] ibid, paras 44, 190, 123. See also J Waldron, *The Right of Private Property* (Oxford, Clarendon Press, 1988) 181, 398.

[29] Man is the word, for it refers to male individuals in most cases. For women's role in social contract theories, see C Pateman, *The Sexual Contract* (New York, Polity Press, 1986) and SM Okin, *Justice, Gender and the Family* (New York, Basic Books, 1989).

[30] LC Becker, *Property Rights: Philosophical Foundations* (New York, Routledge and Kegan Paul, 1977) 32ff.

[31] Locke (n 25) para 25.

[32] ibid, paras 26, 27, 28, 34.

Finally, the third condition establishes that since people need perishable goods to survive, nobody should take more than what they can use.[33]

The right of preservation is essential in justifying property. According to Locke, government needs legal procedures when interfering with the property of its subjects, for property is that which belongs to one and cannot be used without one's consent or the consent of the majority of representatives.[34] And the regulation of property is nothing but the means to achieve an end, public welfare and above all, the preservation of human beings. Moreover, human preservation requires additional support in the right of access to the necessary material conditions to achieve that preservation in political society.[35] The relevance granted by Locke to property in the human body when defining his conception of basic individual rights is related with the idea that these aim, above all, to protect people in order to ensure their preservation.

B. Hegel: Property as Embodiment of Personality

Hegel's starting points differ from those of Locke. There is no social contract, since it makes no sense to Hegel, not even as a counter-factual or imaginary construction. Private property is a fact, and as such is maintained since it enjoys internal rationality. Only what is real is rational.[36] A person is shaped by means of general relations with external things; relations regulated by law:[37]

> Since property is the *embodiment* of personality, my inward idea and will that something is to be mine is not enough to make it my property; to secure this need occupancy is requisite. The embodiment which my willing thereby attains involves its recognisability by others.[38]

The Hegelian construction of a property model is oriented towards a process of formation of identity and recognition of the subjectivity of others. The essential points of Hegel's notion of property could be summarised as: 1) the definition of property in terms of self-development, social recognition and public welfare; 2) the importance of *embodiment* in self-development;

[33] ibid, para 31.

[34] ibid, para 140.

[35] J Tully, *A Discourse on Property: John Locke and His Adversaries* (New York, Cambridge University Press, 1980).

[36] GWF Hegel, *Philosophy of Right* (TM Knox trans, Oxford, Clarendon Press, 1965 [1821]).

[37] See J Ritter, 'Personne et propieté selon Hegel' (1968) 31 *Archives de Philosophie* 179; F Dallmayr, *GWF Hegel: Modernity and Politics* (Newbury Park, SAGE Publications, 1993) 105–11.

[38] Hegel (n 36) s 51.

and 3) the inter-connected idea that a contract reflects a relation, but not all relations are materialised in a contract.[39]

Jeremy Waldron develops his interpretation of Hegel, concluding that the defence of private property carries certain weight even in societies that have evolved towards ethical communities. Further, even though the right to property is not absolute, it does not give in before any claim or merely utilitarian considerations.[40] In Waldron's view, Hegel appeals to the need of psychological development in individuals. Private property entails control of an object and its use, as an exercise of individual will, stability and maturity, which would not be possible any other way.[41]

Fundamental to Hegel's philosophy is the principle that mind or freedom is necessarily embodied. It is very interesting to note a common concern of determining the role and status of the human body raised by Locke and Hegel in their philosophical constructions of the idea of property. In their theories the human body and private property are closely related, the control over the bodies plays an important role in justifying property. The obvious sense in which a human being is embodied is expressed by Hegel as 'I am alive in this bodily organism which is my external existence'.[42] In other words, I am in possession of my body. But that is not sufficient: Waldron tell us that according to Hegel the first step in human development is for the mind to take possession of its body in a strong sense and to fuse it with the will.[43] Accordingly, the idea of self-control is present in Hegel, as is the care and training of the body and its physical and mental capacities to take on complex and delicate activities. This implies that no one is to have control over my body except myself. Controlling the body, its integrity, its *preservation*, is an essential condition for freedom, even in its most primitive stages, as well as for any kind of personal development.[44] Working with different criteria, Hegel develops an idea of property from a perspective that differs from the Lockean approach and can go further than orthodox liberal proposals, as Dickenson suggests.[45]

IV. PROPERTY: A FLEXIBLE CONCEPT

Considerations now turn to a number of concepts of property, looking for the best to deal with the idea of property rights in the human body.

[39] ibid, s 47–51.
[40] Waldron (n 28) 350–51.
[41] ibid, 347–59.
[42] Hegel (n 36) s 47.
[43] Waldron (n 28) 361.
[44] ibid, 362. Hegel (n 36) s 48.
[45] D Dickenson, *Property in the Body: Feminist Perspectives* (Cambridge, Cambridge University Press, 2007) 47–53.

When talking of property we may refer to: objects and material things; relations between persons and things; or relations between persons regarding things. At the beginning of the last century, Hohfeld articulated an analysis of legal concepts in terms of binary relations—rights, privileges, powers and immunities and their opposites (no-right, duty, disability, liability) or correlatives (duty, no-right, liability, disability)—that has become the starting point for a wide range of analytical studies, including the development of the concept of ownership as the 'bundle of rights' discussed below.[46]

A. Property as a Bundle of Rights

Ownership is defined by Tony Honoré as 'the greatest possible interest in a thing which a mature system of law recognizes',[47] and as a 'bundle of rights'. When speaking of ownership, we do not refer to a thing but rather the rights in or to a thing.[48] Honoré retakes the original definition of ownership in Article 544 of the French Civil Code (1804): 'the right to enjoy and dispose of things in the most absolute way, provided one does nothing forbidden by laws or regulations'. The owner's control over the object that is owned is clearly established by the Civil Code, but in its definition of ownership, the existence of possible limits imposed by laws and regulations on enjoyment and disposition is also clear. Ownership thus implies an inherent feature of flexibility 'by which either on account of law or individual will, holders can, in specific cases, be deprived from some of the rights that ordinarily compose it'.[49]

The composition of the 'bundle of rights' that make up the concept of ownership includes: the right to hold exclusive physical control over something; the right to use and enjoy it; the right to decide who will use the thing and how, as in the case of contracts or licenses; the right to yield on the thing in shape of gains, assets or applications; the right to capital, ie the power to alienate the thing, give it away, sell it, mortgage and divide it and the freedom to consume, spoil or destroy the thing; the capacity to transmit or dispose; the right to safety or immunity in face of expropriation and the idea that all transmission has to be consensual; the absence of terms established for this right; the prohibition of making detrimental use of the thing; the possibility of execution in cases of responsibility; and other interests related with legacy, licences and loans.

[46] S Munzer, *A Theory of Property* (Boston, Cambridge University Press, 1990) 17ff.
[47] Honoré (n 2) 108.
[48] ibid, 128–34.
[49] L Diez-Picazo, *Fundamentos de Derecho civil patrimonial VI* (Madrid, Civitas, 2012) 33–35.

However, for James Penner the notion of property as a 'bundle of rights' is a 'deficient concept, whose persistence in the language is to some extent inexplicable', because it converts property into a misguided concept which does not effectively characterise any particular sort of legal relations.[50] One owns property when one has some of the entitlements that make up the bundle, but it is not clear which of these rights are essential, or whether a certain number of them must be present to be able to speak of property.[51] Thomas Merrill adopts a similar position in which he starts off with the origins of the 'bundle of rights' metaphor as a manifestation of hostility towards the idea of property in the American Legal Realism movement.[52] Jurists of the Realist movement pretended, Merrill emphasises, to separate property rights from the idea of natural rights; while, with the metaphor of the 'bundle of rights', the absence or presence of the elements of this bundle and their features of non-essentiality would suggest the futility of granting constitutional protection to property. The so-called 'essentialists' regarding property, amongst whom Merrill situates Penner and himself, claim that there is an undeniable and irrefutable defining feature in the concept of property and that is the *right to exclude*. Their views are seen to contrast with those held by 'nominalists', more in line with the 'bundle of rights', that when there is no such thing as a defining right, the identification of property would become a question of social convention.

Despite Penner and Merrill's critique, Honoré's metaphor 'the bundle of rights', which is flexible and with varying elements, is useful to articulate property in the human body. These 'incidents', if grouped together, may constitute property, although that particular bundle of incidents may not amount to full ownership. Further, each individual incident is not considered as a necessary condition for a person to be appointed the owner of something.[53] Such non-essentialist configuration of property allows the construction of human rights that is respectful of individual decisions, while recognising the *right not to be excluded* from the access to materials such as those related with the human body that can be necessary for people's preservation.[54]

B. The Rights not to be Excluded

Whilst recognising the existence of a paradigm of property as the exclusive use of a thing, CB Macpherson contends that this paradigm should be

[50] JE Penner, *The Idea of Property in Law* (Oxford, Clarendon Press, 1997) 1.
[51] ibid.
[52] T Merrill, 'The Property Prism' (2011) 8 *Economics Journal Watch* 247. S Munzer's reply: 'A Bundle Theorist Holds on His Collection of Sticks' (2011) 8 *Economics Journal Watch* 265.
[53] Honoré (n 2) 124–26.
[54] See generally Dickenson (n 45).

changed: the claim to use or benefit from something entails the impossibility of being excluded, while the possibility of excluding others should be an exceptional case.[55] The idea of property is thus extended:

> I am suggesting that the broader claims will not be firmly anchored unless they are seen as property, for in the liberal ethos which prevails in our liberal democratic societies property has more prestige than has almost anything else; and if the new claims are not brought under the head of property the narrow idea of property will be used with all the prestige of property to combat them.[56]

Macpherson reverses the idea of property as the right to exclude; the starting point for him is that there is nothing related with the right to property to prevent the interpretation of it as the *right not to be excluded*, for the thesis behind MacPherson's proposal is that underlying any idea of property is the classic idea of *self-preservation* that goes hand in hand with the human aspiration of developing a flourishing life. Self-preservation is present in the history of political theory as the foundation of property.

The conception of ownership as a *bundle of rights* is still a liberal approach, however, it is a construction coming from the legal world looking for answers to complex questions and for solutions in controversy surrounding rights and duties concerning property. It is useful when applied to issues concerning property in the human body.

V. RE-EVALUATING THE MEANINGS OF SELF-OWNERSHIP

A. Right-wing Libertarians and Left-wing Libertarians

We cannot forget the irrefutable fact of being corporeal beings, and we often use 'the possessive' when referring to our own bodies. In most legal systems, laws protect body integrity and punish the use of violence against the body of others. There is also a theoretical conception of property as an absolute and inviolable right in the defence of the moral right of people to control the use of their body and mind. It is now time to re-evaluate the meaning of self-ownership discussed earlier on in Locke's discourse, by turning to the work of Robert Nozick.

Nozick's reconstruction of Locke is linked to a specific idea of freedom and autonomy: stating that I own myself is equivalent to saying that nobody has the right to dispose of me or direct my acts. Nozick thus goes further

[55] CB Macpherson, 'Capitalism and the Changing Concept of Property' in E Kamenka and RS Neale (eds), *Feudalism, Capitalism and Beyond* (London, Edward Arnold, 1975) 121; CB Macpherson, *Property, Mainstream and Critical Positions* (Oxford, Basil Blackwell, 1978) chs 1 and 12.

[56] Macpherson, 'Capitalism and the Changing Concept of Property', ibid 122.

than Locke, and this self-dominion implied in the notion of self-ownership even admits the possibility of someone selling himself as a slave.[57] Nozick's re-interpretation of Locke allows him to legitimise not only any acquisition without too many qualms regarding the method used, whether it be labour, merit, occupation, but also any non-fraudulent transfer.[58] Property for Nozick is *dominion* and once acquired is an exclusive right against the world, with full capacity to alienate and to transfer it with full freedom.

There is a particular concern in Nozick, as pointed out by Harris, that we may reach a point of cannibalisation of human beings. From a consequentialist perspective, it could become acceptable to dispose of organs, tissues, blood, marrow and other parts of a person, even at the loss of a person's life, in exchange for saving the life of several people.[59] This would be one strong reason for insisting on self-ownership and the absolute rights of property as side-constraints,[60] and for rejecting '(partial) ownership over other persons and over their work and actions'.[61]

Nozick's position falls within the paradigm of the 'right-wing libertarianism'. However, the idea of self-ownership also appears in authors considered as 'left-wing libertarians'.[62] The difference is that left libertarians accept a right of self-ownership that is not absolute. The left libertarian approach to self-ownership does not forbid 'all unintentional incursions upon one's body', but it is against intentional incursions or threats of incursions without any restrictions, including assaults, aggressions, arrests, detentions or prison.[63] It also articulates a rigorous right to all profits derived from the activity of one's own mind or body, including work done by oneself or through voluntary exchanges with other individuals.[64]

Critics of self-ownership state different reasons. The most classic criticism of self-ownership is that it would place us before a notion that is *incoherent*, since only things can be property and owners can only be persons, nothing can be a thing and a person at the same time; therefore, nobody can be the owner of her/himself.[65] Contemporary authors also argue that

[57] Nozick (n 23) 331.

[58] ibid 157–59; 167–68; 172; 235–36 and 262–68.

[59] ibid 201–07; see also J Harris, 'The Survival Lottery' (1975) 50 *Philosophy* 81.

[60] Nozick considers that justice theories may favour this possibility, mainly the idea that appears in Rawls's theory on talents and capacities. See J Rawls, *Theory of Justice* (Boston, Harvard University Press, 1999) 62–64; 443–48.

[61] Nozick (n 23) 172.

[62] M Otsuka, 'Why Left-Libertarianism Is Not Incoherent, Indeterminate, or Irrelevant: A Reply to Fried' (2005) 33 *Philosophy and Public Affairs* 201.

[63] M Otsuka, *Libertarianism without Foundations* (Oxford, Oxford University Press, 2003) 15.

[64] See ibid 15, 19. For Otsuka, property over external things is conditional to the satisfaction of an equal condition that imposes the existence of equal welfare opportunities.

[65] See K Lippert-Rasmussen, 'Against Self-Ownership: There Are No Fact-Insensitive Ownership Rights over One's Body' (2008) 36 *Philosophy and Public Affairs* 86; I Kant, *Lectures on Ethics* (New York, Harper and Row, 1963[1775–1780]) 165–66; Munzer (n 12) 259–86.

the idea of self- ownership suffers from too much *indeterminacy*, since it only acquires meaning when it appeals to principles or institutions that are morally independent.[66] Other critics consider that the idea of self-ownership fails because it is not tuned in with deep moral beliefs, due to its *counterintuitive* implications.[67] For some critics, the self-ownership thesis would only make sense when separating the rights of control over one's own life and one's own body from the entitlement to the profits obtained from it, because only the former is solidly grounded in moral beliefs.[68]

B. A Non-Libertarian Proposal

The answers as to whether there should be property rights in the human body could be reduced to three possibilities. The first lies in the answer that sustains the bearing of a classic libertarian notion of self-ownership, defending that people are entitled holders of ownership rights over their body, and legitimising the construction of an idea of property as absolute dominion over everything spawning from the activities performed by these bodies. The second relates to the position of those who discard the suitability of this debate, for this would imply the degradation of human beings and the erosion of human dignity.[69] The third is manifested in a tentative proposal, without adopting the libertarian idea of self-ownership, that an idea of property could be applied to human bodies and its parts. This idea would have to be constructed with well-defined features, clearly destined to offer people protection and control over decision capacity regarding their bodies and the elements derived from these bodies.

It is very important to consider property in human bodies in light of the following: libertarians advocate of the idea of self-ownership and place self-ownership in the origin from which autonomy and individual agency would derive, and consequently, that the legitimation and foundation of individual human rights would be a derivation of self-ownership. Non-libertarians, on the contrary, when defending an entitlement to body rights, would invert the foundation of the right over the body, since in their argumentation, ownership entitlement and property rights would be derived from the principle of autonomy and basic human rights, and not the other way round.

[66] BH Fried, 'Left-Libertarianism: A Review Essay' (2004) 32 *Philosophy and Public Affairs* 66; P Vallentyne, H Steiner and M Otsuka, 'Why Left- Libertarianism' (2005) 33 *Philosophy and Public Affairs* 201; R Arneson, 'Lockean Self-Ownership: Towards a Demolition' (1995) 39 *Political Studies* 36; BH Fried, 'Left-Libertarianism Once More: A Rejoinder to Vallentyne, Steiner and Otsuka' (2005) 33 *Philosophy and Public Affairs* 206.

[67] GA Cohen, *Self-Ownership, Freedom and Equality* (New York, Cambridge University Press, 1995).

[68] Lippert-Rasmussen (n 65) 94–95.

[69] See above, s II.

The proposal of those that recognise some kind of property rights in the body also echoes the relevance of making a distinction between different rights such as the distinction between personal rights and property rights, or between *strong* property rights and *weak* property rights.[70] These distinctions entail the acceptance of the complexity of property conceptions and the idea of recognising property in the human body, and seem to take on a consideration of property as a bundle of rights. There would be, however, recognising different types of rights over one's own body that would act as legal advantages translatable into legal entitlements. This proposal requires a careful construction. To start with, two steps would be necessary and neither is simple: a first step would be the creation of a list of people's rights regarding their body, referring to the use, manipulation, disposition, transfer, exclusion of third parties from own body; and a second would be to the necessity to settle whether or not these rights are in fact property rights or something else.

Property rights over the body should be viewed as a special category of property rights, due to the special status of the subject matter. On the one hand, the recognition of property in the human body would certainly empower individuals, as the source of tissues and materials which are used in medical treatment and biotechnological research, and hence legitimise their demand for informed consent in certain types of donations, or when receiving compensation. On the other hand, in light of the concern that subjecting the human body to property may lead to commodification, certain limitations on the exercise of such property rights should be imposed by law and regulation. That said, as discussed previously, defending an idea of property in the human body does not necessarily equate with allowing a free market of transferring human body parts. Detailed discussion on this debate can be found elsewhere.[71]

VI. CONCLUSION

In this chapter we have discussed the controversy surrounding the recognition of an idea of property in the human body and its parts. Thinking of a special configuration of property rights in the human body is the right road to travel and is the best way to explore the possibilities of protecting agency and the self-preservation capacity of people. Perhaps it is somewhat anachronistic to reconsider the idea of self-preservation of human beings, but it is by no means irrelevant to take a look at the implications of this idea. For Locke it is the raison d'être of self-ownership and the conception of

[70] Munzer (n 46) 37–58; see also Waldron (n 28); Dickenson (n 15) and (n 45); and Goold, Greasley, Herring and Skene (n 14).

[71] Munzer (n 46) 48–58; Penner (n 50) 121–27.

property. Leaving aside the theological connotations and deriving debates, we can think of self-preservation as the original right of human beings, the condition *sine qua non* of the human being as a moral agent capable of developing as such as from the autonomy and control of his body. Without a body, there is no human being, without autonomy, there is no moral agent. This is the starting point of human rights. It is obvious that the human body and its protection is at the heart of the construction of law. Locke does not forget this. Neither does Hegel.

Some conceptions of property have been reflected in the lines above in order to clarify meanings and articulate efforts to meet the challenges we are facing. If we think of a justification for an idea of property as a means of human self-preservation, then the absolute refusal to consider human beings as holders of a certain sovereignty over their bodies, translated into some type of ownership entitlement, would be sound. Neither would the disqualifications of this possibility as an attack on human dignity be plausible.[72]

The challenge regarding the articulation of a notion of property rights in the human body is a big one. The difficulty in tackling the specificity of these rights and providing efficient protection to individuals, as manifested in the cases and examples mentioned above, is great. Court decisions sometimes leave us with a feeling of unease when one of the parties, the one claiming rights to control elements proceeding from his or her body, is left in a situation of helplessness.

Increasing privatisation in matters related to health, research and medicine present new challenges that lead us to ask ourselves if the legal system provides enough protection of basic human rights regarding decisions over our bodies. Perhaps in an ideal world, as envisioned by dissenting Judge Broussard in the *Moore* case, health care and research should be generously financed by public funds so as to preserve and improve people's lives without having to give priority to profits-based criterion:

> It is certainly arguable that, as a matter of policy or morality, it would be wiser to prohibit any private individual or entity from profiting from the fortuitous value that adheres in a part of a human body, and instead to require all valuable excised body parts to be deposited in a public repository which would make such materials freely available to all scientists for the betterment of society as a whole.[73]

Does the idea of property contribute to the better protection of people in the present time when dealing with basic human rights such as the rights in their body or over parts of it? The answer is not a simple one. Admitting the possibility of being entitled to property rights over the parts of our body challenges deeply rooted ideas and is full of risks. That said, it is very important to highlight that the recognition of such rights would not stop us

[72] See above, s II.

[73] *Moore v the Regents of the University of California* 51 Cal 3d at 160.

from questioning the legitimacy of the commodification of certain goods. And such recognition may contribute to going deeper into the question of considering the ways in which to decrease the asymmetry between corporations and individuals, between states and individuals, between rich and poor and to increase the protection of basic human rights.

6

Reconciling Lockean Copyright with the Human Right to Education

LEONARDO MACHADO PONTES*

I. INTRODUCTION

COPYRIGHT JUSTIFICATIONS ARE generally based on four clusters of legal doctrines: cultural, instrumentalist, personality and labour theories.[1] Notwithstanding their existence and importance, this chapter goes beyond the current literature to investigate the last of these theories which is derived from the writings of John Locke.[2] It sets out a deontological interpretation of the labour theory of property.[3] According to this interpretation, property acquisition is tantamount to the processing of personhood, coextensive with the projection of one's personality and autonomy through labour. With this as the overriding consideration, this chapter argues that education is of paramount importance for the deontological interpretation of the labour theory, as it assures individual self-realisation and self-awareness, which are pre-conditions for immaterial property acquisition.

This chapter sets out to analyse the relationship between education and copyright, considering the famous Lockean provisos—limits that Locke saw to property acquisition and justification—under the deontological

* The author would like to express his gratitude to Professors C Geiger and CM Correa for their helpful comments.

[1] See W Fisher, 'Theories of Intellectual Property' in S Munzer (ed), *New Essays in the Legal and Political Theory of Property* (Cambridge, Cambridge University Press, 2001) 168. Professor Fisher, from Harvard University, also provides a free copyright course that can be assessed on YouTube, called 'CopyrightX'.

[2] J Hughes, 'The Philosophy of Intellectual Property' (1988) 77 *Georgetown Law Journal* 287; CJ Craig, 'Locke, Labour, and Limiting the Author's Right: A Warning Against a Lockean Approach to Copyright Law' (2002) 28 *Queen's Law Journal* 1.

[3] C Valcke, 'Locke on Property: A Deontological Interpretation' (1989) 12 *Harvard Journal of Law & Public Policy* 941.

interpretation. Locke created three provisos: no-harm, no-waste and charity. The no-harm proviso limits appropriation in situations where the act of appropriation would not qualitatively and quantitatively deprive others from equally appropriating from the commons. The no-waste proviso postulates that even if such an appropriation occurs, the owner has a natural law obligation not to waste his acquired property, since it must produce some social value. Finally, the charity proviso allows for situations where individuals in a desperate situation of poverty must have a just claim on the property held by others. As such, a fundamental question is raised: should education be framed as one of the limits to copyright? If so, how should it be considered within the scope of these provisos?

This chapter argues that there are important human rights considerations within the labour theory that have thus far been neglected in copyright debates, including Lockean ideas and the philosophy of enlightenment, which are recognised as the cornerstone of human rights.[4]

Although Locke's ideas helped to shape eighteenth-century copyright justifications and gave birth to modern human rights theory, the relation between copyright and human rights has only lately been developed, having remained curiously isolated.[5] The same is true of the relationship between Locke, human rights and copyright. Although many scholars consider Locke's theory and its relationship to copyright, they rarely analyse the inherent human rights dimension within that theory. In fact, scholars have been using Locke and the fruits of the author's labour argument to strengthen copyright without acknowledging that Lockean theory supports important human rights claims. His ideas are often unduly appropriated in part, with this biased vision.

This chapter challenges such a conception, considering the relationship between human rights, and in particular education, within the Lockean labour theory. A coherent approach to both the Lockean contributions to copyright and human rights theory is a deontological interpretation of his labour theory, which has the potential to engage copyright with human rights.

Nonetheless, such a new normative framework would remain fruitless if, in practice, it was not reconciled with the Agreement on Trade-Related Aspects of Intellectual Property Rights (TRIPS) and its implications for

[4] See JAL Alves, 'The Declaration of Human Rights in Postmodernity' (2000) 22 *Human Rights Quarterly* 478, 488; JW Nickel, *Making Sense of Human Rights: Philosophical Reflections on the Universal Declaration of Human Rights* (California, University of California Press, 1987) 7.

[5] For a discussion on this isolationism, see LR Helfer, 'Human Rights and Intellectual Property: Conflict or Coexistence?' (2003) 5 *Minnesota Intellectual Property Review* 47; PK Yu, 'EU Economic Partnership Agreements and International Human Rights' in J Drexl, H Ruse-Khan and S Nadde-Phlix (eds), *EU Bilateral Trade Agreements and Intellectual Property: For Better or Worse?* (Berlin, Springer, 2014).

education in developing countries.[6] Education in developing countries is often precarious. That precariousness is well recognised and demonstrated by a study affiliated with UNESCO which states that '[i]n many cases, children and teachers lack access to base learning materials ... over half of grade 6 pupils in many countries—including Malawi, Mozambique, Uganda and Zambia—did not have a single book'.[7] It appears that TRIPS, via a restrictive regime of copyright licensing, constrains people's access to educational material in developing countries.[8] Moreover, a biased version of Lockean theory of property is often manifested in the analysis of the adverse impact of TRIPS on education.[9] Yet, Locke's theory not only supports a copyright regime but also provides room so as to ensure that there is no imposition of unduly restrictive conditions on education.

With this in mind, it is time to do justice to Locke and to recalibrate the current normative justification for intellectual property (IP). One way to do this is to read important rights instruments in conjunction, thus harmonising the interpretation of TRIPS with a more nuanced reading rooted in Lockean ideas. Such harmonisation manifests itself in the fact that Locke was fundamental to the development of copyright, while being involved in the genesis of modern human rights. As a result, we can turn to Article 15(1)(c)

[6] Agreement on Trade-Related Aspects of Intellectual Property Rights, Annex 1C of the Marrakesh Agreement Establishing the World Trade Organization (adopted 15 April 1994).

[7] See the study in LR Helfer, *Human Rights and Intellectual Property: Mapping the Global Interface* (Cambridge, Cambridge University Press, 2011) 333. See also the report of the Commission on the Intellectual Property Rights (CIPR), stating that in Africa '[s]hortages of relevant, low-cost books for use inside and outside school continue to undermine the provision of good quality-education', quoted by M Chon, 'Intellectual Property "From Below": Copyright and Capability for Education' (2007) 40 *UC Davis Law Review* 803, 821; A Adewopo, 'The Development Imperative in the Global IP System: Some Reflections on Developing Africa' in GB Dinwoodie (ed), *Methods and Perspectives in Intellectual Property* (Cheltenham, Edward Elgar, 2013) 248: '[G]lobal regimes are expanding the IPR frontiers without adequate safeguards and with disparate effects on developing and African countries'; D Shabalala, 'Knowledge and Education: Pro-Access Implications of New Technologies' in T Wong and G Dutfield (eds), *Intellectual Property and Human Development: Current Trends and Future Scenarios* (Cambridge, Cambridge University Press, 2010) 258 ('[T]he practical structure of copyright has meanwhile favoured for-profit models of knowledge dissemination even in the field of education').

[8] D Barbosa, 'Droit d'Auteur et Accès à l'Information' in B Remiche and J Kors (eds), *L'Accord ADPIC: dix ans après—Regards croisés Europe-Amérique latine* (Brussels, Larcier, 2007) 416–17 (explaining the high costs imposed by TRIPS and developing countries' difficulties in tagging along the rich countries). See also V Kitz, 'The New Free for Education Licence in Australia' (2005) 36 *International Review of Industrial Property and Copyright Law* 555 ('[A]ltogether, the legal hurdle for a non-infringing use of learning and teaching materials is high'); R Burrell and A Coleman, *Copyright Exceptions: The Digital Impact* (Cambridge, Cambridge University Press, 2006) 128ff; S Picciotto, 'Copyright Licensing: The Case of Higher Education Photocopying in the United Kingdom' (2002) 24 *European Intellectual Property Review* 438 (explaining the high costs and complexity of collective licensing for education materials in UK).

[9] ET Biadgleng, 'The Development-Balance of TRIPS Agreement and Enforcement of Intellectual Property' in J Malbon and C Lawson (eds), *Interpreting and Implementing the TRIPS Agreement: is it Fair?* (Cheltenham, Edward Elgar, 2008) 97.

of the International Covenant on Economic, Social and Cultural Rights (ICESCR),[10] dealing with the rights resulting from intellectual activity and scientific progress, as a means of interpreting the reach of TRIPS.[11] While the provisions of Article 15 would not support a traditional interpretation of Lockean theory, it might support a deontological interpretation. Such a new normative justification of the reading of Article 15 would assist in changing the current justification of TRIPS and to foster pro-education policies. Additionally, it would carve out a coherent human rights justification at the centre of copyright, compatible with the practice of other human rights, and properly justified by Lockean labour theory.

Although the World Trade Organization (WTO) has a limited jurisdictional domain and is a self-contained or *lex specialis* system, the WTO members are required to comply with obligations of international law set out in human rights instruments. Although human rights law cannot modify or trump the rules of the WTO, those rules must be read in light of human rights obligations in such a way as to ensure they do not violate them. Although the WTO does not have jurisdiction to enforce human rights, it has the ability—some might say the obligation—to interpret its own rules in line with legal obligations flowing from international human rights instruments to which Member States of the WTO are bound.[12]

This is made evident by Article 31(3) of the Vienna Convention on the Law of Treaties, which states that the relevant rules of international law, together with other subsequent practices regarding the application of the treaty between the parties, including human rights provisions, must be taken into consideration in a holistic manner, when interpreting the parties' obligations.[13] However, that interpretation is limited by three rules: 1) the non-WTO rule must be definitional in nature, linked somehow to the vagueness of the WTO's terms; 2) the interpretation must not go beyond the clear meaning of the WTO term and; 3) such an interpretation is bound by the norms expressing the common intentions of all the WTO's members.[14] The third requirement is the one most disputed: that human rights

[10] Art 15: '[1]. The States Parties to the present Covenant recognize the right of everyone: (a) To take part in cultural life; (b) To enjoy the benefits of scientific progress and its applications;(c) To benefit from the protection of the moral and material interests resulting from any scientific, literary or artistic production of which he is the author'.

[11] See International Covenant on Economic, Social and Cultural Rights (adopted 16 December 1966, entered into force 3 January 1976) 993 UNTS 3 (ICESCR). See HM Haugen, *Technology and Human Rights—Friends or Foes? Highlighting Innovations Applying to Natural Resources and Medicine* Vol 2 (Dordrecht, Republic of Letters, 2012) 43.

[12] G Marceau, 'WTO Dispute Settlement and Human Rights' (2002) 13 *Journal Européen de Droit International* 753, 773; X Seuba, 'Mainstreaming the TRIPS and Human Rights Interactions' in CM Correa (ed), *Research Handbook on the Protection of Intellectual Property under WTO rules* (Cheltenham, Edward Elgar, 2010) 204–14.

[13] Vienna Convention on the Law of Treaties (23 May 1969)1155 UNTS 331.

[14] J Pauwelyn, *Conflict of Norms in Public International Law: How WTO Law Relates to Other Rules of International Law* (Cambridge, Cambridge University Press, 2003) 273.

obligations are not binding on the WTO legislation, as not all WTO members are party to, in this instance, the ICESCR. For this reason, an alternative interpretation is being put forward, one which substitutes 'common intentions' of Members for 'obligations binding on a large number of members', thus making it possible to conform to the ICESCR.[15] Part II of this chapter analyses copyright scholars' interpretation of Lockean labour theory and its role in justifying copyright, and then sets out the deontological interpretation and how such an interpretation exhibits the potential to justify and enshrine human rights elements into copyright. That done, consideration is given to the criticism of the Lockean theory and the responses to it by showing that the no-harm proviso would not only support education as a limit to copyright, but, in fact, render copyright illegitimate without accepting such a limit. In Part III an analysis is undertaken to consider the implications of the deontological interpretation for the debates over the relationship between human rights and intellectual property, and the Part goes on to consider the impact of TRIPS on education and how it can be harmonised with other human rights instruments and with the normative implications of the labour theory. This Part concludes by demonstrating that the deontological interpretation of Locke's theory is a stronger basis for making claims and justifications for a fundamental right to education.

II. LOCKE AND COPYRIGHT

A. The Labour Theory of Property

This section offers a brief explanation of the labour theory with regard to tangible property. It also considers scholars' attempts to extend such a theory to intangible property, and whether this would make sense taking into account Locke's own writings and political engagement.

i. The Labour Theory and Tangible Property

The fundamental problem for Locke is to explain how property is born without the need of any individual consent: '[I] shall endeavour to shew, how man might come to have a property in several parts of that which God gave to mankind in common, and that *without any express compact of all the commoners*' (emphasis added).[16] His predecessors, most notable Hugo Grotius, saw property as resulting from the common agreement of all

[15] The Appellate Body discussion in *European Communities and Certain Member States—Measures Affecting Trade in Large Civil Aircraft*, WT/DS316/AB/R (June 1 2011) para 845, suggests such an approach.

[16] J Locke, *Two Treatises of Government* Student edn (Cambridge, Cambridge University Press, 1988) 25.

commoners, and as a slow process of occupying land in the state of nature. Such an evanescent tacit agreement that constitutes the basis of property would make no sense, so Locke conceived a moral justification to property rights accrued as the result of labour. It is labour, not occupation, that would justify the acquisition of a title to property.

Even if the beginning of his reasoning is the same as that of his predecessors—everything which exists in the commons was given to man to comfort and support his being—the outcome is crucially different. The rights in the state of the nature are not initially property rights.[17] Therefore, life begins with the absence of property.[18] Common to all men in the state of nature is the right to the common use. According to Mossoff, that would be better described as a right to self-preservation or a claim-right.[19] Indeed, Locke wrote: '[w]hether we consider natural reason, which tells us, that man, being once born, have a *right to their preservation*, and consequently to meat and drink, and such other things as nature affords for their subsistence' (emphasis added).[20] According to Locke, God grants to humanity goods that are maintained in the commons, but they cannot be appreciated fully in its natural state. The work adds value to the goods, a surplus.[21] The commons would be the natural state where all the goods can be appropriated by all through the exercise of labour *inasmuch there is enough left for others*. As long as the commons is not harmed in such a way, everyone can remove from the common the amount on which they are willing to work, '[b]ecause one of the functions of the commons is the allocation of goods in a non-competitive way'.[22] The commons represents a fundamental condition of free interaction and equality—the commons or the public domain is thus a domain of fair interaction.[23] The appropriation of the commons, though, should be subject to the non-waste condition. In simple terms, it is the condemnation of waste, prohibited by natural law. Property should bring, therefore, some value to humanity.[24] Locke wrote '[n]othing was made by God to Man to spoil or destroy'.[25]

Once labour is annexed to the commons the labour value remains. If the commons is then appropriated by others, they are appropriating not only from the commons, but also from the labour of others. This would harm

[17] ibid, 26.
[18] Valcke (n 3) 959.
[19] A Mossoff, 'What Is Property? Putting the Pieces Back Together' (2003) 45 *Arizona Law Review* 371, 387.
[20] Locke (n 16) 25.
[21] ibid 28, 32 and 34.
[22] Hughes (n 2) 288–89.
[23] A Drassinower, 'Capturing Ideas: Copyright and the Law of First Possession' (2006) 54 *Cleveland State Law Review* 191, 198.
[24] Hughes (n 2) 297.
[25] Locke (n 16) 31.

those who worked on the commons. Therefore, one should refrain from interfering with someone else's labour, since such an aggregated labour is someone's property right.[26] It is not any damage type that should be punished in Locke's theory, but just the one that violates the state of nature. Work is associated with pain;[27] that '[s]omeone wants to avoid but nevertheless does because is necessary'.[28] What is condemned is the desire to benefit from the pain of others.

Thus far we have seen the interaction of the no-harm and no-waste provisos in his theory. Appropriation is only valid if others have equal conditions to appropriate; the commons must remain non-depleted or non-scarce. Even if one does appropriate, he must not waste his property, destroying or spoiling it.

I would contribute to this debate by adding to Locke's theory a third proviso, the charity proviso, which has been obscured in the IP debate before Merges.[29] In Chapter IV, Section 42, of the *First Treatise*, Locke wrote what is regarded as the charity proviso.[30] It appears that charity would only apply to physical conditions of subsistence and to horrible situations, such as slavery. He describes situations in which to resort to another's plenty is justified if there is no other way to counter the problem. In Section 110 of Locke's essay *Some Thoughts Concerning Education* he offers another idea of charity that acquiring property for more than one person's needs is the root of all evil. One should be ready to help others; that must be encouraged, inasmuch that one does not lose his or her liberality and be paid afterwards. Charity should be a measure of great mediation and rules of justice.[31]

Locke's religious views would deny an absolute property right because the only reason for property to exist is to permit humanity to flourish. Merges's interpretation of this proviso is that it should be applied as a limitation to IP rights in situations where IP rights limit the survival or sustenance of the poor. While Merges applies this notion to patents, this proviso will be considered in the next Part of this chapter, via its application in the field of copyright. That said, I would disagree with Merges when he argues that the charity proviso is weaker in instances regarding non-physical survival or sustenance, like intellectual or cultural development, what he calls a

[26] WJ Gordon, 'A Property Right in Self-Expression: Equality and Individualism in the Natural Law of Intellectual Property' (1992) 102 *Yale Law Journal* 1533.

[27] J Hughes, 'Locke's 1694 Memorandum (and More Incomplete Copyright Historiographies)' (2010) 27 *Cardozo Arts and Entertainment Law Journal* 555, 562.

[28] Hughes (n 2) 301.

[29] RP Merges, *Justifying Intellectual Property* (Cambridge, Harvard University Press, 2011) 60.

[30] Locke (n 16) 42.

[31] J Locke, *Some Thoughts Concerning Education and Of the Conduct of the Understanding* (Cambridge, Hackett Publishing, 1996) 110.3.

quasi-Lockean argument.[32] As Forde explains, the question of whether the charity duty may be applied in normal situations was never answered by Locke.[33] In his essay *Venditio*,[34] for example, Locke makes the argument that selling goods at the market price which would starve the public to death is tantamount to homicide: a clear limitation to property and patents. But in Chapter V of the *Second Treatise*, this notion of charity does not appear. It is very difficult to grasp, in absence of extreme cases, if charity should apply or if Locke would have imposed it as a positive duty rather than a liberality. However, I argue below that a Lockean deontological framework would support constructing this proviso to encompass intellectual development.

ii. The Labour Theory and Intangible Property

Copyright scholars saw in Locke's moral argument and in the structure of the above theory a tenable justification for the existance of copyright, making even a stronger case for the protection of intangibles. The commons of intellectual property or its natural state would be the public domain, comprised of old works that fell in the public domain and of ideas. Authors, when working on the commons to create expressions, aggregate to such ideas their intellectual labour and create property rights. This would be justified, the argument goes, since public domain resources, such as ideas, are of endless nature, and the ability of others to create would neither be affected by accruing property rights (no-harm), nor would it generate waste (no-waste). Additionally, copyright would create social value by incentivising the creation of more works. Indeed, the idea–expression dichotomy, a major principle of copyright law, firmly states that no ideas can be protected, but only expressions of such ideas which are original and have a modicum of creativity.

Nevertheless, Gordon, like others, questions the ambiguous concept of intangible property in Lockean theory.[35] They argue that Locke's theory was envisioned only for tangible property. I, however, argue that their claim is not completely accurate.

In 1695, Locke was clearly against the monopoly of the Stationer's Company members with regard to the renewal of the Licensing Act,

[32] Merges (n 29) 64; K Himma, 'The Legitimacy of Protecting Intellectual Property Rights: The Irrelevance of Two Conceptions of an Information Commons' (2007) 11 *Journal of Information, Communication and Ethics in Society* 210 (making a similar argument).

[33] S Forde, 'The Charitable John Locke' (2009) 71 *The Review of Politics* 428.

[34] J Locke, *Locke: Political Essays* (Cambridge, Cambridge University Press, 1997) 339.

[35] Gordon (n 26) 1547; D Atlas, 'Lockean Theories of Justice' in A Gosseries, A Marciano and A Strowel (eds), *Intellectual Property and Theories of Justice* (London, Palgrave Macmillan, 2008) 29; B Friedman, 'From Deontology to Dialogue: The Cultural Consequences of Copyright' (1994) 13 *Cardozo Arts and Entertainment Law Journal* 157; J Waldron, 'From Authors to Copiers: Individual Rights and Social Values in Intellectual Property' (1992) 68 *Chicago-Kent Law Review* 841, 879.

which, if approved, would have given publishers continuous control over the publication of books. He wrote a memorandum to Edward Clarke, a member of the Parliament, opposing the perpetual renewal of such rights.[36] Against the monopoly of the Stationers, Locke proposed authors' right of controlling their own works through property rights. He wrote that '[f]rom authors that now live and write, it may be reasonable to limit their property to a certain number of years after the death of the author, or the first printing of the book, as, suppose, fifty or seventy years'.[37] Surprisingly, Locke suggested the protection of what was going to became copyright, for a lifetime of the author, plus 50 or 70 years after his death.

Locke expressly referred to the author's property control regarding the amendments proposals in 1695, '[t]o secure the author's property in his copy, or to whom he has transferred it'.[38] Mossoff notes that at the end of Section 44, Chapter V, of the *Second Treatise*, Locke referred expressly to 'inventions and arts'.[39] Merges also points out that Locke '[d]escribed his own work as labor: I am "employed", he wrote, "as an under-labourer in clearing ground a little, and removing some of the rubbish, that lies in the way to knowledge"'.[40] In his essay *Labour* (1693),[41] Locke acknowledged '[l]abor in mechanical and useful art, making the different concepts of manual labor, artisan labor and intellectual labor'.[42] The words '[c]onveniences of life, arts and inventions' also appear in [this essay], being connected to books, arts and instruments of luxury, invention and arts'.[43] In his *Essay Concerning Human Understanding*, Locke explains the concept of a maker as the one who creates the object according to his idea, which constitutes his own work.[44]

In the final part of Locke's letter to Clark, called *Liberty of the Press* (1694–95),[45] he wrote:

> [The act] shall vest a privilege in the author of the said book ... of solely reprinting and publishing the said book for [blank] years from the first edition thereof, with a power to seize on all copies of the said book reprinted by any other person which by virtue of this Act shall be forfeited to the said author.[46]

[36] Hughes (n 27) 562.
[37] ibid.
[38] A Mossoff, 'Saving Locke from Marx: The Labor Theory of Value in Intellectual Property Theory' (2012) 29 *Social Philosophy and Policy* 283, 309.
[39] A Mossoff, 'The Use and Abuse of IP at the Birth of the Administrative State' (2009) 157 *University of Pennsylvania Law Review* 2001, 2048.
[40] Merges (n 29) 33.
[41] Locke (n 34) 336.
[42] L Zemer, 'The Making of a New Copyright Lockean' (2005) 29 *Harvard Journal of Law & Public Policy* 891, 910.
[43] ibid, 911.
[44] M Buydens, *La propriété intellectuelle évolution historique et philosophique* (Brussels, Bruylant, 2012) 198–99.
[45] Locke (n 34) 329.
[46] Zemer (n 42) 902.

In a passage of his essay *Understanding* (1677), Locke makes clear the importance of inventions, as the instruments that are intrinsically responsible for reducing the need of third parties' labour:

> [H]ere then is a large field of knowledge proper for the use and advantage for men in this world, *viz*, *to find out new inventions of dispatch to shorten or ease our labour*, or applying sagaciously together *several agents and patients to procure new and beneficial productions* whereby our stock of riches (*ie things useful* for the conveniences of life) may be increased or better preserved. (emphasis added)[47]

If Locke recognised authors' property control of their labour, and expressly confined their property to a limited period of time, giving even power to seize books, it is plausible to apply his theory to the immaterial.

B. Applying Locke's Ideas to the Idea–Expression Dichotomy in Copyright

i. Traditional Interpretation

Epstein has demonstrated that IP rights are not forms of inferior property rights. The reasoning of physical property can be applied to intellectual property as well. He explains the idea–expression dichotomy, making an analogy to physical property.[48] He argues that economic monopolies are not an issue, since ideas are free and close substitutes for each work can still be created by competitors, who work on similar ideas and products. Thus, the commons would not be harmed.

According to the tragedy of the commons theory,[49] the law protects copyright and patents because if everybody had free access to the protected works, there would not be enough incentive to sustain its value; each one would just explore and consume until there were no more market for the work.[50] The main argument put forward is that copyright restrictions can be justified in terms of dynamic efficiency that overcomes the measures of static efficiency and productive efficiency. In economic language this argument can be rephrased that these restrictions are incentives to avoid the tragedy, because copyright increases social value:

[47] Locke (n 34) 261.

[48] RA Epstein, 'Why Libertarians Shouldn't Be (Too) Skeptical About Intellectual Property', papers.ssrn.com; ACC Yen, 'Restoring the Natural Law: Copyright as Labor and Possession' (1990) 51 *Ohio State Law Journal* 517; Drassinower (n 23).

[49] G Hardin, 'The Tragedy of the Commons' (1968) 162 *Science* 1243. For an explanation, see MJ Trebilcock, *The Limits of Freedom of Contract* (Cambridge, Harvard University Press, 1997) 13–14.

[50] LR Bradford, 'Parody and Perception: Using Cognitive Research to Expand Fair Use in Copyright' (2004) 46 *Boston College Law Review* 705; RA Posner, 'When Is Parody Fair Use?' (1992) 21 *Journal of Legal Studies* 67. The theory of the tragedy of the commons can be clearly questioned. See eg, S Dusollier, 'The Commons as a Reverse Intellectual Property—from Exclusivity to Inclusivity' in HR Howe and J Griffiths (eds), *Concepts of Property in Intellectual Property Law* (Cambridge, Cambridge University Press, 2013).

> [T]he standards of allocative efficiency and productive efficiency are static measures of wealth inasmuch as they focus on the allocation of a given stock of resources or the use of resources at a particular point in time. In contrast, the standard of 'dynamic efficiency' focuses on the scope for increasing and improving society's stock of resources over time ... it is possible to justify [copyright] restrictions in terms of dynamic efficiency because of the incentives they provide in production of new intangible resources and thus to increase overall wealth over time.[51]

Thus, the traditional interpretation has to do with the balance between moral consequentialism and instrumental justifications that considers the idea–expression dichotomy by means of systematically increasing the social value within a property theory framework. Since the dichotomy allows for the creation of close substitutes for each work and prevents economic monopolies, the intellectual commons would not be harmed by the concession of property rights, untimely aimed at incentivising further works.

ii. Deontological Interpretation

Appropriation for Locke is the means by which the '[a]bstract and the individual are objectified in the world'.[52] For Valcke, though, appropriation for Locke would not be merely a means of providing subsistence; when appropriating, '[m]an does more than simply to struggle for his survival, man affirms his distinctiveness in relation to nature and in relation to other man'.[53] Property is the '[e]xpression of human reason and personality'.[54] Appropriation is part of humanisation because '[m]ore man is freed from his animalism more conscious he becomes by the acts of appropriation of his autonomy'.[55]

Appropriation is better understood by Mossoff's explanation of the relationship between Locke's labour theory of value and Locke's idea of mixing labour:

> Since man is a rational animal he is 'Proprietor of his own Person,' and this is why he has 'in himself the great Foundation of Property,' because it is his rational mind that guides his productive labor. This productive 'labour' is a moral activity because it is what secures his 'support or comfort of his being,' and this does not mean just support of his physical or animal nature; rather, it is support of 'the conveniences of life' — the flourishing life of a rational being.[56]

One can only comprehend the concept of value if one situates it in the context of Locke's ethical natural law foundations. When Locke refers to

[51] A Griffiths, *An Economic Perspective on Trademark Law* (Cheltenham, Edward Elgar, 2011) 40–41.
[52] Valcke (n 3) 953.
[53] ibid.
[54] ibid 954.
[55] ibid 956.
[56] Mossoff (n 38) 303.

property within the self he is talking about personhood and our rational capabilities given by God to intellectually and physically flourish through the exercise of reason and labour. As Radin puts it:

> [p]erhaps property in one's person should be understood to mean simply that an individual has an entitlement to be a person or to be treated as a person. This would probably include the right to self-preservation on which Locke bases the right to appropriate.[57]

In his *Essay Concerning Human Understanding*, Locke describes a *person* as being able to have rational consciousness. So, when he says that man has a *property in his own person*, he actually means that man has a property in his own thoughts and in his own actions.[58]

For Locke, value has to do with productive activities, self-preservation of life and human flourishing.[59] That is what justifies property. One acquires property not because one mixes his or her physical labour with an object, which would raise absurd situations, as the famous examples of Nozick's tomato juice, or Waldron's drying cement ring.[60] Instead, one acquires property by the act of appropriation because man's life and intellectual development are protected.

Although Merges recognises the Hegelian aspect of Locke and the deontological interpretation of his theory, he fails to grasp that Locke's idea of property untimately has to do with the flourishing of the life of the rational man, with his intellectual development created through and as an end of property, *because property is a reflective state of personhood*. Self-preservation, thus, could not mean just physical survival, and that is why Merges's construction of the charity proviso, as not encompassing the rights of intellectual development, is contradictory with his recognition of the Hegelian aspect of Locke.[61] Merges takes this path because he believes that

[57] MJ Radin, 'Property and Personhood' (1982) 34 *Stanford Law Review* 957, 965.

[58] Buydens (n 44) 204–05.

[59] Merges (n 29) 38 ('Property and human flourishing—that is the key relationship'). See also T Palmer, 'Are Patents and Copyrights Morally Justified? The Philosophy of Property Rights and Ideal Objects' in A Mossoff, (ed) *Intellectual Property and Property Rights* (Cheltenham, Edward Elgar, 2013) 836 (claiming that liberty-based arguments of property in Locke's theory are basically the same found in the personality theories). See also S Ang, *The Moral Dimensions of Intellectual Property Rights* (Cheltenham, Edward Elgar, 2013) 82 (arguing that freedom and well-being are the justifications for property rights in Locke's theory).

[60] For criticism on Nozick's and Waldron's reading of Locke's mixing labour argument, see A Mossoff, 'Locke's Labor Lost' (2002) 9 *University of Chicago Law School Roundtable* 155; Merges (n 29) 41–45. It is interesting to note that what Merges calls the Hegelian aspect of Locke, which is missed by Nozick and Waldron, is actually Locke's deontological interpretation; G Hull, 'Clearing the Rubbish: Locke, the Waste Proviso, and the Moral Justification of Intellectual Property' (2009) 23 *Public Affairs Quarterly* 67, 69.

[61] Himma (n 32) 9 and 13 (he states that the notion of survival in Locke's labour theory should not encompass this personhood nature of property, which has to do with an intellectual development. Nevertheless, he recognises the possibility of a minimal intellectual commons argument).

the construction of the charity proviso on grounds of cultural development would reduce considerable copyright.[62]

C. Critiques on the Labour Theory Applied to Copyright and Responses from the Deontological Interpretation

Criticism on a Lockean approach to copyright can be summarised as follows:

- although ideas are infinite, they would be culturally defined for a certain society in a certain time (some would be prevalent in relation to others, which would reduce the commons);
- being denied access to the copy of a book a person will not have access to the ideas of the book, impeding the *gateway idea* (the idea that would be responsible for spreading other ideas), reducing the commons equally;
- even under a Lockean point of view, the defenders of his theory, such as Justin Hughes, are unable to justify it without appealing to notions such as fair use and parody;
- ideas accomplished by intellectual products would be essentially 'social' and not a private property.[63]

The first of Craig's critiques is rebutted easily. Of course nobody in theory has access to all of humankind's ideas. Nevertheless, the idea–expression dichotomy still clears the path. It is dangerous to equate the protection of copyright with the protection of popular culture, or with a passing fashion, what could be called 'cultural contingencies'. The copyright system is much bigger and looks to the bigger picture, considering all kinds of creations.[64]

The second of Craig's critiques is more interesting. Although books are protected against being copied and even if theoretically we can prohibit copying, it does not mean that we can always stop the circulation of ideas. It is impossible to raise a total barrier in relation to literary property. One cannot set up a fence around ideas from a book which circulates and generates social values, independently of its copies being accessed by everyone.[65]

This is one of the premises of Wagner's theory of *incomplete capture*, which demonstrates, paradoxically, that the intellectual property commons tends to increase and to be more powerful where the control over the information is stronger.[66] One can offer a counter-argument, nevertheless,

[62] Merges (n 29) 65.

[63] Craig (n 2).

[64] JL Harrison, 'Creativity or Commons: A Comment on Professor Lessig' (2003) 55 *Florida Law Review* 795, 797.

[65] Similarly, see A Moore, 'A Lockean Theory of Intellectual Property Revisited' (2012) 49 *San Diego Law Review* 1069; Merges (n 29) 37.

[66] RP Wagner, 'Information Wants to Be Free: Intellectual Property and the Mythologies of Control' (2003) 103 *Columbia Law Review* 995.

that circumvention technology, on one hand, and copyright 'shrink-wrap' and 'click-through' licences,[67] on the other hand, which exceed traditional copyright limitations, descramble public domain as well as protected works, thus crippling the idea–expression bar.[68] For example,

> [A] study conducted by the British Library in 2008 of 100 random samples of its contracts with digital publishers revealed that more than 50 per cent conflicted with the exceptions granted under the UK Copyright Act. Many licences were silent on permitted statutory uses, and it was not apparent whether licences distinguished between works still under copyright or in the public domain ...[69]

Even if one could turn a blind eye to such mechanisms, what about the outcasts, those who are even further pushed out of the social circles where ideas can be discussed, accessed and produced, such as public libraries and schools? If they do not have even the means to sustainably access ideas, the structure of copyright becomes unjustified by the idea–expression dichotomy, since to access the commons one needs first minimal property rights and education to permit the transition between the physical and immaterial worlds. As Radin argues:

> [T]he premise underlying the personhood perspective is that to achieve proper self-development—to be *a person*—an individual needs some control over resources in the external environment. The necessary assurances of control take the form of property rights ... Property for personal autonomy or liberty might be a class of objects or resources necessary to be a person or whose absence would hinder the autonomy or liberty attributed to a person.[70]

People from places with precarious access to public education, public libraries, the internet, or rural zones would not buy or access works as do persons from developed places. At least the market share cannot be considered as the same. In fact, the UNCTAD-ICTSD project on 'IPRs and Sustainable Development' urges differential pricing in developing countries.[71]

[67] The term 'click through' derives from the shrink wrap that was used in software boxes. The software's user agreement was written inside the shrink wrap or printed on the outside of the boxes. These agreements stated that, by removing the shrink wrap, the user would assent to the terms of use therein. This removal, without assessing the contractual clauses, was considered as an acceptance of the agreement. The same occurs by downloading or installing software online, and by clicking on the agreement button. These practices have been extended to all kinds of works and often override legal exceptions and impose stringent conduct on the user.

[68] J Ginsburg, 'Copyright or "Infograb": Comment on General Report on Limitations Found Outside Copyright' in L Baulch, M Green and M Wyburn (eds), *ALAI Study Days: The Boundaries of Copyright—its Proper Limitations and Exceptions* (Australian Copyright Council, 1999) 55ff; H Tavani, 'Locke, Intellectual Property Rights, and the Information Commons' (2005) 7 *Ethics and Information Technology* 87.

[69] P Davies, 'Access v Contract: Competing Freedoms in the Context of Copyright Limitations and Exceptions for Libraries' (2013) 35 *European Intellectual Property Review* 402, 406.

[70] Radin (n 57) 957–60.

[71] UNCTAD-ICTSD project on 'IPRs and Sustainable Development' (2008) 119, www.ictsd.org.

Locke had little to say about a pure knowledge system of education, because he was much more interested in the moral development of children, and how this could be put to use by the industrious to serve a purpose in society. For Locke, a young gentleman should not be required to know everything, or to have access to everything, but just to acquire a flavour for education, or to be introduced into a small system of education, because if he really wanted to acquire more knowledge, he should pursue this by his own effort.[72]

Thus, if we understand Locke's idea about an introduction to education, it becomes clear that the no-harm and the charity provisos, regarding property rights, must be reasoned in terms of basic public structures of education. For example, Himma and Moore argue that when we pay for education we would have access to collective ideas, and, as such, what else we create could be a private property, which brings the assumption that basic education is necessary.[73]

If copyright restrictive mechanisms encroach considerably on education, the idea–expression dichotomy principle is harmed, since an intellectual commons of information must remain accessible for students, for this is the necessary condition for any later intellectual property acquisition or development. Without this basic commons, protected by the no-harm and charity provisos, any moral claims on copyright property become illegitimate. Property acquisition, following the deontological interpretation, reflects a state of personhood, autonomy and self-awareness; the justifications of property are the 'conveniences of life' and the flourishing of mankind, but one needs to have the right of accessing this basic pool of knowledge in order to become a 'person'. Without this right, any social value of accruing copyright property is rendered unproductive, generating considerable waste. Locke himself proposed amendments to the legislation regarding the deposit of books in public libraries, which suggests that he would take decisions which could permit the improvement of structures devoted to education.[74]

III. LOCKE AND HUMAN RIGHTS

The traditional interpretation of Locke, by focusing on economic value, would not take into consideration education as a paramount aspect of

[72] Locke (n 31) s 94: '[N]or is it requisite that he should be a thorough scholar, or possess in perfection all those sciences, which it is convenient a young gentleman should have a taste of, in some general view, or short system. A gentleman, that would penetrate deeper, must do it by his own genius and industry afterwards; for nobody ever went far in knowledge, or became eminent in any of the sciences, by the discipline and constraint of a master ... But it is only to open the door, that he may look in, and as it were begin an acquaintance, but not to dwell there ... not think that all lies in Latin and French or some dry systems of logick and philosophy'.

[73] Himma (n 32) 34; Moore (n 65) 38–39.

[74] See Hughes (n 27), explaining the amendments proposals.

property acquisition. However, if we follow the deontological interpretation, in which property and personality are closely related, the building blocks of education are seen as a prerequisite to personhood and to the acquisition of intellectual property. Since many developing countries lack the basic structures of education, to impose rigid and restrictive mechanisms of intellectual property would encroach upon sustainable structures of education, thus violating the idea–expression bar to copyright and Lockean no-harm and charity provisos, ultimately generating waste. In this section, we shall deal with the dynamics of human rights and TRIPS, but also analyse how Lockean theory could construct a new normative justification for copyright, since it could bridge the gaps between human rights, education and copyright.

The debate over the relationship between human rights and copyright is quite extensive.[75] Copyright as a human right can be protected under Article 27(2) of the Universal Declaration of Human Rights (UDHR)[76] and Article 15(1)(c) of the ICESCR. Paragraph 1 of the UN Sub-Commission on Human Rights Resolution 2000/7 states that Article 15(1)(c) of the ICESCR protects copyright as a human right.[77] General Comment 17 of the UN Committee on Economic, Social and Cultural Rights (CESCR),[78] however, distinguishes intellectual property rights from human rights, indicating that Article 15(1)(c) should be read as protecting the personal link of authors with their creation, but not necessarily business or corporate interests.[79] The former interests, the General Comment tells us, do not coincide necessarily with TRIPS and with other international IP instruments.[80] This interpretation prevents equating intellectual property with a full human right, but at the same time could permit human rights protection to the moral dimension of copyright that affects the personality and the living of authors. The relationship between intellectual property and human rights posed by CESCR's interpretation would consider that:

> receiving moral and material benefits derived from human creativity is part of a broader right to culture and its implications must be addressed in that context … additionally, other [core] human rights prevail over the granting of the material benefits derived from authors' and inventors' creativity.[81]

[75] LR Helfer, 'Regime Shifting: The TRIPS Agreement and New Dynamics of International Intellectual Property Lawmaking' in LR Helfer (ed), *Intellectual Property and Human Rights* (Cheltenham, Edward Elgar, 2013); C Geiger, *Droit d'Auteur et Droit du Public à l'Information* (Paris, Litec, 2004) 47–68.

[76] Universal Declaration of Human Rights (adopted 10 December 1948) UNGA Res 217 A (III) (UDHR).

[77] Sub-Commission on the Protection and Promotion of Human Rights, Intellectual Property Rights and Human Rights, E/Cn.4/Sub.2/RES/2000/7 (17 August 2000).

[78] General Comment 17 (art 15 para 1c) of the Covenant E/C.12/GC/17 (21 November 2005) (CESCR).

[79] ibid, para 2.

[80] ibid.

[81] Seuba (n 12) 201.

The Committee's interpretation of Article 15(1)(c) does not support a traditional justification for Lockean copyright,[82] but it could be justified by the deontological interpretation, as explained above. This interpretation encompasses the protection of the moral dimension of authors, and is compatible with other mutually reinforcing human rights, such as education, considering sustainable structures of education as a prerequisite of copyright protection and part of the scope of the no-harm and charity provisos.

One possible interpretation of General Comment 17 states that its provisions can be used to clarify TRIPS obligations.[83] '[T]he issue will not normally be whether a WTO Member has violated a provision of the ICESCR, but rather, what is necessary in terms of relaxation of WTO disciplines for the Member to fulfill its duties under the ICESCR'.[84] Paragraph 35 of General Comment 17 stipulates that '[S]tates parties thus have a duty to prevent unreasonably high costs for access to ... schoolbooks and learning materials, from undermining the rights of large segments of the population ...' Article 15(1)(c) of the ICESCR could be used to clarify TRIPS in three cases: (1) ambiguous norms; (2) when the term has a specific meaning in international law; and (3) when terms are opened and need further reference to public international law.[85] '[T]he principle of decentralization without hierarchy, along with that of giving full effect to international obligations, implies the need to interpret and to develop these regimes in a complementary and consistent fashion to the extent possible'.[86] Courts, thus, when dealing with ambiguous terms from TRIPS transposedinto national law, can interpret these terms by enshrining human rights considerations or the Lockean normative framework so as to make States fulfil their obligations to comply with the ICESCR.[87] Since the ICESCR applies referential terms to copyright and is binding on a large number of WTO members, it can be used to give meaning to the ambiguous terms in TRIPS; so far, however, it has not completely changed these terms. Nevertheless, we could look ahead to some possible developments in the future. In fact, human rights treaties, according to the International Law Commission, enjoy precedence over transactional instruments, since they pose integral obligations, as *erga omnes* rights including education under the evolutionary development of *jus cogens*, which could prevail even in cases involving direct conflict between

[82] Haugen (n 11) 39–40.

[83] ibid, 43.

[84] R Howse and RG Teitel, 'Beyond the Divide: The International Covenant on Economic, Social and Political Rights and the World Trade Organization' in S Joseph, D Kinley and J Waincymer (eds), *The World Trade Organization and Human Rights: Interdisciplinary Perspectives* (Cheltenham, Edward Elgar, 2009) 44–45.

[85] Seuba (n 12) 207.

[86] Howse and Teitel (n 84) 40.

[87] France, Greece, Italy, Portugal, for example, have transposed the test to national laws. Germany, Austria and UK have treated it only as a meta-norm addressed to legislators. See PB Hugenholtz, 'Limits, Limitations and Exceptions to Copyright under the TRIPS Agreement' in Correa (n 12) 329.

TRIPS and the ICESCR.[88] For example, the Doha Declaration, adopted by WTO Members, is clear in framing the right to public health as superior to intellectual property.[89] As Hugenholtz points out, '[TRIPS] cannot apply to exercises of State discretion that are done pursuant to public policy external to copyright issues ... since this would imply an hierarchy of copyright over other domains of law ...'[90]

It is also noted by Geiger that one of the most important questions of recognising copyright as a human right is the framing of copyright 'in perspective'. This framing permits to treat copyright as an equal right as freedom of expression and access to culture, creating the possibility of balancing rights, subjecting copyright to the rule of proportionality, even the general rules of copyright, such as *in dubio pro auctore* and the rule of restrictive interpretation.[91] However, from a deontological point of view of Lockean theory, education is an already inherent limit of copyright. That said, Lockean deontological interpretation does not afford a strong regime of intellectual property, but actually narrows down the regime's scope by considering an intellectual commons for education as a pre-requisite to copyright property.

The problem with my reasoning is the internationalisation of Intellectual Property by the TRIPS agreement,[92] the so-called 'upward harmonisation',[93] which ignores basic levels of educational and economic development while imposing a strong regime of intellectual property. The three-step test created by Article 13 of TRIPS applies to all economic rights guaranteed under it,[94] and also to those provided by Berne Convention *acquis*, except in the case of express limitations, such as quotation, and 'minor reservations'.[95] Article 13 subjects limitations on economic rights to (1) special cases;

[88] Seuba (n 12) 213–14.

[89] ibid, 212.

[90] Hugenholtz (n 87) 331–32.

[91] Geiger (n 75) 49–50. In civil law countries, authors are generally considered as having weaker bargain power. Thus, to protect them, courts and statutes will normally state that copyright dispositions must be read on a strict manner, without applying legal analogies, and that ambiguous terms must be read as always supporting authors' rights. When these rules are applied to analyse copyright's exceptions, for example, they narrow considerable flexibilities.

[92] CM Correa, *Trade Related Aspects of Intellectual Property Rights: A Commentary on the TRIPS Agreement* (Oxford, Oxford University Press, 2007); CM Correa, *Intellectual Property Rights, the WTO, and Developing Countries: The TRIPS Agreement and Policy Options* (New York, Zed Books, Third World Network, 2000); DJ Gervais, *The TRIPS Agreement: Drafting History and Analysis* 4th edn (London, Sweet & Maxwell, 2012); DJ Gervais, I Schmitz and L Anell, *L'accord sur les ADPIC* (Brussels, Larcier, 2010); C Geiger, 'Promoting Creativity through Copyright Limitations: Reflections on the Concept of Exclusivity in Copyright Law' (2009) 12 *Vanderbilt Journal of Entertainment and Technology Law* 515.

[93] Helfer (n 7) 18.

[94] TRIPS expanded on Berne Convention acquis, like the rental right, previously not existing. See J Malbon, C Lawson and M Davison, *The WTO Agreement on Trade-Related Aspects of Intellectual Property Rights* (Cheltenham, Edward Elgar, 2014) 256.

[95] WIPO Standing Committee on Copyright and Related Rights, Study on Limitations and Exceptions of Copyright and Related Rights in Digital Environment, WIPO Doc SCCR/9/7 (5 April 2003).

(2) that do not interfere with the normal commercial exploitation of the work, and (3) which do not cause unreasonably prejudice to the legitimate interests of the right holders. These provisions affect even the scope of compulsory licenses regarding the reproduction of works.[96] Without compensation achieved on voluntary grounds, systematic copying is forbidden by the cumulative application of the test. According to the 1967 Stockholm Revision of the Berne Convention, normal exploitation includes all the forms of exploitation on a work, which have, or are likely to have, considerable and practical economic importance.[97] According to the Stockholm Conference (1967), all forms of important economic trade which compete with the market of the author's work will not pass the test as long as there is no equitable remuneration.

The Appendix of the Berne Convention—'Special Provisions Regarding Developing Countries'—subjects translation rights and reproduction rights to compulsory licences in developing countries, provides that the country, upon becoming a party, declares that it will avail itself of the faculty provided by the Appendix. It states that the statutory licence must not apply where local needs could be assured by the right holders' voluntary actions, and this is not done because of other factors outside the right holder's power. This includes a situation where, if the right holder is not heard before; if the payment is not promptly done; and if the royalties are not consistent with those that would be paid on a voluntary basis, the party is in breach of obligations.[98] For example, Nigeria's Copyright Law imposes that, to translate a book from English using such a system, one must wait three years from its original publication; obtain authorisation from the right holder, which takes a supplementary delay of six months; and pay not the value which would be paid on Nigeria's national market, but a price that would also take into account the licencing fees applied in the other country.[99] If the Nigerian publisher cannot present solid economic conditions, his request will not even be heard by the Copyright Council. Although the meaning of 'solid economic conditions' is not specified, one could speculate that this limitation might only encourage the business of large editorial companies, and not other forms of pro-education policies.

Regarding the reproduction right, the licence under the Appendix is limited to copies for the purpose of instructional activities and can be only enforced if copies have not, within five years of publication, been distributed for this purpose or to the general public at a reasonable price. Regarding works of natural and physical sciences, the period is reduced to three years and in the case of fiction, poetry, drama, music and art books, increased

[96] Gervais (n 92) 89.
[97] Gervais, Schimitz and Anell (n 92) 256.
[98] ibid.
[99] LY Ngombe, *Le Droit d'Auteur en Afrique* (Paris, L'Harmattan, 2004) 66–67.

to seven years.[100] Also, if the right holder makes his work available at a reasonable price after the licence, the licence must terminate, being granted the right to sell the previous works licensed until the stock terminates. There is a need to attempt to locate the right holder and there must be records of this pursuing, or from the absence of authorisation from the right holder.[101] This creates a second class right of the outcasts to have conditions to access the necessary intellectual commons.

Much has been written about the three-step test and criticised its strict economic interpretation. Some have proposed its inverted interpretation;[102] some have pointed out that it should not be treated as different from fair use's holistic approach, considering the steps as factors analysed by courts;[103] while others have made clear that the history behind the Berne Convention is such that it was meant to create the test as a flexible tool to balance limitations and exceptions, a technique typically used in human rights balancing.[104] Since the *acquis* of the Berne Convention sheds light on the interpretation of TRIPS, they argue that such *acquis* provides breathing space for flexibilities.

According to Senftleben, a conflict with a normal exploitation '[a]rises if the authors are deprived of an actual or potential market of *considerable economic or practical importance*' and the 'actual or potential market is solely formed by those possibilities of marketing a work which *typically constitute a major source of income* and, consequently, belong to the *economic core of copyright*' (emphasis added).[105] Hugenholtz's formulation is quite similar regarding each step: '[(1)] are not overly broad; (2) do not rob the right holders of a real or potential source of income that is substantive; and (3) do not do disproportional harm to the right holders'.[106] Senftleben, Geiger and Gervais explain that:

> [s]pecific purpose such as limited copying to increase access to books in schools would likely pass the first and third step. Consideration under the second and

[100] P Goldstein and PB Hugenholtz, *International Copyright: Principles, Law and Practice* 2nd edn (Oxford, Oxford University Press, 2010) 389–90.

[101] Helfer (n 7) 339.

[102] DJ Gervais, 'Towards a New Core International Copyright Norm: The Reverse Three-Step Test' (2005) 9 *Marquette Intellectual Property Law Review* 1. The restrictive interpretation of steps 1 and 2 could reduce considerably the reach of step 3 and its normative implications. In fact, since normative considerations, such as fundamental rights, can be used to interpret terms such as 'legitimate' and 'reasonable', this approach would be more beneficial for human rights adjudication.

[103] Hugenholtz (n 87) 334.

[104] C Geiger, DJ Gervais and MRF Senftleben, 'The Three-Step Test Revisited: How to Use the Test's Flexibility in National Copyright Law' (2013) 29 *American University Law Review* 581; Hugenholtz (n 87) 330.

[105] MRF Senftleben, *Copyright, Limitations, and the Three-Step Test: An Analysis of the Three-Step Test in International and EC Copyright Law* (The Hague, Kluwer Law International, 2004) 193.

[106] Hugenholtz (n 87) 340.

> third step could be given to whether the books at issue are designed to schools—where the case for interference and prejudice may be much stronger—as opposed to material designed for other markets, for which a fine-grained analysis of the evidence would be required.[107]

Since students from non-sustainable schools in developing countries do not touch at the economic core of copyright, and limited copying of materials which are not designed for schools does not deprive the author of its core market, the making of limited copies in schools should be allowed. Nevertheless, the outcome is not foreseeable, since how much of each book could be copied is controversial. We should deal with this question by returning to the Lockean framework. The idea of property is justified as an end of productive activities and human flourishing, since this is the nature of labour, accounts for inherent limits. In fact, a necessary commons of education itself is an internal limitation to copyright, the *almae matres* of the idea–expression rationality. The quantity of copy allowed regarding materials should clearly favour education and not copyright, meaning that it should take into consideration the economic conditions of a particular school and State's budget, varying considerably depending on the country. This means that the more precarious the school, more copying should be allowed for non-educational materials, on one hand, and differential price policies applied for education materials, on the other hand. This would not be incompatible with Paragraphs 23 and 24 of General Comment 16 of the CESCR, which state that compensatory measures are necessary insofar as they fulfil the standard of author's livings. General Comment 16 could be used to give meaning to TRIPS' steps 2 and 3 'normal commercial exploitation', 'legitimate' and 'unreasonably prejudice' by facilitating making available textbooks in schools, but still providing compensation to authors, even if differential, reasonable enough to uphold their living conditions.

TRIPS must be harmonised with the constitution of one's country, with ICESCR, even if this must mean a limitation, because TRIPS ignores different realities of development and inherent limits to private property, as well as the constitutional independence of each country. It is so strict that the US fair use can be seen wrongly as a violation of the three-step test.[108] According to the UN Sub-Commission, Resolution 2000/7, '[a]ny intellectual property regime that makes it more difficult to comply with [ICESCR] core obligations in relation to health, food, [or] *education* … is

[107] Geiger, Gervais and Senftleben (n 104) 611.

[108] A Kur, 'Of Oceans, Islands, and Inland Water—How Much Room for Exceptions and Limitations under the Three-Step Test' (2009) 8 *Richmond Journal of Global Law & Business* 288; R Okediji, 'Toward an International Fair Use Doctrine' (2001) 39 *Columbia Journal of Transnational Law* 75.

inconsistent with the legally binding obligations of the State party'(emphasis added).[109] Also,

> [T]RIPS Agreement does not adequately reflect the fundamental nature and indivisibility of all human rights ... there are apparent conflicts between the intellectual property rights regime embodied in the TRIPS Agreement, on the one hand, and international human rights law, on the other.[110]

IV. CONCLUSION

Someone would say that it is not copyright's problem that individuals do not have access to ideas, or that copyright should not pay the bill of the government's inability to provide basic education. This reasoning, though, has not taken Lockean provisos, human rights or inherent limits to private property into consideration. Education is not just a market. Copyright can be restricted to ameliorate the situation without destroying the economic incentives to authors or their autonomy and self-realisation. This would be safeguarded and justified by the provisos and its deontological interpretation.

Lockean deontological theory provides the framework to bridge the large gap between human rights, education and copyright by unifying ideas from international human right instruments, such as the ICESCR, influenced in its origin by Locke, and also copyright justifications, historically based on his ideas. Additionally, it provides a new framework for courts to interpret copyright obligations, strongly favouring sustainable education structures as a prerequisite to the copyright idea–expression dichotomy bar. If we analyse seriously this question, the dichotomy cannot only be treated as establishing the boundaries of copyright subject matter, but it also plays a role in ensuring an intellectual commons for education, which cannot be constrained either by protected works of authorship or works in the public domain overly restricted to schools.

ICESCR's obligation on parties in making schoolbooks and educational materials accessible must guarantee further inclusive and differential pricing policies for public libraries and schools. If copyright does not allow for such basic educational policies, courts should be able to use the balancing tools of human rights and the deontological interpretation to conform and harmonise TRIPS with States' pro-educational actions.

[109] D Weissbrodt and K Schoff, 'The Sub-Commission's Initiative on Human Rights and Intellectual Property' (2004) 22 *Netherlands Quarterly of Human Rights* 181, 183.

[110] ibid, 186.

7

Filling the Institutional Void Between Fundamental Rights and the Legal Purchase of Goods: What Role for Consumocratic Law?

MARTIN DUMAS

I. INTRODUCTION

WHAT DO CONSUMERS know about the general conditions under which the goods they buy are produced? What are (or what could be) the kinds of information provided to consumers in that respect? In what way could such information be furnished? What are the consequences that attach to the (im)possibility of disseminating such information at the point of sale? At a more concrete level, we might ask if the legal sale of products manufactured with undeniable contempt for human rights, and for the most fundamental rights of workers in particular,[1] is morally acceptable, and if the existing legal framework of this state of affairs is likewise acceptable.

Popular initiatives, behaviour and techniques now commonly referred to as 'fair trade', 'ethical purchasing' and 'societal labelling' remind us that consumers are increasingly exposed to a wider range of information pertaining not so much to market goods themselves as to conditions linked to their

[1] I take the view that not all labour rights are human rights, and that the latter must include the most fundamental labour rights, such as the right to associate (and not to associate), to freedom of expression and mobility (through the prohibition of forced labour) and to decent work for all. The precise identification of such fundamental labour rights remains controversial, but a pragmatic view of the problem suggests that even ILO's *core conventions* should not be treated on an equal footing. See on this: PM Dumas, 'Thickening Soft Law through Consumocratic Law: A Pragmatic Approach' in A Trebilcock and A Blackett (eds), *Research Handbook on Transnational Labour Law* (London, Edward Elgar, 2015, forthcoming). The relative absence of consideration for these rights, in some well-known works of the human-rights literature, is however deplorable—see, for instance, J Donnelly, *Universal Human Rights in Theory and Practice* (New York, Cornell University Press, 2013).

production or usage. Consumers may indeed be called upon to acknowledge some part of responsibility in the persistence of a number of irritants which the sole intervention of the state, in the operation of markets, cannot seem to combat satisfactorily. Informational barriers between the loci of production and consumption, between workers' fundamental rights and buyers' civil rights, have the effect of excluding the act of buying from the sphere of corporate regulation, effectively imprisoning the debate on the social regulation of commerce. A remedial system, by which consumers can exert more authority over corporations by making enlightened choices when purchasing goods (ie the *consumocratic* system) must therefore provide the necessary mechanisms for lowering such information barriers.

I will attempt in this chapter to demonstrate that, despite the potential reinforcement of already rigid barriers to societal information by the advance of international trade and of WTO (World Trade Organization) law, a new model for regulating corporations founded on the gradual elimination of these barriers is practical and able to enhance workers' human rights as well as the apparatus of liberal democracy. By providing consumers with the opportunity to purposefully influence, *ab initio* and outside common political spheres, decision-making processes on matters that affect others in society, the consumocratic system discredits the view that such problems may only be solved ex post, under pre-eminent state care.

II. THE INSTITUTIONAL VOID BETWEEN FUNDAMENTAL RIGHTS AND THE PURCHASE OF GOODS

Under both the common and civil law regimes, the sale of stolen property is (or might be) stained with illegality[2] whereas the sale of a product manufactured under illegal working conditions would not normally be stained with such illegality, whether or not the buyer is aware of the manufacturing conditions. Within this institutionalised rupture between the spheres of production and consumption, goods produced under conditions that violate the workers' fundamental rights can therefore be offered and sold legally on global markets. Workers' most fundamental rights, in effect, attach to individuals in their workplace. We count among these rights the right to physical integrity, and the rights to freedom of mobility and expression.

[2] This relates to a rule that is firmly rooted in both legal traditions: in the common law, one may refer, for example, to the decisions rendered in *Lipkin Gorman v Karpnale Ltd* [1991] 2 AC 548; *R c Ilich* (1987) 69 ALR 231, 244; *Merry v Green* (1841) 7 M & W 623; *Rex v Hutton* (1911) 19 WLR 907 (the simple theft of water might be—or have been—an exception); or, in the civil law, to the French *Code Civil* (arts 1599 and 2279), the Spanish *Codigo Civil* (arts 433, 447, 464 and 1950), the *Code Civil du* Québec (arts 1713 and 1714), the German *Bürgerliches Gesetzbuch* (arts 861, 935 and 1006) as well as the ancient Roman Law I ([*Corpus Juris Civilis, Digest* 47.16]; *de receptatoribus*).

In the labour context, they consist of the right of children to a task and a work environment that do not pose serious risks to their integrity;[3] the right not to be subject to forced labour; the right not to be subject to discrimination; and the right to associate with the goal of agreeing upon suitable working conditions.[4] In no way do they commingle with the rights in those things manufactured by a person at work. Besides, the conditions under which a thing is produced do not legally qualify the traditional status of that same thing. It follows that 'real rights' attach to the thing (from a civilist perspective, more particularly), but are alien to the conditions under which the item was made.

In this context, attempts to alert or inform world consumers of the conditions under which goods are produced, though laudable, face serious challenges under state law. These challenges may reside in the limits inherent to the regulation of commercial speech (section II.A) as well as in the treatment of state-regulated labelling schemes under WTO law (section II.B). They would be more certainly overcome through ongoing developments of market-based, *non-state* labelling systems (section III). These transnational systems of private regulation, termed *consumocratic law* (section III.A), require providing access to other-regarding information, and thus face particular limitations (section III.B).

A. Within the Boundaries of Commercial Free Speech

Let us first differentiate product information from societal information. Information pertaining to the final attributes of consumer goods, namely their price, intrinsic quality and safety, can be referred to as *product information*. Conversely, the peripheral attributes of consumer goods, such as the environmental or work conditions that characterise the general process of their production and use is referred to as *societal information*. More concretely, societal information may relate to various conditions or

[3] The quasi-universal acceptance of the Convention on the Worst Forms of Child Labour, 1999 (Convention 182), in contrast with the status of the Minimum Age Convention (Convention 138, 1973), may be indicative of a closer and more efficient link, underlying the former convention, between the goal of improving children's well-being and the means selected to reach it. For a detailed discussion on this issue, see Dumas (n 1).

[4] These are, more precisely, the rights envisioned in the Freedom of Association and Protection of the Right to Organize Convention, 1948 (Convention 87), the Right to Organize and Collective Bargaining Convention, 1949 (Convention 98), the Forced Labour Convention, 1930 (Convention 29), the Abolition of Forced Labour Convention, 1957 (Convention 105), the Equal Remuneration Convention, 1951 (100), the Discrimination (Employment and Occupation) Convention, 1958 (Convention 111), the Minimum Age Convention, 1973 (Convention 138), and the Worst Forms of Child Labour Convention, 1999 (Convention 182), which are brought out by the ILO Declaration on the Fundamental Principles and Rights at Work (1998).

repercussions observed at the stage of production, distribution or usage of goods (such as the use of child labour, the depletion of the ozone layer or the effect a product may have on human health) and to consumer-sanctioned activities undertaken to improve these conditions. Understood in a broad sense and in relation to the prevention of illegal child labour, for instance, societal information may therefore refer to the use of adult labour in the production of goods, as well as the implementation of consumer-sponsored schools and rehabilitation centres for kidnapped children.[5] It is worth noting that societal information is not confined to information relating to the production process, strictly speaking, under which consumer goods come into being.[6]

Corporations may use the product–process distinction before national courts to avoid some liabilities. When faced with charges of labour exploitation, the Nike Company attempted to officially depict itself as a 'socially responsible employer' but nevertheless sought the protection of the First Amendment to the United States Constitution to isolate this very claim from the false advertising regulation applicable to commercial speech. It contended that commercial speech should not be considered as encompassing attributes other than 'the qualities of a product as such (like its price, availability, and suitability)'.[7] Influential associations in support of the petitioner added that 'only speech that does no more than propose a commercial transaction—that is, speech that does no more than promote *tangible* qualities of a product or service in a *traditional* advertising format—may be treated as commercial speech and subjected to strict liability rules' (emphasis added).[8]

It bears stating the point that Nike's claim was contested as false and misleading, and susceptible of deceiving consumers. Messages supporting the societal value of commodities may prove sensitive indeed, in comparison to those which more freely entertain the code of purely marketing values, hence perhaps the determination of producers and advertisers to exclude societal information from false advertising regulation.[9]

[5] The difference between product and societal information is not always clear. Some peripheral attributes, such as the engineering techniques retained in devising a product (eg, genetically modified food), are very closely associated with the final attributes of goods, since they alter the very nature of the latter.

[6] Yet 'process information' is the expression favoured by the WTO in its appreciation of any information not pertaining to 'products as such', thereby opening the door to potential confusion when it comes to examining relatively constrained state-sponsored labelling schemes (see section II.B).

[7] See *Nike, Inc v Kasky*, 45 P.3d 243 (Cal 2002); 123 S Ct 2554 (2003).

[8] See Brief Amici Curiae of Forty Leading Newspapers, Magazines, Broadcasters, Wire-Services, and Media-Related Professional and Trade Associations in Support of Petitioners, 2003 WL 835613.

[9] In general terms, the societal value of the commodity is typically revealed through an act of non-indifference towards distant people or things—an act of responsibility, more or less consciously and instrumentally carried out. Its basic ingredients, in the form of societal

Rebuffing Nike's pretensions, the California court held that 'when a corporation, to maintain and increase its sales and profits, makes public statements defending labor practices and working conditions at factories where its products are made, those public statements are commercial speech that may be regulated to prevent consumer deception'.[10]

The *Nike* case thus reveals a first caveat in state attempts to link the informational spheres of production and consumption. Even if commercial speech regulations may discourage corporations from spreading misleading statements regarding the conditions under which goods are produced, or their societal attributes, it remains that they cannot do much to prevent a corporation from staying mute about its production methods when they happen to encroach on fundamental rights. WTO law does not prevent this either, but it does tackle some difficult questions raised by the communication to consumers of information related to the (non)enforcement of some fundamental rights along production chains.

B. Labelling under WTO Law: Manipulating the Product–Process Distinction

The product–process distinction can be seen in contrasting ways. It may oppose an instrument of consumer power based on an analysis of products, on the one hand, and on an analysis of processes (more or less broadly defined) on the other. It may equally reflect an institutional attempt to cordon off consumer access to 'process information'. Under the jurisprudence of the WTO Appellate Body, the so-called product–process distinction appears as a controversial formulation designed to distinguish not products from processes, but more precisely between governmental measures aiming either at one or the other. The product–process distinction was notably discussed in the *Tuna/Dolphin* case.[11] Following such distinction, according to

information, may or may not be mixed with the simulacra and imageries of modern marketing. It is less hardly shielded from the results of investigations designed to authenticate its claims. The degree of transparency retained in communicating societal information to consumers may thus lie at the centre of a more highly receptive social interface. The societal value of the commodity differentiates itself from other values in that its ingredients are generally presented under a falsifiable format; it reveals itself in the appreciation of more concrete elements. In general, the promises of societal marketing may be validated and they often are. There is nothing very magical indeed in verifying whether corporations are paying 'decent wages' to their employees, using fishing nets of a certain size, treating waste water, employing adults while funding schools for their children, or else conducting themselves like 'socially responsible' organisations.

[10] *Nike, Inc v Kasky* (n 7) 45 P.3d, 319.

[11] GATT Dispute Panel Report on United States—Restrictions on Imports of Tuna, 16 Aug 1991, GATT BISD (39th Supp) at 155 (1993) [hereinafter *Tuna-Dolphin I*]; *see also* GATT Dispute Panel Report on United States—Restrictions on Imports of Tuna, 16 June 1994, GATT BISD (41st Supp) (1994).

the Appellate Body, peripheral characteristics such as the methods by which tuna is harvested 'could not possibly *affect* tuna as a product' (emphasis added) and—more questionably—imported dolphin-(un)safe tuna could not be compared with '*like products* of national origin' under Article III of the GATT (General Agreement on Tariffs and Trade) (which opens the door to analyses based on the non-discrimination principle between foreign and domestic productions).[12] Literally speaking, 'dolphin-safe tuna' and 'dolphin-unsafe tuna', though physically identical, would then be deemed 'unlike products',[13] meaning that they could not be analysed and accepted under Article III for the reason that process characteristics (and import restrictions regulating them, more precisely) do not *affect* 'products as such'.[14] Although the *Tuna/Dolphin* 1991 ruling and the relevant jurisprudence must now be read in light of more recent decisions of the Appellate Body,[15] the product–process distinction maintained by the WTO remains a major obstacle to non-discriminatory measures that respond to social and environmental

[12] Under WTO jurisprudence, process-based trade restrictions may constitute disguised attempts to discriminate in practice against foreign producers. Such was the conclusion reached by the Dolphin/Tuna 1991 GATT panel after examining a dispute in which Mexican tuna producers failed to comply with provisions of the US Marine Mammal Protection Act. Under these provisions, foreign producers are required to obtain a certificate establishing that the techniques used in the harvest of tuna result in an incidental dolphin kill rate similar to that of the US industry (cf Direct Embargo Provision (§101 (a)(2)) in the Marine Mammal Protection Act). Due to the obvious difficulty for Mexican producers to align their long-term business plans with changing American environmental policies, Mexican products were in effect accorded treatment 'less favourable than that accorded to like products of national origin', under art III (4) of the GATT. The panel however justified its decision on the broader ground that the American regulations were *not* aiming at 'products as such'; that is, products that could be compared with 'like products of national origin' under art III, and whose treatment could then be assessed under the criterion of non-discrimination. As critically observed by Kysar, by adopting a narrow definition of 'like products' and by limiting the applicability of the general exceptions clause of the GATT to trade measures that do not seem to affect extra-jurisdictional practices prima facie, the panel not only prevented governments 'to make non-protectionist distinctions among products based on the methods by which they were manufactured or harvested', but also gave support to the view 'that product regulations not directly related to physical or other tangible characteristics of a product violate the GATT'. See DA Kysar, 'Preferences for Processes: the Process/Product Distinction and the Regulation of Consumer Choice' (2004) *Cornell Law Faculty Publications*, paper 8, 20.

[13] The 'likeness' determination is the subject of growing attention among analysts. For a detailed discussion of the issue, see R Hudec, '"Like Product": The Differences in Meaning in GATT Articles I and III' in T Cottier and P Mavroidis (eds), *Regulatory Barriers and the Principle of Non-Discrimination in World Trade Law* (Michigan, University of Michigan Press, 2000). For our purposes, it suffices to mention that new criteria, such as *direct* health or safety risks posed by a product, also may be considered in determining product likeness (cf WTO Appellate Body Report on European Communities—Measures Affecting Asbestos & Asbestos-Containing Products, WT/DS135/AB/R (12 March 2001), at paras 149–54). *Indirect* risks (eg, to distant people) appear to be excluded from such analysis.

[14] *Tuna/Dolphin I*, 30 I.L.M. at 1618, para 5.14.

[15] Under Art XX (b) (g) of the GATT, trade restrictions may be justified on the ground that they are 'necessary to protect human, animal, or plant life or health' or that they 'relat[e] to the conservation of exhaustible natural resources'. The permissibility of process-based trade restrictions under Art XX is seemingly intended to be and remain exceptional. See Report of

concerns expressed by the public. It could consolidate the view that unilateral trade restrictions should relate to products only—not processes. At the centre of this notion, from a functionalist point of view, therefore lies the potential narrowing or broadening of the sphere of authority for individuals within the framework of markets.

In addition, while the legal status of (government-sanctioned) *mandatory* labelling of goods differentiated on the basis of how they are produced is altogether uncertain under the GATT,[16] the status of *voluntary* programmes hinges more centrally on its likely impact on the targeted populations.[17] The standards developed under these programmes must abide by the provisions contained in the Agreement on Technical Barriers to Trade (the TBT agreement) and, where applicable, the Agreement on Sanitary and Phytosanitary Measures (the SPS agreement). The more general TBT agreement provides for necessity and proportionality tests comparable to, although more refined than, those which have been developed under the Article XX GATT jurisprudence.[18] The SPS agreement aims at a more restricted category of

the Appellate Body, *United States-Import Restrictions of Certain Shrimp and Shrimp Products*, WT/DS58/AB/R (12 Oct 1998) [hereinafter *Shrimp/Turtle 1998*]; WTO Appellate Body Report on United States Import Prohibition of Certain Shrimp and Shrimp Products, WT/DS58/AB/RW (22 Oct 2001) [hereinafter *Shrimp/Turtle 2001*]. *Shrimp/Turtle 1998* exposed a series of cumulative tests (including 'sufficient nexus', 'proportionality', 'necessity', and 'means and ends' tests) which are known to be applied stringently. See D McRae, 'Article XX and the WTO Appellate Body' in M Bronkers and R Quick (eds), *New Directions in International Economic Law: Essays in Honour of John H Jackson* (The Hague, Kluwer Law International, 2000). The GATT further stipulates that trade restrictions shall not be applied 'in a manner which would constitute a means of arbitrary or unjustifiable discrimination between countries where the same conditions prevail, or a disguised restriction on international trade'—the so-called 'chapeau' of Art XX. Although the Appellate Body more recently found that Mexican tuna products and (dolphin-safe) US tuna products originating in the United State are 'like products', it also held the view that 'Mexico has established a *prima facie* case that the US "dolphin-safe" labelling provisions modify the conditions of competition in the US market to the detriment of Mexican tuna products and are not even-handed in the way in which they address the risks to dolphins arising from different fishing techniques in different areas of the ocean' and, therefore, that 'US "dolphin-safe" labelling provisions provide "less favourable treatment" to Mexican tuna products than that accorded to tuna products of the United States and tuna products originating in other countries and are therefore inconsistent with Art 2.1 of the *TBT Agreement*'. See Report of the Appellate Body, United States-Measures Concerning the Importation, Marketing and Sale of Tuna and Tuna Products, WT/DS381/AB/R, 114–15 (16 May 2012).

[16] A measure requiring the labelling of a whole category of imported products on such basis may be tantamount to imposing a blanket ban whose legality could only be saved under the GATT general exceptions clause.

[17] The 'likeness' test is here substituted with a 'relatedness' determination that appears no less problematical: '[T]here has been furious discussion but no consensus view within the WTO about how closely non-mandatory PPM [process and production methods] measures such as eco-labels must be "related" to the product to fall within the scope of the TBT Agreement'. See SE Gaines, 'Processes and Production Methods: How to Produce Sound Policy for Environmental PPM-Based Trade Measures?' (2002) 27 *Columbia Journal of Environmental Law* 383, cited in DA Kysar, 'Preferences for Processes: The Process/Product Distinction and the Regulation of Consumer Choice' (2005) 118 *Harvard Law Review* 525.

[18] TBT agreement, Art 2.2.

product standards and governs product regulations intended to protect life from 'pests, diseases, disease-carrying organisms or disease-causing organisms' or from 'additives, contaminants, toxins or disease-carrying organisms in food, beverages or feedstuffs'.[19] Variations on the tests established under the GATT exceptions clause are also found in the SPS agreement, in addition to requirements that the product regulations be 'based on scientific principles', supported by 'sufficient scientific evidence' and applied 'only to the extent necessary to protect human, animal or plant life or health'.[20] Furthermore, both agreements require the use of existing international standards in the establishment of product regulations unless such standards are found to be ineffective, inappropriate or, in accordance with scientific evidence, too minimalist.[21]

A number of reasons have been invoked against the diffusion of transparent societal information through markets. These arguments are similar to those made against the use of linkages between international trade and more traditional modes of socio-environmental protection (such as state-defined standards, tariffs and quotas, and international agreement frameworks). The fight against protectionism is one of these reasons. One may fear, in a liberal spirit, that access to societal information, and the obligation to communicate it to consumers, will encourage trade discrimination practices to the detriment of foreign producers. It is not rare, in effect, that practices deemed objectionable by large segments of consumers manifest themselves more frequently abroad than on local territories.[22] Because trade and regulatory discrimination by states is no more unusual, under the pretext of encouraging or discouraging certain methods of production, it is feared that such control may reinforce a type of economic nationalism already condemned by the World Trade Organization.[23]

It is not yet impossible to design tests so as to distinguish discriminatory measures from measures aiming justly at the protection of vulnerable people or things. This is not what the WTO supported, interestingly, by

[19] SPS agreement, Annex A.
[20] SPS agreement Art 2.2.
[21] TBT agreement, Art 2.2; SPS agreement, Arts 3.3, 5.
[22] Child labour and certain practices detrimental to the environment are more commonly found in developing regions, as the costs of productive and less polluting technologies are more likely to be prohibitive.
[23] It is recalled that such was the conclusion reached by the *Dolphin/Tuna* 1991 GATT panel after examining a dispute in which Mexican tuna producers failed to comply with the Direct Embargo Provision §101 (a)(2) of the US Marine Mammal Protection Act. Under these provisions, foreign producers are required to obtain a certificate establishing that the techniques used in the harvest of tuna result in an incidental dolphin kill rate similar to that of the US industry. Due to the obvious difficulty for Mexican producers to align their long-term business plans with changing American environmental policies, Mexican products were in effect accorded treatment 'less favourable than that accorded to like products of national origin' (cf GATT Art III (4)).

creating the 'product–process distinction', and rejecting the communication of 'process information' to consumers on the basis that such information did not qualify 'products as such' (suggesting that 'products as such', as opposed to 'processes', are the only elements to be examined by the panel). The *Dolphin/Tuna* 1991 GATT panel justified its decision, indeed, on the broad ground that the American regulations were *not* aiming at 'products as such'; that is, final products that could be compared with 'like products of national origin' under Article III, and whose treatment could then be assessed under the criterion of non-discrimination. In sum, the manipulation of the process–product distinction in international trade law does seem to have prevented a reasoned discourse about how to distinguish appropriate from inappropriate regulations aimed at processes and production methods.[24]

III. WHAT ROLE FOR NON-STATE LABELLING SYSTEMS?

It is largely admitted that the latest wave of free trade, at the world level, has contributed to the destabilisation of various regimes of social protection, developed or supported at state level. An epitome of this phenomenon is the challenge posed to protective state law by the configuration of transnational production networks. Given that WTO law and national laws have hitherto proved inapt to meet this challenge through an adequate apprehension of the complexity and diversity of transnational operations, increased attention has been directed to the role of other regulatory means. One of them involves consumers as agents endowed with regulatory power.

A. On Consumocratic Law

When they act as consumers, adults, like children, are often regarded as the subjects of protective state regulation—potential, manifest or latent victims of corporate negligence, misrepresentations, price-fixing and abusive marketing. The status of consumers may change significantly, though, depending on whether or not the societal value of consumer goods is elicited through markets.[25] Central in this process is the control over the diffusion of societal information on consumer markets. Its understanding requires an

[24] See also in this regard: S Charnovitz, 'Solving the Production and Processing Methods Puzzle' in K Gallagher and J Werksman (eds), *The Earthscan Reader on International Trade and Sustainable Development* (London, Routledge, 2001) and Kysar (n 17).

[25] See in this regard PM Dumas, 'The Malaise of Modernity under Consumocratic Order' (2012) 5 *Economics and Sociology* 75.

examination of the regulatory regime through which citizens are invited to broaden their notion of a desirable good and exercise new forms of authority over corporations. This is done, transnationally, through the operation of codes of conduct the enforcement of which is signaled to consumers via a more or less transparent form of societal marketing.[26] Societal labels are typically placed on the outside of products in order to signal the effects such products or production conditions may have on consumers, other people or the environment. The regulatory capacity of labelling initiatives is thus actuated by the communication to consumers of information pertaining, in general, to the conditions (managerial, financial, social, environmental and ethical) under which goods are produced. The meaning of logos not accompanied by a text description must be conveyed through other media such as the internet, wireless communication and television. A variety of impacts ensue with a degree of directness the state could hardly approach.[27]

An increasing number of independent codes of conduct constitute, in this view, a body of rules, enforced through demand-side market-based mechanisms, and used as instruments of corporate governance (hereinafter referred to as *consumocratic law*).[28] As such, they do not fit well within the 'soft law' regime of corporate voluntary initiatives, nor do they qualify properly as 'reflexive law' rules, since one finds them conditioned by important segments of consumers.[29] In contrast with citizens called to express, ex ante, their preferences for particular socio-economic plans through voting, consumers (or, more precisely, *consumocrats*) are rather called here to play

[26] One may define societal marketing as the marketing of goods or services whereby societal information is signalled to consumers through various means. Societal information in turn pertains to certain conditions or effects observed or to be observed at the stage of production, distribution, or usage of goods, in accordance with the terms of a corporate code.

[27] In the works of regulatory cost–benefit analysis proponents, consumer choices in fact do not lay themselves wide open to bureaucratic inefficiencies, agency capture and paternalism—at least not as openly as political action through voting does. See D Zamir, 'Consumer Preferences, Citizen Preferences, and the Provision of Public Goods' (1998) 108 *Yale Law Journal* 377. See also, for more details regarding the nature and operation of consumocratic law, PM Dumas, 'Three Misunderstandings about Consumocratic Law' (2013) 35 *Comparative Labor Law and Policy Journal* 67.

[28] From *consummare* (Lat), to consume, and *kratos* (Gr), authority. One may be indecisive about whether to refer to consumocratic 'law' or 'regulation'. But as rightly pointed out, 'there is no settled definition of "law" within legal pluralism, just as there is none of regulation. Legal pluralists are agreed that "law" does not solely emanate from the state; just what it is and how it is distinguished from other forms of norm-based social ordering is still contested'. See J Black, *Critical Reflections on Regulation* (CARR Paper 1-27, 2002). A distinctive attribute of consumocratic law, ie, its direct and widely distributed economic sanctioning power, can interestingly be put in contrast with other sanctioning mechanisms in use in governance systems; the threat of consumers' sanctioning power is here analogous to a 'form of legal compulsion'. See M Weber, *The Theory of Social and Economic Organization* (New York, Free Press, 1964) 128.

[29] See R Rogowski, *Reflexive Labour Law in the World* (Cheltenham UK and Northampton MA, Edward Elgar, 2013); C Barnard, S Deakin and R Hobbs, *Reflexive Law, Corporate Social Responsibility and the Evolution of Labour Standards: The Case of Working Time* (ESRC Centre for Business Research Paper, 2004); and Dumas (n 27).

a role ex post, and pronounce themselves on the desirability of certain goods, in comparison to others, following a number of non-traditional criteria already embodied in labelled codes. These codes, therefore, may more appropriately be described as codes of 'second generation', in contrast with more truly voluntary codes of first generation, and may link production and consumption processes in ways that rehabilitate morality in the operation of markets.[30]

B. Providing Access to Other-Regarding Behaviour

When purchasing goods, world consumers are traditionally interested in some identifiable attributes of such goods. It is in reference to these attributes, notably, that they will determine whether or not things newly acquired really *are* what they intended to buy. Traditional attributes such as the safety, availability, suitability and quality/price ratio of a product are considered in decisions regarding the desirability of such product, from a purely individual point of view. But our legal and economic frameworks of analysis become almost obsolete when one examines situations in which consumers are willing to consider the societal attributes of goods—such as respect for the fundamental rights of labour—a process involving the evaluation of other-regarding information.

The elicitation of the societal value of goods largely depends on the fruits of societal marketing and of societal labels, among its primary means. Societal labels are typically placed on the outside of products in order to signal the effects such products or production conditions may have on consumers, other people or the environment. As a general rule, they act as an incentive (as in 'Made by Free Labour') or as a warning (as in 'Secondary Smoke May Cause Cancer').

Let us stress that labels aiming at the protection of consumers' self-interest, understood in a traditional sense, should not be confused with those directed towards the condition of other people or things (for example, distant workers, the environment, animals, future generations). Decisions regarding the desirability of a product from a purely individual point of view, such as the evaluation of its safety or suitability, contrast sharply with decisions involving an evaluation of its social or environmental impact. They first require different forms of expertise. On the one hand, consumers are normally well placed to identify a safety or quality/price ratio that fits their own needs and, in this, they are experts.[31] Deciding what one should do to distant people or

[30] See Dumas (n 25).

[31] It is not assumed that consumers are experts in determining the level of safety attached to the usage of goods. To that end, they need advice. It is in the evaluation of the financial sacrifice

things, on the other hand, is undeniably more complex and the profile of the average consumer, here, appears more dilettantish.[32]

Also, consumocratic law is not immune against the risk of polemical information leaking and reaching the public, without proper contextualisation. The possibility that various flaws or 'grey zones' in the operation of consumocratic law be exposed to the public, indeed, may attract special attention. In the absence of mechanisms designed to translate this complexity to consumers and offer a framework for fruitful exchanges with producers, regulators of societal labelling are exposing their organisations and the beneficiaries thereof to the risks posed by the leaking of sensitive information towards a large, potentially ill-informed audience. Societal labelling standing for one fairly elementary mode of interaction between producers and consumers, it may have to confront the gap between consumers' relatively broad expectations and the harsh reality that often shapes consumocratic initiatives. Ultimately, the vulnerability of the latter rests on the absence of a deliberation or understanding space between consumers and producers, under the risk of increased regulatory transparency, either forced or unexpected.[33]

The quality and transparency of the societal information transmitted to consumers should therefore not eclipse issues concerning the quality of the debates this information is likely to engender—because transparency measures aiming at the satisfaction of information recipients' needs cannot, without unintended consequences, be treated like those aiming at the satisfaction of people usually unknown to information recipients. From a consequentialist perspective, the self–other distinction suggests that increased transparency may help consumers make better, safer choices for themselves, but that it may not generate only positive results on people consumocrats endeavour to support from a distance. It is maintained that, within an effective consumocratic system and absent a proper regulatory platform for

they are prepared to make for proper safety that consumers develop an appreciable level of expertise, having only themselves to please.

[32] Not less importantly, these decisions rest on different motivational bases. Being solicited to influence the conditions of others through rather transparent consumocratic systems is not only an empowering experience; it also signifies a factual departure from the foundations of consumerist capitalism—a phenomenon which, in spite of the challenges it entails, is presented as highly desirable (see for a more detailed discussion see Dumas (n 25)).

[33] Moreover, the portrait of the transparency problem is peppered with contradictory expert debates, a phenomenon too often neglected in regulation studies. That experts may be better placed than dilettantes to make an informed decision, in the face of a complex situation, is a well-defended opinion shared by policy makers and academics. An obstacle to the future development of regulation on consumer access to societal information nonetheless is the fact that experts do not inevitably come into agreement with each other. The situation is all the more troubling since incompatible positions on important questions—such as the enforcement of children's fundamental rights—are being advocated. It further brings into light a regulation problem which, in spite of its centrality under the rise of private governance of standards, has been largely neglected. See Dumas (n 1), for a pragmatic view of this problem.

deliberation and understanding, consumers should not be informed of all they may naturally be curious about the people they purport to help and, more precisely, about some details of how help is brought to people.

Finally, greater regulatory transparency could hardly emerge without genuine efforts to contextualise (a priori doubtful or potentially controversial) decisions taken by the regulators of societal labelling in the course of their activities. Such contextualisation, however, would inevitably expose the flaws of their organisations in the formulation, execution and interpretation of their own rules. It is the obligation of contextualising societal information, within a more transparent framework, which would then command a regulatory reform of consumocratic initiatives on both the substantive and procedural planes. In the absence of such reform, higher levels of transparency would most likely trouble local regulators and consumers alike, putting the consumocratic missions at risk. From a pragmatic and consequentialist point of view, maintaining a certain degree of opacity, while fighting power abuses insofar as possible, would be advisable before a reform takes place. A successful and transparent consumocratic regime would thereafter represent an important step towards the creation of a veritable deliberation space between producers and consumers and, plausibly, towards a more globally democratic alignment of the policies which model transnational markets.

IV. CONCLUSION

This research has been inspired by, and has been set against the background of, a relatively promising, though rather unstable, vision of social realities. It is a promising vision, for if a critical mass of consumers manifest an interest in sending economic signals embodying the promotion of other people's interests—and not only their own—the motivational foundations of capitalism (deemed deprived of any spirit of solidarity) may have to be redefined. We have seen that a developing consumocratic system, through a lowering of information barriers between the loci of production and consumption, could in fact enhance the apparatus of liberal democracy and workers' human rights. In a context arguably marked by a global democratic deficit and the political disenchantment of voters, these new political economic signals do seem to open some avenues of hope.

In the short term, it is possibly a rather unstable vision, also, because the maintenance of such openness, expressed through markets and not via state action, lies in the end on the credibility of rather transparent messages of responsible marketing. It has been demonstrated that transparency in matters of societal marketing, absent an appropriate regulatory framework for public debates, is vulnerable from an instrumentalist point of view. It is likely indeed that the communication of accurate facts to a critical mass of people may turn out to compromise the achievement of nonetheless well-intentioned objectives, such as the protection of workers' most fundamental rights, and that regulators may instead dissimulate or alter some potentially controversial information so as to comfort consumers. But this regulation scenario is not ineluctable in theory. Difficult local choices under global scrutiny give rise to various scenarios of governance and, necessarily, to different ways of mediating between principles of state law and consumocratic law. It has been shown that a more appropriate regulatory platform between producers and consumocrats could better frame polemic (re)actions expected to occur at the transnational level. The challenge would indeed consist in abandoning the comfort of regulatory opacity to meet that of (a priori) discomforting transparency, in a more sophisticated world polity.

In sum, the emancipatory goal of the consumocratic system, in the spirit of 'historical hope',[34] can be seen as releasing consumers from the uninformed fog in which they find themselves and which forecloses any resort to ethical or political reasoning in their purchasing decisions. By giving politically disenchanted consumers the opportunity to safeguard human rights and exert new authority on enterprises through a more enlightened selection of consumer goods, the consumocratic law system may be viewed here as the centre of a nascent political economic order or a structured social space offering regulatory bulwarks against hegemonic interests.

[34] See RM Unger, *Democracy Realized: The Progressive Alternative* (London, New York, Verso, 1998) and C Gomes and RM Unger, *O Próximo Passo* (Rio de Janeiro, Topbooks, 1996) for a sensible evocation of such a spirit.

8

Development, Property and International Investment: The Double-edged Sword of Human Rights

BRUCE WARDHAUGH

THIS CHAPTER IS an examination of the relationship among human rights, property rights and international investment protection regimes, in the light of recent critical discourse. This discourse often paints the latter regimes as being over-protective of the rights of (foreign) investors, thus handcuffing host country governments in their attempts to regulate in their citizens' interests.[1] When these limits to regulation appear to adversely affect the host country's ability to regulate in the interests of public health, the environment or the disadvantaged, such limits are portrayed as human rights concerns. These concerns then become reflected in subsequent discourse regarding investor's property rights trumping the human rights of host country citizens.[2]

This chapter argues that dichotomising human and property rights is misplaced. Development concerns promoted by investment are commonly addressed by market measures. It is through market-driven investment that host nations' infrastructure can be developed, hence facilitating raising of its citizens' standards of living. But the market requires reasonably secure property rights to function, and this security will facilitate investment decisions which can promote the development agenda. Paradoxically, to advance a domestic human rights agenda, securing property rights for investors may not be merely desirable, but necessary. Without such protection, the (human rights advancing) investment may not be made, thus hindering (or even frustrating) domestic efforts to advance these rights.

[1] See, eg, B Bland and S Donnan, 'Indonesia to Terminate More Than 60 Bilateral Investment Treaties' *Financial Times* (London, 26 March 2014).

[2] See, eg, B van der Zee, 'Legal Weapon that Gives Corporations the Edge on Governments' *The Guardian* (London, 4 November 2011).

The remainder of this chapter is structured in three sections. The first section examines the relationship between development, trade and international investment stressing the liberal understanding of the ability to achieve wealth gains through comparative advantage. This underlies much recent thinking regarding development and the use of trade and international investment to enhance the wellbeing of developing countries. However, any market response to a problem presupposes security of property rights.

The second section examines security of property rights within the context of the international investment protection regime. I argue that much of this regime is devoted to securing property rights for potential foreign investors. This allows a better calculation of risk in assessing investment opportunities, which thus facilitates foreign investment. As this foreign investment can relate to infrastructure projects which have a direct bearing on the human rights to water and health of the host country's citizens, this risk alleviation is significant. It can make a difference whether the investment (and hence essential service) is provided; and, if so, for what price.

The third section of this chapter is a case study of the *Suez/Vivendi* investment dispute[3] regarding the development of the water and sewer system for Buenos Aires. This project provided expanded access to potable water and sanitation facilities for that city's residents. However, due to subsequent austerity measures imposed by the Argentinian government, the project collapsed, leading to claims of human rights violations. I argue that this is a mistaken interpretation of events. It was not the privatisation of water facilities, the influence of foreign investors, nor the investment protection regime which led to this collapse. Indeed these elements worked as intended. Rather it was Argentina's own actions which adversely affected its own citizens' ability to access water and sanitary facilities.

I. DEVELOPMENT AND TRADE: MARKETS AND PROPERTY

The standard view of the relationship between trade and development rests in the ability of a trading country to exploit the opportunities available from comparative advantage. Simply put, if a particular country can produce a particular good less expensively than its trading partner can, it makes sense for both countries for the former to produce the good, and the latter to purchase the good using resources obtained from the production of goods (or services) for which the latter has a factor advantage. This is old news. Adam Smith argued this in his 1776 treatise *The Wealth of Nations*.[4] David Ricardo's insight regarding absolute advantage (namely that gains can still

[3] *Suez, Sociedad General de Aguas de Barcelona SA and Vivendi Universal SA v The Argentine Republic* ICSID Case No ARB/03/19, Judgment 30 July 2010.

[4] A Smith, *The Wealth of Nations* (1776) Part IV, Chapter iii, Sections 11–12.

be made even if a country is more efficient at producing everything than its trading partners) cemented this insight.[5] Ricardo's famous two-good example of Portuguese productive superiority over England in the making of both wine and cloth illustrates this point.[6]

This classical vision of trade shows the potential for the benefit of trade in advancing development. A country with comparative advantages in labour uses the fruits of that factor in a production process, and in turn use the savings to purchase (from abroad) goods that it could not produce as efficiently. Similar gains can be made by exploiting other endowments, such as natural resources or environmental conditions. Natural resources can be extracted, (possibly, but not necessarily) refined and traded on the international market. Climatic advantages can underlie the production of agricultural commodities which can then be traded in a similar fashion: Canadian maple syrup and Honduran bananas satisfying northern European tastes are two such examples of the latter.

Foreign investment, particularly direct investment, can underlie and complement the gains through trade. For instance, the location of a factory can utilise local advantages in labour (of appropriate skill level),[7] likewise the development of agricultural plantations or facilities to extract natural resources permits the host country to take advantage of its relevant endowments. In addition to directly benefitting the host country in this manner, there are additional indirect benefits, through skill and technology transfer. Indeed, the Preamble to the World Bank's *Guidelines on the Treatment of Foreign Direct Investment* opens with the following paragraph:

> *Recognizing* that a greater flow of foreign direct investment brings substantial benefits to bear on the world economy and on the economies of developing countries in particular, in terms of improving the long term efficiency of the host country through greater competition, transfer of capital, technology and managerial skills and enhancement of market access and in terms of the expansion of international trade ...[8]

Development, through relying on the gains obtained through trade and the private sector's role in this process, became a cornerstone of the so-called 'Washington Consensus'[9] surrounding the vision of economic development

[5] D Ricardo, *Principles of Political Economy* (1817) Ch VII.

[6] See also A Maneschi, 'International Trade Theory and Comparative Advantage' in J Linarelli (ed), *Research Handbook on Global Justice and International Economic Law* (Cheltenham, Edward Elgar, 2013) 278–88 for a formal exposition of Ricardo's example.

[7] Consider, for instance, skill differentials required in electronics assembly and garment manufacture and the influence which this differential may have in the location of an assembly plant.

[8] World Bank, *Legal Framework for the Treatment of Foreign Investment Volume I Report to the Development Committee and Guidelines on the Treatment of Foreign Direct Investment* (Washington, World Bank Group, 1992) 35.

[9] See J Williamson, 'What Washington Means by Policy Reform' in J Williamson (ed), *Latin American Adjustment: How Much Has Happened?* (Washington, Peterson Institute

and responses to financial and economic stability of countries in economic crisis which became the dominant school of thought in the post-1990s.

This is, of course, a market-based response to development. It is premised on the vision of gains from liberalised trade stemming from the thought of Smith and Ricardo. To the extent that such a market response permits countries to enhance their national income and wealth, particularly as measured by the traditional economic yardsticks (eg Gross National Product (GNP), per capita GNP, Gross National Income, and Value Added as a percentage of GNP) this link between trade and development is obvious. In addition to this wealth-enhancing function of market transaction, there is an additional—normative—feature present in market responses. This normative feature is the value which a market ordering can accurately reflect an individual's choice of how they wish to conduct their life

A liberal society recognises individual rights and is predicated on the need and desirability to protect and advance these rights[10] and to provide those living in such a society with dignity and the freedom that they need to order their lives. It is in this context of liberalism that talk of human rights makes sense. A market-based system of distribution permits this individually directed ordering of one's life. Indeed, in his discussion of the nature of a just state, the American philosopher John Rawls comments on the normative advantages of the market:

> A further and more significant advantage of the market system is that, given the requisite background institutions, it is consistent with equal liberties and fair equality of opportunity. Citizens have a free choice of careers and occupations. There is no reason at all for the forced and central direction of labor ... There is no necessity for comprehensive direct planning. Individual households and firms are free to make their decisions independently, subject to the general conditions of the economy.[11]

Yet market freedoms are just one set of those rights which are hallmarks of a liberal society.

There is a reasonably well-recognised set of core values inherent in liberal societies, which also operate to enhance a country's developmental progress. This position has been influentially advocated by Amartya Sen:

> [I]n the context of the narrower views of development in terms of GNP growth or industrialization, it is often asked whether certain political or social freedoms,

for International Economics, 1990). On the history of this, see J Williamson, 'From Reform Agenda to Damaged Brand Name' (2003) 40 *Finance and Development* 10.

[10] Liberalism is not to be confused with libertarianism. The latter as a political ideology places strong emphasis on individual freedom, faith in unregulated markets, limited government and international isolationism. The former shares a similar view regarding freedom, but may be more amenable to market regulation, and may take different positions regarding the latter two tenets.

[11] J Rawls, *A Theory of Justice* revised edn (Cambridge MA, Harvard University Press, 1999) 240–41.

> such as the liberty of political participation and dissent, or opportunities to receive basic education, are or are not 'conductive to development.' ... As it happens, these freedoms and rights are *also* very effective in contributing to economic progress ... But while the causal relation is indeed significant, the vindication of freedoms and rights provided by this causal linkage is over and above the directly constructive role of these freedoms in development.[12]

Sen's argument is persuasive and has influenced, for instance, the United Nations Development Program in its strategy.[13]

As remarked earlier, this market-based, trade facilitated, means of development can be furthered through direct investment in a host state. In a simple case, a factory can be located to take advantage of savings in labour costs. This in turn provides a needed economic benefit for the host state. But development needs are also satisfied through foreign development of the host country's infrastructure and a significant amount of investment in the least developed countries is of this sort.

From the perspective of the host country, encouraging such infrastructure development from abroad is a very rational decision. The needed infrastructure facilitates trade and the benefits of trade: roads, sea- and airports facilitate the movement of goods. Further, infrastructure which improves the basic health and welfare conditions of the host country's citizens can increase their standard of living and health (thereby enhancing life expectancy, a measure of development)[14] but also further support and advance the citizens' human rights to inter alia health. By 'importing' the infrastructure in this way, the host country can benefit from the established expertise available elsewhere: the wheel need not be reinvented and this sort of private provision of services may also bring with it efficiencies in their supply to the host country's citizens.[15]

Yet in spite of these advantages, the private supply by foreign commercial entities of such infrastructure is often to navigate between Scylla and Charybdis. There is a need to provide such services at a price to ensure an

[12] A Sen, *Development as Freedom* (Oxford, Oxford University Press, 1999) 5.

[13] See eg The United Nations Development Program, *The Human Development Report 2005: International Cooperation at a Crossroad—Aid, Trade Security in an Unequal World* (New York, UNDP, 2005) vii.

[14] See, eg the UN Development Program's Human Development Index which uses life expectancy at birth as part of its measure of a country's development.

[15] See Williamson's comments ('What Washington Means' (n 9)): 'However, the main rationale for privatization is the belief that private industry is managed more efficiently than state enterprises, because of the more direct incentives faced by a manager who either has a direct personal stake in the profits of an enterprise or else is accountable to those who do. At the very least, the threat of bankruptcy places a floor under the inefficiency of private enterprises, whereas many state enterprises seem to have unlimited access to subsidies'. See also R Pritchard, 'Privatisation and Private Provision of Infrastructure' in R Pritchard (ed), *Economic Development, Foreign Investment and the Law* (London, Kluwer Law and International Bar Association, 1996) 76–92.

adequate return for the project's investors. But there is an equally compelling demand to recognise that the very provision of such services can affect the fundamental interests of those receiving the services. This is strikingly so when the infrastructure underlies public health interests of, say, water and sanitation facilities. It is no surprise that not only are disputes regarding this sort of infrastructure a frequent source of arbitration,[16] but they are also the sorts most likely to raise human rights concerns.[17] When the provision of, say, clean water by a private entity becomes unaffordable, criticism of this means of supply can be veiled in terms of a human rights violation. To the extent that the supplier of this necessity is seen as a large foreign company, the rhetorical force of such claims of a rights violation is magnified.

However, notwithstanding concerns which such investment might raise there are beneficial consequences to trade and inward investment in advancing a development agenda. However, this trade agenda is fundamentally market-based, as a result of which these benefits can only be assured within this context. Underlying a market context is the need for a system of property rights. A well-running market presupposes the existence of secure, well defined, and enforceable property rights. Williamson, in his outline of the Washington Consensus remarks:

> In the United States property rights are so well entrenched that their fundamental importance for the satisfactory operation of the capitalist system is easily overlooked. I suspect, however, that when Washington brings itself to think about the subject, there is general acceptance that property rights do indeed matter. There is also a general perception that property rights are highly insecure in Latin America ...[18]

As insecure property rights will add an element of risk to any transaction, for a market to function well, security of property rights is essential. This is particularly so the greater the timeframe of the investment. The risk over time resulting from the insecurity of property rights borne by a purchaser of goods for export is significantly less than the risk which an owner of a factory or an infrastructure facility with a lifetime (and amortised cost) of many decades has. Indeed, in the former case the contractual regime surrounding the sale of goods can be structured in a manner to shift a significant amount of this risk from the purchaser.[19] This is not necessarily the case with investments that are by their nature immobile, hence other means of mitigating risk are needed.

[16] See the *Suez/Vivendi* case study in s III, below.

[17] See the Amicus Curiae Submission in *Suez/Vivendi* (n 45) below.

[18] Williamson, 'What Washington Means' (n 9).

[19] CIF (cost, insurance and freight) contracts for sales of goods accompanied by related requirements in the corresponding letter of credit can remove most of the insecurity of property rights in the exporting country.

II. INVESTMENT, OWNERSHIP AND PROTECTION OF PROPERTY

A. Investment and Risk

It is trite to note that private investments are made so that their owners receive an appropriate return[20] on capital, and this is the case whether the investment is made in the owner's jurisdiction or abroad. In describing the desired return on capital, I have intentionally described it using the nicely vague adjective 'appropriate.' This ambiguity captures the lack of consensus regarding the scope of corporate social responsibility beyond the maximisation of profit for the owners.

Milton Friedman famously argued that (corporate) business have no social responsibilities beyond obtaining the maximum return for their owners (shareholders). He further argued if management assumes such a duty on behalf of the corporation, this represents both an illegitimate substitution of management's social preferences on the owners and an imposition of a tax on the owners to subsidise management's choices.[21] While Friedman's minimalism regarding corporate social responsibility may be a viewpoint held only by a small minority, his position represents a starting point for any discussion about the set of social responsibilities appropriate to be imposed on or assumed by a corporate entity.

It is not the purpose of this chapter to engage in a discussion of the appropriate content of the set of corporate social responsibilities. We only need to make the following observations: at minimum the goal of the entity is to achieve some return (or profit) for its owners. The adequacy of this return is ultimately a matter for the owners to decide. If dissatisfied with such a return (or the means by which the return is obtained), shareholders can theoretically advocate a change in corporate policy, or more realistically 'vote with their feet' and sell their holdings. 'Appropriate' is thus suitably vague. It neutrally describes the varying extension of sets of social responsibilities without prescribing their content, and permits their evaluation to be conducted by the owners (shareholders) themselves. This adjective also implies (correctly) that it is the ownership itself which is to determine the scope of

[20] 'Return' is used in the economist's sense of the risk-weighted payment which the owner received for the use of their money during the course of the investment: the greater the risk, the higher the return. If the efficient market hypothesis is correct, this risk-weighted return is in equilibrium. Were super-normal returns available in certain market sectors, this would attract investment opportunities from other sources of capital, which would then force down prices (and hence returns) to the market equilibrium. Return is to be contrasted with the accountant's conception of 'profit,' that being the difference between income and expenses. The latter concept does not account for risk; hence a more profitable enterprise is possibly characterised by its operation in a riskier environment.

[21] M Friedman, 'The Social Responsibility of Business is to Increase its Profits' *The New York Times Magazine* (New York, 13 September 1970).

the set of duties deemed to be socially responsible. Ownership may wish to eschew certain productive practices for, say, environmental concerns, adopt 'industry leading' labour practices to advance a human rights agenda or advance other goals to fulfil a given agenda.

In some instances there may be a compelling business case to promote these socially responsible practices: different production methods can serve to distinguish one set of products from another putting them into a different product market appealing to different consumer preferences.[22] There may be reasons that ownership may wish to make sacrifices regarding the return on investment—this could include an enhanced psychic return as a result of the chosen production methods. Nevertheless, the significance is that the shareholders will be seeking some form of return on investment, whether this return is exclusively a monetary return, or a combination of monetary and psychic gains. If the return is inadequate, the investment will either not be made, or if originally made, will be mitigated through sale of shareholdings.

The point of the preceding is to indicate the trite proposition that any investment is made with an eye towards a return. This return includes a monetary benefit, which may be accompanied by other, possibly psychic, benefits. Any monetary return will be risk-related. This is best explained in the accountant's sense: the greater the risk, the higher the profit.[23] This trite proposition has one significant consequence: the riskier (or more costly) it is to produce a product, the more expensive the product will be.

This conclusion follows as a matter of elementary microeconomic theory. In a competitive market, goods or services will be priced at the marginal cost of their production. In addition to the more visible inputs into a good, such as raw materials and labour, there is the cost of capital which, as noted, is risk-dependent. As with every input, the more expensive the cost of capital is, the greater the cost and hence the price of the good. It thus follows that products manufactured in an environment in which there is less risk to capital can, all other things being equal, be manufactured at less cost. This savings in cost—in a competitive market—will in turn be passed on to consumers in the form of lower prices (as the goods will be sold at a price which is identical to their cost of production).

B. Investment Regimes as a Means of Risk Reduction

Public international law is hostile to the idea of protection of shareholdings. This is among the conclusions which can be drawn from the *Barcelona*

[22] Consider, for instance, organic products which are in a different product market from their non-organic counterparts.

[23] To the economist, the return will be equalised for risk: See n 20 above.

Traction Case.[24] There, the court recognised the legal personality of the corporation, and held that while there may in some circumstances be a justification for piercing the corporate veil,[25] that case was not one of them. Indeed, the International Court of Justice held:

> The Court considers that the adoption of the theory of diplomatic protection of shareholders as such, by opening the door to competing diplomatic claims, could create an atmosphere of confusion and insecurity in international economic relations. The danger would be all the greater inasmuch as the shares of companies whose activity is international are widely scattered and frequently change hands.[26]

In international law, the protection of foreign shareholders is a matter for those shareholders' own state, which is a matter of purely domestic concern.[27]

Perhaps the most sceptical of the views regarding the protection of foreign investors (in the form of shareholders) can be found in two remarks in Judge Padilla Nervo's separate opinion in *Barcelona Traction*, where he remarks:

> Investors who go abroad in search of profits take a risk and go there for better or for worse, not only for better. They should respect the institutions and abide by the national laws of the country where they chose to go.[28]

And:

> If the defence of the national wealth could be the legal foundation of the State's own right to diplomatic or judicial intervention [on behalf of its citizens who are shareholders of undertakings with investments abroad], the rules concerning the treatment of foreigners would be, in fact, substituted by vague and undefined concepts regarding non-existing duties of the territorial State to guarantee against loss, the investment, by a person, of money which the national State could, arbitrarily, claim was originally part of its national wealth when the investor sent his money abroad.[29]

Barcelona Traction is not the only case in which the ICJ considered the ability of shareholders (of a nationality different from the host state) to receive diplomatic protection under customary international law.[30]

Since the 1970s, perhaps at least in part due to the doctrine of *Barcelona Traction*, states and investors have devised other means to fill this lacuna in international law. Bi- and multilateral treaties and contracts between states and investors are now the primary means of governing the relationship of

24 *Barcelona Traction, Light and Power Company, Limited, Judgment*, ICJ Reports 1970, 3.
25 ibid, paras 56–58.
26 ibid, para 96.
27 See ibid, para 97.
28 ibid, 250.
29 ibid, 265.
30 See *Guinea v Democratic Republic of Congo, Judgment*, ICJ Reports 2007, 582.

investors to host state.[31] Indeed, there has been a veritable explosion of bi- and multilateral treaties which have as their object the protection of investments abroad. One text notes:

> Since 1959, when the first BIT [bilateral investment treaty] was negotiated between Pakistan and the federal Republic of Germany, the number of IIAs [international investment agreements] increased steadily until 1990, when the rate of increase jumped. With under 400 BITs in force by the beginning of 1990, by 1995, the number was over 1000, and by 2000 there were over 1800. Today, with over 6000 IIAs, the peak of negotiations might have been reached, but the end is not foreseeable.[32]

This wave of investment treaties has been a market response to the desire of (if not need for) host countries to attract foreign investment on mutually beneficial terms.

Foreign investment is long-term, involves high sunk costs (for the investor) and high transaction costs (for both parties) and is conducted in an environment of shifting risk, and potentially long term political uncertainty. Schefer describes this market, and the responses:

> The structure of foreign investment is characterised by a long-term relationship between a private person and a government in which the negotiating power of the parties shifts between the negotiating stage and the project implementation stage. For the government the relationship means that it must attract the private party to put money, time, and effort into the relationship with its country. As money, time, and effort are scarce resources, the private party will normally have to choose a single country with which to have this relationship. Thus the would-be host has to market its location.
>
> For the investor, the long term nature of the relationship means that it must spend money immediately ... with the hope of making a profit in the future. This entails a risk that something will occur between the putting in of financial resources and the getting back of financial profits. The profit-making potential of the factory or production facilities, however, is not just contingent on the normal risks of business ... but also on the official or unofficial actions of the government that is the host of the investment. Such governmental actions often were not, or even cannot be, foreseen at the time the investor made its decision to invest.[33]

IIAs (international investment agreements) thus serve as a means by which potential host states can attract investment, by providing assurances to potential investors that particular risks can be mitigated.

Such mitigation is typically provided in the form of guarantees towards the protection of investment form expropriation and is often accompanied

[31] See R Dolzer and C Schreuer, *Principles of International Investment Law* 2nd edn (Oxford, Oxford University Press, 2012) 57.

[32] KN Schefer, *International Investment Law: Text, Cases and Materials* (Oxford, Hart Publishing, 2013) 1.

[33] ibid, 2–3.

by a treaty-based or a contractual stabilisation clause, which crystallises the host country's regulatory regime affecting the investment at the time of the investment.[34] While the early generations of such treaties did not directly protect shareholding, arbitral tribunals were soon to hold that the concept of 'investment' included, by necessary implication of the term, shareholdings. Indeed, in an oft-quoted passage from *Alex Genin v Estonia*[35] the Tribunal held:

> The term 'investment' as defined in Article I(a)(ii) of the BIT clearly embraces the investment of Claimants in EIB. The transaction at issue in the present case, namely the Claimants' ownership interest in EIB, is an investment in 'shares of stock or other interests in a company' that was 'owned or controlled, directly or indirectly' by Claimants.[36]

Other cases have extended this point. In *CMS v Argentina*, the Tribunal rejected Argentina's argument that protection was due only to majority shareholders' interests. It held that state practice has changed the older view, by including minority and non-controlling shareholdings within the scope of protected investments.[37] Indeed, subsequent practice in the negotiation of such investment treaties is to explicitly incorporate protection for shareholders in these terms.

The US's 2012 Model BIT (bilateral investment treaty) is illustrative of this: 'investment' is defined to include 'shares, stock, and other forms of equity participation in an enterprise.'[38] Under the model treaty, investors—hence shareholders—are guaranteed national treatment, most favoured nation treatment, and treatment in accord with customary international law.[39] Similar definitions of investors to cover shareholders are found in other BITs.[40]

The utility of protecting shareholders in the 'market for international investment' is evident. As the ICJ noted in *Barcelona Traction*, shareholdings are diverse, internationalised and frequently change hands. Protecting shareholders permits the easy flow of capital among potential (individual)

[34] See Dolzer and Schreuer (n 31) 81–82: 'It is not surprising that investors have sought to negotiate stabilization clauses in particular with those states whose political and legal regime has in the past been subject to frequent changes or volatility. Governments of such states may have reason to agree to such clauses because they wish to attract foreign investment and because stability serves to facilitate this goal. For the host country, a stabilization clause may be more attractive than a treaty, which requires lengthy international negotiations and ratification processes'. (footnote omitted)

[35] *Alex Genin v Estonia*, Award 25 June 2001, 6 ICSID Reports 241.

[36] ibid, para 324.

[37] *CMS v Argentina*, Decision on Jurisdiction, 3 August 2004, (2005) 138 ILM 788 at paras 47–48, Tribunal's footnotes omitted.

[38] US Model BIT 2012, Art 1 (b).

[39] ibid, Arts 3–5.

[40] See, eg German Model BIT 2008, and Canada Model BIT 2004.

investors, thereby minimising the costs of capital.[41] Shareholders are protected when their country of nationality has ratified an investment treaty with the host country. Additionally, to attractively market itself to foreign investors, risk imposed on minority shareholders will need to be mitigated. Further, a larger-scale investment may occur in the form of a joint venture with enterprises from the host country, and the project as a whole operated through a legal entity incorporated in the host nation.[42] As a consequence of this incorporation in the host country, the joint venture would be unable to avail itself of the protection of any IIA, however, its shareholders may. Likewise, the joint venture may be a consortium of investors, none of whom have a majority of shareholding: The possibility of divergent interests over the long term would justify protection of minority shareholders to reduce their risk, making investment in the host country a more attractive option.

Protecting shareholders through these treaty provisions is just another way of stating that the host country is making itself more attractive to inward investment by attempting to reduce the climate of risk facing foreign investment. The economic consequences of this reduction of risk for investment are immediately apparent. First, by providing this protection to shareholders, shareholdings in companies engaged in these foreign-oriented activities are less risky, thus it is less costly to raise capital. Second, and of importance to the host country, as the cost of capital is an input into the (cost of) the good or service produced, the less expensive this capital is to raise, the less expensive the good will be. This is particularly significant when the intended good or service produced by the foreign investment will be marketed in the host country itself.

Similar economic consequences follow from stabilisation clauses. By crystallising the regulatory regime at a known point in time a potential investor can be insulated from the risk of volatile shifts in regulation. In a political environment which may have been historically hostile, the possibility of such risk may make investment prohibitively expensive. If the product is in turn destined for host nation consumption, the result is that it may be more expensive than otherwise need be, or simply too expensive to market. If the investment involves infrastructure which relates to more essential public needs (eg water and sewer provision), the concerns are of a different order than mere frustrated consumption of a non-essential good.

[41] Difficulty in selling (hence mitigating) an investment acts to increase the cost of the investment. In terms of a shareholding, it would have the effect of making it more expensive to raise capital.

[42] As was done in *Suez/Vivendi*, see s III, below.

III. A PROPERTY—HUMAN RIGHTS CONFLICT? A CASE STUDY

The *Suez and Vivendi v Argentina*[43] case arose in the climate of the economic and political instability (and even civil unrest)[44] of South America in the 1980s and 90s. In this case foreign entities received water and sewer concessions. This was a response to chronic under-investment in such infrastructure, which resulted in poor to non-existent services. As this matter involved access to potable water and sanitation facilities, the ensuing disputes had human rights implications, in response to which NGOs (non-governmental organisations) sought participation through the use of Amicus Curiae submissions. Of significance, the parties agreed that the Tribunal could receive the brief.[45]

The purpose of this chapter is not to diminish or denigrate the right of potable water or effective sanitation. These are most certainly essential human needs. Argentina was correct in its assessment that they needed to ensure that such services were supplied to their citizens. Given the state of the existing infrastructure and that there were no credible domestic suppliers of such services,[46] the Argentinian government was further correct in its need to go abroad to find an appropriate provider. While, as it turned out, the provision of these services in this case may not have been as ideally desired, as this case study will show, the reason for this does not rest with the international investment regime, but rather with the host countries' conduct and unwillingness to respect the rights of their citizens.

The case involved the provision of drinking water to and wastewater management of Buenos Aires. The Tribunal describes the background thus:

> Prior to the granting of the concession in this case, the provision of water and sewage services in Argentina had been the responsibility of State-owned and managed entities. From 1912 until 1980, *Obras Sanitarias de la Nación* (OSN), a corporation owned by the federal government, provided water and sewage services throughout most of the territory of Argentina. In 1980, the government of Argentina decentralized water and sewage services, transferring this function to provincial authorities, with the exception of the City of Buenos Aires and certain surrounding municipalities, which remained the responsibility of OSN.
>
> During the 1980s, the Argentine economy and particularly the country's public enterprises suffered severe problems. The country experienced extremely high

43 Above (n 3).

44 ibid, para 257.

45 See *Suez/Vivendi* (n 3) para 18, Amicus Curiae Brief of Centro de Estudios Legales y Sociales (CELS), Asociación Civil por la Igualdad y la Justicia (ACIJ), Consumidores Libres Cooperativa Ltda. de Provisión de Servicios de Acción Comunitaria, Unión de Usuarios y Consumidores, Center for International Environmental Law (CIEL), dated 4 April 2007.

46 ibid, para 18.

> inflation, steep budgetary and fiscal deficits, a serious lack of investment capital, and no less than four currency crises, each resulting in a currency devaluation of over 90%. Its public enterprises, such as OSN, also ran large deficits, suffered from under-investment in their plants and services, and in general were not managed efficiently. With respect to OSN, the result of this situation was deterioration in the quality and quantity of water and sewage services provided to the public and the inability to expand the service to all inhabitants of the area, a situation that raised concern in the public and the press with respect to the health and safety of the population.[47]

In 1990 the federal government sought to privatise the provision of water and sewage supply, and to seek the assistance of foreign, private-sector parties.[48] In 1992, the claimants successfully bid for the concession for the Buenos Aires water and sewer system. The primary reason the claimants were chosen was that 'they proposed to charge the lowest tariff among all the other bidders'.[49]

The concession, for a 30 year period, was awarded in 1993.[50] This was done through a corporate vehicle of an Argentinian company (AASA) some of whose shares were held by the claimants.[51] Due to the state of the existing infrastructure, AASA had to make substantial investments to expand and upgrade the system. By 2001, approximately US$1.7 billion had been invested into the concession.[52] Recognising the long-term nature of the concession, and Argentina's antecedent political instability, the Concession Contract included a provision requiring the parties 'to establish and maintain a fluid relationship that facilitates the performance of this Concession Contract'.[53]

The investment appeared to pay off for the citizens of Buenos Aires. The Tribunal noted:

> Evidence offered by the Claimants and not challenged by the Respondent indicates that between 1993 when AASA assumed the Concession, and 2005 when the Concession was near its end the population with access to drinking water increased from 5,559,270 persons to 7,859,000 persons (an increase of 41.37%) and the population with access to sewage services increased from 4,532,856 persons to 5,989,000 persons (an increase of 32.12%). Moreover during that same period the production of drinking water increased from 3,398,000 cubic meters a day to 4,700,000 cubic meters a day (an increase of 33%), the sewage treatment capacity increased from 27,305,000 cubic meters a day to 80,334,603 cubic meters a day (an increase of 194.20%), and the water network expanded

[47] *Suez/Vivendi*, ibid paras 27–28.
[48] ibid, para 30.
[49] ibid, para 33.
[50] ibid, para 34.
[51] ibid, para 33.
[52] ibid, para 35.
[53] ibid, Concession Contract Art 5.7, quoted ibid, para 103.

from 11,913 kilometers to 16,459 kilometers (an increase of 38.16%). It would therefore seem that as a result of the Concession the Respondent achieved at least some of the goals that it had sought in undertaking the privatization of the water and waste water treatment systems of Buenos Aires.[54]

However, by 2000 Argentina was to face severe financial and economic difficulties which had a direct impact on its citizens.[55] Among the consequences of the financial crisis were austerity programmes, the devaluation of the peso and taxes on bank accounts. To soften the effect of such measures on the public, the Argentinian Ministry of Economy issued a decree freezing the tariffs of industries regulated by them, including AASA.[56]

For AASA, the consequences of these measures resulted in a decrease in collections, the tax on bank accounts and the devaluation of the peso increased ASSA's costs.[57] Indeed in February 2003, its costs increased 63 per cent, without an offsetting increase in revenue.[58] All of this contributed to the worsening of AASA's bond rating, raising its costs of funding. Additionally, in July 2003, AASA 'was required to provide water and sewage services to areas that were not originally within its concession'.[59] In spite of repeated requests by ASSA to renegotiate the concession (including the tariff level) and intermittent discussions over time, no resolution was achieved.[60] AASA's shareholders requested termination in September 2005, the Argentinian Government refused this request three months later, only to open up an investigation on 17 March 2006 which resulted in the Government terminating the concession four days later.[61]

In attempting to justify its conduct, Argentina raised several defences focusing on how the severity of the economic crisis constrained the options open to it, particularly given its responsibilities to safeguard its citizens' access to water and sanitary facilities. In suggesting that its actions did not fall below the 'fair and equitable' standard required under the relevant BITs, the Government mounted a two-pronged defence. First, it asserted that it acted in a reasonable, fair and non-discriminatory manner in light of the economic circumstances which it faced, taking only legitimate action

54 ibid, para 36.

55 These are outlined by the Tribunal, ibid, paras 41–49.

56 ibid, para 47.

57 'A particular source of increased costs and therefore losses was the fact that by virtue of the loans it had secured from multilateral lending agencies it was required to make loan service payments in United States Dollars, the costs of which in Argentine pesos had tripled'. ibid, para 50.

58 ibid.

59 ibid, para 49.

60 It is worth noting that during the period between 1993 and 2001, ie before the financial crisis, AASA and the Government successfully negotiated two significant adjustments to the concession—which included changes to the tariffs—to reflect increased investments and costs, see ibid, paras 35–40.

61 ibid, paras 50–56.

within the police powers of a sovereign State.[62] It further argued that given its economic history, it was foreseeable that it would take measures which would affect investment to continue these sorts of public services.[63] As the Tribunal was to rightly find, neither of these arguments should carry much weight.

The context of the parties' negotiation of the Concession was significant. The Tribunal noted:

> The Concession Contract and the legal framework of the Concession described above clearly meet the conditions proposed in the cases just referred to. They set down the conditions offered by Argentina at the time that Claimants made their investment; they were not established unilaterally but by the agreement between Argentina and the Claimants; and they existed and were enforceable by law. Like any rational investor, the Claimants attached great importance to the tariff regime stipulated in the Concession Contract and the regulatory framework. Indeed, their ability to make a profit was crucially dependent on it. The importance of the tariff regime was underscored even before the bidding took place, as shown inter alia by the redrafting ... to take into account changes in financial costs and a legal modification of the exchange rate parity provided by the Convertibility Law ... In view of the central role that the Concession Contract and legal framework placed in establishing the Concession and the care and attention that Argentina devoted to the creation of that framework, the Claimants' expectations that Argentina would respect the Concession Contract throughout the thirty-year life of the Concession was legitimate, reasonable, and justified. It was in reliance on that legal framework that the Claimants invested substantial funds in Argentina.[64]

Rejecting Argentina's claim that given its previous history of instability, the claimants should have expected that country to act in the way it did, the Tribunal observed that much of Argentina's actions towards potential investors were designed to reassure investors of the safety of their investment.[65] The Tribunal's analysis was as it should be.

The claimants make a calculated decision to enter into a long-term arrangement. The return which they could obtain on their investment was determinative of their decision to invest. This decision would be based on projections of matters which would affect the Concession's revenue (particularly the tariffs) and expenses. As any change in revenue or expenses would have a bearing on the viability of the investment, renegotiation of the terms of the concession over its lifetime is a foregone conclusion. The parties' agreement to renegotiate in good faith[66] and Argentina's conduct in the 1990s to reassure potential

62 ibid, para 202, quoting from para 892 of the Respondent's Counter Memorial.

63 ibid, para 203.

64 ibid, para 231.

65 ibid, para 234: 'Indeed, one can say without exaggeration that Argentina's various actions toward foreign investors in the 1990s were intended to overcome its negative economic history in the minds of the international financial and business community'.

66 See text accompanying n 53 above.

foreign investors of the security of investing in Argentina were obvious influences in the decision not just to bid, but also in regard to the terms of the bid. This enabled the claimants to offer the lowest tariff among the bidders, which resulted in the Government's award of the concession.

This on-going obligation to negotiate was a key to the success of the endeavour. This endeavour, it must be recalled, had as it purposes not just the generation of an income stream to the concessionaires, but also the provision of water to the residents and businesses of Buenos Aires. Meaningful participation in this dialogue of negotiation by the Government would protect the interests of its citizens.

The Tribunal recognised this point. Strongly rebuking Argentina's conduct, it noted that Argentina could have been more flexible in its response to the claimants. Such flexibility could consist in relieving AASA from some of its commitments, or permitted cross subsidisation of tariffs to ensure less wealthy customers could afford the services. Indeed, 'Argentina might have taken measures to assure that its own governmental organizations paid their legitimate debts to AASA. All of these options were suggested to the Argentine authorities and all were rejected'.[67] Rather than abandoning its citizens, had the Argentinian Government engaged in a discussion process which, at minimum, may have had the effect of providing a temporary remedy for the financial problems suffered by AASA, the citizens of Buenos Aires may have had access to needed water and been provided with appropriate sanitary facilities.

Notably there was a dissent among the Tribunal members. Although all members of the Tribunal felt that Argentina's conduct violated the standards expected of it by both international law and under the terms of its agreement with the investors, the dissent was merely in regards to how Argentina violated its obligations. Two members held that crux of the violation involved a frustration of the claimants' reasonable expectations,[68] the dissent held that Argentina failed to exercise due diligence in its treatment of the investment.[69] Nevertheless, even the dissent recognised that the although the re-negotiation process did not violate Argentina's obligations, the Government's continued freeze of the tariffs during the period of negotiation, when AASA's financial difficulties were known, violated the obligation of fair and equitable treatment.[70]

[67] *Suez/Vivendi* (n 3) para 235.
[68] ibid, para 288.
[69] ibid, and dissent paras 43–50.
[70] ibid, dissent para 50: 'What, to my way of thinking, has no satisfactory explanation is that while that prolonged negotiation process was being extended tariffs were kept frozen without arbitrating even a temporary remedy for the well-known financial difficulties that AASA was undergoing, as was requested by the latter repeatedly and insistently. That fact constitutes, without doubt, a violation of the obligation of fair and equitable treatment of the Claimants' investment'.

The lesson from this case study is significant. The citizens of Buenos Aires required an upgrade to their water and sewer facilities. As local expertise and resources were not credibly available, this project was put out for tender internationally. Given the nature of the project and the amount of infrastructure investment required it was clear from the start that the investment's timeframe would be a matter of decades. Any investor embarking on such a project would require assurance of predictability of revenue and costs and reassurances of the general stability of the climate for investment. The claimants received this, and relying on these assurances, made their successful bid.

This bid provided the services at the lowest tariff of any competing bids. The needed improvements to infrastructure were made, and over a 12 year period, access to drinking water and sewage services increased by over 41 and 32 per cent respectively. Until the Government in response to a financial crisis imposed fiscal measures, there is no evidence to suggest that these services were unaffordable. The population was provided the services it needed, and to the extent that these services enhanced the access to water and vital public health facilities, these basic needs (if not human rights) were advanced. The impact of the government's response to the crisis was the imposition of fiscal measures which raised AASA's costs without providing them the correlative ability to raise revenue.

It would thus be somewhat disingenuous to place the blame for the post-crisis failure on either the investment regime or the claimants. The international legal regime provided sufficient guarantees of stability to induce the investment which induced the provision of needed services. As a result, the population of Buenos Aires was far better off. Indeed, it may be reasonably suggested that without the guarantees provided by the BITs the needed infrastructure improvements and subsequent delivery of water and sanitation services would never have been made, or—if made at all—would have been made under different terms than they were. While one can only speculate on what these different terms would be, however, it would be safe to suggest that they would include some combination of lower infrastructure investment and a higher tariff rate. The immediate consequence of this is fewer people would have benefited from the project.

Similarly, to place the entirety of the blame on the claimants is also unwarranted. These undertakings bid for the concession based upon assurances provided by the government. The claimants relied on these assurances to cost their bid, which provided the lowest tariff. The claimants would thus have viewed the return from the investment as adequate. There is no evidence that the claimants entered into this venture for altruistic reasons, or that the Argentinian government sought the claimants' assistance for charitable purposes. This was a simple business proposition, motivated by an expectation of mutual benefit which underlies all commercial transactions.

Further, the privatisation per se of water supply is also not an appropriate target for condemnation. It is noteworthy that the Amicus Curiae brief makes the following observations:

> According to the ESCR Committee, when water services 'are operated or controlled by third parties, States parties must prevent them from compromising equal, affordable, and physical access to sufficient, safe and acceptable water.'
>
> The UN Special Rapporteur on Housing stated: 'While human rights law does not prevent the provision of services—including water, education, electricity and sanitation—through private companies, States have the responsibility to ensure that such privatization does not infringe on the human rights of the population.' Also the Special Rapporteur on Water has identified as '[a] particular concern … the phenomenon of companies' raising prices when the local currency is devalued. Any concession contracts should specify that the risk of devaluation shall not be borne by the poorest consumers.[71]

Unfortunately, the Brief next makes the following leap of reasoning: 'In this sense, if Argentina had not frozen the tariffs, water would have become unaffordable for millions of people in the province of Buenos Aires. In light of the human rights treaties in force in Argentina, this three-fold increase in the price of water would have constituted a breach of Argentina's international human rights obligations'.[72]

The consensus appealed to by the amici does not rule out the private provision of essential services such as water. Indeed, the experiences of countries such as the UK have shown that a private sector model is a viable means of providing such a service. Rather the consensus shows that the obligation on the state is to ensure that the privatisation does not infringe the human rights of the population. This is nothing more than a specific application of a principle that the state has a human rights obligation to ensure the provision of these services, by whatever means chosen. This further entails that measures which are a consequence of any sort of economic or fiscal restructuring are done in a manner so that their effects on the ability of the poorest to obtain these services is mitigated. All of this is almost certainly uncontroversial.

However, the subsequent leap in reasoning is highly contentious. The missing premise that justifies the conclusion is that Argentina had no alternative but to freeze the tariffs. This is demonstrably false, as the Tribunal noted in its reasoning. There were multiple options open to the government, from permitting the tariffs to be raised and incorporating a means of cross-subsidisation among the users to mitigate the effects on the poorer consumers, a reduction of any demands beyond those specified in the contract for enhanced provision of services, to even ensuring that its agencies

[71] Amicus Curiae Brief (n 45), 12, references omitted.
[72] ibid, 13.

paid AASA's invoices on time. All of these options are within the context of the two parties cooperating and working together in good faith to ensure that these fundamental needs are provided.

Privatisation, whether by domestic or international concerns, is not the problem with the supply of water and appropriate sanitation facilities. A careful analysis of the *Suez/Vivendi* case indicates the difficulty in the supply rested with the conduct of the parties after the crisis developed. The Tribunal put the blame for the breakdown in the parties' relationship on the shoulders of the Argentinian government. For our purposes, the assignment of blame is irrelevant; rather our lesson shows the need for sensitivity by all parties to the agreement to ensure the goal of the agreement is achieved: The service is delivered in a manner which ensures a reasonable return for the investor. Long-term contracts will require renegotiation as times change. Parties entering such contracts are aware of this. The lesson is that the delivery of essential services requires the parties to take these responsibilities to renegotiate seriously and in good faith.

IV. CONCLUSION

This chapter has shown that human rights are a two-edged sword in concerns of development. Property rights, as a human right, are essential for any market based relationship, and hence any market based solution which may alleviate poverty and/or promote basic human rights, including rights to water and sanitary facilities. Development needs may require that such infrastructure be provided using capital and knowhow which can only be found outside of the host country. Foreign investment must be obtained.

Yet, the companies investing in (or providing) such capital or services do so on behalf of their shareholders. While there may be a set of corporate social responsibilities beyond maximising the return on investment for shareholders, all companies have both a moral and legal obligation to keep their shareholders' interests in mind when conducting their affairs. Shareholders demand risk-weighted return on their investment: the greater the risk, the greater must be the return. Additionally, if an investment is above the shareholders' risk threshold, the investment will not be made.

Regulatory crystallisation reduces risk. Investors are put on notice at the outset of their investment not of only the scope of the legal regime which will affect their investment, but they are also assured that no changes will be made to this regime. This eliminates the risk of regulatory uncertainty. This uncertainty, if priced into the investment, may either make the provision of the service more expensive (and thus less affordable to citizens of the host state); or, if the risk were too great, the service would not be provided.

Property rights thus not only underlie the justification for this sort of investment, but also serve to ensure that appropriate investment is made in the host state in the first place, to guarantee the provision of services access to which is a basic human right. The making of such an investment in turn ensures that the citizens of host countries have access to the services or economic benefits resulting from the foreign investment. Yet to the extent that these benefits enhance the host country's citizens' wellbeing, they are predicated on the protection of the investors' property rights. Contrary to much critical discourse, recognition and protection of the property rights of investors thus enables investment to be made, enhancing economic opportunities for host state citizens and thereby furthering their own economic and human rights.

Wholesale condemnation of the international investment protection regime on the basis that by focusing on protecting the investor's property interests it leads to wholesale human rights violations, is thus unmerited. This is the very lesson which our analysis of *Suez/Vivendi* has taught us. Indeed it is by this very focus on the right to property that this investment protection regime can ensure that essential services and development enhancing investment are provided, thus furthering the human rights interests of the citizens of the host countries. Human rights and property rights should not be seen as somehow in opposition – rather the latter should be seen as a means of enhancing the former.

9

The Reach of Human Rights

DAVE COWAN AND SALLY WHEELER

IN THIS CHAPTER, our concerns are with the ways in which the international community seeks to *responsibilise* transnational corporations and other business enterprises not just by encouraging them to accept human rights norms and values but also by suggesting that they promulgate the same to other commercial actors such as those with which they trade or to whom they lend money. We offer a critique of UN principles-based initiatives (such as the UN Global Compact and UN supported process based initiatives,[1] like the UN Principles for Responsible Investment (UNPRI) and the Guiding Principles on Human Rights), which have close affinities with the critique of corporate social responsibility. That is, although there are external drivers that push corporate actors towards the adoption of such policies,[2] their adoption is part and parcel of the drive for greater profits through establishing a 'business case', while being used to underlie the socio-moral concerns of corporations—without any recognition that these are two really quite different things.

That said, we go further by drawing on a particular case study to develop a more micro-critique. When one takes a sector, like UK housing, issues are presented that become problematic for the free flow of capital and the fiduciary duties of company directors or trustees (of pension funds, for example). The conflict between profit-making and human rights can be problematic, particularly when there is clarity in the former objective but obscurity as regards the latter.

In considering UK housing, we look closely at three recent moments: the purchase of low rent property in London by an international investor, institutional investment in social housing and the private finance initiative in social housing. These moments clearly point to this micro problem as between

[1] This follows the typology of corporate responsibility initiatives proposed in D Gilbert, A Rasche and S Waddock, 'Accountability in a Global Economy: the Emergence of International Accountability Standards' (2011) 21 *Business Ethics Quarterly* 23.

[2] D Vogel, 'Private Global Business Regulation' (2008) 11 *The Annual Review of Political Science* 261; and T Bartley and C Child, 'Shaming the Corporation: The Social Production of Targets and the Anti-Sweatshop Movement' (2014) 79 *American Sociological Review* 653.

profit and rights. We could have chosen any other infrastructure project across the world, but our position is that the UK provides an interesting test-bed for such global principles because it is a country where 'rights have been brought home'—our argument might be put that, while rights have been brought home, they appear to have been stopped in the Arrivals Lounge and in Parliament.[3] It is also the case that we have selected housing as opposed to other infrastructure projects because, despite the UK's well-defined welfare state, housing has always been regarded as its 'wobbly pillar'.[4]

Our analysis is in four sections. In the first section, we outline the relevant UN principles that form the focus of this chapter. Our argument is that the UN Guiding Principles on Business and Human Rights are written and adopted with productive industries in mind—extraction and garment industries for example—rather than the seemingly clean hands world of finance. The references the Principles contain to mechanisms such as 'the courts of public opinion' which will assess a corporation's 'social license to operate' would seem to suggest that an end product and a consumer audience for that product are required.[5] However the effects of finance capital on the human rights of individuals are likely to be as egregious as those of productive capital even though empirically speaking this remains under-observed.[6] The very mobility of finance capital allows it to move quickly and decisively in search of investment and return.[7] Individuals and practices that offer weak investment opportunities and risky returns on capital are excluded or included only on payment of a premium.[8]

We then move on to discuss the globalisation of capital, drawing out two points: first, the state remains an important and sometimes neglected element in globalisation narratives, and, second, that finance capital operates on a different circuitry to productive capital within these networks. Richard Falk's observation that the interests of capital drive globalisation over the interests of most people is pertinent for our purposes.[9] Our analysis then

[3] Home Office, *Rights Brought Home: The Human Rights Bill*, Cm3782 (London, Home Office, 1987); Human Rights Act 1998.

[4] P Malpass, 'The Wobbly Pillar? Housing and the British Postwar Welfare State' (2003) 32 *Journal of Social Policy* 589.

[5] *Protect, Respect and Remedy: A Framework for Business and Human Rights* UN Doc A/HRC/8/5 (7 April 2008) para 54, www.business-humanrights.org/SpecialRepPortal/Home/ReportstoUNHumanRightsCouncil/2008.

[6] M Dowell-Jones, 'Financial Institutions and Human Rights' (2013) 13 *Human Rights Law Review* 423.

[7] S Dierckx, 'After the Crisis and Beyond the New Constitutionalism? The Case of the Free Movement of Capital' (2013) 10 *Globalizations* 803.

[8] S French and A Leyshon, 'Dead Pledges: Mortgaging Time and Space' in K Knorr Cetina and A Preda (eds), *The Oxford Handbook of the Sociology of Finance* (Oxford, Oxford University Press, 2012) 357.

[9] R Falk, 'The Making of Global Citizenship' in J Brecher, J Childs and J Cutler (eds), *Global Visions* (Boston, South End Press, 1993) 39; see our case study below at n 91 and the text which follows.

shifts to the neo-liberal state and how shifts in the political economy have dramatically opened up new roles for finance capital, particularly after the global financial crisis of 2008 (GFC). In this section, we examine the existing critique of the enfolding of finance capital and the state provided by Michael Likosky. Likosky's work predated the UN initiatives we are examining, and our question is the extent to which those initiatives impact on his narrative.

Our case study is in the final section. A potential tension for finance capital, as our case study explains, is that its commitment is a long term one—long in the sense of 20 to 30 years—whereas many previous investment decisions have been about taking profit in the short term and diversifying risk across a large portfolio—with short term being defined as quarterly performance assessment of asset managers.[10] There are various risks to capital involved, principally from changing regulatory regimes, reputational issues, and other externalities, including the financial capacity and housing needs of existing and new occupiers. Ultimately, the question is whether the court of public opinion has any real purchase as a regulatory and/or adjudicatory tool in the context set out by the case study.

I. UN PRINCIPLES

By the UN Global Compact, which draws on various international treaties, corporations are asked 'to embrace, support and enact, within their sphere of influence, a set of core values in the areas of human rights, labour standards, the environment and anti-corruption'.[11] By joining, corporations commit themselves to aligning their operations to 10 principles concerned with human rights, environmental concerns and anti-corruption activities. Aligned with the Global Compact is the investor-led United Nations Principles of Responsible Investment (UNPRI), which recognises investors' fiduciary duties in relation to environmental, social and corporate governance (ESG). The UNPRI involves signatory asset owners and their investment managers committing to incorporate ESG into their investment choices, to engage investee companies on these issues and to promote these issues within the investment community. The choice of particular ESG factors focused on rests with the subscribing investor.

For its part, the Guiding Principles on Business and Human Rights[12] are addressed to all corporations, irrespective of size or whether they operate

[10] The OECD estimated that the period investors held assets for had declined steadily over a 20 year period from an average of over five years to just two months, OECD (2011) *Promoting Longer-Term Investment by Institutional Investors: Selected Issues and Policies* OECD Discussion Note for EUROFI High Level Seminar at p6 www.oecd.org/dataoecd/37/42/48281131.pdf.

[11] www.unglobalcompact.org/AbouttheGC/TheTENPrinciples/.

[12] UN, *Guiding Principles on Business and Human Rights: Implementing the United Nations 'Protect, Respect, and Remedy' Framework* (New York and Geneva, UN, 2011).

transnationally.[13] Corporations are asked to respect human rights by avoiding infringing the rights of others and addressing adverse impacts with which they might be associated. They do not create new rights but, rather, highlight certain points. So, for example, although states are not responsible for human rights abuses of private actors, they are in breach 'where such abuse can be attributed to them, or where they fail to take appropriate steps to prevent, investigate, punish and redress private actors' abuse'. States should be proactive in setting out best practice for corporations. Corporations themselves are required to avoid human rights abuses, and prevent or mitigate abuses even those to which they have not contributed.[14] Corporations are enjoined to the promotion of human rights through high level statements of principle, due diligence practices and external communications.[15] States and corporations must also provide appropriate remedies and grievance redress.[16] The Guiding Principles tread an uneasy line between, on the one hand, influence-based responsibility and, on the other hand, impact-based responsibility, which illustrates the difficulties inherent in a system seeking to respond to the complex mechanics of global production.[17] The Framework is silent on whose social expectations will be used as the measure but it does indicate particular sites of judgement—investors, employees, communities, consumers, civil society.

On one level asking corporations and investors to respect, and then report on, that respect for minimum standards of ESG and human rights is a very different requirement and policy focus from voluntarily adopting corporate social responsibility (CSR) policies of their choice for strategic reasons.[18] But that is a discussion about the philosophical basis of the two practices.[19] When considered at a different level, from the position of the relationship between the state, individual citizen and the corporate/investor sector around regulation and ideas of *responsibilisation* for socio-economic conditions, what is occurring looks very similar. These instruments all represent the triumph of networked governance which shifts traditional functions of

[13] However, such factors are relevant in assessing the extent to which corporations can have responsibility for such abuses: Principle 14.

[14] Principle 13.

[15] Principles 16 and 17.

[16] Pt III.

[17] See S Wheeler, 'Global Production, CSR and Human Rights: the Courts of Public Opinion and the Social License to Operate' (2015, forthcoming) *The International Journal of Human Rights*, **DOI:**10.1080/13642987.2015.1016712.

[18] R McCorquodale, 'Corporate Social Responsibility and International Human Rights Law' (2009) 87 *Journal of Business Ethics* 391.

[19] F Wettstein, 'CSR and the Debate on Business and Human Rights: Bridging the Great Divide' (2012) 22 *Business Ethics Quarterly* 739 and T Campbell, 'A Human Rights Approach to Developing Voluntary Codes of Conduct for Multinational Corporations' (2006) 16 *Business Ethics Quarterly* 255.

the state to other actors, in this instance the corporate/investment sector.[20] Ruggie, the progenitor of the Guiding Principles, makes exactly this point in relation to those principles. He refers to them as an exercise in polycentric governance as opposed to the rights-based hierarchy that is preferred by rights activists. For him, the Guiding Principles are drawing on social compliance mechanisms in circumstances where human rights abuses by corporations are risks to the legitimacy of their business model.[21]

These UN initiatives do expose corporate conduct to scrutiny by NGOs (non-governmental organizations), consumers and others[22] and this point should not be lost when expounding the view that they represent the ceding of the governance of issues of public importance that should be met by public authority and action to private interests. None of these initiatives are constitutionally concerned with verification or improving compliance with human rights standards. They are facilitative mechanisms that seek to improve the transparency of corporate activity for the individual citizen and civil society more broadly. They add credence and support to corporations' claims of responsibility and normalise their activities while pushing the possibility of protecting and enforcing human rights claims onto individuals or activists.[23]

The initiatives are all politically feasible but minimal interventions—they make palatable the anti-democratic activities of the corporate/investor sectors in the context of the neo-liberal political rationality about the limited role of the state.[24] The retreat of the state from various social and welfare functions and the pushing of those functions into the market place has been accompanied by what Shamir characterises as a 'moralisation' and 'responsibilisation' of the market[25] and its corporate participants. That has resulted

[20] V Haufler, 'Globalisation and Industry Self-regulation' in M Kahler and DA Lake (eds), *Governance in a Global Economy: Political Authority in Transition* (Princeton NJ, Princeton University Press, 2003) 226–52.

[21] J Ruggie, 'Global Governance and "New Governance Theory": Lessons from Business and Human Rights' (2014) 20 *Global Governance* 5. There is a powerful critique of Ruggie's approach made by T Melish, 'Putting "Human Rights" Back into the UN Guiding Principles on Business and Human Rights: Shifting Frames and Embedding Participation Rights' in C Rodriguez-Garavito (ed), *Business and Human Rights: Beyond the Beginning* (Netherlands, Brill, 2015 forthcoming).

[22] A major debate around the adoption of voluntary standards is the extent to which they represent real policy adoption and operational change in the corporate sector. See T Melish and E Meidinger, 'Protect, Respect, Remedy *and Participate*: "New Governance" Lessons for the Ruggie Framework' in R Mares (ed), *The UN Guiding Principles on Business and Human Rights* (Leiden, Martinus Nijhoff, 2012) 311f.

[23] S Soederberg, 'Taming Corporations or Buttressing Market-Led Development? A Critical Assessment of the Global Compact' (2007) 4 *Globalizations* 500.

[24] L Baccaro and V Mele, 'For the Lack of Anything Better? International Organisations and Global Corporate Codes' (2011) 89 *Public Administration* 451.

[25] R Shamir, 'The Age of Responsibilisation: on Market-Embedded Morality' (2008) 37 *Economy and Society* 1.

in a neo-liberal imagination that 'grounds and refines socio-moral concerns from *within* the instrumental rationality of capitalist markets'.[26] His argument is that through privatisation, franchising, outsourcing, deregulating and general withdrawal from frontline engagement, governments have become facilitators of private authority that now enjoys a similar status to state authority without the support of coercive sanctions. Private sector authority is augmented by codes of conduct, principles and standards that are not laws supported by the power of the state[27] but instead are the result of processes such as 'multi-stakeholder dialogue' or negotiated as 'best practice solutions'. Industry based codes governing employment practices[28] and environmental standards[29] are useful examples of this. The various UN interventions described above form part and parcel of making such corporate/investor interventions palatable and subject to the semblance of control and accountability. We now turn to discuss the more general question of the complexities in the global flow of finance to address whether the structures that protect human rights are sufficiently flexible to operate outside binary divides.

II. GLOBALISATIONS AND FINANCE

For our purposes here, the defining feature of globalisation has been its recalibration of scale. Economic power is not centred in particular geographical locations and it does not operate on particular binary divides such as global and local, north and south and private and public. Instead there are conglomerations of all of these interests operating across different scales in a fluid process.[30]

Descriptive accounts of the evidence of globalisation have become more sophisticated over time. It is no longer the case that we are surprised by, or indeed satisfied by, observations that the scale of corporate power has moved beyond the physical borders of states, or that global convergence is occurring around capital structures and a compression of distance.[31]

[26] ibid, 3.

[27] D Kinderman, '"Free Us Up So We Can Be Responsible!" The Co-Evolution of Corporate Social Responsibility and Neo-liberalism in the UK, 1977–2010' (2012) 10 *Socio-Economic Review* 29.

[28] D Hoang and B Jones, 'Why do Corporate Codes of Conduct Fail? Women Workers and Clothing Supply Chains in Vietnam' (2012) 12 *Global Social Policy* 67.

[29] O Boiral and Y Gendron, 'Sustainable Development and Certification Practices: Lessons Learned and Prospects' (2011) 20 *Business Strategy and the Environment* 331.

[30] P Dicken, P Kelly, K Olds and H Yeung, 'Chains and Networks, Territories and Scales: Towards a Relational Framework for Analysing the Global Economy' (2001) 1 *Global Networks* 89.

[31] See eg, T Friedman, *The World Is Flat: A Brief History of the Twenty-First Century* (New York, Farrar, Straus and Giroux, 2005).

For example, global business in terms of foreign direct investment (FDI) flows is now much more complex and granular than early accounts suggested. Capital in the form of FDI no longer flows inexorably from the global North to the global South.[32] Therefore, it is no longer sufficient to talk just in terms of the regulatory relationship between host state and inward investing multinational corporation (MNC), or about home state responsibility for outward moving capital. Various other external factors have to be added to the mix—the role of bilateral investment treaties[33] and free trade agreements, the rise of global value chains[34] and the emergence of new national economies as well as MNCs based within them.

What emerges from this are complex networks of power and policy that intertwine market (corporate) concerns with the foreign and domestic policies of states. These networks, in Hardt and Negri's typically politically trenchant terms, 'directly structure and articulate territories and populations … transnational corporations directly distribute labor power over various markets, functionally allocate resources, and organise hierarchically the various sectors of world production'.[35] At the corporate level, this means that a variety of different scales come into play as the corporate actor seeks to manage a number of local contexts alongside an international commercial operation.[36]

The position of the individual citizen is that they are more exposed to the market and corporate power. Their exposure comes not just from the consequences of global production resulting in changed employment patterns for example;[37] but also from the rise of finance capital as a distinct form of capital. By this, we mean not only the emergence of specialised financial markets and centres which have grown in power as innovative mathematical algorithms and legal design of financial instruments has produced ever

[32] A Rugman, 'How Global are TNCs from Emerging Markets' in K Sauvant (ed), *The Rise of Transnational Corporations from Emerging Markets* (Cheltenham, Edward Elgar, 2008) 86.

[33] Bilateral investment treaties have the potential to influence if not restrict a state from developing its domestic policy, see M Sheffer, 'Bilateral Investment Treaties: A Friend or Foe to Human Rights' (2011) 39 *Denver Journal of International Law and Policy* 483. These treaties often include land tenure and use reform under the descriptor of 'official development assistance' which potentially leads to mass evictions and consequent hardships, see R Künnemann and S Suárez, 'International Human Rights and Governing Land Grabbing: A View from Global Civil Society' (2013) 10 *Globalizations* 123. For a rather different pro-investment and pro-treaty stance see G Foster, 'Investors, States and Stakeholders: Power Asymmetries in International Investment and the Stabilising Potential of Investment Treaties' (2013) 17 *Lewis & Clark Law Review* 361.

[34] G Gereffi, 'Global Value Chains in a Post-Washington Consensus World' (2014) 21 *Review of International Political Economy* 9.

[35] M Hardt and A Negri, *Empire* (Cambridge MA, Harvard University Press, 2001) 31.

[36] K Meyer, R Mudambi and R Narula, 'Multinational Enterprises and Local Contexts: The Opportunities and Challenges of Multiple Embeddedness' (2011) 48 *Journal of Management Studies* 235.

[37] M Hart-Landsberg, *Capitalist Globalization* (New York, Monthly Review Press, 2013) 13–69.

more complicated financial products,[38] aided and abetted by technological advances which allow large volume high speed trading;[39] but also the pursuit of finance led growth and profit in non-financial firms.[40] Enron remains the most notorious example of this probably by reason of its spectacular failure.[41] The activities of capital markets have, as Saskia Sassen describes them, become a 'distinct institutional order to be differentiated from other ... systems such as global trade'.[42]

Finance capital operates on a different circuitry to productive capital within these networks.[43] Their topology is fundamentally different—finance capital has no visible physical locus (we distinguish financial trading centres such as New York, Chicago and London which have their own individual and distinct spatial logics)[44] and so is scaled against the nation state and the individual citizen as more mobile and inherently more flexible than both;[45] classically Harvey's spatial fix.[46] At the level of nation state, finance capital's emergence as the dominant influence over leading economies, such as the UK and US,[47] means that it is subject to continuous efforts to regulate its presence within national borders to particular standards of conformity;[48] and globally to ensure that economic shocks and economic volatility are

[38] An account of the development of algebraic finance innovation, its drivers and its consequences is provided by E Engelen, I Ertürk, J Froud et al, *After the Great Complacence* (Oxford, Oxford University Press, 2011) 36–65. A documentary play written by David Hare, *The Power of Yes* (Faber and Faber, London) based on interviews Hare had done with banking and investment firm executives and regulators, and premiered at the National Theatre in December 2009, famously hinted that the packaging of risk within algebraic finance produced financial innovation that few individuals understood.

[39] L Snider, 'Interrogating the Algorithm: Debt, Derivatives and the Social Reconstruction of Stock Market Trading' (2014) 40 *Critical Sociology* 747.

[40] G Krippner, 'The Financialisation of the American Economy' (2005) 3 *Socio-Economic Review* 173.

[41] As Bratton explains Enron transformed itself from a company the main business of which was managing energy infrastructure such as gas and water pipelines into a company that traded energy futures; W Bratton, 'Enron and the Dark Side of Shareholder Value' (2002) 76 *Tulane Law Review* 1275. See also L Fox, *Enron: The Rise and Fall* (New York, Wiley, 2002).

[42] S Sassen, 'Global Finance and its Institutional Spaces' in Knorr Cetina and Preda (n 8) 18.

[43] J Comaroff and J Comaroff, 'Alien-Nation: Zombies, Immigrants and Millennial Capitalism' (2002) 101 *South Atlantic Quarterly* 779, 784.

[44] C Zaloom, 'Trading on Numbers' in M Fisher and G Downey (eds), *Frontiers of Capital: Ethnographic Reflections in the New Economy* (Durham, Duke University Press, 2006) 58.

[45] S French, A Leyshon and T Wainwright, 'Financialising Space, Spacing Financialisation' (2011) 35 *Progress in Human Geography* 798.

[46] D Harvey, 'Globalisation and the "Spatial Fix"' (2001) 2 *Geographische Revue* 23.

[47] A Nesvetailova, 'Innovations, Fragility and Complexity: Understanding the Power of Finance' (2014) 49 *Government and Opposition* 542.

[48] At national level in the UK, for example, this has involved in the recent past the creation of various agencies and regulatory bodies all of which are charged with either safe guarding Government investment in supported banks and other financial institutions; UK Financial Investments Ltd—or insuring economic stability and effective regulation of finance capital without triggering capital flight; the Financial Conduct Authority, the Prudential Regulation Authority and the Bank of England's Financial Policy Committee.

kept to a minimum.[49] Finance capital has a particular aura of inviolability and mysteriousness about how it works that means that it is subject to lower levels of scrutiny in regulatory and popular debates about human rights standards. The regulatory debates around human rights standards and how traction for them can be garnered with actors other than nation states tend to focus on productive capital and its consequences for the individual rather than finance capital.

III. THE NEO-LIBERAL STATE[50]

States have increasingly declined to insulate the individual from the consequences of corporate power and its networks.[51] From the latter part of the twentieth century onwards, states opened up new service markets for corporations by privatising state monopolies under the blueprint offered by proponents of the new public management school.[52] Agencification and contracting out, both delivery mechanisms lauded by proponents of the less government and more governance approach to service delivery,[53] created a further disambiguity between the state and individuals. In the post GFC era, there has been a further wave of stripping back state functions in favour of private sector provision, not necessarily for any particular ideological reason but to serve the interests of austerity in cutting public debt in the face of rising social support bills in a global recession and the cost to states of bank bailouts.[54] The absence of driving political ideology at this juncture does not, of course, mean that there is not an evolving politics around the relationship of state, private capital and citizen. The state, as we demonstrate below, is ceding some of its key protective obligations to the private sector in the realm of economic and social rights, particularly in the areas of housing, health, food and education.

[49] G Chesini and E Giaretta, 'Regulating High-Frequency Trading: An Examination of European, US and Australian Equity Market Structures' in T Lindblom, S Sjögren and M Willesson (eds), *Financial Systems, Markets and Institutional Changes* (Basingstoke, Palgrave Macmillan, 2014) 152 provide an analysis of national and supra national efforts to regulate a global practice.

[50] Accounts of this, like globalisation, abound but a particularly well balanced and broad cross-sector (as in impact on family life, work life, welfare systems and concepts of public life) narrative is provided by J Clarke, 'Dissolving the Public Realm: The Logics and Limits of Neoliberalism' (2004) 33 *Journal of Social Policy* 27. J Peck and A Tickell, 'Neoliberalising Space' (2002) 34 *Antipode* 380 provide the best account of neoliberalism in process and policy terms.

[51] R Goldman and S Papson, *Landscapes of Capital* (Cambridge, Polity, 2011) 64–104.

[52] A Crane, D Matten and J Moon, *Corporations and Citizenship* (Cambridge, Cambridge University Press, 2008) 64f.

[53] R Rhodes, *Understanding Governance: Policy Networks, Governance, Reflexivity and Accountability* (Buckingham, Open University Press, 1997).

[54] M Kitson, R Martin and P Tyler, 'The Geographies of Austerity' (2011) 4 *Cambridge Journal of Regions, Economy and Society* 289.

In addition to agencification and the relinquishment, through privatisation,[55] of state held monopolies in areas like utilities supply and telecommunications, states took the opportunity to rearrange new infrastructure development and existing infrastructure maintenance so as to engage the loan raising capability of the private sector. Known as the Private Finance Initiative in the UK (and as Public Private Partnerships in the rest of the world), these were projects where a private sector actor or consortium undertook to finance, design, build, as well as often operate and maintain a large infrastructure development such as a new hospital or school.[56] The public sector leased back the facility and either paid rent over a period of 25 years or so, or passed the cost on to direct users who paid at the point of use. The finance was procured from banks on a loan basis. These arrangements became popular with numerous national Governments[57] for a variety of reasons.[58] Simultaneously they also incurred the ire of commentators as the promises of shared risk taking and mutual benefit[59] failed to outweigh perceived inappropriate allocations of risk between public and private sectors leading to overstated levels of efficiencies and savings.[60]

Using private finance in this way re-orientates the discourse around infrastructure development. The traditional roles of the state have been to improve and enhance citizens' lives; provide economic stimulus to its national economy; and take responsibility for human rights protections in social and ecological terms before, during and after construction. By contrast, in the discourse of the market, such values and protections are not necessarily given the same weight as profit needs to be generated to produce a contractually agreed return on investment. It is also the case that a state is likely to be prepared to take more risks around design and realisation of a project than private sector investors. The state is likely to be more flexible

[55] Between 1984 and 1990 the UK Government for example placed in the hands of private shareholders the telephone service, the gas industry, airports, the water and electricity industries and the rail service.

[56] International Financial Services London, *PFI in the UK & PPP in Europe* (London, IFSL Research, 2008) report that at the start of the GFC 23.2% of PFI projects by value were in the health sector with the next largest sector being education on 15.5%; and 11.7% in housing, discussed below in the case study at n 91 and the text which follows.

[57] D Grimsey and M Lewis, *Public-Private Partnerships: The Worldwide Revolution in Infrastructure Provision and Project Finance* (Cheltenham, Edward Elgar, 2004).

[58] Public private finance partnerships allow infrastructure development to take place without compromising the level of public sector borrowing (known as the PSBR), reduce pressure on the public sector budget and allegedly provide a better value delivery mechanism.

[59] *HM Treasury, Partnerships for Prosperity: the Private Finance Initiative* (London, Treasury Taskforce Private Finance Policy Team, 1997).

[60] For a comprehensive review of PFI and its position as an emanation both of the state and from the state see J Froud, 'The Private Finance Initiative: Risk, Uncertainty and the State' (2003) 28 *Accounting, Organisations and the State* 567; Y Kwak, Y Chih and C Ibbs, 'Towards a Comprehensive Understanding of Public Private Partnerships for Infrastructure' (2009) 51 *California Management Review* 51 offer a synthesis of research on PPP/PFI that compares the various definitions and tests employed in assessing success and failure.

in its subsequent utilisation of the infrastructure assets it controls; it is not tied to the need to raise a particular amount of revenue and can respond to different policy imperatives.[61] The link between public property at the point of use and private property as a commercial asset generating revenue from that use requires us to think about which actors stand in a relationship of rights recognition and protection in relation to other actors, and how those relationships are formalised.

Seeking an answer to that potentially incommensurable mix, Michael Likosky provides three case studies drawn from state financed, private financed and partnership financed infrastructure developments, analysed through the lens of human rights risk. He sees the articulation of human rights as a risk to project completion,[62] whereas conversely we would see human rights risk as the risk of the project itself to rights bearers in areas like access to food, housing, health and education and the right to non-discrimination.[63]

Likosky's conclusion is that it was not only public accounting issues and neoliberal ideology that drove the withdrawal of the state and the rise of private finance in the wake of that withdrawal but also the success of human rights enforcement against states engaged in infrastructure development. The move to private finance externalises human rights risks onto the most vulnerable. However, as he points out, the state does not retreat entirely from these projects—that would be to suggest a false binary. The state is still present in the form of sovereign wealth fund investment, collaboration in regional development banks and the provision of functions like export credit. But the state is absent from the vehicle that faces the individual citizen most directly, replaced instead by a revenue driven special purpose vehicle (SPV).[64] This provides a further reason why housing is such a good case study—whereas in most infrastructure projects, there are no prior rights bearers just objects (like a road or hospital) and future customers; in housing there are lengthy, complicated political histories and, most significantly, rights-bearing occupiers with which the SPV has to deal.[65]

[61] P O'Neill, 'The Financialisation of Infrastructure: the Role of Categorisation and Property Relations' (2013) 6 *Cambridge Journal of Regions, Economy and Society* 441.

[62] M Likosky, *Law, Infrastructure and Human Rights* (Cambridge, Cambridge University Press, 2006) 46f.

[63] Ö Kahale, 'Project Finance and the Relevant Human Rights' in S Leader and D Ong (eds), *Global Project Finance, Human Rights and Sustainable Development* (Cambridge, Cambridge University Press, 2011) 37.

[64] M Likosky, 'Mitigating Human Rights Risks Under State-Financed and Privatised Infrastructure Projects' (2003) 10 *Indiana Journal of Global Legal Studies* 65.

[65] See generally, S Hodkinson, 'The Private Finance Initiative in English Council Housing Regeneration: A Privatisation Too Far?' (2011) 26 *Housing Studies* 911; S Hodkinson, 'Housing Regeneration and the Private Finance Initiative in England: Unstitching the Neoliberal Straitjacket' (2011) 43 *Antipode* 358.

Likosky was writing in 2003 and in our case study we consider whether any of the initiatives that have emanated from the UN or from the market itself since that time have changed, or have the potential to change, the rescaling of rights protection and the creation of human rights 'risks' that Likosky identified. As discussed above, these initiatives look at the 'responsibility' of private sector actors in relation to human rights observance. The idea of responsibility is standing in as a replacement for the 'obligation' that attaches to states under the Universal Declaration of Human Rights (UDHR).

Just as the GFC put pressure on the ability of states to deliver welfare and social support,[66] it also put pressure on the ability of the private sector globally[67] to participate in public–private partnership infrastructure delivery.[68] A lack of liquidity and loss of confidence in the banking sector ended the possibilities of loan syndication which had an adverse impact on the ability of the private sector to raise loan finance. Debt became both more expensive and less available, requiring at best a banking consortium as opposed to the pre-GFC era when a single funding source would have been available,[69] together with a higher level of equity.[70] In the UK, in 2008, only 34 Private Finance Initiative (PFI) arrangements were agreed, half the level of activity seen in 2007 and the lowest for a decade.[71] In 2006, the OECD (Organisation for Economic Co-operation and Development) forecast that, taking into account development needs, infrastructure spending would account for in excess of 3.5 per cent of the world's GDP (Gross Domestic Product) annually in the years to 2030.[72] The collapse of one of the most popular ways of achieving infrastructure development for states

[66] N Hossain, R Fillaili and G Lubaale, 'Invisible Impacts and Lost Opportunities: Evidence of the Global Recession in Developing Countries' (2010) 18 *Journal Of Poverty and Social Justice* 269 and C Pollitt, 'Cuts and Reforms—Public Services as We Move into a New Era' (2010) 32 *Society and Economy* 17.

[67] D Hall, 'A Crisis for Public-Private Partnerships (PPPs)?' (2009) gala.gre.ac.uk/1709/1/2009-01-crisis-2.pdf and A Boardman and A Vining, 'Assessing the Economic Worth of Public-Private Partnerships' in G Hodge, C Greve and A Boardman (eds), *International Handbook on Public-Private Partnerships* (Cheltenham, Edward Elgar, 2010) 159.

[68] P Burger et al, 'The Effects of the Financial Crisis on Public-Private Partnerships' (2009) IMF Working Paper Washington, www10.iadb.org/intal/intalcdi/PE/2009/03918.pdf.

[69] PWC (Pricewaterhouse Coopers), *Infrastructure Finance—Surviving the Credit Crunch* (London, 2008), www.pwc.com/cz/en/verejna-sprava-zdravotnictvi/infrastructure-finance-surviving-the-credit-crunch.pdf.

[70] Equity in this context is essential risk capital, as it is comprised of shares and shareholders' loans in the company set up to execute the project. If this company fails then this capital is repaid only after the debt finance has been paid out. Pre the GFC equity finance would have been required at a ratio of 90:10 loan capital to equity capital. Changing this gearing renders financing of the project more difficult and less attractive, see NAO, *Financing PFI Projects in the Credit Crisis and the Treasury's Response* (London, 2010), www.nao.org.uk/wp-content/uploads/2010/07/1011287.pdf.

[71] www.ft.com/cms/s/0/3d73dfda-e1ab-11dd-afa0-0000779fd2ac.html?siteedition=uk#axzz3AmeRF1nb.

[72] OECD, *Infrastructure to 2030: Telecom, Water Land, Transport and Electricity* (2006).

has severe knock on consequences for economic growth both in terms of the economic activity that infrastructure construction creates and the opportunities for economic expansion that result from the infrastructure installation itself notwithstanding a view that many of the structures used for public–private partnerships are a politically unpalatable methodology for financing infrastructure.[73]

The global tightening of bank support occurred at a time when the UK Government was also under pressure to review its private finance partnership structures and management practices in the wake of a critical assessment from the National Audit Office[74] and the Treasury Committee.[75] Its response to both of these drivers was to trial a variety of new approaches[76] to attract the £200 billion required from private finance to enable infrastructure development that had been labelled as needed from 2011 to 2015.[77] One of these approaches included seeking the participation of pension funds[78] and insurance companies in their role as institutional investors in an activity in which, in the UK at least,[79] they have not previously participated for the structural reason referred to above—long term lock-in of funds is required and the dominant pattern of investment for these investors previously was short term. FDI from institutional investors and sovereign wealth in UK infrastructure has occurred for some time.[80] John Allen and Michael

[73] A Leyshon and N Thrift, 'The Capitalisation of Almost Everything: The Future of Finance and Capitalism' (2007) 24 *Theory Culture and Society* 97.

[74] National Audit Office, *Lessons from PFI and Other Projects*. April 2011 www.nao.org.uk/report/lessons-from-pfi-and-other-projects/; in relation to housing, the NAO produced an extremely critical report: *PFI in Housing*, 2010.

[75] Treasury Committee, *Private Finance Initiative*, July 2011 publications.parliament.uk/pa/cm201012/cmselect/cmtreasy/1146/1146.pdf.

[76] C Connoly and T Wall, 'The Impact of the Global Financial Crisis on Public-Private Partnerships: A UK Perspective' in C Greve and G Hodge (eds) *Rethinking Public Private Partnerships: Strategies for Turbulent Times* (London, Routledge, 2013) 33 and HM Treasury, *A New Approach to Public Private Partnerships*, December 2012 www.gov.uk/government/uploads/system/uploads/attachment_data/file/205112/pf2_infrastructure_new_approach_to_public_private_parnerships_051212.pdf.

[77] HM Treasury, *National Infrastructure Plan 2011*, www.gov.uk/government/uploads/system/uploads/attachment_data/file/188337/nip_2011.pdf.

[78] In November 2011 the National Association of Pension Funds and the Pension Protection Fund signed a Memorandum of Understanding with the UK Government to create a climate (appropriate credit ratings, guarantees and gilt structure) that would facilitate pension fund investment in infrastructure, see www.gov.uk/government/uploads/system/uploads/attachment_data/file/220996/foi_memorandum_of_understanding.pdf.

[79] OECD, *Pension Funds Investment in Infrastructure: A Survey* (2011) identified Canada, Australia and the US as all securing a 10% or better contribution to infrastructure funding from institutional investors, as opposed to the UK which saw 1–3% from its institutional investors. See also RD Croce, 'Trends in Large Pension Fund Investment in Infrastructure' (2012) *OECD Working Papers on Finance, Insurance and Private Pensions*, No 29, OECD Publishing.

[80] Details of the level of overseas investment, in particular infrastructure projects since 2010, are detailed in HM Treasury's *National Infrastructure Plan* 2013 www.gov.uk/government/uploads/system/uploads/attachment_data/file/263159/national_infrastructure_plan_2013.pdf, 87–88.

Pryke use the story of Thames Water and its complex corporate structure which incorporates holdings owned by Dutch, Canadian, Australian, Spanish and UAE investment funds to illustrate how infrastructure investment by these funds is predicated not on the value of the asset itself, but on the return that the asset offers in terms of a regular and reliable income stream from householders using the water supply to the detriment of their customers.[81] These customers are captured by the commercial enterprise that Thames Water has become in the sense that there is no alternative supply of water that they can use. The state facilitates this capture by legitimating this form of investment structure and delegating regulatory responsibility to an independent entity.

It is the case that institutional investors in the UK already hold and trade shares in listed companies that regularly invest in or participate in infrastructure projects such as power, water and transport sector companies and through asset managers invest in general infrastructure funds. However, in this initiative, they are being targeted as direct investors in what for them is a new asset class. The significance of this at a level above the ability of pension funds to manage a different asset class competently[82] is the interaction it brings with the various mechanisms designed to protect human rights. Standing as shareowners at one remove allows the option of a market-based exit if trustees decide that the ESG risks really do outweigh the gains for fund beneficiaries. Direct investment in the SPV set up to deliver the project and maintain it thereafter is potentially a much more complex management task involving engagement with a variety of non-professional audiences around human rights impact assessments—consumers and NGOs, for example—and monitoring the activities of the SPV rather than requesting asset managers to apply particular screening policies to potential and existing shareholdings or to ensure that the UNPRI are complied with.[83]

The current financing arrangements for infrastructure provide a very effective example of the scales involved in globalisation and the presence of networks of relationships as opposed to binary divides. Infrastructure in its

[81] J Allen and M Pyrke, 'Financialising Household Water: Thames Water, MEIF, and "Ring-Fenced" Politics' (2013) 6 *Cambridge Journal of Regions, Economy and Society* 419.

[82] G Clarke, *Pension Fund Capitalism* (Oxford, Oxford University Press, 2000) explores this issue in ch 9.

[83] There are a number of institutional investors that have a policy of making investment decisions based upon a positive screening in, or a negative screening out of particular corporations or industries based upon their end products or the production methods employed by them. For example the stated investment strategy might exclude corporations that make weapons, alcohol or tobacco products, and include corporations which undertake to behave responsibly in relation to supply chain procurement. Others use a 'best in class' approach therefore permitting themselves to invest in industries which might otherwise be screened out. Some investment brokers have designed particular products for principally the individual retail market that target only screened funds or investee companies.

immediate physical location is intensely local. It is embedded in a community, often providing a key service for that community. It depends on local knowledge for the choice of prime location, but on a wider geographical and more specialised knowledge base for the current and future regulatory and legal landscape, for information about population demographics now and in the future and for information on renewal and reinvestment requirements over the lifetime of the investment.[84] On an expanding scale, it draws down investment on an international basis and increasingly in the UK from nationally-based pension funds. A range of professional groups within this investment class—bankers, fund managers, finance ministry officials, asset managers and pension fund trustees—do the calculations about projected returns on investment.

The presence of UK pension funds adds a further scale and an additional dimension to the network. These pension funds represent in a funded scheme the retirement savings of thousands of individuals, and, in an unfunded scheme,[85] the hopes for a financially sustainable retirement of thousands of individuals whose contributions are being marketised.[86] Some of these individuals might be users of the infrastructure funded by these invested contributions. In an unfunded pension scheme, members might find themselves torn between paying to use a particular facility and worrying about the market value of their pension. Some pension fund members might have particular political views about infrastructure funding and management, take a position on the obligations owed to members of society in human rights terms perhaps, or have concerns about climate change and the environment more generally. These concerns will be the province of the SPV created to manage the infrastructure investment and secure value for the fund and pension fund trustees. The obligation that is primary for pension fund trustees is to make investment decisions that maximise the returns available for fund members. That is what acting as a fiduciary means in this context.

Involvement of the private sector, as Likosky argues, means that the state has less of a central role in citizen's lives. In descriptive terms, there is a shift in modes of governance, which means that the state has become a mere part

[84] M Torrance, 'The Rise of a Global Infrastructure Market through Relational Investing' (2009) 85 *Economic Geography* 75.

[85] A funded scheme is a defined benefit scheme. Employer and employee contribute to the scheme and the employer assumes responsibility of managing a pool of assets within the pension fund on the understanding that an agreed benefit will accrue to an employee reaching retirement age (often in practice, a percentage of either final salary or average salary across the tenure of employment). An unfunded scheme is a defined contribution scheme. Again employee and employer contribute but contribute considerably less as the final benefit paid depends not on a contractually agreed sum ex ante but on the ex post investment returns on contributions.

[86] For an insightful but concise account of the marketisation of pension funds and risks for the individual saver, see K Strauss, 'Financialisation and Gendered Risk in Occupational Pensions' in G Clark, A Dixon and A Monk (eds), *Managing Financial Risks* (Oxford, Oxford University Press, 2009) 258.

of the ring around an individual rather than being at its centre. The state has not shrunk under neo-liberalism; rather it has changed shape. Where there was once provision, now there is a facilitated and regulated market[87] in which individuals have to hope that there are sufficient safeguards for their wellbeing. The call for corporations to recognise and protect human rights from the UN and the broader NGO community is a predictable response that is symptomatic of these changing paradigms of governance. The question is whether the move to this articulation of human rights should be seen in the Polyanian sense of an anti-market[88] and state avoidance[89] response to the huge social and political disruptions that have resulted from the marketisation of not just the economy but of existence itself[90] or whether human rights discourse is not so much a counterweight to neoliberalism but in fact one that gives it strong support and validity. It is this question which we address in our case study.

IV. A CASE STUDY: UK HOUSING

Although this is not the place for a full analysis of UK housing policy,[91] certain key distinguishing features relevant to our themes in this chapter should be highlighted. First, the UK has a significant proportion of households in owner-occupation. It has been the tenure of choice, largely propped up by open-market lending and a benign policy environment, which supports it. Securitisation was not a prominent feature of that market, although the New Labour government sought to encourage it.[92] One result of the GFC has been a decline in the availability of mortgage finance, so that lower income households have had difficulties accessing it. Governments have sought to respond by creating further incentives for ownership, through various initiatives including government-backed mortgages. However, as

[87] J Braithwaite, *Regulatory Capitalism: How it Works, Ideas for Making it Better* (Cheltenham, Edward Elgar, 2008) 24.

[88] J Best, 'From the Top-Down: The New Financial Architecture and the Re-Embedding of Global Finance' (2003) 8 *New Political Economy* 363.

[89] For a review of the extent to which anti-market social movements are state avoidance mechanisms, see B King and N Pearce, 'The Contentiousness of Markets: Politics, Social Movements, and Institutional Change in Markets' (2010) 36 *Annual Review of Sociology* 249.

[90] G Burchell, 'Liberal Government and Techniques of the Self' (1993) 22 *Economy and Society* 267.

[91] See D Cowan, *Housing Law and Policy* (Cambridge, Cambridge University Press, 2011).

[92] 'The key question in relation to securitisation in this country is why it is not happening already': DETR, 'Quality and Choice: A Decent Home for All—Housing Green Paper' (London, DETR/DSS, 2000) para 4.13; T Wainwright, 'Laying the Foundations for a Crisis: Mapping the Historic-Geographical Construction of Residential Mortgage Backed Securitisation in the UK' (2009) 33 *International Journal of Urban and Regional Research* 372.

Ray Forrest and Yosuke Hirayama demonstrate,[93] there has been a shift from home ownership as a social, aspirational asset, to a financialised asset from which more households are excluded, as finance is not available to those on lower incomes. This is one consequence of increased controls on the lending abilities of lenders.[94]

Other tenures, which were seen as feeders for home ownership, have now become more prominent in their own right and form the focal point of this case study. We consider two such tenures, private renting and social housing, which together account for around 30 per cent of UK households. This proportion is growing. Although we refer to the UK, its devolved governments have differing responsibilities for the regulation of housing. However, what has been a common feature has been large-scale legislative reform in the devolved regions and a static legislative base at Westminster. This has left a sense in which, broadly, the devolved regions have increased occupier rights and controls on landlords over the Westminster housing settlement.

A. Private Renting

For the last 30 years, governments have struggled to persuade institutional investors to participate in private renting. Landlords have tended to become such as an accident (such as inheritance) or as a sideline business. Most landlords have owned less than five properties in the sector, and the cottage industry nature of the sector was intensifying even before the GFC as a result of corporate and institutional withdrawal from the sector.[95] That having been said, the sector was growing even before the GFC as a result of a combination of factors, most notably the rise of the small-scale buy-to-let landlord, underpinned by the development of financial products between the landlord associations and lenders.[96] As Forrest and Hirayama put it,

> For those who can … the sensible financial strategy is to own your own home and somebody else's as well. Thus, private landlordism is itself becoming increasingly financialised with new corporate investment and as middle to high income

[93] R Forrest and Y Hirayama, 'The Financialisation of the Social Project: Embedded Liberalism, Neoliberalism and Home Ownership' (2014) 52 *Urban Studies* 233; J Montgomerie and M Budenbender, 'Round the Houses: Homeownership and Failures of Asset-Based Welfare in the United Kingdom' (2015) 20 *New Political Economy* 386.

[94] Financial Services Authority, *Mortgage Market Review: Feedback on CP11/31 and Final Rules* (London, FSA, 2012).

[95] J Rugg and D Rhodes, *The Private Rented Sector: Its Contribution and Potential* (York, Centre for Housing Policy, 2008) 9.

[96] K Scanlon and C Whitehead, *The Profile and Intentions of Buy-to-Let Investors* (London, CML, 2005).

> households seek new ways to generate income flows and pensions. A new breed of private landlords has little interest in property other than as investment vehicles in a situation of low savings rates and volatile stock markets.[97]

One key factor said to underlie the growth of private renting has been the sector deregulation in the Housing Act 1988.[98] This was a watershed moment—from providing security of tenure and rent control or regulation since 1915, the 1988 Act provided limited security of a maximum of six months coupled with the provision of market rents. This has been coupled with a variety of (unsuccessful) schemes to engage institutional investors in the sector,[99] the most recent of which are real estate investment trusts, designed to lever pension funding into the sector (again, unsuccessfully).[100] The Montague review found that 'the strength of the owner-occupier market, the lack of developments of scale, and the challenges to net yields have constrained the range of opportunities available to investors to invest in new schemes'.[101] Although the yield question is significant, there are a number of examples of pension scheme investments. So, for example, the Greater Manchester pension fund, a public sector pension scheme, joined with Manchester local authorities to develop land for private renting; Orbit, a social housing provider, has made a similar investment.[102] As suggested in the previous section, the pension scheme role is ambivalent in the sense that it is unclear whether these types of developments are what are wanted by the scheme beneficiaries. So, for example, the Manchester development represents a further example of demunicipalisation—the new properties are managed by a (social) housing association's private rental management subsidiary.[103] Islington Council is using its pension scheme to build private

[97] Forrest and Hirayama (n 93) 7.

[98] The significance of the 1988 Act is disputed in the literature, but it cannot be denied that the subsequent discourse around the Act has contributed to its success—see Cowan (n 91) ch 3.

[99] A Crook and P Kemp, 'Housing Investment Trusts: A New Structure of Rental Housing Provision?' (2002) 17 *Housing Studies* 741.

[100] C Jones, 'Private Investment in Rented Housing and the Role of REITS' (2007) 7 *European Journal of Housing Policy* 383.

[101] A Montague, *Review of the Barriers to Institutional Investment in Private Rented Homes* (London, DCLG, 2012) para 32; see also House of Commons Communities and Local Government Committee, *Financing of New Housing Supply* 11th Report of Session 2010–12 (2012) HC 1652, para 17. For a critical discussion of the role of policy makers' mistaken assumptions about institutional investment, see H Pawson and V Milligan, 'New Dawn or Chimera? Can Institutional Financing Transform Rental Housing?' (2013) 13 *International Journal of Housing Policy* 335.

[102] P Apps, 'Social Landlord Enters Private Rented Sector' *Inside Housing* (London, 7 November 2014). The CE is reported as saying, 'This is a new step for us but it is certainly one we must take. With the current housing market impacting the tenure requirements of our customers, housing providers need to be smarter and develop their customer offer to meet the needs of the market'. The following section of this chapter on 'social housing' picks up on this comment.

[103] C Stothart, 'Landlord's PRS Subsidiary to Manage Manchester Homes' *Inside Housing* (London, 11 December 2013).

rented properties outside that borough, because otherwise there would be too much investment risk.[104]

However, perhaps the most egregious example of the marketisation and financialisation of the sector is the example of New Era Estate, which comprises 96 flats and 12 shops in Hackney, North London. This estate was sold (for the first time since it was constructed in the 1930s) to a US real estate development firm, Westbrook, which owns and manages property across the world and is funded by numerous pension schemes, including US teachers and public employees. Westbrook initially were partnered by the Benyon Estate, a family trust managed by Peter Benyon MP. After negative publicity, the Benyon Estate pulled out of the purchase.[105] The agent's particulars of sale for the New Era Estate, which by some accounts had been managed largely as a social project by a charitable trust, said that 'Gross current income of £754,098 per annum with the opportunity to substantially increase rents through asset management'.[106] And that is precisely what it is reported Westbrook have done—increase rents from substantially below market rent to market rent.[107] In doing so, it is unlikely that they are breaking the law. The occupiers are likely to have Housing Act 1988 tenancies and, if they cannot afford the rent, they will have to move (like anybody else). The point is that this substantial profit was made possible by the state regulatory intervention in the 1988 Act, which created a benign climate for investment. Although that investment has not been from institutional finance capital, the government and other agencies, which have struggled long and hard through different investment formats to encourage such investors in to the sector, cannot really challenge the fact that Westbrook sought to take advantage of that exhortation. It is fulfilling their desires and needs.

This is not a breach of the occupiers' human rights per se—or, at least, not those contained in the Human Rights Act 1998 or indeed the International Covenant; indeed, the legal rights are all on the side of Westbrook, which has simply made a good investment and is entitled, in the hallowed tomes of property law, to do with it what it will. The commitment to vague ESG principles, even if they are of relevance to this context, can hardly deny the excellent investment—indeed, perhaps Westbrook paid more for the estate because of the riskiness of the investment. It is unclear, of course, what

[104] P Apps, 'Council to Invest £150m from Pension Scheme in Housing' *Inside Housing* (London, 3 December 2014).

[105] C Johnston, 'Tory MP's Family Firm Pulls Out of Hoxton's New Era Estate over Rent Row' *The Guardian* (London, 13 November 2014).

[106] docs.novaloca.com/55664_634635368173071250.pdf.

[107] A Chakraborty, 'The Story of the Millionaire Tory MP and the Tenants Facing Homelessness' *The Guardian* (London, 10 November 2014), 'New Era Estate Scandal: Families at the Mercy of International Speculators' *The Guardian* (London, 19 November 2014).

the pension scheme investors make of Westbrook's actions, but a plausible response is that they should be applauded for the business risk and substantial profits they will make from their investment.

B. Social Housing: Housing Associations[108]

As foreshadowed in the previous section, the state, which was formerly responsible for enabling public housing to be constructed and managed by local government, has largely withdrawn from such large-scale funding (certainly from local authority construction). Indeed, no longer do we talk about 'public' housing but 'social' housing, perhaps in recognition of the fact that the majority of this type of housing provided at below market rents to households in housing need, is provided by housing associations.[109]

Since the mid-1980s, housing association development has been mixed funded. Such developments are pioneers of the public private funding model explained above. This was not, as Likosky might suggest, because the state was seeking to contract out of its human rights obligations. Indeed, nowhere until recently has human rights been discussed, and never in relation to the funding sources. The principal reason for this mixed funding approach was to create more social housing for less public investment. Initially, such private funding was fairly standard loan finance, but, over time, the housing association sector has become big business and loan packages have altered. There is an irony here—the sector was originally chosen as the investment vehicle by the Conservative government because it was local and small scale; the big business element, however, has led to mergers, complex group structures and, as we have seen, diversification of the portfolio across housing sectors.[110]

The diversification of the loan packages can be seen in the fact that just a quarter of private finance to the sector came from standard loan packages in 2012, partly as a result of the GFC. As Hal Pawson, David Milligan and Tony Gilmore suggest, the predominant sources of funding are 'bond issues

[108] The term 'housing association' is used in this chapter because it is well-known and internationally transferable; however, these organisations are now known in England as 'private registered providers of social housing'; and, in other parts of the devolved governments, as 'registered social landlords'.

[109] In England, in 2014, local authorities owned 1.67 million dwellings; housing associations owned 2.67 million: DCLG, *Local Authority Housing Statistics: Year ending March 2014* (London, DCLG, 2014); HCA, *Private Registered Provider Social Housing Stock in England: Statistical Data Return 2013/14* (London, HCA, 2014).

[110] D Mullins and L Craig, *Testing the Climate: Mergers and Alliances in the Housing Association Sector* (Birmingham, National Housing Federation and University of Birmingham, 2005); H Pawson, 'Restructuring England's Social Housing Sector Since 1989: Undermining or Underpinning the Fundamentals of Public Housing?' (2006) 21 *Housing Studies* 767; H Pawson, D Mullins, and T Gilmore, *After Council Housing: Britain's New Social Landlords* (Basingstoke, Palgrave MacMillan, 2010).

involving multiple investors or bilateral deals with insurance companies and pension funds through so-called "private placements"'.[111] Housing associations are now as worried about their business plans and innovation strategies as they are about their social mission. A competitive ethos dominates the sector.[112] Although in a formal sense they are private organisations, they are nevertheless subject to government control through the regulator and the policy passporting power of central government in relation to rent rises.[113] This can cause policy mishaps. Recently, for example, central government has given up on its longstanding policy of rent convergence with the local authority sector, on which business plans had been based, leading to the potential loss of millions and ratings downgrades.[114] So, this is an example of the enfolding of global capital, private organisations and state regulation.

Perhaps the most significant ESG and human rights concerns arise as a result of the potentially increasing eviction rates, declining security of tenure and the association-specific allocations schemes. Finance capital has had major effects on each of these, reducing and removing the social and human rights of occupiers, in terms of rights to a home within the occupiers' means.

As regards eviction rates, housing associations, unlike local authorities, are entitled to evict occupiers on the basis of mandatory grounds of two months' rent arrears. They tend to have increased motivations to exercise their right to possession because their business plans and finance are predicated on a certain proportion of rent collection. It is a paradoxical effect of finance capital levered in to the sector that associations' social mission, and the sustainability of a person's home, can be subjugated to the business plan.

So, some associations have developed increasingly managerial rent collection policies, appointed credit control professionals from outside the sector, and greater attention has been given to requiring occupiers to manage their rent accounts by 'income maximisation officers'.[115] After a period in which actual evictions had declined, it appears that they are now increasing.[116]

Security of tenure has declined because housing associations now usually use 'starter tenancies', which are the same types of tenancy as exist in the private rented sector. However, the key intervention by the Coalition government was the introduction of 'affordable rent', which applies across

[111] Pawson and Milligan (n 101) 338.

[112] T Manzi, 'Cultural Theory and the Dynamics of Organisational Change: The Response of Housing Association in London to the Housing Act 1988' (2006) 24 *Housing, Theory and Society* 251.

[113] Housing and Regeneration Act 2008.

[114] P Apps, 'Landlords Face Losing Millions after Giving Up on Waivers' *Inside Housing* (London, 17 November 2014).

[115] H Pawson et al, *Investigation of Rent Arrears Management Practices in the Housing Association Sector* (London, HCA, 2010).

[116] HCA, *Private Registered Provider Social Housing Stock in England* (London, HCA, 2014).

the social sector. This programme, which formed the basis of the affordable housing plan from 2011–15,[117] essentially required associations to set rents at 80 per cent of market level (far higher than they had previously done) and use fixed term tenancies. It is a programme mirrored across the social sector, and represents a fundamental change of policy. It has coincided with major retrenchment in the welfare budget, including benefit caps, reductions in allowable benefit for under-occupiers and annual reductions in the uplift to benefits.[118] Many poor people are poorer, the effects are disproportionately affecting the most vulnerable poor, and there is less money available to pay the rent; hence rent arrears are rising (and threatening business plans).[119] As Jacobs and Manzi suggest, 'It is evident from even the most cursory reading of government policy documents that the long-term aim of the Coalition government is to reframe public housing as a transitional mode of housing until tenants can exit to the private rental or owner occupied sector, and thereby reconfigure the view of public housing as a residual tenure'.[120] This is a significant shift which clearly impacts on social and human rights, with mandatory eviction thereafter.

As regards allocation schemes—that is, how housing association homes are allocated—what is becoming increasingly evident is the exclusion of large swathes of households. In short, housing need is insufficient to be allocated accommodation; indeed, housing need may itself be a bar, if the association is seeking to allocate housing to people who are less risky—thus, local authority nominees for a housing association tenancy can be rejected by that association for a range of reasons, including housing debt as low as £50.[121] Exclusions from allocations has clear impacts on peoples' social and human rights to a home.

C. Social Housing: Councils and 'Decent Homes'

There has been historic underinvestment in the repair of local authority housing. In 2000, a repair programme to make good this deficiency ('Decent Homes') left authorities with stark choices about how to fund it. Central

[117] HCA, *Affordable Homes Programme 2011 to 2015: Guidance and Allocations* (London, HCA, 2011).

[118] See eg, N Harris, 'Welfare Reform and the Shifting Threshold of Support for Disabled People' (2014) 77 *Modern Law Review* 888.

[119] HCA, *Sector Risk Profile 2014* (London, HCA, 2014) s 3.60–3.65.

[120] K Jacobs and T Manzi, 'Investigating the New Landscapes of Welfare: Housing Policy, Politics and the Emerging Research Agenda' (2014) 31 *Housing, Theory and Society* 213, 219; see also S Hodkinson and G Robbins, 'The Return of Class War Conservatism? Housing under the UK Coalition Government' (2013) 33 *Critical Social Policy* 57, in which it is noted that social housing has become regarded as a privilege for the deserving poor.

[121] See D Cowan et al, 'Risk, Trust and Betrayal: A Social Housing Case Study' (2009) 72 *Modern Law Review* 157.

government offered them three options: Transfer their stock to a housing association; transfer their management to an arm's length organisation (but this option was only available to high performing authorities); or participate in the PFI initiative (which had been running since 1998).[122] Around 50 PFI schemes have been approved (although 15 were subsequently rejected as not providing value for money following a government review after the GFC).

As suggested above, PFI in housing has not been without its problems. There has been the jejune approach of the relevant government department, including the lack of oversight—apparently, just four civil servants were responsible for housing PFI which was a £4.8billion investment.[123] Housing PFI is different from other PFIs because it usually relates to an already existing physical asset, which is in need of demolition or repair and ongoing maintenance. The costs are, therefore, hard to predict at the outset when they are fixed, but there have been delays at various stages which meant that the construction costs escalated. The main beneficiary appears to be the different exchange professionals—accountants, consultants, advisors etc. There are occupiers, who can challenge schemes and who can destroy the financial underpinnings through exercising their right to buy (something which, ironically, central government has further encouraged by reintroducing high discounts). Business plans have been adversely affected by lengthy delays in approvals. It might be thought that one could compare the different elements of the Decent Homes programme, but that is impossible in part because of the 'serious deficiencies' in the regulatory environment, the self-certification of the 'Independent Certifier', who is paid by the SPV. Hodkinson reports concerns about low inspection rates by the certifier and corruption.[124]

Those occupiers, however, have been treated in some cases with less than candour. Since the 1970s, tenant empowerment has been a strong ethic in social housing, one that has been much encouraged by both central and local government.[125] Tenant participation in housing management provides an important focal point of the ESG in the social sector.[126] If the council

[122] For critical discussion, see D Cowan and M McDermont, *Regulating Social Housing: Governing Decline* (London, Routledge, 2006).

[123] National Audit Office, *PFI in Housing* (London, NAO, 2010); Hodkinson, 'The Private Finance Initiative in English Council Housing Regeneration' (n 65) 911, 923.

[124] Hodkinson, ibid 924.

[125] See eg, L Cairncross et al, *Housing Management, Consumers and Citizens* (London, Routledge, 1997).

[126] For discussion in addition to Cairncross et al, ibid, see I Cole and R Furbey, *The Eclipse of Council Housing* (London, Routledge, 1994) ch 8; R Furbey, B Wishart and J Grayson, 'Training for Tenants: "Citizens" and the Enterprise Culture' (1996) 11 *Housing Studies* 251; Communities and Local Government (CLG), *Local Choice, Local Control: Statutory Guidance on Tenant Management for Local Authorities and Local Authority Tenants* (London, CLG, 2008); Communities and Local Government (CLG), *Resident's Choice: Guidance on Tenant Management and Other Options Supported through the Tenant Empowerment Programme* (London, CLG, 2008).

seeks to transfer its housing stock to a housing association, occupiers have a right of veto through a vote. However, no ballot is required for a PFI housing contract, merely consultation, and such consultation is likely to be thin because of the complexity of the process. As Hodkinson puts it,

> PFI's complexity makes it difficult for tenants and other community stakeholders to have meaningful input into a highly technical process driven by project managers and corporate consultants. This could mean weekly meetings of two hours or more for years on end, enormous documents written in jargon, constant battles with local authority officers over the minutes of meetings or unmet demands for information, and the perennial problem of time with officers always aware that delays could create 'affordability gaps'.[127]

When tenants have been entitled to have a ballot, they have voted no but their votes have been by-passed by local authorities.[128]

V. CONCLUSIONS

What our discussion shows is that the implementation of the various international treaties, compacts, agreements and other devices must take place in a complex globalised system in which finance capital, as opposed to productive capital, flows in complex ways. States are seeking and relying on ever-increasing shares of that capital as they withdraw from direct and indirect provision of goods and services. We might say that human rights and ESG are likely to be sacrificed to the fiduciary principle, but our analysis has also shown that it is not quite so simple as this binary suggests. The flexibility in human rights and ESG gives considerable leeway, even if organisations subscribe to these ideals beyond mere lip service. The other interests—pension scheme beneficiaries and others—are assumed and this gives rise to perhaps counter-intuitive investment strategies (such as the Islington Council pension scheme purchasing properties outside its borough).

What our case study provides is a series of examples in which the obscurity of human rights and ESG can be subverted to the profit motive so as to feed the corporate and institutional investment sectors. The original identity of UK social housing as providing low cost accommodation to households in need has been re-envisaged: Exclusions from social housing (whether by means of eviction or ineligibility in the first place) are growing;[129] security

[127] Hodkinson, 'The Private Finance Initiative in English Council Housing Regeneration' (n 65) 927–28.

[128] S Hodkinson, 'From Popular Capitalism to Third Way Modernisation: The Case of Leeds, England' in S Glynn (ed), *Where the Other Half Live: Lower Income Households in a Neoliberal world* (London, Pluto, 2009).

[129] So, for example, some social landlords sought to exclude homeless households from obtaining reasonable preference on their housing lists, a practice declared unlawful recently: *R (Jakimaviciute) v Hammersmith and Fulham LBC* [2014] EWCA Civ 1438.

of tenure is being loosened and rents increased so that there can be greater reliance on institutional investment. Some of these processes have been in train for some time, at least since the 1970s, but have been exacerbated in this century by a combination of New Labour and Coalition governments. Housing 'rights' are far from the epicentre of the current housing policy dynamic. There is no right to a decent home—indeed, decent homes are paradoxically the cause of some of the issues—and certainly no unqualified right to the income to pay for a decent home.

Part Three

Community and Human Rights

10

Communal Property Rights in International Human Rights Instruments: Implications for De Facto Expropriation

TING XU AND WEI GONG*

I. INTRODUCTION: DE FACTO EXPROPRIATION AND THE LIMITS OF EXPROPRIATION LAW

IN THE CONTEXT of globalisation, expropriation has taken on new forms, such as 'land grabs', which depart from our traditional understanding manifested at the domestic level: Expropriation involves the acquisition and transfer of legal title of ownership. This chapter argues that these new forms of 'hidden expropriation'[1] should be regarded as de facto expropriation; as the exercise of power that directly or indirectly contributes both to the deprivation of *access to* land and other natural resources, and to the weakening of *control over* land and other natural resources by people who may just hold nothing but user rights to land and natural resources. Such de facto expropriation adversely affects communal property rights, and therefore locating communal property rights within an international human rights paradigm may help both to establish global standards and norms needed to protect these rights, and to force a rethink of expropriation law.

* Thanks to Jean Allain and Thomas Muinzer for their helpful comments on earlier drafts of the text. All errors remain the author's responsibility. Part of the research is funded by the British Academy International Partnership and Mobility Scheme on 'Diversifying Ownership of Land?' 2014–2017.

[1] See T Xu, 'Hidden Expropriation in Globalisation and Soft Law Protection of Communal Property Rights' in B Hoops, E Marais, L Verstappen, H Mostert and J Sluysmans (eds), *Context, Criteria and Consequences of Expropriation Law* (The Hague, Boom/Eleven Law Publishers; Cape Town, Juta Law Publishers, 2015 forthcoming).

Expropriation usually refers to the taking of property from its owner by the state or an authority for public use or interest.[2] For example, in the UK, expropriation often takes the form of 'compulsory purchase',[3] that is, 'the compulsory purchase of any land under powers conferred by or under any statute'.[4] In the US, expropriation takes the form of 'eminent domain',[5] which is the process through which a government acquires a resource for a public use and pays compensation to private parties.[6] Expropriation, or simply, 'taking', is an exercise of state power of taking private owners' property, either by force, by consent or by a mix of the two.

Expropriation can be divided into two categories: 'Individual' and 'general' expropriation.[7] The former refers to a single action of taking, usually for purposes of constructing public facilities; the latter concerns large-scale taking for general purposes, as is the case with agrarian reforms whereby expropriated property may be transferred to another private individual, or as is also the case with 'nationalisation' whereby expropriated property is transferred to state ownership.[8]

Expropriation in the international context, in particular general expropriation engaging international investment, often involves disputes between foreign investors and capital-importing countries. While it is generally accepted that the expropriating state is obligated to pay compensation for the expropriated property in cases pertaining to individual expropriation, disputes often arise in cases concerning general expropriation, where the expropriating state may deny any obligation to compensate foreign property holders.[9] For example, the Mexican government recognised no duty to compensate when it nationalised oil properties owned by foreign companies

[2] Oxford Online Dictionary, www.oxforddictionaries.com/definition/english/expropriate?q=Expropriation#expropriate__15.

[3] See eg, T Allen, 'Controls over the Use and Abuse of Eminent Domain in England: A Comparative View' in RP Malloy (ed), *Private Property, Community Development, and Eminent Domain* (Aldershot, Ashgate, 2008) 75–100. The origin of compulsory purchase lies in the Town and Country Planning Act (1947). Other pieces of major legislation include the Land Compensation Act (1961), the Compulsory Purchase Act (1965), Town and Country Planning Act (1990), Planning and Compulsory Purchase Act (2004).

[4] The Law Commission, 'Towards a Compulsory Purchase Code: (1) Compensation, An Overview' Consultation Paper (2004), No 165 (Overview) 4.

[5] Eminent domain refers to 'the power of any government body to compel a private owner to sell at a price fixed by a court. When government pays for property it is free of the constraint of the taking issue'. See RH Platt, *Land Use and Society: Geography, Law, and Public Policy* (Washington DC, Island Press, 2004) 278.

[6] Indeed the idea that eminent domain should be coupled with compensation at 'fair market value' has been entrenched in the US constitution: 'Nor shall private property be taken for public use, without just compensation' (the last clause of the Fifth Amendment).

[7] A Rafat, 'Compensation for Expropriated Property in Recent International Law' (1969) 14 *Villanova Law Review* 1, 3.

[8] ibid, 3.

[9] ibid, 3–4.

in 1938;[10] nor did the Soviet Union in similar instances.[11] As a result of these nationalisation ventures, some principles and mechanisms have been developed in international law that seek to strike a balance between the competing interests of foreign investors and host countries. These principles allow that nationalisation may be justified if it meets three standards: It is in the public interest; it is non-discriminatory; and it affords adequate compensation.[12] Beyond these general principles, a large number of Bilateral Investment Treaties (BITs) adopt the standard that a host state is obligated to pay 'prompt, adequate and effective' compensation to foreign investors for expropriated investments.[13] 'Stabilisation clauses' are also included in investment contracts as 'a risk-mitigation tool' to 'protect foreign investments from such sovereign risks as nationalisation, expropriation, or the obsolescence bargain'.[14] The fact that these clauses may 'insulate investors from environmental and social legislation' by the host state has raised many human rights concerns, especially with regard to the negative impact of stabilisation clauses in instances where developing countries occupy the role of host state.[15] In general, international law and international investment law afford protection for foreign investors' property rights in cases where their property is subject to expropriation.

Yet, structural imbalances exist in the international legal system, for 'while international law has gone a long way towards strengthening the protection of foreign investment, it offers little protection to rural people who may be adversely affected by investment flows'.[16] The traditional conception of expropriation is not broad enough to capture new forms of interference with property rights, in particular large-scale land acquisitions that have been negotiated through contracts on behalf of foreign governments or corporations (domestic or transnational) worldwide. In many parts of the developing world, in particular Sub-Saharan Africa, much of the land is state-owned; land users have no titles to the land they cultivate, and their use rights to the land are vulnerable to acquisition by the state.[17] Under such

[10] US Department of State, Office of the Historian, 'Mexican Expropriation of Foreign Oil, 1938', history.state.gov/milestones/1937-1945/mexican-oil.

[11] Rafat (n 7) 4.

[12] ibid, 53.

[13] SH Nikièma, 'Compensation for Expropriation' the International Institute for Sustainable Development, March 2013, www.iisd.org/pdf/2013/best_practice_compensation_expropriation_en.pdf, 9.

[14] 'Stabilisation Clauses and Human Rights', a research project conducted for IFC and the United Nations Special Representative of the Secretary-General on Business and Human Rights, 27 May 2009, www.ifc.org/wps/wcm/connect/9feb5b00488555eab8c4fa6a6515bb18/Stabilization%2BPaper.pdf?MOD=AJPERES, v, vii.

[15] See ibid, viii.

[16] L Cotula, *The Great African Land Grab?: Agricultural Investments and the Global Food System* (London, Zed Books, 2013) 12.

[17] O De Schutter, 'Large-Scale Land Acquisitions and Leases: A Set of Minimum Principles and Measures to Address the Human Rights Challenges' 28 December 2009, www.oecd.org/site/swacmali2010/44031283.pdf.

circumstances, the state has unfettered power to reallocate land, leaving the rights of land users, in particular those of indigenous peoples and local communities, largely unprotected. Furthermore, the process of globalisation has eased transnational capital flows and enabled possession of land by foreign investors.[18] In many instances this has led to displacement and dispossession of indigenous peoples and local communities. This phenomenon encompasses examples that include long-leases, investment in agriculture in the name of food production, manipulation of agricultural value chains and the financing of large-scale land acquisitions.

The use of long leases is widespread. For instance, in Mozambique, more than 70 per cent of the population's livelihood depends on small-scale farming, fishing and pastoralism, while the state offers leases to foreign governments and corporations for agribusiness or extractive industrial projects that are renewable for up to 99 years.[19] In Cambodia, more than 70 per cent of arable land has been leased out.[20] In such cases, the use rights of the land are transferable and the distinction between purchases and leases is blurred.[21] 'It therefore makes sense to consider a lease as a land acquisition—even though, strictly speaking, landownership does not change'.[22] In comparison to long leases, other cases that lead to dispossession in indirect ways are less visible. Individual investors, hedge funds[23] and sovereign funds[24] invest in agriculture in the name of food production. Foreign investment begins to transfer community-controlled and biodiversity-based food systems into company-controlled food systems (for example, palm oil production).[25] This leads to the commodification of land and transforms the nature of land into a vehicle of production that generates global commodities such as grains, coffee and palm oil. Traders and processors have gained in power through

[18] S Murphy, 'Land Grabs and Fragile Food Systems: The Role of Globalisation', Institute for Agriculture and Trade Policy, 20 February 2013, www.iatp.org/documents/land-grabs-and-fragile-food-systems, 3.

[19] See eg, S Tramel, 'Mozambican Peasants vs. the Great African Land Grab' *Huffington Post*, 7 October 2014, www.huffingtonpost.com/salena-tramel/mozambican-peasants-vs-th_b_5943776.html.

[20] A Simms, 'Unprecedented Case Filed at International Criminal Court Proposes Land Grabbing in Cambodia as a Crime against Humanity' *Huffington Post* (London, 7 October 2014) huffingtonpost.co.uk/andrew-simms/land-grabbing_b_5938500.html.

[21] Cotula (n 16) 37.

[22] ibid.

[23] C Badgley, 'When Wall Street went to Africa' *Foreign Policy* (Washington DC, 11 July 2014) www.foreignpolicy.com/articles/2014/07/11/bruce_wrobel_cameroon_palm_oil_herakles_greenpeace_logging.

[24] Murphy (n 18) 5.

[25] Down to Earth, 'Report Accuses India-born Businessman of Unchecked Land Grabbing across Continents', 8 October 2014, www.downtoearth.org.in/content/report-accuses-india-born-businessman-unchecked-land-grabbing-across-continents. Small-scale farmers still produce more than 80% of the food consumed in Asia and Sub-Saharan Africa. See Simms (n 20). See also, K Manalo, 'Investors, Hedge Funds Flock around Opportunities in Agriculture' *Opalesque* (Nicosia, 7 October 2014) www.opalesque.com/652824/Investors_hedge_funds_flock_around_opportunities_in_agriculture282.html>.

the extraction of value by manipulating agricultural commodity prices; as a result, farmers' control over farming decisions has been severely weakened.[26] Furthermore, banks' financing of international land acquisitions has galvanised dispossession; for example, small farmers have been evicted from their land by sugar plantations financed by banks.[27] In these various forms of hidden expropriation, land has become 'an investible asset'.[28]

Some terms have been coined in order to characterise large-scale land acquisitions, such as 'land grabs', and are employed mostly by the media in order to describe 'large-scale purchase or leases of agricultural or forest land on terms that do not serve those already living on the land' that lead to displacement and dispossession.[29] However, such terms are not legal concepts and as a result they are not very useful where indigenous peoples and local communities seek to assert their legal rights. Indeed, the cases discussed above are not considered to constitute expropriation in the traditional sense. However, these instances constitute de facto expropriation: foreign governments or transnational corporations expropriate land use rights with the help of an agent such as the host state, the holder of the legal title of ownership. Furthermore, there is often a lack of recognition of traditional tenure systems that are predominantly communal, and a denial of any state obligation to protect such tenure systems. The lands occupied by indigenous peoples and local communities are often regarded as 'underused' or 'underdeveloped' and are therefore vulnerable to expropriation. As a result, local communities can be: deprived of access to, or control over, land and natural resources; excluded from the process of consultation (if any) on land deals; and denied fair compensation.[30]

De facto expropriation in the context of globalisation involves different interests, tensions and conflicts and reveals imbalances that exist in the current expropriation laws at local, regional and global levels. The global scale of de facto expropriation calls for the formulation of global standards and rules in order to reconcile these conflicts and redress these imbalances, taking into account marginalised groups such as minorities and indigenous peoples and their property rights. A human rights approach has provided some possibilities to achieve this goal.[31] This approach has many merits, as Richard Falk points out, '[for it takes] into account cultural pluralism,

[26] Cotula (n 16) 26.

[27] 'Farmers Protest at ANZ Bank against Land Grabs', *Yahoo News*, 1 October 2014, uk.news.yahoo.com/video/farmers-protest-anz-bank-against-061750076.html.

[28] Cotula (n 16) 176.

[29] Murphy (n 18) 3–4.

[30] International Work Group for Indigenous Affairs, 'Fact Sheet: Indigenous peoples' Right to Land—The Threat of Land Grabbing', www.iwgia.org/publications/search-pubs?publication_id=693.

[31] See eg, C Golay and I Cismas, 'Legal Opinion: The Right to Property from a Human Rights Perspective', SSRN Scholarly Paper (Rochester NY, Social Science Research Network, 2010), http://papers.ssrn.com/abstract=1635359.

group rights, duties to the community, the unheard voices of indigenous peoples, and giving due weight to the hitherto insufficiently influential non-Western civilisations';[32] however, it also has limits. The dominant human rights approach is essentially individualistic, affording only limited scope for the protection of communal or collective rights, which are often understood to contrast with individual rights. Indeed treating communal property rights as a fundamental human right is highly contentious.

This chapter locates communal property rights in international human rights instruments, and analyses the prospects and limits of using a human rights approach to protect communal property rights in situations of de facto expropriation. Several studies of the right to property in international human rights instruments already exist.[33] Moving the current debate forward, section II of this chapter focuses on the evolution of peoples' rights, duly broadening the parameters within which human rights are traditionally thought about, and laying in the process a legal foundation for recognising communal property rights at the international level. This legal foundation is based on the notion that access to, use, management and conservation of land resources by indigenous peoples and local communities are recognised as forms of property rights. Following this, section III points to the fact that such recognition of communal property rights is operative to an uneven extent in different regions of the world, with the analysis focusing upon the status of communal property rights in three major regional human rights instruments: The European Convention on Human Rights, the American Convention on Human Rights and the African Charter on Human and Peoples' Rights. The chapter then concludes with a consideration of this study's implications for leveraging global guidance to redress the imbalances in the international legal framework concerning de facto expropriation.

II. HUMAN RIGHTS AND PROPERTY RIGHTS: TRANSCENDING THE BOUNDARIES

A. The Right to Property in the 1948 Universal Declaration of Human Rights (UDHR) and the International Covenants on Human Rights

Article 17 of the UDHR reads: 'Everyone has the right to own property as well as in association with others' and 'No one shall be arbitrarily deprived

[32] RA Falk, *Human Rights Horizons: The Pursuit of Justice in a Globalizing World* (London, Routledge, 2000) 2.

[33] Eg, TRG van Banning, *The Human Right to Property* (Antwerp, Intersentia, 2002); Golay and Cismas (n 31); A Rosas, 'Property Rights' in A Rosas, J E Helgesen and D Goodman (eds), *The Strength of Diversity: Human Rights and Pluralist Democracy* (Dordrecht, Martinus Nijhoff, 1992) 133–58.

of his property'.[34] The reference 'in association with others' in Paragraph 1 of the Article was proposed by the Soviet Union and inserted in order to cover collective forms of property.[35] Paragraph 2 of Article 17 does not place a strong limitation on state action, as it only prohibits the 'arbitrary' deprivation of property. Therefore, it permits 'a considerable margin of discretion for states in adopting national laws relating to property of various kinds'.[36] Nevertheless, it entails a general rule that the taking of property shall not be justified without any compensation.[37]

The drafters of the UDHR include Eleanor Roosevelt (1884–1962), the first Chair of the newly established UN Commission on Human Rights in 1946, and French jurist René Cassin (1887–1976), who later won the Nobel Peace Prize in 1968. During the drafting process, Cassin drew upon many models including the English Bill of Rights (1689), the US Declaration of Independence (1976), and France's Declaration of the Rights of Man and of the Citizen (1978).[38] Indeed, under these influences the articulation of the protection of property has been underpinned by an emphasis on the essential role that property takes in securing individual freedom.[39] This approach to the perception of property associates the abuse of individual freedom with the promotion of 'collective rights', and as such it reminded the drafters of the UDHR of the horrors experienced with regard to totalitarianism and European fascism. Therefore, they were dubious about any possible priority that might be given to collective rights and to the 'notion of duties'.[40] Although the final draft of the Article applies to both individual and collective ownership, the status of collective/communal property rights has been further undermined by the individualist approach to human rights, that is, the approach asserting that human rights are essentially the rights of the individual rather than the rights of peoples or groups. Yet, such a conception of property rights proves problematic for many under-developed countries where the notion of property is often associated with their unique histories, cultures and customs, and where it is also often collective or communal in nature, albeit that the legal title, in the main, is vested in the state. For people in these countries, the individualist conception of property rights

[34] Some aspects of the right to property such as intellectual property rights have been given protection in the UDHR. For example, Art 27 (2) provides that the author's right to the protection of the moral and material interests resulting from his or her scientific, literary or artistic production is safeguarded, and a corresponding provision is included in Art 15 (c) of the International Covenant on Economic, Social and Cultural Rights (ICESCR).

[35] Rosas (n 33) 137.

[36] ibid, 137–38.

[37] ibid.

[38] R Maran, 'The Universal Declaration of Human Rights at 40' (1989) 16 *Social Justice* 146, 147.

[39] See eg, T Bethell, *The Noblest Triumph: Property and Prosperity through the Ages* (New York, St Martin's Press, 1998).

[40] T van Boven, 'Can Human Rights Have a Separate Existence from Peoples' Rights?' (1989) 16 *Social Justice* 12, 13.

is also seen as the root of many economic, social and political problems. Further, it is often linked to poverty, inequality and the exploitation of local resources by transnational companies.[41]

Various proposals concerning the form of the property clause in the UDHR went through different iterations and amendments as a consequence of influence exerted by the US, UK, France, the Soviet Union and Chile, amongst others.[42] The UK and Australia, in fact, were opposed to the incorporation of this sort of article into the UDHR, due to their resistance to the idea that national controls concerning both the scope of property rights and the state power of expropriation might be limited by international norms.[43] In addition to the provisions in Article 17, 'property' is included in the list of impermissible grounds of distinction in Article 2 of the UDHR; the states reserve considerable power to expropriate property and regulate the use of property. This echoes Falk's argument that 'to make the governments of these strong states the target of international law arguments has generally seemed futile'.[44] This observation has been corroborated by the failure of the endeavour to include a free-standing property provision when the UN General Assembly adopted the International Covenant on Civil and Political Rights (ICCPR) in 1966, although 'right to housing' is provided in Article 17 of the ICCPR[45] and the prohibition of discrimination/distinction on the basis of property is also included.[46]

Likewise, the right to property was also discussed in connection with the International Covenant on Economic, Social and Cultural Rights (ICESCR) 1966, but no free-standing provision was included, although Article 11, Paragraph 1 makes reference to the right to 'housing'.[47] It is difficult to establish a clear connection between the right to property and civil and political rights, while, as will be discussed below, there are barriers to associating property rights with economic, social and cultural rights. The ultimate reason for not including a property clause in the covenants was a challenge to the wording on the limitation of state power to expropriate that

41 C Krause and G Alfreðsson, 'Article 17' in GS Alfreðsson and A Eide (eds), *The Universal Declaration of Human Rights: A Common Standard of Achievement* (The Hague, Martinus Nijhoff Publishers, 1999) 360.

42 Krause and Alfreðsson, ibid 361–62; Rosas (n 33) 136.

43 Krause and Alfreðsson, ibid 364; Rosas (n 33) 137.

44 R Falk, 'United States Foreign Policy as an Obstacle to Realising the Rights of Peoples' (1989) 16 *Social Justice* 57, 58.

45 Art 17 of the ICCPR: 'No one shall be subjected to arbitrary or unlawful interference with his privacy, family, home or correspondence, nor to unlawful attacks on his honour and reputation. Everyone has the right to the protection of the law against such interference or attacks'.

46 ICCPR, Art 2(1) provides that 'State Party to the present Covenant undertakes to respect and to ensure to all individuals within its territory and subject to its jurisdiction the rights recognized in the present Covenant, without distinction of any kind, such as race, colour, sex, language, religion, political or other opinion, national or social origin, property, birth or other status'. Art 2(2) of the ICESCR provides a similar prohibition.

47 van Banning (n 33) 44; Rosas (n 33) 138.

was mounted by the Soviet Union and some of its allies, although they did not oppose the inclusion of a property clause in a general sense.[48] Objections persisted on both the limitation of the right and restrictions on state power concerning expropriation. The 1995 UN Secretary-General's annotations on the text of the draft International Covenants on Human Rights summarise best the mindset of the drafters:

> While no one questioned the right of the individual to own property, some doubted the advisability of including an article on the right of property in the covenants. It was stated that there were considerable differences of opinion with regard to the concept of property and the restrictions to which the right of property should be subject ...[49] It was generally admitted that the right to own property was not absolute. At the same time it was recognised that the limitations on the right varied from time to time and from country to country. Consequently, it was difficult to reach agreement not only on the extent of the limitations to be included in the article, but also on the manner in which such limitations were to be defined.[50] While there was wide agreement that the right to own property was subject to some degree of control by the State, it was felt that certain safeguards against abuse must be provided. However, there was considerable difficulty in reaching agreement on such safeguards.[51]

B. Categories of Human Rights

Despite the recognition that all human rights are 'indivisible, interdependent, and interrelated',[52] there are different categories of identifiable human rights, such as civil and political rights, as distinguished from economic, social and cultural rights, or individual rights, as distinguished from collective rights.[53] Thinking about the nature of human rights in terms of categories and classifications is exemplified in the 'three generations of human rights', proposed by Karel Vasak, the first Secretary-General of the International Institute of Human Rights in Strasburg and former UNESCO legal adviser:

> The first generation rights were those rights which emerged from the American and French revolutions. They were aimed at securing the citizen's liberty from arbitrary action by the State. They correspond by and large to the *Civil and Political Rights* in the International Bill of Rights. They are said to be negative rights in that they call for restraint from the State.

[48] Rosas (n 33) 138.

[49] Annotations on the text of the draft International Covenants on Human Rights, 1 July 1995, UN Doc A/2929, para 197.

[50] ibid, para 202.

[51] ibid, para 206.

[52] Vienna Declaration and Programme Action, A/CONF.157/23, adopted by the World Conference on Human Rights in Vienna on 25 June 1993, Part I, para 5.

[53] T van Boven, 'Categories of Rights' in D Moeckli, S Shah and S Sivakumaran (eds), *International Human Rights Law* 2nd edn (Oxford, Oxford University Press, 2014) 144.

> The second generation rights emerged with the Russian revolution and were echoed in the welfare state concepts which developed in the West. They correspond largely to the *Economic, Social and Cultural rights* and they require positive action by the State.
>
> The third generation of rights ... are a response to the phenomenon of global interdependence. Individual States acting alone can no longer satisfy their human rights obligations. The problems that are now being faced require international cooperation for their resolution. These problems include the maintenance of peace, the protection of the environment and the encouragement of development. The third generation rights necessarily benefit *individuals and peoples*.[54] (emphases added)

Vasak's thesis of the stages of human rights development is not without criticism.[55] For example, the division of rights into civil, political, economic, social and cultural rights in the UDHR presents problems concerning the negotiation of the status of the right to property within the international human rights framework.[56] Moreover, the property clause (Article 17) in the UDHR is located alongside provisions on civil and political rights; the property clause (Article 14) appears in the African Charter on Human and People's Rights between provisions on civil and political rights (Articles 3–13) and provisions on economic, social and cultural rights (Articles 15–18). Such binary thinking undermines the 'mixed character of property rights'.[57]Although it is subject to conceptual limitations, the classification of the 'generations' of human rights points to the evolution of group/collective rights, in particular peoples' rights in human rights discourse; and, therefore, it speaks to the recognition of a spectrum of property—from private property to communal property and mixed forms of property—in the discourse of property rights.[58]

[54] K Vasak, 'A Thirty Year Struggle—the Sustained Efforts to Give Force of Law to the Universal Declaration of Human Rights', UNESCO Courier, November 1977, summarised by R Rich, 'The Right to Development: A Right of Peoples' in J Crawford (ed), *The Rights of Peoples* (Oxford, University of Oxford Press, 1988) 41.

[55] Rich, ibid 41.

[56] Maran (n 38) 40; PH Olsson, 'Every Natural or Legal Person Is Entitled to the Peaceful Enjoyment of His or Her Possessions: Article 1, Protocol 1 to the European Convention on Human Rights' in F Dorssemont, K Lörcher and I Schömann (eds), *European Convention on Human Rights and the Employment Relation* (Oxford, Hart Publishing, 2013) 382. For the vague conceptions of these categories of rights, see also B Felice, 'Rights in Theory and Practice: An Historical Perspective' (1989) 16 *Social Justice* 35.

[57] Rosas (n 33) 145.

[58] See eg, A Lehavi, *The Construction of Property: Norms, Institutions, Challenges* (Cambridge, Cambridge University Press, 2013), in particular ch 3 'Private-Common-Public: The Promise of Property Hybrids'; H Dagan and M Heller, 'The Liberal Commons' (2001) 110 *Yale Law Journal* 549.

C. The Evolution of Group Rights and Recognition of Communal Property Rights

Despite the fact that the right to property only appears in both covenants as part of the non-discrimination clause, Article 1 of both the ICCPR[59] and the ICESR recognises the rights of all peoples to self-determination. This paves the way for the emergence of communal/group rights, which are 'intended to protect a group (for example, a people[60]) from discrimination and oppression as *a group*' (emphasis added).[61] As of 1984, this provision on self-determination has been reiterated in a consensus adopted by the Human Rights Committee, the supervisory body established under the ICCPR:

> The right of self-determination is of particular importance because its realisation is *an essential condition for the effective guarantee and observance of individual human rights* and for the promotion and strengthening of those rights. It is for that reason that States set forth the right of self-determination in a provision of positive law in both Covenants and placed this provision as article 1 apart from and before all of the other rights in the two Covenants.[62] (emphasis added)
>
> Article 1 enshrines an *inalienable* right of all peoples as described in its paragraphs 1 and 2. By virtue of that right they freely 'determine their political status and freely pursue their economic, social and cultural development'. The article imposes on all States parties corresponding *obligations*. This right and the corresponding

[59] Para 1: 'All peoples have the right of self-determination, including the right to determine their political status and freely pursue their economic, social and cultural development'. Para 2: 'All peoples may, for their own ends, freely dispose of their natural wealth and resources without prejudice to any obligations arising out of international economic co-operation, based upon the principle of mutual benefit, and international law. In no case may a people be deprived of its own means of subsistence'.

[60] See one of the definitions of 'people' in the Final Report and Recommendations of an International Meeting of Experts on the Further Study of the Concept of the Right of Peoples for UNESCO, SNS-89/CONF.602/7 (22 February 1990). In terms of 'indigenous peoples', there is no formal definition. The UN Working Group on Indigenous Populations lists several factors to understand the meaning of 'indigenous':

> Priority in time, with respect to the occupation and use of a specific territory;
> The voluntary perpetuation of cultural distinctiveness, which may include the aspects of language, social organization, religion and spiritual values, modes of production, laws and institutions;
> Self-identification, as well as recognition by other groups, or by State authorities, as a distinct collectivity; and
> An experience of subjugation, marginalization, dispossession, exclusion or discrimination, whether or not these conditions persist.

Working Group on Indigenous Populations, Working paper by the Chairperson-Rapporteur, Mrs Erica-Irene A Daes, on the concept of 'indigenous people', E/CN.4/Sub.2/AC.4/1996/2 (1996).

[61] R McCorquodale, 'Group Rights' in Moeckli, Shah and Sivakumaran (n 53) 334.

[62] Human Rights Committee, General Comment 12, Art 1 (Twenty-first session, 1984), Compilation of General Comments and General Recommendations Adopted by Human Rights Treaty Bodies, UN Doc HRI/GEN/1/Rev.1 at 12 (1994).

> obligations concerning its implementation are interrelated with other *provisions of the Covenant and rules of international law.*[63] (emphasis added)
>
> Paragraph 2 affirms a particular aspect of the economic content of the right of self-determination, namely *the right of peoples*, for their own ends, freely to 'dispose of their natural wealth and resources without prejudice to any obligations arising out of international economic cooperation, based upon the principle of mutual benefit, and international law. In no case may a people be deprived of its own means of subsistence'. This right entails *corresponding duties for all States and the international community* ...[64] (emphasis added)

The provision on self-determination in both covenants and the highlighted parts of the above quotation reaffirm the human rights obligations imposed on states and the importance of international cooperation in order to fulfil these obligations. However, the adoption of that article and its emphasis on peoples' rights go against the western perception of rights, which are inherently individualistic, and give rise to the 'fear that peoples' rights are detrimental to the realisation and enjoyment of individual rights'.[65] Furthermore, the right to self-determination is controversial, as it may involve different claims such as sovereignty or 'at least the right to exert effective control over one's *collective destiny*' (emphasis added).[66] The fear is that recognising self-determination at this level will lead to fragmentation, jeopardising the unity of sovereign states.[67] There has been a persistent struggle for self-determination below the level of the state after de-colonisation, that is, self-determination by indigenous peoples, ethnic or religious minorities, etc.[68] As a result, the international consensus on the scope of self-determination has been narrowed down to 'its human rights role of ensuring equitable treatment within existing state structures of authority',[69] encompassing those rights including the right to national resources, the right to economic, social and cultural development, self-government, etc. This position has now been reaffirmed in Articles 3 and 4 of the United Nations Declaration on the Rights of Indigenous Peoples 2007 (hereinafter the UN Declaration 2007). Although it has raised significant controversy, the scope of self-determination within the international human rights framework such as the recognition of the right to natural resources allows for a connection between group rights and communal property rights. Other important international documents that have recognised peoples' rights include: The 1986 United Nations Declaration on the Right to Development;[70] the UNESCO

[63] Art 2, ibid.
[64] Art 5, ibid.
[65] van Boven (n 40) 12–13.
[66] Falk (n 32) 98.
[67] ibid, 102–13.
[68] ibid, 102.
[69] ibid, 103.
[70] GA Res 41/128 (4 December 1986).

1987 Declaration on Race and Racial Prejudice, which has explicitly recognised 'the right to be different';[71] as well as the 1981 African Charter on Human and Peoples' Rights. The 1993 Vienna World Conference on Human Rights considered the denial of the right of self-determination as a violation of human rights.[72]

Recognising peoples' rights provides significant grounds for establishing a new legal basis for affording protection to communal property in de facto expropriation. It also serves 'to affirm [that] the rights of peoples is an expression of legal, moral, and political support *on a transnational basis* for popular struggles against various contemporary forms of oppression' (emphasis added).[73] Since the 1980s, indigenous peoples' communal relationships and their perception of property have been recognised by the development of major international law and international human rights instruments,[74] cumulating in the adoption of the UN Declaration 2007,[75] although this takes the form of 'soft law'.[76]

The UN Declaration 2007 recognises indigenous peoples as rights-holders, and the right to self-determination is one of the key rights being acknowledged: 'indigenous individuals are entitled without discrimination to all human rights recognised in international law and … [to] possess collective rights which are indispensable for their existence, well-being and integral development as peoples'.[77] Article 3 of the Declaration reads: 'indigenous peoples have the right to self-determination. By virtue of that right they freely determine their political status and freely pursue their economic, social and cultural development'. The Declaration 'brings together peoples' rights and individual rights in a spectrum of mutual relationship and reach'.[78] Provisions in the Declaration have been reflected in the decisions of the Inter-American Court of Human Rights.[79]

Other 'soft' instruments relating to human rights protection of communal property rights include the 2007 Basic Principles and Guidelines on

[71] Art 1, Para 2, the Declaration on Race and Racial Prejudice, UNESCO, 27 November 1987.

[72] Above (n 52) para 2.

[73] Falk (n 44) 58.

[74] See T Koivurova, 'Jurisprudence of the European Court of Human Rights Regarding Indigenous Peoples: Retrospect and Prospects' (2011) 18 *International Journal on Minority and Group Rights* 1, 1.

[75] Important international treaties regarding indigenous peoples prior to the 1980s include the ICCPR. Art 27 provides: 'In those States in which ethnic, religious or linguistic minorities exist, persons belonging to such minorities shall not be denied the right, in community with the other members of their group, to enjoy their own culture, to profess and practise their own religion, or to use their own language'.

[76] Due to the present chapter's space limitations, a detailed discussion of 'softness' in the global normative system is not engaged. For a detailed study, see Xu (n 1).

[77] GA Res 61/295 (13 September 2007) preamble.

[78] van Boven (n 53) 146.

[79] See eg, IACtHR, *Case of Kichwa Indigenous People of Srayaku v Ecuador*, Judgment of 27 June 2012, Series C No 245, para 217.

Development-Based Evictions and Displacement. These apply to acts and/or omissions involving the coerced or involuntary displacement of not only individuals, but also *groups* and *communities*, from home and/or lands and *common property resources* that were *occupied or depended upon* (eg, Articles 16, 23, 28, 32, 36, 52, 56, 64, 68). This gives recognition to indigenous peoples' 'dependency on and attachment to informally held land'.[80] Protection for most socially and economically vulnerable and marginalised sectors of society, including women, children, minorities and indigenous peoples is emphasised. Further, states are meant to 'carry out comprehensive reviews of relevant national legislation and policy with a view to ensuring their conformity with international human rights provisions' (Article 24). The 2007 Principles also emphasise the role of the international community in protecting the human right to housing, food and property. The international community includes different bodies and entities such as international organisations (international financial, trade, development, and other related institutions and agencies, and member or donor states that have voting rights within such bodies), as well as transnational corporations and other business enterprises (Chapter VIII, the 2007 Principles).

The ILO (International Labour Organisation) Convention Concerning Indigenous and Tribal People in Independent Countries in 1989 (hereinafter ILO Convention 169) recognises the rights of ownership and possession of indigenous peoples and the state obligation to protect such rights (Article 14). Article 1(1)(a) of that Convention recognises tribal peoples as communities 'whose status is regulated wholly or partially by their own customs or traditions or by specific laws or regulations'. Article 13 of the ILO Convention 169 provides that the collective aspects of the peoples' relationship with their lands carry important cultural and spiritual values. Article 14 recognises 'access to land': for the indigenous peoples, the right to property is not about exclusive possession but refers to traditional access to land for their subsistence and traditional activities. Where the relocation of these peoples is necessary, it shall take place with their free and informed consent, and they shall be provided with lands of equal quality and legal status or be fully compensated (Article 16). Prior, free and informed consultation procedures should be applied where a project is attempted to dispossess local communities of their land (Articles 6, 15, 17, 22, 27 and 28). However, it should be noted that the ILO Convention 169 has only 22 ratifications by March 2015.

[80] The Guiding Principles on Internal Displacement (1998) contains similar provisions. Principle 21 reads: 'No one shall be arbitrarily deprived of property and possessions'. Principle 9 provides: 'States are under a particular obligation to protect against the displacement of indigenous peoples, minorities, peasants, pastoralists and other groups with a special dependency on and attachment to their lands'. E/CN.4/1998/53/Add.2.

III. COMMUNAL PROPERTY RIGHTS IN REGIONAL HUMAN RIGHTS INSTRUMENTS

A. The European Convention on Human Rights (ECHR)

The drafting and adoption of the ECHR and its Protocol 1 came about after a period of authoritarian rule in Europe and marked a shift in the endeavour to constrain state power to expropriate.[81] States began to acknowledge 'the social function of property', which entails that 'the right to property is also a social right thereby implying a substantial and active role of the State' in securing the public interest. At the same time, however, states were reluctant to submit political decisions on issues such as expropriation to the review of the courts, in particular nationalisation, which is often carried out in agrarian reform or associated with other economic and social reforms.[82] As a result, the ECHR affords some protection against expropriation, but it grants states a very wide 'margin of appreciation'. The right to property has been included in Article 1, Protocol 1 (hereinafter A1P1), adopted in 1952:

> Every natural or legal person is entitled to the peaceful enjoyment of his possessions. No one shall be deprived of his possessions except in the public interest and subject to the conditions provided for by law and by the general principles of international law.
>
> The preceding provisions shall not, however, in any way impair the right of a State to enforce such laws as it deems necessary to control the use of property in accordance with the general interest or to secure the payment of taxes or other contributions or penalties.

This Article can be broken down into 'three distinct rules': A general right to property (the first sentence of the first paragraph); a set of principles concerning the deprivation of possessions (the second sentence of the first paragraph); and a right of states to control the use of property (the second paragraph).[83] The second paragraph of A1P1 reserves to states the right to enact such laws as they deem necessary to control the use of property according to general interest.[84] The initial assessment of whether there exists a public interest in justifying the taking of property is often left to the national authorities. Furthermore, compensation is not specified in A1P1.[85]

[81] Golay and Cismas (n 31) 5.

[82] van Banning (n 33) 79.

[83] *James v United Kingdom*, App No 8793/79, Judgment of 21 February 1986, §37; *J A Pye (Oxford) Ltd and J A Pye (Oxford) Land Ltd v The United Kingdom*, App No 44302/02, (GC) Judgment of 30 August 2007, § 52.

[84] *Pye v The United Kingdom*, ibid §55.

[85] In the EU Charter of Fundamental Rights, protection of the right to property (Art 17) is along the lines of A1P1 of the ECHR, with an addition that deprivation of possessions is subject to 'fair compensation being paid in good time'. Proclaimed in 2000, the Charter has become legally binding on the EU with the entry into force of the Treaty of Lisbon, in December 2009.

The developing jurisprudence of the European Court of Human Rights (ECtHR) concerning group rights, in particular the rights of indigenous peoples, is rather limited. Several cases involving indigenous peoples heard before the Court show that the ECHR is not very effective where it is applied to cases pertaining to communal relationships and communal property. The cases usually involve disputes in which modern economic development activities penetrate into the traditional community (often with the permission of the state), resulting in reduced access to communal resources by indigenous peoples, or, in extreme cases, their forced relocation. Indigenous peoples also carry the burden of proof to argue for their 'immemorial use rights' over local resources.[86] Moreover, the protection afforded by the ECHR is mostly procedural rather than substantive, and indigenous complaints have primarily relied on Articles 6 and 8 and A1P1 of the ECHR. There has been a lack of landmark cases decided by the ECtHR in favour of indigenous peoples.[87]

In *Hingitaq 53 and Others v Denmark*,[88] the Thule tribe claimed compensation for reduced hunting and fishing opportunities as a result of the establishment of an air base. The ECtHR found that the national authorities successfully struck a balance between the general interest of the community and the proprietary interests of the persons concerned and therefore there was no violation of A1P1. While 'non-pecuniary damage' by the interference of colonial power on an isolated indigenous tribe and 'collective rights' were recognised, the debate focused on the status of the Thule tribe. A reference was made by the Court to the ILO Convention 169. However, the ruling of the ECtHR supports the argument by the Supreme Court of Denmark that the Thule tribe does not 'retain some or all of its own social, economic, cultural and political institutions'; therefore, the Thule tribe is not a distinct indigenous people and does not fall within Article 1(1)(b) of the ILO Convention 169, and does not hold separate rights under the Convention.[89] The ECtHR did not fulsomely recognise aspects of communal relationships that are not necessarily expressed by formal institutions, but that may instead have been formed by custom, tradition and long-time use of land and other resources. Nor did the Court assess the tribe's hunting and fishing activities in direct cultural terms, despite the fact that they are important elements of the tribe's lifestyle and identity.

In *Chagos Islanders v UK*,[90] the ECtHR declared the Chagos islanders' case to be inadmissible on the grounds that the applicants had previously

[86] See Koivurova (n 74) 4.

[87] ibid, 1.

[88] *Hingitaq 53 and Others v Denmark*, App No 18584/04, Judgment of 12 January 2006.

[89] This resonates with the common law's recognition of local customary rights 'only if they are ancient, certain, reasonable and continuous'. See K Gray and SF Gray (eds), *Elements of Land Law*, 5th edn (Oxford, Oxford University Press, 2009) 1360. If the continuity is broken, local customary rights may be easily dismissed.

[90] *Chagos Islanders v UK*, App No 35622/04, Judgment of 11 December 2012.

accepted compensation from the British government and had therefore effectively renounced their right to bring any further claims (§81). The battle between the Chagos Islanders and the UK government began in the 1960s when the UK government, which owns the territory, leased Diego Garcia, the largest part of the Chagos Islands, to the United States. In 1982, under pressure from Chagossian campaigners, the UK government offered a compensation package with a payment of £4 million ($6 million) and provision of land worth £1 million ($1.5 million) by Mauritius. However, controversy surrounding the compensation centred on the fact that many islanders did not receive compensation, and that those who did receive it were not aware that accepting the compensation meant 'signing away their right to return'.[91] More importantly, monetary compensation did not truly reflect a more genuine sense of the islanders' loss. The deportation from the island adversely affected around 2000 local residents who had formed a community over generations. Many fell into poverty and lost the sense that they still belonged to their old community.[92] Clearly the deportation had an adverse social, cultural, environmental and spiritual impact on not only the islanders as individuals but also the local community as a whole. However, the compensation package did not take such losses into account. These decisions reveal the Court's ambivalent attitude toward the recognition of communal property rights that are based on customs and long-term use 'from time immemorial', and also its ambivalent attitude toward the perception of collectives or communities as a separate category of right-holders.

B. The American Convention on Human Rights (ACHR)

The American Convention on Human Rights (Article 21, 'Right to Property') provides: 'Everyone has the right to the use and enjoyment of his property' (Article 21(1)). Immediately after this provision, it acknowledges the social function of property, asserting that 'the law may subordinate such use and enjoyment to the interest of society'.[93] However, restrictions on state actions are imposed: 'No one shall be deprived of his property except upon payment of *just compensation*, for reasons of public utility or social interest' (emphasis added) (Article 21 (2)). The article also cautions against the abuse of exercising private property rights by prohibiting 'usury and any other form of exploitation of man by man' (Article 21 (3)), thereby

[91] J Wan, 'Chagos Islanders Lose the European Court Battle but the Struggle Continues' *Think Africa Press* (London, 20 December 2012) thinkafricapress.com/legal/chagos-islanders-lose-european-court-battle-struggle-continues.

[92] Prior to the ECtHR ruling, several cases regarding the removal of Chagos Islanders had been heard in the UK courts, culminating with the House of Lords ruling in *R (Bancoult) v Secretary of State for Foreign and Commonwealth Affairs (No 2)* [2008] UKHL 61.

[93] van Banning (n 33) 62.

acknowledging the manner in which property engages the relationship between persons, that is, everyone's right to property is limited by other people's right to property.

The jurisprudence of the Inter-American Court of Human Rights recognises the evolution of peoples' rights and associated communal property rights, and establishes a much broader scope of 'possession'. In *Sawhoyamaxa Indigenous Community v Paraguay*, indigenous peoples' rights of possession are summarised as follows:

> 1) traditional possession of their lands by indigenous people has equivalent effects to those of a state-granted full property title; 2) traditional possession entitles indigenous people to demand official recognition and registration of property title; 3) the members of indigenous peoples who have unwillingly left their traditional lands, or lost possession thereof, maintain property rights thereto, even though they lack legal title, unless the lands have been lawfully transferred to third parties in good faith; and 4) the members of indigenous peoples who have unwillingly lost possession of their lands, when those lands have been lawfully transferred to innocent third parties, are entitled to restitution thereof or to obtain other lands of equal extension and quality. Consequently, possession is not a requisite conditioning the existence of indigenous land restitution rights.[94]

Case law allows for the recognition of the communal or collective property rights of indigenous peoples. In *The Mayagna (Sumo) Awas Tingni v Nicaragua*,[95] property rights are protected 'in a sense which includes, among others, the rights of members of the indigenous communities within the framework of communal property':[96]

> Among indigenous peoples there is a communitarian tradition regarding a communal form of collective property of the land, in the sense that ownership of the land is not centred on an individual but rather on the group and its community [...] For indigenous communities, relations to the land are not merely a matter of possession and production but a material and spiritual element which they must fully enjoy, even to preserve their cultural legacy and transmit it to future generations.[97]

Kichwa Indigenous People of Srayaku v Ecuador[98] confirms that as one category of communal property, indigenous communal property is different from the classic concept of property, which is perceived as individualist and exclusive. The case affirms that the ways in which communal property is

[94] IACtHR, *Case of the Sawhoyamaxa Indigenous Community v Paraguay*, Judgment of 29 March 2006, para 128.
[95] IACtHR, *Case of the Mayagna (Sumo) Awas Tingni v Nicaragua*, Judgment of 31 August 2001, Series C, No 79.
[96] ibid, para 148.
[97] ibid, para 149.
[98] Above (n 79).

used and managed by indigenous peoples should be protected as property rights:

> This notion of land ownership and possession does not necessarily conform to the classic concept of property, but deserves equal protection under Article 21 of the American Convention. Disregard for specific forms of use and enjoyment of property, based on the culture, uses, customs and beliefs of each community, would be tantamount to holding that there is only one way of using and disposing of property, which, in turn, would render protection under Article 21 of the Convention illusory for millions of people.[99]

Furthermore, the decision of *The Moiwana Community v Suriname*[100] extends the scope of communal property rights beyond indigenous peoples, and recognises other groups of individuals as right holders (paragraph 111). This position has been reaffirmed in *Saramaka People v Suriname*, a case in which the Saramaka people's property rights were deprived by Chinese and multinational logging and mining companies with the government's permission.[101] The Court recognises that although 'the Saramaka people are not indigenous to the region they inhabit', members of the Saramaka people should be treated as 'a distinct social, cultural and economic group with a special relationship with its ancestral territory'.[102] Therefore 'the State shall delimit, demarcate, and grant collective title over the territory of the members of the Saramaka people, in accordance with their customary laws, and through previous, effective and fully informed consultations with the Saramaka people'.[103]

C. The African Charter on Human and Peoples' Rights (AfCHPR)

The African Charter on Human and Peoples' Rights 'reflects African approaches' to human rights and the interface between human rights and peoples' rights.[104] It specifies different categories of peoples' rights at the international level including self-determination, the free disposal of wealth and natural sources, the right of all peoples to economic, social, and cultural development, the right of all peoples to national and international peace and security and the right to a generally satisfactory environment.[105]

[99] Above (n 79), para 145.
[100] IACtHR, *Case of Moiwana Community v Suriname*, Judgment of 15 June 2005, Series C No 124.
[101] IACtHR, *Case of Saramaka People v Suriname*, Judgment of 28 November 2007, Series C No 172.
[102] ibid, para 79.
[103] ibid, para 194.
[104] van Boven (n 40) 15.
[105] ibid, 15.

Categories of peoples' rights in relation to property rights that were often violated in the colonial history of Africa and that are still being infringed under the conditions of recent and increasing African land acquisition are delineated in Article 21:

1. All peoples shall freely dispose of their wealth and natural resources. This right shall be exercised in the exclusive interest of the people. In no case shall a people be deprived of it.
2. In case of spoliation, the dispossessed people shall have the right to the lawful recovery of its property as well as to an adequate compensation.
3. The free disposal of wealth and natural resources shall be exercised without prejudice to the obligation of promoting international economic cooperation based on mutual respect, equitable exchange and the principles of international law.
4. State Parties to the present Charter shall individually and collectively exercise the right to free disposal of their wealth and natural resources with a view to strengthening African Unity and solidarity.
5. State Parties to the present Charter shall undertake to eliminate all forms of foreign exploitation particularly that practised by international monopolies so as to enable their peoples to fully benefit from the advantages derived from their national resources.

This presents an almost identical interpretation of the communal property rights of indigenous peoples to the interpretation offered in the ACHR. Following the setting up of a Working Group on Indigenous Populations/Communities in 2001, the African Commission on Human and Peoples' Rights issued an Advisory Opinion in 2006, which engaged certain fundamental issues relating to the African countries, including: The definition of indigenous populations, the issue of self-determination and the issue of land ownership and the exploitation of resources.[106] 'A special attachment to and use of their traditional land' is construed as an important element of that which constitutes the identity of 'indigenous peoples'.[107] In the *Endorois* case,[108] a landmark ruling on indigenous land rights, the Commission

[106] Advisory Opinion of the African Commission on Human and Peoples' Rights on the United Nations Declaration on the Right of Indigenous Populations, adopted by the African Commission at its 41st Ordinary Session held May 2007 in Accra, Ghana.

[107] Para 12, the concept of 'indigenous peoples' embodies the following constitutive elements or characteristics:

a) Self-identification;
b) A special attachment to and use of their traditional land whereby their ancestral land and territory have a fundamental importance for their collective physical and cultural survival as peoples;
c) A state of subjugation, marginalization, dispossession, exclusion, or discrimination because these peoples have different cultures, ways of life or mode of production than the national hegemonic and dominant model.

[108] *Centre for Minority Rights Development (Kenya) and Minority Rights Group International on behalf of Endorois Welfare Council v Kenya*, Case No 276/2003, 25 November 2009.

ruled on 4 February 2010 that the Endorois' eviction from their traditional land for the purposes of tourism development violated their human rights. The judgment echoed the position adopted in the case law developed by the Inter-American Court of Human Rights;[109] it has been asserted that 'possession is not a requisite conditioning the existence of indigenous land restitution rights'.[110] Furthermore, the Commission expanded the jurisprudence concerning indigenous peoples' communal property rights by linking these rights to an understanding of 'cultural integrity': 'tribal land, in addition to securing subsistence and livelihood, is seen as sacred, being inextricably linked to the cultural integrity of the community and its traditional way of life'.[111]

Yet the AfCHPR does not rule out the subordination of property rights to expropriation 'in the interest of public need or in the general interest of the community and in accordance with the provisions of appropriate laws' (Article 14). The safeguards on state action in expropriation remain very weak,[112] as the interpretation of public interest is largely dependent on the state. As a result, various forms of de facto expropriation driven primarily by the commercial interests of investors rather than by 'public interest' may still occur with state permission, as outlined earlier in this chapter.

IV. CONCLUSION: IMPLICATIONS FOR DE FACTO EXPROPRIATION

This chapter has addressed the relationship between communal property rights and human rights. It has done this by locating provisions that concern the right to property in general and communal property rights in particular within certain key international human rights instruments. Compared to other 'absolute' rights that are safeguarded by various international human rights instruments, the protection afforded to the right to property in a human rights context seems highly 'relative' in nature. Yet, the evolution of peoples' rights, and the interface of this evolution with property rights, in particular communal property rights, has important implications. It has broadened the scope of property rights. As witnessed in the adoption of both the ACHR and AfCHPR, and also in the development of the relevant jurisprudence, the concept of property is beginning to become disassociated from 'exclusive possession'. Instead, it is coming to encompass long-term communal use of and access to land, based on shared customs, traditions

[109] See eg, *Sawhoyamaxa Indigenous Community v Paraguay* (n 94) para 128.

[110] *Centre for Minority Rights Development (Kenya) and Minority Rights Group International on behalf of Endorois Welfare Council v Kenya* (n 108), para 209.

[111] ibid, paras 16 and 19.

[112] GJ Naldi, 'Limitation of Rights under the African Charter on Human and Peoples' Rights: The Contribution of the African Commission on Human and Peoples' Rights' (2001) 17 *South African Journal on Human Rights* 109.

and cultures, wherein 'the customary character of the right to property' is acknowledged.[113] Indigenous peoples and other groups and communities have been recognised as right holders. Human rights law protection engaging communal property rights has also improved the standard of compensation in cases where communities have been dispossessed of their lands: To compensate these communities for their losses, it is inadequate to merely offer monetary compensation, even if that form of compensation is at the market price; the package of compensation needs to take various factors into account, including the social, cultural and environmental impact of de facto expropriation on these communities. By placing more obligations on states and limiting state power in cases of expropriation, the international human rights paradigm has introduced a process of negotiation on the global scale that lends a voice to marginalised groups of people, although the recognition of communal property rights is still operative to an uneven extent in different regions of the world. As such, this international human rights paradigm exhibits a potential to recognise the following matters as forms of property rights at the global level: Access to, use, management and conservation of land resources by indigenous peoples and local communities. Further, it presents a need to redefine the concept of expropriation as the exercise of power in a way that directly or indirectly contributes to the deprivation of access to land and other natural resources, and/or to the weakening of control over land and other natural resources. This definition gives various forms of 'land grabs' a legal meaning, in particular interference with communal property rights (use rights), and therefore helps to redress the imbalances in the international legal framework concerning de facto expropriation.

[113] Golay and Cismas (n 31) 10.

11

Property Right to Rural Land in Ethiopia: A Human Rights Perspective

BELACHEW FIKRE

I. INTRODUCTION

UNDER THE CURRENT land tenure system of Ethiopia, an individual may hold land either as a peasant,[1] as an urban dweller having the right of use of the land for house construction through the lease system,[2] or as an investor using land for industrial, agricultural, service or real estate development purposes based on a lease contract.[3] Apart from these, as guaranteed by the Constitution, pastoralist and semi-pastoralist communities may also hold communal land for grazing and other purposes.[4] Therefore, free access to rural land holding is guaranteed in the country and at present, a massive adjudication and certification process of existing holdings is underway. This is said to help to clarify holding rights of individuals, reduce land-related conflicts and ultimately entrench tenure security.[5]

[1] This is as per the federal and the various regions' rural land administration laws that provide for free access to rural land use by peasants which reflect also the constitutional provision. Art 40(4) and (5) of the 1995 Federal Democratic Republic of Ethiopia Constitution Proclamation 1/1995 (1995 FDRE Constitution); see also Art 5(1) of Federal Rural Land Use and Administration Proclamation 456/2005 (Proclamation 456/2005).

[2] According to Art 5(1) of the Urban Land Lease Holding Proclamation, 'no person may acquire urban land other than the lease holding system provided under this Proclamation'. Urban Lands Lease Holding Proclamation 721/2011 (Proclamation 721/2011).

[3] Both the rural land administration and urban land lease holding Proclamations provide for land holdings by investors, all of which are to be based on the lease arrangements. See, for instance, Art 5(4) (a) of Proclamation 456/2005 with regard to rural land. Art 11(7) of Proclamation 721/2011 imposes a duty on Regional governments and City Administrations to prepare in advance plots of urban land to be assigned through tender to private investors that plan to construct 'higher education institutions, hospitals, health research institutions, four star and above hotels and mega real estate developments'.

[4] Art 40(5) of 1995 FDRE Constitution.

[5] D Rahmato, 'Land Rights and Tenure Security: Rural Land Registration in Ethiopia' in JM Ubink, AJ Hoekema and WJ Assies (eds), *Legalising Land Rights: Local Practices, State*

The literature with respect to these potential benefits of Ethiopia's rural land certification process, particularly relating to securing tenure, show mixed results.[6] While the formalisation process continues to attract a wide range of research interest that investigates aspects of tenure security,[7] gender implications[8] and impacts on investment,[9] its human rights implications are hardly considered. The process evokes critical concerns from human rights perspectives specifically in relation to the rights of indigenous groups/pastoralists and women's equality rights. In this chapter some of the factors affecting these two sections of society are explored to reveal the extent to which land certification in Ethiopia inadvertently overlooks people's human rights. In the first section, the human rights framework relating to property both at global and national level are examined. The second section provides a brief description of the certification process that explains the legal basis, approaches and the coverage of the process. In the third section the chapter examines the human rights implications of the process on women and pastoralists. This shall be followed by a concluding section.

II. HUMAN RIGHT TO LAND

The human right to property, first in the sense of 'the right to own property,' and second in the sense of 'the right to peaceful enjoyment of possessions' has long been debated.[10] Although whether or not there should be a human right to own property that warrants a claim against a State to provide access

Responses and Tenure Security in Africa, Asia and Latin America (Leiden, Leiden University Press, 2009) 59.

[6] For a critical assessment of the tenure insecurity implications of the registration process see Rahmato, ibid. K Deininger et al, on the other hand, have a more positive finding of enhanced tenure security as a result of the certification process. K Deininger, DA Ali and T Alemu, 'Impacts of Land Certification on Tenure Security, Investment and Land Market Perception: Evidence from Ethiopia' (2011) 87(2) *Land Economics* 312.

[7] K Deininger, DA Ali, S Holden and J Zevenbergen, 'Rural Land Certification in Ethiopia: Process, Initial Impact, and Implications for other African Countries' (2008) 36(1) *World Development* 1786.

[8] M Bezabih, ST Holden and A Mannberg, 'The Role of Land Certification in Reducing Gender Gaps in Productivity in Rural Ethiopia' (2012) Norwegian University of Life Sciences, Centre for Land Tenure Studies; ST Holden, K Deininger and H Ghebru, 'Tenure Insecurity, Gender, Low-Cost Land Certification and Land Rental Market Participation in Ethiopia' (2011) 47(1) *Journal of Development Studies* 31.

[9] ST Holden, K Deininger and H Ghebru, 'Impacts of Low Cost Land Certification on Investment and Productivity' (2009) 91(2) *American Journal of Agricultural Economics* 359; Deininger et al (n 6).

[10] This classification could be gathered from Art 17 of the Universal Declaration of Human Rights (UDHR) that provides, in two subsections, first the human right of everyone to own property alone or in association with others, and second the right not to be arbitrarily deprived of one's property. Universal Declaration of Human Rights (adopted 10 December 1948) UNGA Res 217 A(III) (UDHR) Art 17.

to resources such as land remains widely contested, the recognition of a human right to the peaceful enjoyment of property is less controversial.[11] Tom Allen explains this distinction in the context of the European human rights system which, under article 1 of the First Protocol to the European Convention on Human Rights, guarantees the right to the peaceful enjoyment of possessions.[12] Allen describes the Convention as only recognising property and not guaranteeing an 'entitlement to property' which, according to him, 'exists prior to any human rights law, rather than being constituted by State response to basic needs'.[13]

One of the most debated points among the United Nations Human Rights Commission members during the drafting process of the Universal Declaration of Human Rights (UDHR) was the recognition of the right to property as a human right. At a time when the world was divided, on the one hand, into the socialist bloc with command economies as its guiding principle and, on the other, capitalist states with free market economies, the inclusion of the right to property in the UDHR was not an easy task. When the world community, acting through the UN, sought a stronger human rights commitment by upgrading the Declaration to a Covenant, the old debate on recognising the human right to property once again resurfaced, though this time with more fierceness because of the international politics of the Cold War.[14]

This debate led, in part, to the classification of human rights into socio-economic rights, on the one hand, and civil and political rights on the other hand, resulting in the adoption of two separate covenants despite the fact that the UDHR had insisted on the indivisibility and interdependence of human rights. The disagreement basically related to the nature of the obligations of state parties emanating from these two types of rights and

[11] Under the Regional human rights mechanisms the second aspect of the right to property in terms of protection against arbitrary interference is given recognition. See, for instance, Art 1 of the Protocol to the European Convention on Human Rights, Paris, 20.III.1952; Art 21 of the American Convention on Human Rights (adopted November 22, entered into force 18 July 1978) (1970) 9 ILM 673 (ACHR); Art 14 of the African Charter on Human and Peoples' Rights (adopted 27 June 1981, entered into force 21 October 1986) (1982) 21 ILM 58.

[12] The provision states, 'Every natural or legal person is entitled to the peaceful enjoyment of his possessions. No one shall be deprived of his possessions except in the public interest and subject to the conditions provided for by law and the general principles of international law. The Preceding provisions shall not, however, in any way impair the right of a State to enforce such laws as it deems necessary to control the use of property in accordance with the general interest or to secure the payment of taxes or other contributions or penalties'. See Art 1 of the First Protocol to European Convention on Human Rights. T Allen, 'Liberalism, Social Democracy and the Value of Property under the European Convention on Human Rights' (2010) 59(4) *International and Comparative Law Quarterly* 1055.

[13] Allen, ibid 1065.

[14] This was because the socialist bloc, headed by the Soviet Union, espoused public ownership of all factors of production whereas the capitalist bloc regarded public ownership as an anti-thesis to capitalism and free market ideals. See generally M Craven, 'The International Covenant on Economic, Social and Cultural Rights—A Perspective on its Development' (DPhil thesis, University of Nottingham, 1992).

resistance to the recognition of socio-economic rights, particularly from the capitalist bloc led by the US which, until this date, remains a non-party to the International Covenant on Economic, Social and Cultural Rights (ICESCR).[15] While neither the International Covenant on Civil and Political Rights (ICCPR) nor the ICESCR have provided for the human right to property, as was done under Article 17 of the UDHR, both do have a provision which is effectively identical and which, in Nickel's words, speaks about 'national property rights'.[16] The common article 1 of the two covenants speaks about the collective right to self-determination of people, and its sub-article 2 states that 'all people may ... freely dispose of their natural wealth and resources ... In no case may a people be deprived of its own means of subsistence'. This paragraph of the two covenants has been described as addressing the economic aspects of the right to self-determination.[17] The reference in this provision to 'a people' makes it automatically inapplicable to individuals, a fact that has been repeatedly affirmed by the Human Rights Committee based on its mandate under the Optional Protocol.[18]

Accordingly, the two covenants were drafted without acknowledging a human right to property, which is the only substantive right not to succeed in being upgraded to a covenant right from the UDHR. Van Banning expressed this gap as a 'failure' of the world community acting through the UN.[19] Thus, we can say that at the international level, the human right to property as such cannot be clearly supported within the context of international human rights treaties. In the context of the right to land, however, the UN normative framework has evolved and now special significance is attached to recognising indigenous people's rights to their lands, territories and resources.[20] Accordingly, the United Nations Declaration on the

[15] C Tomuschat, *Human Rights: Between Idealism and Realism* 2nd edn (Oxford, Oxford University Press, 2008).

[16] JW Nickel, *Making Sense of Human Rights: Philosophical Reflections on the Universal Declaration of Human Rights* (California, University of California Press, 1987) 152. See also the International Covenant on Economic, Social and Cultural Rights (adopted 16 December 1966, entered into force 3 January 1976) 993 UNTS 3 and International Covenant on Civil and Political Rights (adopted 16 December 1966, entered into force 23 March 1976) 999 UNTS 171 (ICCPR) Art 1.

[17] See for instance, the UN Human Rights Committee, 'General Comment No 12' in 'Note by Secretariat, Compilation of General Comments and General Recommendations Adopted by Human Rights Treaty Bodies' (13 March 1984) UN Doc HRI/GEN/1/Rev.1, para 5.

[18] *Mikmaq tribal society v Canada*, Communication No 78/1980 (30 September 1980), UN Doc Supp No 40 (A/39/40) at 200 (1984), *Ivan Kitok v Sweden*, Communication No 197/1985, CCPR/C/33/D/197/1985 (1988) and *Lubicon Lake Band v Canada*, Communication No 167/1984 (26 March 1990), UN Doc Supp No 40 (A/45/40) at 1 (1990) in all of which cases the Committee declined from granting a violation of Art 1 of the ICCPR merely because the Optional Protocol only permits submission for alleged violations of individual rights, while this provision is all about 'a people's right'.

[19] TRG Banning, *The Human Right to Property* (Antwerp, Intersentia, 2002) 46.

[20] UNGA, Declaration on the Rights of Indigenous Peoples, 13 September 2007, A/RES/61/295, Art 26.

Rights of Indigenous Peoples (UNDRIP) has accorded a special place for Article 17 of the UDHR with respect to property rights to the land of indigenous people.

A. Land Rights of 'Indigenous' People

Where communities are concerned, international human rights law further recognises indigenous people's special need for the protection of their traditional lands. According to Article 26 of the UNDRIP, indigenous peoples are guaranteed 'the right to the lands, territories and resources which they traditionally owned, occupied or otherwise used or acquired', and states are obliged to protect the same with 'due respect to their customs, traditions and land tenure systems'.[21] This special protection is justified, according to the Declaration, because of 'their political, economic, social structures and their cultures, spiritual traditions, histories and philosophies'.[22] The Declaration, however, does not contain a definition of 'indigenous people', and according to the African Commission on Human and People's Rights (ACHPR), 'a definition is not necessary or useful, as there is no universally agreed definition of the term and no single definition can capture the characteristics of indigenous populations'.[23]

In the Ethiopian context, there are no references in the Constitution or any other laws having a bearing on the subject of indigenous character. For example, the rural land administration laws, both at the federal and regional levels, do not make even a single reference to indigenous populations and/or their peculiar land rights. Although the Constitution and the regional laws speak of communal land rights, including pastoralists, 'they all failed to come up with clear and enforceable instruments for collective land rights of traditional communities'.[24] The author's attempt to locate any state policy justification for this silence ended with no concrete finding. Nonetheless, the African view on the conceptualisation of the indigenous population, which perhaps explains the Ethiopian position, is best described by the ACHPR in the following terms:

> in Africa, the term indigenous populations does not mean 'first inhabitants' in reference to aboriginality as opposed to non-African communities or those

[21] UNDRIP Art 26(1) and (3).

[22] UNDRIP, Preamble, para 7.

[23] Advisory Opinion of the African Commission on Human and Peoples' Rights on the UN Declaration on the Rights of Indigenous Peoples, 41st Ordinary Session, (16–30 May 2007) para 10.

[24] F Thornberry and F Viljoen, *Overview Report on the Constitutional and Legislative Protection of the Rights of Indigenous Peoples in 24 African Countries* (International Labour Organisation and the African Commission on Human and Peoples Rights, 2009) 91.

> having come from elsewhere. This peculiarity distinguishes Africa from the other continents where native communities have been almost annihilated by non-native populations. Therefore, the ACHPR considers that any African can legitimately consider him/herself as an indigene on the continent.[25]

In line with this understanding, the Ethiopian constitution bestows sovereignty on the 'nations, nationalities and peoples'[26] of Ethiopia as a whole, defined as 'a group of people who have or share a large measure of a common culture or similar customs, mutual intelligibility of language, belief in a common or related identity, a common psychological make-up, and who inhabit an identifiable, predominantly contiguous territory'.[27] Again, it does not recognise any indigenous status or minority status emerging from national, ethnic, religious and linguistic backgrounds.[28] Therefore, when the law, for instance, refers to pastoralists in Ethiopia, what it implies is solely the type of livelihood as being dependent fully or partially on livestock production, without any special recognition of indigenous character.[29]

B. Human Right to Land as a Derivative Right

One can infer a derivative right to property, however, from various provisions of the ICESCR and the ICCPR. Indeed, in relation to land, the existence of an indirect recognition within the global human rights regime of the right to property becomes quite explicit. The primary starting point is the right to self-determination, which stipulates the right of people 'not to be deprived of its means of subsistence,' which no doubt encompasses property.[30] Furthermore, one can adopt a derivative approach based on the

[25] Advisory Opinion (n 23) 13. For further examination on the meanings and related matters of indigenous peoples in Africa, see R Home, 'Culturally Unsuited to Property Rights?: Colonial Land Laws and African Societies' (2013) 40(3) *Journal of Law and Society* 403; J Gilbert, 'Indigenous Peoples' Human Rights in Africa: The Pragmatic Revolution of the African Commission on Human and Peoples Rights' (2011) 60(1) *International and Comparative Law Quarterly* 245; V van Genugten, 'Protection of Indigenous Peoples on the African Continent: Concepts, Position Seeking and Interaction of Legal Systems' (2010) 104(1) *The American Journal of International Law* 29.

[26] Art 8(1) of 1995 FDRE Constitution.

[27] Art 39(4) of 1995 FDRE Constitution.

[28] UNGA, Report of the Independent Expert on Minority Issues, A/HRC/4/9/Add.3, 28 Feb 2007, Gay McDougall (Mission to Ethiopia, 28 Nov–12 Dec 2006) para 7.

[29] Arts 2(8) and 2(9) of Proclamation 456/2005 define pastoralist and semi-pastoralist respectively as meaning 'a member of a rural community that raises cattle by holding rangeland and moving from one place to the other', and 'the livelihood of himself and his family is based mainly on the produce from cattle; "Semi-Pastoralist" means a member of a rural community whose livelihood is based mainly on cattle raising and to some extent on crop farming'.

[30] Art 1(2) of ICESCR; see also F Coomans, 'Agrarian Reform as a Human Rights Issue in the Activities of United Nations Human Rights Bodies and Specialized Agencies' (2006) 24(1) *Netherlands Quarterly of Human Rights* 7.

conception of the interdependence of rights,[31] and in this way a human right to land is derived as a consequence of other fundamental rights and freedoms. The most significant of these are the right to adequate food,[32] the right to adequate housing,[33] minorities' rights[34], the right to work,[35] the right to development[36] and the rights of women.[37] Moreover, 'a key principle which would apply to all types of legislation, policies and programmes in the field of property-related rights is the prohibition of discrimination'.[38]

III. CURRENT CERTIFICATION PROCESSES IN ETHIOPIA

The current task of measurement, registration and certification of rural land holding rights in Ethiopia is undertaken by the regional governments and has two stages. The first level certificate involves the provision of simple and temporary landholding certificates without geo-referencing or mapping of land parcels. In the second level, meanwhile, a permanent certificate is issued, with geo-referencing and mapping of individual parcels, with the objective of further enhancing tenure security for smallholder farmers and stimulating greater investment by farmers in sustainable land management

[31] The UNGA 'Vienna Declaration and Programme of Action' (Vienna, 14–25 June 1993) UN Doc A/CONF. 157/23.

[32] This is as provided under Art 11(1) of the ICESCR. See also Report of the UN Special Rapporteur on the Right to Food, J Ziegler, A/56/210, 23 July 2001. This message has been reiterated by the current Special Rapporteur on the subject, UNGA 'Report of the Special Rapporteur on the right to food Olivier De Schutter on access to land and the right to food' GAOR 66th Session (A/65/281) (11 August 2010); FAO, 'Voluntary Guidelines to Support the Progressive Realisation of the Right to Food in the Context of National Food Security' (adopted by the 127th Session of the FAO Council) (November 2004).

[33] Art 11(1) of the ICESCR. See also UNCHR (Sub-Commission), 'Report by Special Rapporteur Mr Rajindar Sachar 1995/12' UN Doc E/CN.4/Sub.2/1995/12, paras 54 and 55; UN Human Rights Council (UNHRC) 'Report of the UN Special Rapporteur on the Right to Adequate Housing as a Component of the Right to an Adequate Standard of Living Mr M Kothari' (5 February 2007) UN Doc A/HRC/4/18, paras 25–31; UN-HABITAT Habitat Agenda Goals and Principles, Commitments and Global Plan of Action (3–14 June 1996, Istambul, Turkey) <http://ww2.unhabitat.org/declarations/documents/The Habitat_Agenda.pdf> accessed 07 June 2014.

[34] Art 27 of the ICCPR; also see ILO Convention C169 Concerning Indigenous and Tribal Peoples (adopted 27 June 1989, entered into force 5 September 1991) particularly see Part II and General Recommendation No 23 by the UN Human Rights Committee on Art 27 of the ICCPR (1994), para 7.

[35] Art 6 of the ICESCR as 'access to land enables peasants to exercise their right to work.

[36] Declaration on the Right to Development, specially Art 8(1) which obliges states to 'undertake at national level all necessary measures for the realisation of the right to development and shall ensure, *inter alia*, equality of opportunity for all in their access to basic resources …' which naturally includes land. UNGA, Declaration on the Right to Development, Res 41/128 (4 December 1986) UN Doc A/RES/41/128.

[37] Convention on the Elimination of All Forms of Discrimination against Women (adopted 18 Dec 1979, entered into force 3 September 1981) 1249 UNTS 13 (ICEDAW) Art 14(2) g.

[38] Coomans (n 30); see also Art 2 of ICESCR and Arts 2 and 26 of ICCPR, which prohibit discrimination on the grounds of, among others, property.

practices.[39] Issuing first level holding certificates started in 1998 in the Tigray Region, in 2003 in the Amhara Region and in 2004 in the Oromia and Southern Nations, Nationalities and Peoples' Regional State (SNNPRS).[40] In early 2005, the country's second phase poverty reduction strategy paper reported that out of a total of about 13 million rural households, 6,216,819 had received a first level land holding certificate.[41] This covered the four regions of Oromia (2,484,693 households certified), Amhara (2,400,000 households certified), Tigray (632,000 households certified) and SNNPRS (700,126 households certified).[42] Although the so-called 'emerging regions' of Afar, Benishangul Gumuz and Gambella have issued rural land administration and use proclamations, they are yet to commence implementation.[43]

The country's development plan, called the Growth and Transformation Plan (GTP), that replaces the previous Plan for Accelerated and Sustained Development to End Poverty (PASDEP)[44] was issued in 2010/11 with a five year timeframe and outlines ambitious plans for transforming the country's poverty conditions.[45] The GTP has given attention to the certification process by promising the completion of the first level certification by certifying the holdings of 3.09 million households and the issuance of the second level holding certificate for 12.7 million households spread over the five year plan period.[46] Therefore, the perpetual holding right that the laws guaranteed is to be represented by the certificate, the registers of which are to be kept by the local level land administration offices. As detailed by Deininger et al, the process involves traditional methods of determining the size of plots 'either using ropes or relying on knowledge of the number of "*timads*" of a plot'.[47] Once determined, the plot is described by naming the neighbours bordering it from east, west, south and north. The process of certification is carried out, as affirmed by Deininger and Feder, 'with high levels

[39] S Bezu and S Holden, 'Unbundling Land Administrative Reform: Demand for Second Stage Land Certification in Ethiopia' (2013), Norwegian University of Life Sciences, Centre for Land Tenure Studies Working Paper 03/13, 7.

[40] Holden et al (n 9) 361.

[41] Federal Democratic Republic of Ethiopia Ministry of Finance and Economic Development, *Ethiopia, Building on Progress: Plan for Accelerated and Sustained Development to End Poverty (PASDEP), 2005/06–2009/10*, 87.

[42] ibid.

[43] The World Bank Report, The World Bank Report, *Federal Democratic Republic of Ethiopia-Options for Strengthening Land Administration* (2012, Washington) Report No 6163.

[44] PASDEP (n 41).

[45] The Federal Democratic Republic of Ethiopia, Growth and Transformation Plan (GTP) 2010/11–2014/15.

[46] ibid (Vol II, Policy Matrix) 8.

[47] K Deininger, J Zevenbergen and DA Ali, 'Assessing the Certification Process of Ethiopia's Rural Lands' (Colloque International, Montpellier, 2006) 4. The word '*timad*' is used as a local unit of measurement of land according to which 4 *timad* equals 1 hectare. It simply means the amount of land that can be ploughed with a pair of oxen in a day.

of community participation'.[48] It is a process by which the three important questions, as suggested by Ho and Spoor, are answered: 'whose land is it? How much is it? And where is it located?'[49]

The certification is targeted not only at individual holdings but also those of governmental and non-governmental organisations, private investors and social institutions.[50] Moreover, a certificate of holding over communal land will also be issued in the name of the beneficiary community and then be kept at Kebele Administration office.[51] Both private and communal holdings will therefore have a certificate of holding to be issued in the name of the beneficiaries both individually and collectively. However, even if registration of communal holdings has been undertaken as part of the ongoing first-level certification process in the Regions of Amhara, Oromia, SNNPRS and Tigray, the boundaries of this land are not recorded, and the communal land overall is registered in the name of the Kebele and not in the name of specific local groups as the laws anticipate.[52]

IV. IMPLICATIONS ON WOMEN AND PASTORALIST COMMUNITIES

A. Rural Land Rights of Women

Women are exposed to various forms of discriminatory social and legal conditions that require special treatment. This is especially true for rural women who are victims of multi-layered exclusion and marginalisation, both within the public and household domain. In Ethiopia, 49 per cent of the population is female and 84 per cent of these are defined as rural.[53] Despite this, the number of female landholders, as well as their productivity, is abysmally low compared to their male counterparts. According to the World Bank, in Ethiopia, as elsewhere in Africa, providing access to land and other productive resources would improve women's agricultural yields, which at present are 26 per cent less than those of male farmers in Ethiopia by 10 to 30 per cent.[54]

[48] K Deininger and G Feder, 'Land Registration, Governance and Development: Evidence and Implications for Policy' (2009) 24(2) *The World Bank Research Observer* 245.

[49] P Ho and M Spoor, 'Whose Land? The Political Economy of Land Titling in Transitional Economies' (2006) 23 *Land Policy* 580.

[50] Art 6(8) of Southern Nations, Nationalities and Peoples' Regional State Rural Land Administration and Utilisation Proclamation 110/2007 (Proclamation 110/2007).

[51] Art 6(12) of Proclamation 110/2007.

[52] The World Bank Report (n 43) 48.

[53] 2007 Population and housing census, Ethiopian statistics Agency, www.csa.gov.et/newcsaweb/images/documents/surveys/Population%20and%20Housing%20census/ETH-pop-2007/survey0/data/Doc/Reports/National_Statistical.pdf.

[54] This is high compared to Kenya's 4%, and relatively better compared to Nigeria, where the average gender difference in productivity is 40%. The World Bank, *World Development*

Even if the purposes of the certification of rural land holdings are clear, relevant and timely, however, the process primarily benefits those who already have land holdings based on the previous regime's land distribution measures, which were carried out in the late 1970s after the promulgation of the ground-breaking law to nationalise all land and extra houses. This historic distribution was enacted based on household units as beneficiaries and thus it was households, represented by their heads—husbands—rather than individuals per se that obtained land use rights.[55] This largely excluded women from obtaining land since the husband was normally the head of the family or household and the title was therefore issued in his name. Second, because of the fact that they cannot plough land by themselves, there was no way that even those female headed families would have had the opportunity to obtain title. The combination of the patriarchal laws that made the husband alone the head of the family and the tradition that undermined the agency of women in agriculture has served to exclude women from accessing land. In consequence, the certification process is in reality merely measuring, certifying and granting land possession certificates to those persons who already have land holdings provable by and to the members of the land administration committee members and is thus perpetuating these historic inequalities.

The framework legislation issued by the federal legislature has specific provisions that seek to acknowledge the equal rights of women and men in respect to access to and control of rural land. For instance, the provision that lays down the guiding principles relating to the acquisition and use of rural land declares 'women who want to engage in agriculture shall have the right to get and use rural land'.[56] In a sense, it is a legislative acknowledgement of the reality that prevails in our rural society in which women do not normally plough and, in cases where they have holdings of their own, the norm is for them to contract it out to male farmers under share-cropping or other similar schemes.[57] Even the rental arrangements are far from being fair because, as observed by Bezabih and others, women are 'persuaded into renting out land to relatives and in-laws, who assume informal access rights

Report 2012: Gender Equality and Development (World Bank, 2012) 202; see FK Byamugisha, *Securing Africa's Land for Shared Prosperity: A Program to Scale up Reforms and Investments* (The World Bank, 2013) 14.

[55] The Public Ownership of Rural Lands Proclamation 31/1975 (Proclamation 31/1975) Art 4 provided for important principles on distribution of privately owned rural lands. It had stipulated the principle of equality and non-discrimination, the maximum size of land to be allotted to a particular family and a prohibition on the use of hired labour to cultivate one's holding. Particularly, Art 4(3) stated, 'the size of land to be allotted to any farming family shall at no time exceed 10 hectares.' Therefore, it was a 'farming family' rather than an individual that was taken as a beneficiary of the holding right.

[56] Art 5(1)(c) of Proclamation 456/2005.

[57] Under previous regime's Proclamation 31/1975 too, the use of hired labour to cultivate land was exceptionally permitted for 'a woman with no other adequate means of livelihood'.

towards the land'.[58] In a comparative research on gender and governance in rural services carried out on Ghana, India and Ethiopia, it was also stated about Ethiopia's women that:

> Anyone who has spent time in rural Ethiopia can readily observe that in most parts of the country women are intimately involved in all aspects of agricultural production, marketing, food procurement, and household nutrition. Despite this reality, the view is widely held that 'women do not farm.' This cultural perception remains strong even though numerous agricultural tasks are deemed 'women's work,' including weeding, harvesting, preparing storage containers, managing all aspects of home gardens and poultry raising, transporting farm inputs to the field, and procuring water for household use and some on-farm uses.[59]

Therefore, when the law stipulates the right of access to rural land to women who want to engage in agriculture, it is a reflection of this perception of considering farming as a male-only engagement. In any event, this guarantee of equal access to agricultural land for women is reinforced by a further proclamation which allows the joint certification of possession rights over land that belongs to both husband and wife. This provision states that 'where land is jointly held by husband and wife ... the holding certificate shall be prepared in the name of all the joint owners'.[60] This piece of legislation, however, omitted what its predecessor had established as an important principle of land administration, namely in Article 5(4) which reads:

> The land administration law of a Region shall confirm the equal rights of women in respect of the use, administration and control of land as well as in respect of transferring and bequeathing holding rights.[61]

It is difficult to understand why there has been this regression in respect to the establishment of a comprehensive equality framework within the new legislation. One area where this general equality clause would have served a purpose is, for instance, in guiding the regional laws to ensure gender balance in constituting the various land administration institutions, particularly the Kebele-level Land Administration Committees (LAC).[62]

[58] Bezabih et al (n 8) 6.

[59] The World Bank and International Food Policy Research Institute, *Gender and Governance in Rural Services: Insights from India, Ghana and Ethiopia* (The World Bank, 2010) 62.

[60] Art 6(4) of Proclamation 456/2005.

[61] Art 5(4) of the Federal Proclamation 89/1997 which has been expressly repealed by Art 20(1) of Proclamation 456/2005.

[62] It is particularly a common practice in traditionally patriarchal societies to impose legal minimums of female membership in various institutions that are empowered to make crucial decisions on matters as vital as land. For instance in neighbouring Uganda the Land Act requires land management bodies and institutions to have women representation. 'The Uganda Land Commission must include at least one female among its five members, one-third of the membership of the District Land Boards must be female, and Land Committees at the parish level must have at least one female among their four members'. J Asiimwe, 'Making Women's Land Rights a Reality in Uganda: Advocacy for Co-Ownership by Spouses' (2001) 4(171) *Yale Human Rights & Development Law Journal* 177–78.

The LAC is composed of five to six elected members of the community who are expected to be traditional leaders and of high standing in the particular locality. These committees have the highest responsibility in the implementation of the certification in terms of identification of individual plots, demarcation, boundary marking, validation of their findings through popular participation, measurement of plots and recording of personal details once they are validated, and then forwarding of the information to the Kebele for purposes of registration and issuance of the certificate. The composition of the LACs however rarely includes even a single woman member and it is suggested that 'the heavy workload demands on members of the LAC, and the need at times to stay overnight in distant locations may have limited the inclination of woman to undertake such an assignment'.[63]

B. Polygamy and Rural Land Administration

According to the Federal Criminal Code, as a rule, the act of polygamy is punishable by a term of imprisonment of up to five years.[64] The Code however makes an exception from this general prohibition under Article 651 stating, 'the preceding Article shall not apply where bigamy is committed in conformity with religious or traditional practices recognised by law'. Therefore, for a polygamous act to be condoned under this provision, the existence of a law acknowledging the particular religious or traditional practice must be proved. This was likewise stipulated under the 1957 Penal Code and the Civil Code had also categorically prohibited acts of plural marriages.[65] The original position taken under the 1957 Penal Code (which remains unchanged under the 2004 Criminal Code when it comes to the crime of bigamy) was meant to create a compromise, because of the prevalence of polygamy, in such a way that 'Muslims would be allowed to practice polygamy in what was basically a monogamous society'.[66] A polygamous marriage, therefore, is always a crime in Ethiopia though it is only punishable if it occurs in a region where the family law expressly prohibits that form of behaviour. The recognition or proscription of polygamy has occupied a central place in discussions of family law revision in Ethiopia and there have been instances where express permission for polygamy in one of the regional family laws has later been rescinded.[67] As the family laws

[63] The World Bank Report (n 43) 47.

[64] Art 650 of the Federal Criminal Code of Ethiopia Proclamation No 414/2004.

[65] Arts 616 and 617 of the Penal Code of the Empire of Ethiopia, Proclamation 157/1957; see also the Art 585 of the Civil Code of Ethiopia.

[66] NJ Singer, 'Islamic Law and the Development of the Ethiopian Legal System' (1971) 17 *Howard Law Journal* 130.

[67] Art 32 of the repealed Tigray Family Law Proclamation 33/1998, 10 November 1998.

stand now, all the regions contain an express prohibition on polygamy and accordingly it continues to be punishable under the criminal law. When one looks at the certification of rural land holding practices, however, this prohibition appears to have been set aside. Here, a brief overview of two regions' (Oromia and SNNPRS) practices of registration and certification of rural land holdings is presented to show the complexities and the ensuing rights violations involved in situations where a person has more than one wife.

The certification processes in the Oromia and SNNP Regional States are conducted in a slightly different manner when it comes to certifying the land holdings of a person who is living within multiple marriages. They have each adopted different standard certificates with regard to the right holder's particulars' entry, photographs, and the manner of registering a title holder married to more than one person at the same time. Under the Oromia region's certificate, a person's holding is to be entered in his own name as 'holder's name.' And the second whose name is to be entered into the certificate will be the wife or wives' name or names. With this regard, the model certificate numerates one to four downwards.[68] At the back of the document is a space to post one person's picture, ie that of the holder's. Accordingly, the registration is done in such a way that a man will have his name mentioned as holder and then his wife's/wives' names are listed, with, finally, his picture alone posted on the back. Having one's picture at the back, from a lay person's perspective, symbolises exclusivity, security and a sense of superiority. Thus, the practice, unlike the SNNPRS and Amhara practices, makes the certificate remain of value only to the husband. According to the World Bank report referred to at the beginning of this chapter, this practice undermines women's rights, commenting:

> While less than 9% of certificates are in the husband's name in Amhara, 58% and 21% are so in Oromia and the South, respectively. Analysis to identify reasons for such differences would be desirable. An intriguing possibility is that the requirement to include women's picture on the certificate in Amhara and the South but not in Oromia is at the source of the neglect of women's rights in the latter.[69]

When we look into the SNNPRS' approach to the matter, there are differences to Oromia. In the SNNPRS certificate the title holders will be two where it is a couple's property,[70] and the entry is to be done in the order of

[68] Whether that caps the maximum wives one may have or just describes the Share'a law's maximum number of wives that one may possess is unclear. One may even say that it just is meant to be economical in the use of the paper space and more may also be welcomed.

[69] Deininger et al (n 7) 1800.

[70] A land could be the common property of the spouses because one of the spouses has decided to make it a common property upon the conclusion of the marriage, because they have obtained it through donation from a person in common, or because either of them has obtained it through succession or donation personally and has not requested for it to be a separate property to that of the spouse. See Art 62 of the Federal Family Code which is similarly endorsed by the various Regional family laws.

holder number one and holder number two. By default the husband's name is to be written first with the wife's following. Legally speaking, however, this has no effect whatsoever and there is no legal requirement that it should be the husband's name that comes first. The picture is to be posted at the front page of the certificate just above the names' list and here lies the second difference because the certificate has to carry the picture of both the husband and the wife. Where a polygamous marriage exists, here too the land administration bureau is not in a position to refuse certification. It achieves this in a slightly different way, however, and with some form of novelty distinct from the countrywide practice of possession certifications. The husband has to decide which one of the wives is the primary one in his married life and then gives her the chance of being registered as second to his name in the landholding where his name appears as holder number one. For the remaining wives, parcels will be allocated and each one of them will be registered in a separate certificate and in one or more parcels and in these circumstances, the wife's name is to be written as the first holder with the husband as the second on the list. This makes the assertion of inferior–superior relations between the holders more valid because in writing the second wife's name first, and not second, shows some distinct status. In this manner, therefore, the person remains married to multiple wives and in cases where division of the property is tabled, each one of them goes with her possession for which her name has been registered.

Primarily, the law prohibiting polygamy and this land certification practice directly contradict each other because the former's prohibition has been disregarded by the latter. Furthermore, well established rules on legal construction have it that where two rules on the same topic conflict, meaning must be sought by construing the status of laws *in pari materia*, and the one having higher authority must be given precedence over the other. In this specific situation, the land certification process is conducted based on some form of administrative decision or directive.[71] Accordingly, the family laws' provisions regarding polygamy must be observed. As simple a solution as this might appear, its practicality cannot be underestimated.

Polygamy, contrary to the legal prohibitions, is a widely practised act, particularly in the eastern and southern parts of the country.[72] And as reported by Holden and Tefera, the original attempt by the Oromia and SNNPRS to have the husband registered in one certificate and only with one wife was highly resisted by the rural land holders eventually compelling the land

[71] An attempt to find any authoritative legal instrument that stipulates this form of registration process has not been successful except the model certificate that can at least be considered as an administrative directive of the respective Regional councils.

[72] Singer (n 66).

administration institutions to design this system of registration with multiple wives.[73] The law on polygamy and the practice are therefore incompatible in that polygamy continues to prevail even in the face of clear legal proscriptions. Therefore, the rural land administration system operates within such a social setting and, as affirmed by the World Bank Report, 'proper rural land administration can be a very effective instrument to empower women socially and economically'.[74] Although women are generally disadvantaged in the division of property, particularly following divorce, research has found that women in polygamous households are in a more disadvantaged position.[75] Therefore, the alliance the rural land administration system has made with the practice of polygamy by issuing land holding certificates for a person with multiple wives exacerbates gender biases in the society and seriously undermines their human rights.

The family law on polygamy and the rural land administration should have been made to work in harmony. For instance, under the Amhara system of registration, where a person has multiple wives, he will not be allowed to register the landholding as belonging to husband and wives. Rather the registration will be made as a common holding of all those three or four.[76] This approach maintains a neutral position towards polygamy without affecting the rights of women to have their holding rights recognised. By definition, common holding gives rise to an equal use right over the land.[77] This is better than the registration system of the Oromia Region that simply lists the wives as 'wives' of the holder-husband and affixes only the latter's photo at the back of the certificate. It is also preferable compared to the SNNPRS that registers the husband as first holder, the first wife as second holder, and then with the rest of the wives having the husband as second holder after putting the other wife as the first, which is repeated in the successive certificates to be issued based on the number of wives he marries. Holden and Tefera have argued that the approach of these two regions creates differentiation between wives according to the timing of their marriage:

> There was also a difference in the perceptions of the first wife vs. later wives of polygamous men. Thirty-five percent of the first wives perceived their positions had been strengthened in cases of divorce and death of the husband, while 51% of the later wives perceived so. The difference may be due to the weaker initial

[73] S Holden and T Tefera, *Land Registration in Ethiopia: Early Impacts on Women* (UN-HABITAT 2008) 5.

[74] The World Bank Report (n 43) 17.

[75] Y Adal, 'Rural Women's Access to Land in Ethiopia' in D Rahmato and T Assefa (eds), *Land and the Challenge of Sustainable Development in Ethiopia* (Addis Ababa, Forum for Social Studies, 2006) 34.

[76] Amhara Region Rural Land Holding Registration and Updating Guideline (April 2008 Amhara National Regional State Environmental Protection Land Administration and Use Authority-EPLAUA), on file with the author.

[77] Art 2(10) of the Amhara Proclamation 133/2006.

> position of later wives as compared to the first wives. We found evidence that the polygamous wives had a weaker position than other wives and that the later wives of polygamous households had even weaker position than the first wife of such households, as measured by their expectations about how much land they would keep upon divorce.[78]

Moreover, by taking a firm position on polygamy, the rural land administration system would contribute towards the enforcement of the law prohibiting such an act that is said to degrade women's positions 'as low-rank wives' and thereby 'reducing their agency and well-being'.[79] This has become, under the African context, a human rights concern as can be gathered from the protocol to the African Charter on Human and Peoples' Rights. This protocol, which also replicates most of the provisions of the United Nations Convention on the Elimination of all Forms of Discrimination against Women, enunciates in Article 6 those rights as they relate to marriage. Specifically, the protocol imposes an obligation on Member States to enact appropriate laws to guarantee that:

> monogamy is encouraged as the preferred form of marriage and that the rights of women in marriage and family, including in polygamous marital relationships are promoted and protected.[80]

Here the authors of the protocol are not confident enough to proscribe polygamy and declare monogamy as the exclusive norm. What the provision does is to set a 'norm of aspiration' for state parties which must do their best to encourage monogamy and at any rate to promote and protect women's right in any form of marital relations, polygamous marriages included. This is therefore an area where national legislation will have to take precedence in determining the right path, but with adequate regard being given to ensuring gender equality. The laws and practices of African countries also differ on this subject.[81] They range from express legalisation

[78] Holden and Tefera (n 74) 5–6.

[79] World Bank, *World Development Report 2012*, 163.

[80] African Union, *Protocol to the African Charter on Human and People's Rights on the Rights of Women in Africa*, 11 July 2003, Art 6(d). It is important to mention that Ethiopia, though a signatory, is yet to ratify this Protocol.

[81] For instance, Art 143 of the Code of Individuals and Family of Benin allows a man to marry more than one woman and not vice versa. Accordingly, the Constitutional Court of Benin reviewed the legislation on the basis of Art 26(1) and (2) of the country's constitution that declares 'the state ensures for all equality before the law without distinction … of gender … Men and women have equal rights …' See Benin Constitutional Court, Decision DCC 02-144, 23 December 2002, reported in the *African Human Rights Law Review*, Vol 127 (2004). In the case of *Bhe and Others v Magistrate, Khayelitsha and Others*, the Constitutional Court of South Africa has also considered, albeit tangentially, the issue of polygyny and fails short of declaring polygamy as a legally recognised act. *Bhe and Others v Magistrate, Khayelitsha and Others*, Constitutional Court of South Africa, CCT 49/03, decided on 15 October 2004, paras 124 and 125.

as is the case in Uganda to the express prohibition as we have seen in the laws of Ethiopia.[82] Indeed, in 2013, a new Marriage Bill was introduced to the Kenyan Parliament that defines marriage as 'the voluntary union of a man and a women whether in a monogamous or polygamous union and registered in accordance with this Act'.[83] In polygamous societies ensuring equity among the land right holders, as was found to be the case in Uganda by Diana Hunt, becomes very difficult.[84] The Amhara system of registering the holdings of a person with more than one wife as a joint holding brings all those mentioned in the certificate as joint holders to a presumption of equal right and to a degree conforms to the overall legal position taken towards polygamy in the region as well as in the country.

C. Pastoralists and Certification of Holdings

The pastoralists have been considered for a long time as 'the others' in a country where agriculture is the mainstay of rural livelihoods. In policy formulation and infrastructure development, the pastoralist way of life is regarded as a challenge, and at times a security threat, because of the absence of a localised existence. The previous regime's efforts to demarcate and allocate communal land rights through the introduction of group ranches, on the basis of the pastoralists' kinship, neighbourhoods and other associational grounds, have been mainly successful.[85] However, this has not been further capitalised and carried out in a more systematic and sustainable manner. Davies and Bennett describe the challenges facing pastoralists in Ethiopia where they say the State has failed to put poor people at the centre of development planning by recognising their goals and aspirations, which requires 'a sound knowledge of poverty and of what people lack when they are impoverished'.[86] There is visible discordance between traditional pastoralist rules relating to land utilisation for pasture and water and the government's policy of transforming the 'nomadic' way of life to settled agriculture.[87] What is crucially missing in Ethiopia's approach to the

[82] Under the Ugandan Customary Marriage (Registration) Act, 1973, s 4(2) declares that 'customary marriage may be polygamous'.

[83] Republic of Kenya Bill for the Introduction into the National Assembly, the Marriage Bill, 2013, Kenya Gazette Supplement, 5 July 2013, Nairobi, s 3(1).

[84] D Hunt, 'Unintended Consequences of Land Rights Reform: The Case of the 1998 Uganda Land Act' (2004) 2(22) *Development Policy Review* 173.

[85] F Beyene, 'Dismantling of Common Property, Land Use and Pastoral Livelihoods in Eastern Ethiopia' (2011) 3(1) *Journal of Development and Agricultural Economics* 475.

[86] J Davies and R Bennett, 'Livelihood Adaptations at Risk: Constraints and Opportunities for Pastoral Development in Ethiopia's Afar Region' (2007) 43(3) *The Journal of Development Studies* 491.

[87] Beyene (n 85) 476.

pastoralists is an understanding of the mobility of pastoralists in Ethiopia and elsewhere in search of pasture and water for their livestock. Little et al aptly explain this problem of the government policy that simply aspires to totally resettle the pastoral communities in the following words:

> The problem is not that Ethiopia has a pastoral settlement policy, but that it has a settlement policy that does not acknowledge the critical importance of mobility. By rural Ethiopian standards, pastoralists tend to be reasonably well off … Reasonably well off pastoralists have no reason to want to become poor peasants, and since Ethiopia already has a surplus of poor peasants, the national economy has little to gain from creating more of them. Simply settling people is no solution.[88]

By and large, the land tenure of the pastoralists has become less secure as the current registration and certification process has totally overlooked the pastoralists' land use pattern, which is characterised by mobility. This is essentially because of the absence of clear policy and implementation tools for certifying those holdings which are distinct from the settled farming household land use patterns. It is estimated that 'more than 40 percent, that is, an estimated 21 million plots, have not yet undergone first-level certification', which predominantly relates to pastoralist areas and those relating to communal holdings.[89] In other words, the architectural design of the certification process itself is suited only to private holdings of farming households, with only a legal declaration that communal holdings are also to be certified.[90]

State policy on transforming this way of life into the northern Ethiopian style of settled agriculture and animal husbandry underestimates the difficulty involved in this process of change. The GTP has treated the conditions of pastoral areas at relative length. It correctly asserts the intertwining of the pastoralist livelihood with livestock resources.[91] Most radical in terms of pastoralists' future is the GTP's policy agenda that plans to execute voluntary settlement programmes, in order to enable pastoralists to lead a settled livelihood.[92] This desire to transform their way of life has already been in place under the 'Commune Centre Development Plan and Livelihood Strategy', otherwise known as the 'Commune Programme' or 'Villagisation'.[93] This plan involves moving as many as four million people in the most

[88] PD Little, R Behnke, J McPeak and G Gebru, *Pastoral Economic Growth and Development Policy Assessment, Ethiopia (Reports 1–4)* (Future Agricultures, 2010) 10.
[89] The World Bank Report (n 43) 9.
[90] See for instance Art 6(12) of Proclamation 110/2007 which anticipates the issuance of communal holding certificate in the name of the beneficiary community which however has never been put into use so far.
[91] The GTP, Volume I (n 45) 46.
[92] ibid.
[93] DFID, USAID, UN and Irish Aid, 'Multi-agency "Villagisation" Mission to *Gambella* Regional State, Ethiopia Report' (3–8 June 2012) 3.

underdeveloped Gambella, Benishangul-Gumuz, Afar and Somali regions into new communities, or 'development centres', with the alleged objective of 'benefiting the people of the developing Regional states from sustainable and good governance outcomes'.[94] Since these areas are home to the large pastoralist communities in Ethiopia, the objective that underpins the villagisation programme is clearly part of the government's plan to change pastoralists' way of life. One official was quoted to have said with this respect, 'at the end of the day we do not really appreciate pastoralists in the forest like this ... pastoralism is not sustainable ... we must bring commercial farming, mechanised agriculture, to create job opportunities to change the environment'.[95]

This top-down and paternalistic approach by the government significantly undermines the communities' agency to control their own future and to decide either their continuation with or re-orientation away from their past. The joint donors' mission report by Department for International Development (DFID), United States Agency for International Development (USAID), UN and Irish Aid found that half of the people interviewed at the 'development centres' said they did not want to move, and there were reports of 'some pressure used'.[96] With the widespread allegation that the process is a measure of clearing the land for the purposes of transferring it to investors, the total absence of the concerned community's participation in the programme has left them disempowered and disfranchised.

The communities who are being moved, either under the villagisation programme or because of the need to clear the land for investment purposes, do not have any legal title to the land, and therefore their claims for compensation may not be tenable.[97] This particularly flows from the fact that there are no communal land certificates or otherwise provable titles on which basis compensation claims could be made. The joint research report of the International Labour Organization (ILO) and the African Commission on Human and Peoples Rights has, after expressing concern to the forced removal of pastoralists from their land, also indicated that even if an estimated '1.9 million hectares of pastoral grazing land have been taken for agriculture and 466,000 hectares for national parks, the right to be compensated "commensurate to the value of property" has not been implemented'.[98]

[94] ibid.

[95] Oakland Institute, *Understanding Land Transfer Deals in Africa: Country Report, Ethiopia* (Oakland CA, 2011) 6.

[96] DFID et al (n 93) 8.

[97] Though the constitution makes no distinction among types of holdings and forms of livelihoods in matters of entitlements to compensation during expropriation, the implementing legal and institutional framework systematically excludes pastoralists from this right. See Art 40(8) of 1995 FDRE constitution.

[98] Thornberry and Viljoen (n 24) 95.

Little et al's suggestions with regard to improving the land tenure of Ethiopia's pastoralists is worth paying attention to in ensuring their empowerment and sustainable livelihood. As they reiterate, what is required is to build upon existing customary systems and clarify their relationship to government, 'a process of legal and administrative evolution, not radical change'.[99] Citing the positive practices in Mali, they underscore the risks associated with the sedentarisation agenda that does not take into account mobility.[100] Accordingly, they put forward three topical agendas that the Ethiopian government needs to seriously consider which relate to *recognition of livestock mobility*; *protection of pastoral resources* which are threatened, among other things, by the large scale agricultural transfers and they propose with this respect a communal or group 'registration format that secures pastoral land and water rights, but does not compromise mobile pastoralism'; and setting up, through the promulgation of procedural and substantive land law, *arbitration and enforcement procedures*.

V. CONCLUSION

Formalising land rights in Ethiopia undermines the human rights of women who have historically been marginalised from landholding rights in the country. The household-based holding distribution of the former regime did accord land access only to male members of the society as legally recognised heads of the family. In acknowledging the existing holdings and issuing certificates as legal titles to those holdings, the process, if anything, only confirms the exclusion of women. This raises a fundamental rights violation as recognised under the various international human rights instruments discussed in this work. Moreover, polygamy is sanctioned by the certification process which is an act the criminal law has proscribed. The absence of uniformity in issuing a joint certificate in the name of the husband and wife also contributes to women's rights violations.

Apart from women, the partial coverage of the process that has failed to accommodate communal holdings continues to violate pastoralists' rights. The certification has only given emphasis to individual holdings and lacks both legal and institutional arrangements to adjudicate, register and certify pastoralist holdings with due regard to peculiarities involved in these

[99] Little et al (n 88) 8.

[100] According to Mali's law, 'pastoral routes are classified as part of the public domain and under government protection, and movement is sanctioned for purposes of nomadism or transhumance across the whole national territory "subject to restrictions on protected areas and animal sanitation requirements"'. Little et al (n 88) 8. See also L Cotula and P Mathieu (eds), *Legal Empowerment in Practice: Using Legal Tools to Secure Land Rights in Africa* (IIED and FAO, 2008) 47.

types of land use patterns. Even though the legal framework promised the registration to cover communal holdings instructing the administrative institutions to issue certificates in the name of the communities using the land, this has never been put into practice. Therefore, a principled approach must be adopted to address the plight of the pastoralist communities in Ethiopia whose land holdings and way of life is being threatened by both large-scale agricultural land transfer deals as well as the government's top-down policy of wanting to impose, rather than suggest, a settled livelihood.

12

Customary Land Rights, Indigenous Rights and Land Expropriation in Cameroon: Ecosystem Services as a Possible New Approach in Valuing Compensation

WALTERS NSOH*

I. INTRODUCTION

ECOSYSTEMS SUCH AS forests are recognised as an important part of cultural and natural heritage.[1] Different countries have different ways of preserving the ecosystem services from forests and ensuring that they are managed in a way that is beneficial to the public. One approach that is increasingly being considered is Payment for Ecosystem Services (PES), a system that aims to recognise the contribution of landowners and managers in enhancing these ecosystem services around the world. In other words, PES is a mechanism whereby payment is provided to encourage landowners and managers to refrain from land management practices that have a negative impact on these services, thereby providing benefits for the public or specific beneficiaries.

In Cameroon, the current approach to preserving forests' ecosystem services also entails the expropriation of the forest land to secure its management in the public interest subject to the payment of some form of

* Thanks to Professor Rosalind Malcolm and Professor Alison Clarke (School of Law, University of Surrey), Professor Colin T Reid and Ms Elizabeth Kirk (School of Law, University of Dundee), Professor Robert Home (Anglia Law School, Anglia Ruskin University) for their comments on the draft of this chapter, and to the anonymous reviewers for their incisive comments on another version of this chapter.

[1] For more on the nature and extent of forest ecosystem services, see A Shvidenko, CV Barber and R Per, 'Forest and Woodland Systems' in R Hassan, R Scholes and N Ash (eds), *Ecosystems and Human Well-Being: Current State and Trends: Findings of the Condition and Trends Working Group* Vol 1 (Washington DC, Island Press, 2005) 587–621.

compensation for the work that has been done to the land over the years. Although the expropriation procedure was initially designed to only affect private property,[2] it is increasingly being used to supplement the forestry laws and to place forested land (where customary rights may still apply) that is valuable either as a commercial asset for timber or for other reasons, such as the protection of biodiversity, under the control of the State. One key feature of this process is the limitation on who can or cannot be compensated for the loss of their interests in the land. Such expropriation is subject to the payment of compensation. However, the law does not recognise all those with a vital interest in the land as having legal rights entitling them to compensation. Even when there is a right to compensation, the valuation tests used do not take into account the different interests that contribute to the value of the land. Under the current law, compensation for expropriation is comprised of the value of crops, the value of 'worthy' buildings and other installations, the selling price of undeveloped land in urban areas and the cost of obtaining a land certificate for land that was held under customary tenure. This means that the 'real' value of the land is ignored, with the law taking account of only a very narrow and artificially created set of 'commercial' interests and market values attributed to only a few of the uses and interests affected by the expropriation. This system of valuation misses on occasion the value of land as providing livelihoods to others and benefits to the community as a whole.

The question as to what amounts to 'just and equitable' compensation has already given rise to litigation under the European Convention on Human Rights and as the law on the rights of indigenous people to land and natural resources develops, there is likely to be further litigation; strengthened by the increasing recognition of the role of the natural environment as providing vital ecosystem services that can no longer be ignored. Within this context, the aim of this chapter is to challenge the Cameroonian position both in terms of it being a misapplication of the current law and by arguing for a change in the law. Specifically it is argued that although not recognised as legal rights under the expropriation regime, customary rights remain part of the land tenure system in Cameroon. The valuation tests used to calculate the different interests that contribute to the value of the land to the customary owners and others are also considered, and, using examples from the United States of America (USA) and South Africa, it is argued that the existing set of interests and values considered in the payment of compensation does not reflect the true value of the land expropriated. The concept of

[2] In Cameroon, lands subject to private property rights include lands already registered under the preceding State land administration systems as privately owned: Ordinance No 74-1 of 6 July 1974 to establish rules governing land tenure, Art 2.

ecosystem services as a new interest in land[3] might provide a basis of getting beyond the narrow and artificially created set of 'commercial' interests and market values attributed to only a few of the uses and interest in land; but such an attempt is hampered by the challenges with valuing ecosystem services.

II. 'VALUE' OF EXPROPRIATED FOREST LAND

Forest resources are important from different perspectives and for a variety of purposes. Although extremely difficult to gauge, the economic value of the ecosystem services of the world's forests is vast. The importance of forests in the provision of vital ecosystem services is evident from the percentage of the world's population directly or indirectly associated with or dependent upon forests. According to World Bank estimates, more than half a billion people living in extreme poverty depend on forests for some part of their livelihoods.[4] While the forest product industry is a source of economic growth and employment, the international trade in global forest products is nonetheless estimated in the order of US $270 billion, of which developing countries account for 20 per cent.[5]

Biologically, World Bank estimates show that forests are home to at least 80 per cent of the world's remaining terrestrial biodiversity and are a major carbon sink that regulate the global climate.[6] Forests are also known to help in maintaining the fertility of the soil, protecting watersheds and reducing the risk of natural disasters such as floods and landslides.

Socially, forests are even harder to classify. They may support isolated pockets of traditional life or lands absorbing uprooted people with nowhere else to go. Forests may be refuges for indigenous cultures. They almost never represent the centres of wealth, power or culture of the modern Nation-State, yet people in those centres of power may see forests as having symbolic or moral values absent in the great cities. These are just some of the ecosystem services attached to the various uses of the forest.

Specifically within Cameroon, the more than 20 million hectares (ha) of tropical rainforest[7] acts as a huge carbon sink in the global fight against

[3] AI Davis, 'Ecosystem Services and the Value of Land' (2010) 20 *Duke Environmental Law & Policy Forum* 339; J Williams, P Martin and C Stone, *Using Ecosystem Services as a Means to Diffuse Political Land Use Decisions in Peri-Urban Regions*, CRC for Irrigation Futures(Armidale, University of New England, 2010).

[4] World Bank, 'Forests and Forestry Sector' (World Bank, 2010) www.go.worldbank.org/VIQE69YFZ0.

[5] ibid.

[6] ibid.

[7] B Mertens et al, *Interactive Forestry Atlas of Cameroon (version 2.0): An Overview* (A World Resources Institute Report Prepared in Collaboration with the Cameroon Ministry of Forestry and Wildlife, Washington DC, 2007) 1.

climate change. In economic terms, the Cameroonian forestry sector is the second largest export revenue source, with timber exports amounting to about six and a half per cent of the Gross Domestic Product (GDP).[8] The forest is also home to several heterogeneous groups of people including the indigenous Pygmy population, who have one of the oldest cultures on earth.[9] The importance of the services provided by the Cameroon forest to poverty reduction is reflected in various policy documents such as the different versions of the Poverty Reduction Strategy Paper (PRSP)[10] under the headings of economic diversification and development of the private sector.

Over the years, the indigenous Pygmy population, who were one of the first settlers in the Cameroonian forests,[11] and other forested communities have, through their lifestyle choices and management practices, enhanced the value of these ecosystem services. As will be argued below, schemes designed to reward land managers whose land management practices enhance the provision of these ecosystem services recognise this contribution to the overall value of land. However, to what extent does the system of paying compensation recognise these vital interests in land when the expropriation procedure is triggered?

III. COMPENSATION AND INDIGENOUS CULTURES

Compensation is an important measure of fairness and justice, although the issue of what amounts to just, fair and equitable compensation remains controversial.[12] As a universal principle, it aims at making amends for any loss or damages suffered—in this case as a result of the action of the State or someone authorised by the State (for example, a logging company). Given

[8] Economist, *Economist Intelligence Unit Country Report Cameroon* (London, 2008). Other sources estimate that the Cameroon's forest sector is the second largest export revenue source for the economy, contributing eg, almost 10% of GDP in 2005, and representing 25% of all export earnings (see VERIFOR, 'Cameroon' (VERIFOR, 2007) www.verifor.org/background/case-studies/cameroon.html.

[9] See sources cited in PR Oyono, 'From Diversity to Exclusion for Forest Minorities in Cameroon' in CJP Colfer (ed), *The Equitable Forest: Diversity, Community, and Resource Management* (Washington DC, RFF Press, 2005) 114–15.

[10] The latest of these reports was prepared by the government of Cameroon in 2009. See IMF, *Cameroon: Poverty Reduction Strategy Paper—Growth and Employment Strategy Paper 2010/2020* (IMF Country Report No 10/257, Washington DC, IMF, 2009). This was a follow-up document to a previous one in 2003 and builds on a Vision 2035 (MINEPAT, *Cameroon Vision 2035—Working Paper* (Yaounde 2009)) policy document prepared earlier by the government. See also IMF, *Cameroon: Poverty Reduction Strategy Paper*, IMF Country Report No 03/249 (Washington DC, IMF, 2003) esp 34–54.

[11] E Mveng, *Histoire du Cameroun* Vol 2 (CEPER, Yaoundé, 1984) cited in Oyono (n 9) 114–15.

[12] See, eg OG Amokaye, 'Compensation for Compulsory Acquisition of Land for Mining Activities in Nigeria: The Search for a Viable Solution' in R Home (ed), *Essays in African Land Law* (Pretoria, Pretoria University Law Press, 2011) 171–87.

the spiritual attachment of indigenous forested communities to their lands and forests,[13] compensation for expropriation of land or damage to land is either not possible or, where it is possible, may never be sufficient. However, this does not mean that it is irrelevant. In fact, no amount of material support can remove the sense of loss of indigenous lands. But what is even worse is the prospect of losing one's land without any such financial compensation at all.[14] And it is significant to note that the loss may arise either as a result of expropriation or where such lands have been assigned for other purposes.[15] If that happens, the right to occupy or use that customary land holders may have does not include the right to use or exploit the forests on such lands except for domestic subsistence.[16]

The desire for sustainable forestry that protects the economic, ecological and cultural values of (forested) land and the need to pay compensation in case of expropriation are not mutually exclusive. Indeed, viewed from an indigenous rights perspective, Article 28 of the United Nations Declaration on the Rights of Indigenous Peoples[17] provides that:

1. Indigenous peoples have the right to redress, by means that can include restitution or, when this is not possible, just, fair and equitable compensation, for the lands, territories and resources which they have traditionally owned or otherwise occupied or used, and which have been confiscated, taken, occupied, used or damaged without their free, prior and informed consent.
2. Unless otherwise freely agreed upon by the peoples concerned, compensation shall take the form of lands, territories and resources equal in quality, size and legal status or of monetary compensation or other appropriate redress.

This requirement is laudable and underscores the human rights dimension to the issue of just and equitable compensation. Nonetheless, we must also

[13] For more on the spiritual connections between the Pygmies and their lands and forests, see Survival International, 'The Pygmies' (*Survival International*, 2011) www.survivalinternational.org/tribes/pygmies accessed 14 September 2011; M Kisliuk, 'Performance and Modernity Among BaAka Pygmies: A Closer Look at the Egalitarian Foragers in The Rain Forest' in B Diamond and P Moisala (eds), *Music and Gender* (Urbana, University of Illinois Press, 2000) 25–46; N Ohenjo et al, 'Health of Indigenous People in Africa'(2006) 367 *The Lancet* 1937, 1939; S Chakma and M Jensen (eds), *Racism against Indigenous Peoples* (Copenhagen, IWGIA, 2001) 312–26. See, also J Sheehan, 'Towards Compensation for the Compulsory Acquisition of Native Title Rights and Interests in Australia' (Paper presented at the FAO/USP/RICS Foundation South Pacific Land Tenure Conflict Symposium, University of the South Pacific, Suva, Fiji, 10–12 April 2002).

[14] See, eg C O'Faircheallaigh, 'Resource Exploitation and Indigenous People: Towards a General Analytical Framework' in P Jull and S Roberts (eds), *The Challenge of Northern Regions* (North Australia Research Unit, Northern Territory Australian National University, 1991) 244.

[15] Ordinance No 74-1, Art 17(3).

[16] Law No 94-1 of 20 January 1994 to lay down Forestry, Wildlife and Fisheries Regulations (hereinafter, the 1994 Forestry Law), s 8(1) defines logging or customary right as 'the right which is recognised as being that of the local population to harvest all forest, wildlife and fisheries products freely for their personal use, except the protected species'.

[17] United Nations Declaration on the Rights of Indigenous Peoples (adopted 13 September 2007) A/RES/61/295.

be conscious of the possibility that the payment of adequate monetary compensation can actually hasten the decline of indigenous cultures. One such prospect is that benefits from compensation could further facilitate access to western lifestyles that have already significantly contributed to the cultural disintegration of the indigenous Pygmy culture over the years.[18]

The debate on the interconnectedness between culture and economic, political and social change (development) perhaps resulting from such monetary compensation has been increasingly apparent in contemporary events such as the emergence of indigenous rights movements.[19] The challenging task therefore, is not only how to get the benefits from compensation in a balanced way,[20] but also how to increase the substantive freedoms that the indigenous people have, by providing support for cultural traditions that they may want to preserve while also protecting them from cultural influences that facilitate the disintegration of their cultures. This is a real dilemma even as further research also remains to be done on the distinct implications for compensation beneficiaries of the different aspects of culture.[21] Nevertheless the worst possible solution might seem to be to destroy their culture and not give them compensation.[22] In any case, the decision as to this can only properly be taken by the indigenous people themselves, hence the need for free, prior and informed consent in environmental decisions.[23]

Against this background, this chapter is concerned only with the tests used to value the different interests in land for compensatory purposes within the context of land expropriation for forestry operations. But what does the real value of land involve? The next section considers the grounds on which ecosystem services add to the value of land. Obviously, there are difficulties on how to value such services, and these difficulties have been well documented.[24] The subject of the analysis here is not to focus on these

[18] IA Mbakogu, 'Is There Really a Relationship Between Culture and Development?'(2004) 6 *Anthropologist* 37, 38.

[19] Eg SA Radcliffe and N Laurie, 'Culture and Development: Taking Culture Seriously in Development for Andean Indigenous People'(2006) 24 *Environment and Planning D: Society and Space* 231.

[20] Sen has made the economic argument of how to get the benefits of globalisation on a more shared basis in AK Sen, *Development as Freedom* (Oxford, Oxford University Press, 1999) 13–145.

[21] SA Radcliffe (ed), *Culture and Development in a Globalising World: Geographies, Actors, and Paradigms* (London, Routledge, 2006) 1–29.

[22] Mbakogu (n 18) 43.

[23] EE Watson, 'Culture and Conservation in Post-Conflict Africa: Changing Attitudes and Challenges' in Radcliffe (n 21) 58–82; A Olasunkanmi, 'Development in Africa: The Need for a Culture-Sensitive Approach' (2011) 2 *Journal of Sociology and Social Anthropology* 97, 101.

[24] See, eg KH Redford and WM Adams, 'Payment for Ecosystem Services and the Challenge of Saving Nature'(2009) 23 *Conservation Biology* 785–87; CT Reid, 'Between Priceless and Worthless: Challenges in Using Market Mechanisms for Conserving Biodiversity' (2013) 2 *Transnational Environmental Law* 217; D Helm and C Hepburn, 'The Economic Analysis of Biodiversity: An Assessment' (2012) 28 *Oxford Review of Economic Policy* 1.

difficulties, but rather on the need to consider such an approach in calculating compensation for land expropriated, especially when it concerns customary landowners who have contributed to enhancing these ecosystem services, but who have not necessarily made improvements to the land that fit with the narrow set of 'improvements' that the current Cameroonian law requires.

IV. THE CONCEPT OF ECOSYSTEM SERVICES AND THE VALUE OF LAND

The concept of ecosystem services has emerged in the literature and in practice elsewhere in the world as one way of valuing land[25] whether that be for the purpose of compensating landowners and land managers, or for other reasons. The contribution that ecosystem services make to the overall value of land is now recognised to the extent that in the United States, for example, it has even been suggested that property owners with ecosystem services on their land should have the land purchased by the government.[26] At the moment though, the discussion is mainly focused on payment for ecosystem services as a mechanism whereby a source of income is provided to those who, by managing land in a particular way—for example, maintaining it in a 'natural' state rather than cutting down trees, building houses or converting land to intensive agriculture—are providing benefits for the public or specific beneficiaries.[27] However, if the benefits are of such public interest that the State may decide to initiate the expropriation procedure in order to better protect them, then the valuation tests used must take into account the value of maintaining land in its 'natural' state. This requires moving away from the very narrow and artificially created set of 'commercial' interests and values used to recognising the true value of land even in its 'natural' state as providing livelihoods to others and benefits (economic, social and ecological) to the community as a whole.

Four broad categories of ecosystem services are recognised at the international level. These include: provisioning services such as food, timber, fresh water and plant-derived medicines; regulating services such as those that affect water quality through the filtration of pollutants by wetlands, climate regulation through carbon storage and water cycling, and protection from disasters and disease; cultural services that provide recreation, spiritual and aesthetic values, education; and supporting services such as soil formation,

[25] See, eg Davis (n 3); Williams, Martin and Stone (n 3). See also J Sheehan and G Small, 'Biota and the Problem of Property' (2005) 22 *Environmental and Planning Law Journal* 158.

[26] J Salzman, 'Creating Markets for Ecosystem Services: Notes from the Field' (2005) 80 *NYU Law Review* 870, 937.

[27] For an overview see, Forest Trends and Katoomba Group, *Payments for Ecosystem Services—Getting Started: A Primer* (Washington DC, Forest Trends, The Katoomba Group & UNEP, 2008).

photosynthesis and nutrient cycling.[28] Studies[29] identify the great economic and spiritual value of the natural environment to society. Harnessing the benefits that the natural environment offers is central to the 'more holistic approach'[30] to the management of land that is now being encouraged through international law; an approach that requires a shift in both the mindset and practices of many of those who manage and use land. Besides the general acceptance of the need to shift our policy and practices to reflect the value of land in providing ecosystem services, a starting point is to calculate in economic terms the value of such services and to ensure that this is properly taken into account when decisions on land use are being taken.

There are challenges with valuing ecosystem services. While ecosystem services such as producing food, timber and energy have an explicit economic value reflected in the market price of the goods produced, other ecosystem services such as the protection or provision of biodiversity, valued by society cannot readily be priced.[31] The difficulty of valuing ecosystem services means that the rate of payments for the provision of ecosystem services under most Payment for Ecosystem Services (PES) schemes are not calculated based on the value of the services. They are valued in comparison to the land area or income forgone by adopting specified land management practices. Nonetheless, the approach adopted and the payment rates demonstrate the extent to which ecosystem services are seen as adding value to land.

Under the US Conservation Reserve Program (CRP), for example, payments are provided to farmers for planting long-term, resource-conserving covers on eligible farmland to improve the quality of water, control soil erosion and develop wildlife habitat.[32] Although payment rates are based on the relative productivity of the soils within each county and the average dry land cash rent or cash rent equivalent, determining the amount to pay is still largely dependent on the area of land to be placed under the scheme.

[28] The Economics of Ecosystems and Biodiversity (TEEB), *The Economics of Ecosystems and Biodiversity: Mainstreaming the Economics of Nature: A Synthesis of the Approach, Conclusions and Recommendations of TEEB* (2010) 7, and Annex 2 and the sources referred to there. See generally the website of the TEEB project www.teebweb.org and United Nations, 'Millennium Ecosystem Assessment' (2005) www.unep.org/maweb/en/index.aspx.

[29] See, eg Defra, *Securing a Healthy Natural Environment: An Action Plan for Embedding an Ecosystems Approach* (London, Defra, 2007) 7; UK National Ecosystem Assessment, *The UK National Ecosystem Assessment: Synthesis of the Key Findings* (Cambridge, UNEP-WCMC, 2011); and HM Government, *The Natural Choice: Securing the Value of Nature*, CM 8082 (London, The Stationery Office, June 2011).

[30] Convention on Biological Diversity, COP 5 (2000) Decision V/6 Ecosystem Approach, para 6, Principle 5.

[31] Reid (n 24) 217.

[32] See the website of the Conservation Reserve Program (CRP) www.fsa.usda.gov/FSA/webapp?area=home&subject=copr&topic=crp. For an overview of the history and development of the CRP, see ch 9 of JB Ruhl, SE Kraft and CL Lant, *Law and Policy of Ecosystem Services* (Washington, DC, Island Press, 2007) 186–92.

Yet, lands that offer greater environmental benefits calculated according to the Environmental Benefits Index (EBI)[33] and for which landowners are willing to accept the maximum productivity adjusted payments, are automatically accepted into the scheme. The rates per acre paid for such lands are also significantly higher than those for land without such environmental benefits. Although the scheme has its weaknesses,[34] there has also been progress in creating habitat for different species of wildlife.[35] The higher rental rates for land with greater environmental benefits reflect the increased flow of ecosystem services and their value, as well as the opportunity cost to the producer of placing this land in the programme.[36] Therefore, if land placed under the CRP, for example, is the subject of a market transaction, its market value is likely to reflect the potential of higher rental rates for the land as a result of the ecosystem services it produces.

If ecosystem valuation were included in the calculation of compensation for expropriation or land damaged it would have a significant benefit for those with a customary interest in undeveloped land. It would particularly benefit those where traditional market value approaches have failed to come up with any reasonable amount of compensation. And there are precedents for this approach being used in other countries. Specifically, the United States Court of Claims has held that, with regards to aboriginal interest:

> This method of valuation takes into consideration whatever sales of neighboring lands are of record. It considers the natural resources of the land ceded, including its climate, vegetation, including timber, game and wildlife, mineral resources and whether they are of economic value at the time of cession, or merely of potential value, water power, its then or potential use, markets and transportation—considering the ready market at that time and the potential market.[37]

Thus, in the determination of the 'market value' of the land subject to 'recognised' aboriginal interests, numerous factors need to be taken into account by the courts which go beyond a simple assessment of the economic value

[33] For more in the index see, Farm Services Agency (FSA), 'Fact Sheet: Conservation Reserve Program Sign-Up 43 Environmental Benefits Index (EBI)' (2012) www.fsa.usda.gov/Internet/FSA_File/gs43ebi.pdf; Farm Services Agency (FSA), 'Conservation Reserve Program Sign-up 41 Environmental Benefits Index (EBI)' (2011) www.fsa.usda.gov/Internet/FSA_File/crp_41_ebi.pdf; and Farm Services Agency (FSA), 'Conservation Reserve Program General Sign-up 33 Environmental Benefi ts Index' (2006) www.fsa.usda.gov/Internet/FSA_File/crp33ebi06.pdf. See further Ruhl, Kraft and Lant, ibid 190–91.

[34] eg, issues have been identified with the design structure, land eligibility criteria, and the pressure to qualify for the program that all contribute to decrease the chances of significant ecosystem service provision. See Salzman (n 26) 892–94.

[35] Farm Services Agency (FSA), 'News Release: Conservation Minded' www.fsa.usda.gov/FSA/printapp?fileName=ss_ia_artid_617.html&newsType=crpsuccessstories. For the reported State-by-State benefits of the CRP, see Farm Services Agency (FSA), 'Conservation Success Stories' www.fsa.usda.gov/FSA/webapp?area=home&subject=copr&topic=crp-20.

[36] Ruhl, Kraft and Lant (n 32) 190–91.

[37] *Otoe and Missouria Tribe of Indians v United States*, 131 Ct Cl 593, 131 F Supp 265 (CT CI, 1955) [290].

of the aboriginal activities carried out on the land. The fair value of the land is to be ascertained, taking into account all pertinent factors including the timber, game, wildlife and agricultural potential of the land. Although not expressly stated by the Court, fair market valuations that consider these factors are actually ecosystem services valuations. The recognised aboriginal interests in the USA and the customary (indigenous) interests in Cameroon have much in common, and this decision underscores the need to look beyond a narrow set of interests when valuing compensation.

The move away from the narrow set of interests is further underlined by the remarkable provisions of the South African Constitution, under which specific factors must be taken into account when different interests are balanced, including what the market value is.[38] The interests of those affected are classified under the following heads:

(a) Current use of the property;
(b) the history of the acquisition and use of the property;
(c) market value of the property;
(d) the extent of direct State investment and subsidy in the acquisition and beneficial capital improvement of the property; and
(e) purpose of expropriation.[39]

Under these different heads, public interest is classified to include the nation's commitment to land reform and to reforms to bring about equitable access to all South Africa's natural resources.[40] Market value is thus one of the factors to be considered, rather than the prime factor. This approach to the calculation of compensation is in line with other jurisdictions, for example Germany, Sweden, the United Kingdom, Ireland, Australia, Japan[41] and Canada.[42] By this approach, the interests of the landowners may increase the compensation to above market value, but this may be balanced by the fact that the public interest may reduce the compensation to an amount less than market value. Just and equitable compensation is therefore the sum total of the value of the interest of those affected by expropriation, minus the value of the public's interest. Although the list of interests given in the South African example does not expressly include ecosystem services as interests that must be valued, it was not intended to be a closed list of interests and

[38] Constitution of the Republic of South Africa Act No 108 of 1996, s 25(3).

[39] NS Terblanche, 'The Challenges to Valuers with Regard to Compensation for Expropriation and Restitution in South African Statutes' (PRRES Tenth Annual Conference, Bangkok, Thailand, 25–28 January 2004) 19–21.

[40] Constitution of the Republic of South Africa, s 25(1).

[41] See, eg DLC Miller and A Pope, *Land Title in South Africa* (Cape Town, Juta & Co, 2000) 302.

[42] AF Hacault, 'A Primer on Expropriation: Are You Missing Elements of Compensation?' (Prepared for the Annual Conference of the Appraisal Institute of Canada, Mont-Tremblant, Quebec, 27–30 May 2009) 5–14.

unconventional property interests (including those that require protection under international law) other than those listed in the section 25(3) of the Constitution may also be considered.[43]

V. 'JUST AND EQUITABLE' COMPENSATION AND HUMAN RIGHTS

The South African approach suggests that 'just and equitable' compensation involves a balancing of interests; a view which is in line with major international human rights instruments, some of which Cameroon is a signatory to. In addition to the provisions of Article 28 of the UN Declaration on the Rights of Indigenous Peoples,[44] which call for 'just, fair and equitable' compensation in case of expropriation or damage of the lands, territories and resources which indigenous peoples have traditionally owned or otherwise occupied or used, Article 21(2) of the African Charter on Human and Peoples' Rights[45] enjoins that where any 'people'[46] have been dispossessed of their 'wealth and natural resources'[47] they shall be entitled to the lawful recovery of their 'property as well as to adequate compensation'. There is tacit recognition in these provisions that indigenous people who have traditionally occupied or used lands and resources have made a significant contribution in maintaining and enhancing the ecosystem services derived from the lands and resources, and that 'just, fair and equitable' compensation should not be limited to those who 'legally' own the lands and resources.[48] The scope for consideration before the threshold for infringement of the human rights of indigenous peoples is therefore wide, both in terms of who may be entitled to compensation and the different interests taken into account when such compensation is calculated. But this is not always the

[43] *Ex parte Chairperson of the Constitutional Assembly: In re Certification of the Constitution of the Republic of South Africa* 1996 (4) SA 744 (CC). See further, D Kleyn, 'The Constitutional Protection of Property: A Comparison Between the German and the South African Approach'(1996) 11 *SA Public Law* 402.

[44] Cameroon was one of the 143 countries that overwhelmingly voted in favour of the Declaration.

[45] African (Banjul) Charter on Human and Peoples' Rights (adopted 27 June 1981, in force 21 October 1986) OAU Doc CAB/LEG/67/3 rev 5, 21 ILM 58 1982. Cameroon ratified the Charter on 20 June 1989. It should be noted that Act No 96-06 of 18 January 1996 amending the 1972 Constitution of Cameroon vested human rights with genuine constitutional status by incorporating into its preamble certain provisions of the Universal Declaration of Human Rights and the African Charter on Human and Peoples' Rights.

[46] For the meaning of the term 'people', especially within the African context see, eg RN Kiwanuka, 'The Meaning of "People" in the African Charter on Human and Peoples' Rights'(1988) 82 *American Journal of International Law* 80.

[47] Either through expropriation or the resource is spoiled by human activities such as timber exploitation.

[48] For more on the implications of these provisions, see eg J Gilbert and V Couillard, 'International Law and Land Rights in Africa: The Shift from States' Territorial Possessions to Indigenous Peoples' Ownership Rights' in Home (n 12) 47–67.

case, especially when expropriation is designed to serve a legitimate environmental interest.[49]

Even when expropriation in pursuit of environmental goals can be deemed legitimate without the express requirement for compensation[50] as case law from the European Court of Human Rights shows, the decision on whether there has been a breach of the Convention still rests on ideas such as a fair balance of interests and whether the interference with the individual's rights can be justified as a proportionate measure to achieve a permissible public goal.[51] For example, the taking of property without payment of an amount reasonably related to its value would normally constitute a disproportionate interference with property rights, and cannot be considered justifiable under Article 1 of the First Protocol.[52] However Article 1 does not guarantee a right to compensation or full compensation in all circumstances and provided the State could properly take the view that legitimate objectives of 'public interest', such as those pursued in measures of economic reform or measures designed to achieve greater social justice, may call for less than reimbursement of the full economic value or no compensation at all.[53] Again this stresses the need for the compensation and the time and manner of payment to reflect an equitable balance between the public interest and the interests of those affected.

From the above examples, there appears to be greater recognition that the expropriation law 'market value at the time of taking' approach is inappropriate to adequately compensate for the infringement of the customary interests in land. Even so, there seems to be a need to also consider the potential future value of the land. Therefore, an approach that takes into account the ecosystem services' present and future value to the land is of particular importance. This is particularly relevant in cases such as that of Cameroon where land subject to customary title or necessary for the exercise of customary rights is expropriated.

By their very nature many customary and indigenous rights to occupation or use, for example subsistence farming, logging and hunting

[49] On the lack of consistency in deciding when compensation was due see J Rowan-Robinson and A Ross, 'Compensation for Environmental Protection in Britain: The Legislative Lottery' (1993) 5 *Journal of Environmental Law* 245, written before the Human Rights Act 1998 gave effect to the European Convention on Human Rights within the UK.

[50] Art 1 of First Protocol of the European Convention on Human Rights does not expressly require compensation for expropriation.

[51] eg *Fredin v Sweden* (1991) 13 EHRR 784; *Tre Traktörer AB v Sweden* (1989) 13 EHRR 309; *Matos e Silva Lda v Portugal* (1997) 24 EHRR 573. See also *United Kingdom Association of Fish Producer Organisations v Secretary of State for Environment, Food and Rural Affairs* [2013] EWHC 1959 (Admin).

[52] *R (Trailer & Marina (Leven) Ltd)* [2004] EWCA Civ 1580, [2005] 1 WLR 1267 [58].

[53] Ibid [58]. See also, G Budlender, J Latsky and T Roux, *Juta's New Land Law* (Cape Town, Juta & Co, 1998) 1–57 and 1–65 cited in Terblanche (n 39) 21.

require land sufficient to ensure their proper exercise. The expropriation of the land for other purposes or the limitation on the exercise of the right in extreme cases, can lead to the demise of the customary activity that the right intends to protect. Such infringements affect in many cases not only those local communities exercising the right at the time the infringements are first carried out, but also all future generations of the customary communities who could have benefited from the exercise of the right. The *sui generis* character of customary ownership rights generally, and particularly the collective, cultural and historic nature of these rights,[54] strongly suggest that the loss of the exercise of the right and the lost land be compensated not only in present value terms, but also in terms which take into account the loss of the future uses of the land and the consequential long term impacts on the affected local society. This is an idea that finds support in the concept of sustainable development: a concept from which the ecosystem approach has evolved, as well as core international human rights instruments.

VI. VALUING COMPENSATION FOR LAND EXPROPRIATION UNDER CAMEROONIAN LAW

Dealing with the problems of unsustainable exploitation of forest resources, and inequality in the distribution of benefits generated by the forest sector among the local populations and the indigenous forest peoples, has seen the Cameroonian State through the introduction of successive laws governing forestry and land issues, increasingly affirm its sovereignty over land, forest resources and their related profits.[55]

Under the Constitution of the Republic of Cameroon,[56] the right to every Cameroonian to use, enjoy and dispose of property is guaranteed,[57] but the right is limited with the power and duty to manage natural resources vested in the State.[58] As in many other countries, effective exercise of this government power for forestry and other public purposes requires the expropriation of land and subsequent allocation to logging companies. Compulsory

[54] HR Berman, 'Are Indigenous Populations Entitled to International Juridical Personality?' (1985) 79 *American Society of International Law Proceedings* 189, 193.

[55] This is set out in the Preamble of the 1972 Constitution of the Republic of Cameroon, which has been maintained in subsequent amendments. The appearance of increasing numbers of commercial and industrial logging companies has further consolidated this: Oyono et al (n 9) 8. See further AJ Njoh, 'Indigenous Peoples and Ancestral Lands: Implications of the *Bakweri* Case in Cameroon' in Home (n 12) 69–90.

[56] The Constitution of Republic of Cameroon of 2 June 1972 as amended by Law No 96/06 of 18 January 1996 and Law No 2008/001 of 14 April 2008 (hereinafter, the Constitution of Cameroon).

[57] ibid, para 5 of the Preamble.

[58] ibid, para 3 of the Preamble.

expropriation, except for public purposes, should invoke the constitutional obligation to pay compensation to the landowner under conditions determined by law. However the expropriation procedure applicable makes it very easy to leave a vast majority of customary landowners without any security or compensation paid.

In addition to the Constitution, the ownership of, and property rights in forest are set out in the 1994 Forestry Law and its 1995 Decree of Implementation[59] and is strictly governed by the land tenure system.[60] Before examining the provisions of the forestry regulations as they deal with the expropriation of forest law, it is important to first look at the restrictions on land ownership by the regulations governing land tenure and State lands.

Land in Cameroon is governed by a set of laws collectively referred to as the Land Ordinances. These ordinances, which have been in force since 1974 are the basis of the country's land law, and include:

— Ordinance No 74-1 of 6 July 1974 to establish rules governing land tenure;
— Ordinance No 74-2 of 6 July 1974 to establish rules governing State Lands; and
— Ordinance No 74-3 of 6 July 1974 concerning the procedure governing expropriation for a public purpose and the terms and conditions of compensation.[61]

The enactment of these Ordinances aimed to bring into parity the divergent systems of land tenure that had existed in the country prior to 1974.[62] However the land reforms did not bring about any real change both on the western value system based aspects of the land tenure system and the efforts to erode and replace the indigenous or customary land tenure systems of the country.[63] The various shortcomings of the Land Ordinances have been

[59] Decree No 95-531-PM of 23 August 1995 to determine the conditions of implementation of the forestry regulations (hereinafter, 1995 Decree of Implementation).

[60] Law No 94-1 of 20 January 1994 to lay down Forestry, Wildlife and Fisheries Regulations (hereinafter, the 1994 Forestry Law) s 6.

[61] Hereinafter referred to as the Land Ordinances.

[62] Before the 1974 Land Ordinances, many other laws, decrees and orders had been enacted after 1963, all aimed at consolidating the State's grip on land. For example, Law No 66-3-COR of 7 July 1966 and its Decree of application, Decree No 66-307 of 25 September 1966 emphasised that there must be what was called '*la mise en valeur des terres*', requiring every individual, including the customary 'holders' to apply for a land title, irrespective of the nature of the tenure.

[63] AJ Njoh, 'The Political Economy of Urban Land Reforms in a Post-Colonial State'(1998) 22 *International Journal of Urban and Regional Research* 408, 411–12. Here, Njoh observes that 'Contemporary land laws like those that prevailed during the colonial era seek not only to place as much land as possible under the direct ownership of the state, but also to replace the traditional [customary] land tenure system with one rooted in a western value system'.

highlighted in numerous articles.[64] The law illustrates the widespread inconsistencies in Government decision making, and, coupled with other practical difficulties such a dysfunctional judiciary it places serious limits on property rights. But who owns what and to what extent are customary rights still recognised under the 1974 Land Ordinances when it comes to how compensation of land expropriation is valued?

The common feature here is the division of land into three broad categories: private property, public property and 'national lands'. Private property now covers only land for which a land certificate has been issued[65] while public property consists of all personal and real property which, by their very nature (for example, coastlands; waterways; sub-soil and air space) or intended purpose (for example, easements), is set aside either for the direct use of the public or for public services.[66] Land that has not been registered as private or public property reverts to the common pool of 'national lands'.[67] This land is administered by the State 'for the public good', and the law explicitly includes untitled lands occupied or used by rural communities by virtue of a customary tenure as 'national lands'.[68] For the purposes of this chapter, untitled lands still held by customary tenure are of particular importance.

VII. LEGALITY OF THE CUSTOMARY INTEREST IN LAND

To define 'national lands', Articles 14 and 15 of Ordinance No 74-1 state that:

> (1) National lands shall as of right comprise lands which at the date on which the present Ordinance enters into force, are not classed into the private or public property of the State and other public bodies. (2) National lands shall not include lands covered by a private property right ...[69]

National lands shall be divided into two categories:

> (1) Lands occupied with houses, farms and plantations and grazing lands, manifesting human presence and development; (2) Lands free of any effective occupation.[70]

[64] See, eg C Anyangwe, 'Land Tenure and Interest in Land in Cameroonian Indigenous Law' (1984) 27 *Cameroon Law Review* 29; CN Ngwasiri and YN Nje, *Advocacy for Separate Land Legislation for the Rural Areas of Cameroon* (Yaounde, A PVO-NGO/NRM Cameroon, 1995) 3–15; CN Ngwasiri, 'The Impacts of the Present Land Tenure Reforms in Cameroon'(1984) Editions Clé *Cameroon Law Review* 73, 76; Njoh (n 63) 411. See also the case of *Amidu Lukong v Razel Road Construction Co Ltd and MINAT* [2001] 1 CCLR Part 7 81.

[65] See Ordinance No 74-1, Arts 2, 3 and 4.

[66] Ordinance No 74-2, Art 2.

[67] Ordinance No 74-1, Art 14.

[68] ibid, Art 15.

[69] ibid, Art 14.

[70] ibid, Art 15.

This means that occupied and unoccupied lands that are not registered are included in the category of national lands. The effect of this all-embracing notion of 'national lands' is that a vast majority of Cameroonians who held land under customary law without any State-recognised document of title found their lands absorbed into national lands. It has been argued that this is sufficient to divest all customary rights holders of their customary ownership rights,[71] but not necessarily other rights (such as the rights to harvest timber products from such lands). However, a vast majority of the citizens have continued to occupy and use land as though customary ownership rights still exist and, as will be seen below, subsequent legislation is still drafted on the basis that such ownership does still exist.

Article 17 of Ordinance No 74-1 gives customary communities and individuals the right to continuous occupation or use of lands that they had been peacefully occupying or using prior to the entry into force of the Ordinance. It also gives them the right to convert such interest into a land certificate. But a land certificate is not required to guarantee the right to peaceful occupation and use by customary communities and individuals. Nevertheless, in order to succeed with any application, the customary communities and individuals have to prove that they were in effective occupation or effectively exploiting the lands (including any forest lands) by 5 August 1974.[72] For some communities such as the indigenous Pygmy populations, even if they could afford the cost of applying for a land certificate,[73] proving that they have been in effective occupation or effectively exploiting the forest (land) is very difficult due to their traditional hunter-gatherer lifestyles.[74] The situation is even more complicated for individuals and customary communities on land classified as 'unoccupied', where the only rights available to them are hunting and fruit picking rights which may also be limited if the land is assigned for different purposes.[75] For such lands, no land certificate can be issued even if occupation or use was claimed by these individuals or customary communities. It has, however, been held that where land is in the possession of another, no land certificate can validly be issued in respect of that

[71] Ngwasiri and Nje (n 64) 3–15; Ngwasiri (n 64) 75–76; and Njoh (n 63) 411.

[72] For a detailed analysis of the various procedures, see CF Fisiy, *Power and Privilege in the Administration of Law: Land Law Reforms and Social Differentiation in Cameroon* (Leiden, African Studies Centre, 1992) 42–47.

[73] Without taking into account other incidental costs, obtaining a land certificate in Cameroon requires an application which includes inter alia a postal order of about 5,000 CFA francs (about US $10.00) to cover the application filing fees and a postal money order of 27,000 CFA francs (about US $55.00) to cover the cost of topographic works: See, eg AJ Njoh, 'Equity, Fairness and Justice Implications of Land Tenure Formalization in Cameroon' (2013) 37 *International Journal of Urban and Regional Research* 750, 760–61. While these amounts may seem insignificant by western standards, completing the land certificate application process could easily take up the majority of the annual income of most rural households in Cameroon.

[74] On the implications for equity, fairness and justice in the land titling process as they relate to access to land in Cameroon, see Njoh, ibid 750–68.

[75] Ordinance No 74-1, Art 17(3).

land without first revoking the right of the original occupier.[76] In the case where those lands are possessed by customary communities and individuals the only possible source of such rights would be customary title.

The implication of the above argument is that customary owners are still holding land under the customary land tenure system.[77] This is significant because, although a land certificate is what now confers ownership, it has also been held that this is not the only possible proof of ownership.[78] In other words, even if it could be argued that a land certificate is the only objective proof of ownership, it is not the only basis of ownership since customary holding is one way of acquiring a certificate, implying that customary ownership rights are still recognised. The continuous occupation or use of land which has been absorbed into the category of national land grants customary communities and individuals a legal right to own the land. It is therefore fair to say that this right should be recognised in all legislation dealing with land ownership regardless of whether or not a land certificate exists. This is not however the case, as for the purposes of expropriation and compensation, customary lands are treated as national lands and not as a distinct category of lands entitled to appropriate compensation.

The need for compensation may arise as a result of compulsory expropriation of land for forestry operations or as a result of damage done in the course of logging operations (for example, as a result of breach of the specifications of the logging contract or of the management plan for a permanent or community forest).[79] Despite the legal status of customary ownership, the concept of expropriation on the grounds of public interest and the possibility of compensation that arises from that only apply to private lands.[80] In other words, they do not apply to lands held under customary ownership.

The procedure for land expropriation is set out in Ordinance No 74-3 and involves the extinguishment of existing titles and use rights over the land in question for overriding public interest,[81] and in such cases subject to

[76] See the case of *Chief Molinge & 3 Others v Chief Musenja & 8 others* [2000] 2 CCLR 1. See also the case of *Adje Robert Acho v Rev Ngwane Ediage Thomas* [1998] 4 CCLR 109, 112 where the Appeal Court upheld the decision of the Court of First Instance that Bernard Epie Ntungwe (a family member) who allegedly sold a piece of land to the Appellant 'was not the family head of the Kome-Mgome family'. He therefore, 'had no right of possession and could not dispose of any part thereof without the consent of other family members particularly the head of the family'.

[77] The conditions for obtaining a land title are set out in Decree No 76-165 of 27 April 1976 to establish the conditions for obtaining land certificates and are generally cumbersome and expensive for the customary land owner to fulfil. See further Anyangwe (n 64) 29–30.

[78] See *Mobit Jerry Docta v Alhadji Zakari Mana & 3 others* [2000] 1 CCLR 9.

[79] Law No 94-1 of 20 January 1994 to lay down Forestry, Wildlife and Fisheries Regs, s 65.

[80] Ordinance No 74-1, Art 18, as amended by Ordinance No 77-1 of 10 January 1977.

[81] Ordinance No 74-3, Art 1(1). Questions have been raised over what the phrase 'public purpose' really means (see, eg M Prouzet, 'L'Expropriation pour le Cause d'Utilisé Publique au Cameroun' (1972) 1 *Cameroon Law Review* 27, 27–33) and abuses of this notion have been widely documented: Fisiy (n 72) 49–50; *Fouda Mballa v Etat Fédéré du Cameroun Oriental* [1971] Arrêt No 160/A/CFS/CAY (Federal Supreme Court) of 8 June 1971.

the payment of adequate compensation.[82] On the surface compensation for land expropriated does not seem to raise any issue of equity with regards to what is covered.[83] According to the provisions of Ordinance No 74-3 of 6 July 1974, expropriation for a public purpose shall confer the right to monetary compensation (Article 7) and such compensation shall be related to the direct, immediate and certain material damage caused by the eviction (Article 8). However, the provisions relating to how compensation is calculated do raise questions of equity. Article 9 of the Ordinance provides that:

> Subject to the provisions of Article 13(2)[84] of the Ordinance to establish rules governing land tenure [ie Ordinance No 74-1], compensation for expropriation shall comprise the following:
>
> — The value of the crops destroyed calculated in accordance with the scale in force;
> — The value of the buildings and other installations calculated by the valuation commission ...;
> — The value of the undeveloped land calculated as follows:
>
> a) In the case of urban lands officially allocated subject to payment, compensation may not exceed the official price of public lands in the particular town centre;
> b) In the case of lands held by virtue of a normal transaction under ordinary law, compensation shall be the purchase price to which shall be added the ancillary costs of the purchase and of obtaining title;
> c) In the case of lands held by virtue of customary tenure under which a land certificate has been issued, compensation may not exceed the amount of the expenses incurred by the issue of the said certificate.

From the above provisions, it is clear that expropriation of land provides for the payment of compensation for the land acquired itself. However where there is no improvement on the acquired land as defined under the Ordinance (that is, no valued crops, no worthy buildings and other installations), no compensation is payable. For undeveloped land, compensation can only be paid to the value of the purchase price of the land if it has ever been bought or sold or for the cost of obtaining a land certificate for land that is held under customary law. As argued earlier, this provision excludes a vast majority of citizens without a land certificate, but with a legal right to compensation.

In addition, even when there is a right to compensation, the valuation test used does not take account of the real value of the land to the customary owners and others. Instead the law takes account of only a very narrow set

[82] Ordinance No 74-2, Art 7.
[83] Njoh (n 73).
[84] Ordinance No 74-1, Art 13(2) states that, '[n]o compensation shall be payable for the destruction of dilapidated buildings liable to collapse, or buildings erected contrary to town planning regulations'.

of market values attributed to only a few of those affected, missing the value of land as providing livelihoods to others and benefits to the community as a whole. In most of the forested areas of Cameroon, the land is undeveloped and there are no structures on them, hence no compensation can be paid to the villagers if such land is acquired.[85] Yet expropriation may remove their rights to hunt, to gather fruits, farm or even practice their culture; things which they rely on for their livelihood.[86]

With regards to the 1994 Forestry Law, compensation for the expropriation of forested land is not expressly mentioned. This is due to what appears to be the unwritten objective of the law—to nationalise all forests except non-permanent forests. Non-permanent forests are made up of communal forests, community forests and forests belonging to private individuals.[87] With the exception of private forests, communal and community forests are still part of the national forests, which belong to the State.[88] However, community forests are allowed to be managed, preserved and exploited by the approved community in its own interest and subject to an approved management plan.[89] Its effect is to place title to all forests and forest lands in the State. There is therefore, no need to initiate the expropriation procedure prior to designating the forests as permanent forest estates (State or council forests).[90] Non-permanent forests can be expropriated and classified as State or council forests, which the State then controls and manages in the 'public interest', although in theory, they are categorised as 'non-State' forests.[91] For example, if a forest that was initially classified under the non-permanent forest domain is later considered to fulfil most of the characteristics of a permanent forest, the expropriation process is triggered and the forest reclassified. Nevertheless, the procedure allows for the payment of compensation under the rules defined by the Ordinance No 74-3 as explained above. Specifically, Section 26 of the 1994 Forestry Law provides that:

(1) The instrument classifying State forest shall take into account the social environment of the local population, who shall maintain their *logging rights*.
(2) However, such rights may be limited if they are contrary to the purpose of the forest. In such case, the local population shall be entitled to compensation according to the conditions laid down by decree.
(3) Public access to State forests may be regulated or forbidden.

85 T Greiber and S Schiele (eds), *Governance of Ecosystem Services: Lessons Learned from Cameroon, China, Costa Rica, and Ecuador* (Gland, IUCN, 2011) 27–28.
86 Rights may be limited as a result of the forest being reclassified, but in extreme cases expropriation can lead to the complete loss of the land and all associated rights.
87 1994 Forestry Law, s 34.
88 ibid, s 35.
89 ibid, ss 37 and 38.
90 s 20(2) of the 1994 Forestry Law provides that, '[p]ermanent forest shall comprise lands that are used solely for forestry and/or as a wildlife habitat'.
91 1995 Degree of Implementation, Art 19(2).

Section 27 further states that 'A forest may be classified only after compensating persons who had carried out investments therein before the start of the administrative classification procedure.'

The above provisions again reveal that any payment of compensation is not for the true value of the expropriated land, but only for the very narrow set of interests and values attributed to the local population and others, including their *logging rights*.[92]

The focus of the current law on economic improvements as the basis for paying compensation could be traced to the time when the 1974 Land Ordinances were promulgated. At the time, the debate on land reform was driven mainly by economic objectives, especially in the agricultural sector, rather than environmental and social ones.[93] However, as environmental issues have increasingly become part of the national debate the same laws are still being used to justify the non-payment of compensation for the expropriation of land for economic and even environmental programmes. This is the case when land is set aside for forestry purposes as defined by the Forestry Law, even though its main aim is to ensure the sustainable conservation and use of the forestry resources and of the various ecosystems within the framework of an integrated management approach.[94] In so doing the true value of the land in providing vital ecosystem services and the role of the local population in sustaining these services is being ignored.

VIII. CONCLUSION

An ecosystem services approach involves making sure that the benefits provided by the environment are recognised and sustained whilst delivering other economic and social goals.[95] There are different ways of achieving this objective.[96] Meeting this objective might be simplest if most lands providing ecosystem services were public property that could be set aside for forestry or other public use, but they are not. The reality is that customary ownership remains one of the main facets of the Cameroon land tenure system, although the existing land tenure system has sought to abolish customary ownership by 'nationalising' all lands occupied or used customarily and for which a land certificate has not been issued. Whether or not such

92 These logging rights are limited usufruct rights to harvest forest products for individual and community use: 1994 Forestry Law, s 8(1).

93 See, eg S Melone, *La Parenté et la Terre dans la Stratégie du Développement, l'Expérience Camerounaise: Etude Critique* (Paris, Klincksieck, 1972) 184; AD Tjouen, *Droits domaniaux et techniques foncières en droit camerounais: étude d'une réforme législative* (Paris, Economica, 1982) 37.

94 1994 Forestry Law, s 1.

95 Convention on Biological Diversity, COP 5 (2000) Decision V/6 Ecosystem Approach.

96 See, eg The Scottish Government, *Applying an Ecosystems Approach to Land Use: Information Note* (Edinburgh, The Scottish Government, 2011) 2.

customary ownership titles are recognised by the expropriation law, private lands (which will include lands held customarily in Cameroon) are vital for the provision of most services including biodiversity conservation.[97] The placement of certain forest land under a management agreement indicates recognition of this fact, but the expropriation law fails to recognise all these vital interests and values in the land. For example, without expropriation, where customary individuals or communities are able to control access to a region—as might be the case with sacred forests—it may be possible for them to successfully recoup conservation costs by charging tourists to visit the area and view the native flora and fauna as well as witness some cultural practices.

It follows that whether the subject of a purchase or an expropriation proceeding, the value of the land should not be based only on the houses built and crops found on the land or the cost of obtaining a land certificate as is currently the case, but should also take into account the benefits to the public and specific beneficiaries' present and future of maintaining the land in its 'natural' state. Although this can go a long way to resolving some of the fundamental issues of equity in the system of paying compensation as a result of the expropriation of land especially for conservation purposes in Cameroon, there are obvious problems with an ecosystem services approach.[98] The most important in this case would be how to value the present and future ecosystem services and any improvements to them made by the customary owners and occupiers over the years. Despite this difficulty, the strong human rights implications for the non-payment of compensation that can be considered 'just, fair and equitable' to the indigenous people who have traditionally owned or otherwise occupied or used the lands, territories and resources certainly adds weight to the need for a new approach in the valuation of compensation when these lands and resources are expropriated.

This chapter has drawn examples from the compensation valuation approaches in the United States, South Africa and other countries which generated some useful lessons on how compensation may be calculated taking account of ecosystem services. However it is not in any way suggested that the approach is going to automatically work for Cameroon, particularly due to the differences in political and legal contexts. While further research is needed to find solutions to the problems with this approach, the core principle of the ecosystem services approach provides a significant way in which some of the equity issues in the payment of compensation for the expropriation of land in Cameroon could be addressed. For this to work,

[97] D Farrier, 'Conserving Biodiversity on Private Land: Incentives for Management or Compensation for Lost Expectations?'(1995) 19 *Harvard Environmental Law Review* 303, 310.

[98] Redford and Adams (n 24) 785.

however, it will require both that the valuation system used to calculate compensation payable to owners takes account of the value of ecosystem services and that customary ownership is recognised for the purposes of providing compensation. These changes must be incorporated in tandem given the key role played by customary land owners in the provision and maintenance of ecosystem services in Cameroon, while bearing in mind the payment of monetary compensation may actually hasten the decline of such indigenous cultures and the further degradation of the lands.

Bibliography

Adal, Y, 'Rural Women's Access to Land in Ethiopia' in D Rahmato and T Assefa (eds), *Land and the Challenge of Sustainable Development in Ethiopia* (Addis Ababa, Forum for Social Studies, 2006) 19–43.

Adam, J, 'Land Reform, Dispossession and New Elites: A Case Study on Coconut Plantations in Davao Oriental, Philippines' (2013) 54 *Asia Pacific Viewpoint* 232.

Adamopoulos, T and Restuccia, D, *Land Reform and Productivity: A Quantitative Analysis with Micro Data*, Working Paper 509, University of Toronto Department of Economics, 4 April 2014.

Adewopo, A, 'The Development Imperative in the Global IP System: Some Reflections on Developing Africa' in GB Dinwoodie (ed), *Methods and Perspectives in Intellectual Property* (Cheltenham, Edward Elgar, 2013) 245–60.

Agrawal, PK, *Land Reforms in India: Constitutional and Legal Approach (with Special Reference to Uttar Pradesh)* (New Delhi, MD Publications, 1993).

Alexander, GS, 'Property as a Fundamental Constitutional Right? The German Example' (2003) 88 *Cornell Law Review* 733.

Allain, J, 'Slavery and the League of Nations: Ethiopia as a Civilised Nation' (2006) 8 *Journal of the History of International Law* 213.

—— *The Slavery Conventions: The Travaux Préparatoires of the 1926 League of Nations Convention and the 1956 United Nations Convention* (Leiden, Martinus Nijhoff, 2008).

—— 'On the Curious Disappearance of Human Servitude from General International Law' (2009) 11 *Journal of the History of International Law* 303.

—— '*Rantsev* v *Cyprus and Russia:* The European Court of Human Rights and Trafficking as Slavery' (2010) 10 *Human Rights Law Review* 546.

—— 'The Legal Definition of Slavery into the Twenty-First Century' in J Allain (ed), *The Legal Understanding of Slavery: From the Historical to the Contemporary* (Oxford, Oxford University Press, 2012) 205–06.

—— *Slavery in International Law: Of Human Exploitation and Trafficking* (Leiden, Martinus Nijhoff, 2013).

—— and Hickey, R, 'Property Law and the Definition of Slavery' (2012) 61 *International and Comparative Law Quarterly* 915.

Allen, J and Pyrke, M, 'Financialising Household Water: Thames Water, MEIF, and "Ring-Fenced" Politics' (2013) 6 *Cambridge Journal of Regions, Economy and Society* 419.

Allen, S, 'Looking Beyond the *Bancoult* Cases: International Law and the Prospect of Resettling the Chagos Islands' (2007) 7 *Human Rights Law Review* 441.

Allen, T, *The Right to Property in Commonwealth Constitutions* (Cambridge, Cambridge University Press, 2000).

—— *Property and the Human Rights Act 1998* (Oxford, Hart Publishing, 2005).

—— 'Compensation for Property under the European Convention on Human Rights' (2006–07) 28 *Michigan Journal of International Law* 287.

—— 'Controls over the Use and Abuse of Eminent Domain in England: A Comparative View' in RP Malloy (ed), *Private Property, Community Development, and Eminent Domain* (Ashgate, Aldershot, 2008) 75–100.
—— 'Liberalism, Social Democracy and the Value of Property under the European Convention on Human Rights' (2010) 59 *International and Comparative Law Quarterly* 1055.
Alves, JAL, 'The Declaration of Human Rights in Postmodernity' (2000) 22 *Human Rights Quarterly* 478.
Amokaye, OG, 'Compensation for Compulsory Acquisition of Land for Mining Activities in Nigeria: The Search for a Viable Solution' in R Home (ed), *Essays in African Land Law* (Pretoria, Pretoria University Law Press, 2011) 171–87.
Andreasson, S, 'Stand and Deliver: Private Property and the Politics of Global Dispossession' (2006) 54 *Political Studies* 3.
Ang, S, *The Moral Dimensions of Intellectual Property Rights* (Cheltenham, Edward Elgar, 2013).
Ankersen, TT and Ruppert, TK, 'Defending the Polygon: the Emerging Human Right to Communal Property' (2006) 59 *Oklahoma Law Review* 681.
Anyangwe, C, 'Land Tenure and Interest in Land in Cameroonian Indigenous Law'(1984) 27 *Cameroon Law Review* 29.
Appiah, KA, *Cosmopolitanism: Ethics in a World of Strangers* (London, Penguin, 2006).
Apps, P, 'Social Landlord Enters Private Rented Sector' *Inside Housing*, 7 November 2014.
—— 'Landlords Face Losing Millions After Giving Up on Waivers' *Inside Housing*, 17 November 2014.
—— 'Council to Invest £150m from Pension Scheme in Housing' *Inside Housing*, 3 December 2014.
Arneson, R, 'Lockean Self-Ownership: Towards a Demolition' (1991) 39 *Political Studies* 36.
Arrighi, G, *The Long Twentieth Century: Money, Power and the Origins of Our Times* (London, Verso, 1994).
Asiimwe, J, 'Making Women's Land Rights a Reality in Uganda: Advocacy for Co-Ownership by Spouses' (2001) 171 *Yale Human Rights & Development Law Journal* 4.
Atlas, D, 'Lockean Justifications of Intellectual Property' in A Gosseries, A Marciano and A Strowel (eds), *Intellectual Property and Theories of Justice* (London, Palgrave Macmillan, 2008) 29–56.
Austin, G, *The Indian Constitution: Cornerstone of a Nation* (Oxford, Oxford University Press, 1966).
—— *Working a Democratic Constitution: A History of the Indian Experience* (Oxford, Oxford University Press, 2003).
Baccaro, L and Mele, V, 'For the Lack of Anything Better? International Organizations and Global Corporate Codes' (2011) 89 *Public Administration* 451.
Baka, J, 'Biofuels and Wasteland Grabbing: How India's Biofuel Policy is Facilitating Land Grabs in Tamil Nadu, India', Paper presented at the International Conference on Global Land Grabbing 6–8 April 2011, Institute of Development Studies, University of Sussex.

Baldwin, C and Morel, C, 'Rights of Indigenous Peoples in Litigation' in S Allen and A Xanthaki (eds), *Reflections on the UN Declaration on the Rights of Indigenous Peoples* (Oxford, Hart Publishing, 2011) 132–38.

Barbosa, D, 'Droit d'Auteur et Accès à l'Information' in B Remiche and J Kors (eds), *L'Accord ADPIC: dix ans après—Regards Croisés Europe -Amérique Latine* (Brussels, Larcier, 2007) 373–446.

Barkhuysen, T and Lindenbergh, SD, *Constitutionalisation of Private Law* (Leiden, Brill, 2006).

Bartley, T and Child, C, 'Shaming the Corporation: The Social Production of Targets and the Anti-Sweatshop Movement' (2014) 79 *American Sociological Review* 653.

Barzel, Y, *Economic Analysis of Property Rights* (New York, Cambridge University Press, 1989).

Baxi, U, 'The Constitutional Quicksands of Kesavananda Bharati and the Twenty-Fifth Amendment' (1974) 1 *SCC* (Jour) 45.

Becker, LC, *Property Rights. Philosophic Foundation* (London, Routledge and Kegan Paul, 1977).

Benvenisti, E, 'Reclaiming Democracy: The Strategic Uses of Foreign and International Law by National Courts' (2008) 102 *American Journal of International Law* 241.

Berman, HR, 'Are Indigenous Populations Entitled to International Juridical Personality?'(1985) 79 *American Society of International Law Proceedings* 189.

Berman, S, *The Primacy of Politics: Social Democracy and the Making of Europe's Twentieth Century* (Cambridge, Cambridge University Press, 2006).

Barnard, C and Deakin, S et al, *Reflexive Law, Corporate Social Responsibility and the Evolution of Labour Standards: The Case of Working Time* (ESRC Centre for Business Research Paper, 2004).

Bernas, Fr JG (ed), *The 1987 Constitution of the Philippines, A Commentary* (Manila, Rex Book Store, 2003).

Best, J, 'From the Top-Down: The New Financial Architecture and the Re-Embedding of Global Finance' (2003) 8 *New Political Economy* 363.

Bethell, T, *The Noblest Triumph: Property and Prosperity through the Ages* (New York, St Martin's Press, 1998).

Beyene, F, 'Dismantling of Common Property, Land Use and Pastoral Livelihoods in Eastern Ethiopia' (2011) 1 *Journal of Development and Agricultural Economics* 3.

Bezabih, M, Holden, ST and Mannberg, A, 'The Role of Land Certification in Reducing Gender Gaps in Productivity in Rural Ethiopia' (2012) Norwegian University of Life Sciences, Centre for Land Tenure Studies.

Bezu, S and Holden, S, 'Unbundling Land Administrative Reform: Demand for Second Stage Land Certification in Ethiopia' (2013) Norwegian University of Life Sciences, Centre for Land Tenure Studies Working Paper 03/13.

Bhattacharya, S, 'Swaraj and the Kamgar: The India National Congress and the Bombay Working Class, 1919–1931' in R Sisson and S Wolpert (eds), *Congress and Indian Nationalism: The Pre-Independence Phase* (Berkeley, University of California Press, 1988) 223–49.

Biadgleng, ET, 'The Development-Balance of TRIPS Agreement and Enforcement of Intellectual Property' in J Malbon and C Lawson (eds), *Interpreting and Implementing the TRIPS Agreement: is it Fair?* (Cheltenham, Edward Elgar, 2008) 97–130.

Black, J, *Critical Reflections on Regulation* (CARR Paper 1-27, 2002).

Blake, J, 'On Defining Cultural Heritage' (2000) 49 *International & Comparative Law Quarterly* 61.

Blackstone, W, *Commentaries on the Laws of England, Volume I, Of the Rights of Persons* (Oxford, Clarendon Press, 1766).

Blakeney, M, 'The Protection of Traditional Knowledge Under Intellectual Property Law' (2000) 22 *European Intellectual Property Law Review* 251.

—— 'Protecting Traditional Cultural Expressions: The International Dimension' in F Macmillan and K Bowrey (eds), *New Directions in Copyright Law: Volume 3* (Cheltenham, Edward Elgar, 2006) 3–14.

—— 'Protecting the Spiritual Beliefs of Indigenous Peoples—Australian Case Studies' (2013) 22 *Pacific Rim Law & Policy Journal* 391.

Blandy, S, 'Collective Property: Owning and Sharing Residential Space' in N Hopkins (ed), *Modern Studies in Property Law: Volume 7* (Oxford, Hart Publishing, 2013) 152–72.

Boardman, A and Vining, A, 'Assessing the Economic Worth of Public-Private Partnerships' in G Hodge, C Greve and A Boardman (eds), *International Handbook on Public-Private Partnerships* (Cheltenham, Edward Elgar, 2010) 159–86.

Boiral, O and Gendron, Y, 'Sustainable Development and Certification Practices: Lessons Learned and Prospects' (2011) 20 *Business Strategy and the Environment* 331.

Bowrey, K and Anderson, J, 'The Politics of Global Information Sharing: Whose Cultural Agendas are Being Advanced?' (2009) 18 *Social & Legal Studies* 479.

Boyle, J, *The Public Domain: Enclosing the Commons of the Mind* (New Haven, Yale University Press, 2008).

Bradford, LR, 'Parody and Perception: Using Cognitive Research to Expand Fair Use in Copyright' (2004) 46 *Boston College Law Review* 705.

Braithwaite, J, *Regulatory Capitalism. How it Works, Ideas for Making it Better* (Cheltenham, Edward Elgar, 2008).

Bratton, W, 'Enron and the Dark Side of Shareholder Value' (2002) 76 *Tulane Law Review* 1275.

Brown, MF, *Who Owns Native Culture?* (Cambridge, Harvard University Press, 2003).

—— 'Heritage Trouble: Recent Work on the Protection of Intangible Cultural Property' (2005) 12 *International Journal of Cultural Property* 40.

Brüggemeier, G, Ciacchi AC, Commandé, G (eds), *Fundamental Rights and Private Law in the European Union, Vol I A Comparative Overview* (Cambridge, Cambridge University Press, 2010).

Bruncevic, M, *Fixing the Shadows: Access to Art & the Legal Concept of Cultural Commons* (PhD Thesis, University of Gothenberg, 2014).

Budlender, G, Latsky, J and Roux, T, *Juta's New Land Law* (Cape Town, Juta & Co, 1998).

Burchell, G, 'Liberal Government and Techniques of the Self' (1993) 22 *Economy and Society* 267.
Burger, P, et al, *The Effects of the Financial Crisis on Public-Private Partnerships* (Washington, IMF Working Paper, 2009).
Burrell, R and Coleman, A, *Copyright Exceptions: The Digital Impact* (Cambridge, Cambridge University Press, 2006).
Buydens, M, *La Propriété Intellectuelle évolution Historique et Philosophique* (Brussels, Bruylant, 2012).
Byamugisha, FK, *Securing Africa's Land for Shared Prosperity: A Program to Scale up Reforms and Investments* (The World Bank, 2013).
Cairncross, L et al, *Housing Management, Consumers and Citizens*, (London, Routledge, 1997).
Campbell, T, 'A Human Rights Approach to Developing Voluntary Codes of Conduct for Multinational Corporations' (2006) 16 *Business Ethics Quarterly* 255.
Carpenter, KA, Katyal, S and Riley, A, 'In Defense of Property' (2009) 118 *Yale Journal of Law* 1022.
Chakma, S and Jensen, M (eds), *Racism against Indigenous Peoples* (Copenhagen, IWGIA, 2001).
Chakraborty, A (2014) 'The story of the millionaire Tory MP and the tenants facing homelessness' *The Guardian*, 10 November 2014.
—— 'New Era Estate Scandal: Families at the Mercy of International Speculators', *The Guardian*, 19 November 2014.
Charnovitz S, 'Solving the Production and Processing Methods Puzzle' in K Gallagher and J Werksman (eds), *The Earthscan Reader on International Trade and Sustainable Development* (London, Routledge, 2001) 227–62.
Chesini, G and Giaretta, E, 'Regulating High-frequency Trading: An Examination of European, US and Australian Equity Market Structures' in T Lindblom, S Sjögren and M Willesson (eds), *Financial Systems, Markets and Institutional Changes* (Basingstoke, Palgrave Macmillan, 2014) 152–87.
Chibber, V, 'Organized Interests, Development Strategies, and Social Policies' in R Nagaraj (ed), *Growth, Inequality and Social Development in India: Is Inclusive Growth Possible?* (Basingstoke, Palgrave Macmillan, 2012) 168–93.
Chon, M, 'Intellectual Property "From Below": Copyright and Capability for Education' (2007) 40 *UC Davis Law Review* 803.
Choudhry, S, 'The *Lochner* Era and Comparative Constitutionalism' (2004) 2 *International Journal of Constitutional Law* 1.
Christman, J, *The Myth of Property: Toward an Egalitarian Theory of Ownership* (New York, Oxford University Press, 1994).
Ciervo, A, *I Beni Comuni* (Rome, Ediesse, 2013).
Clarke, A, 'Creating New Commons: Recognition of Communal Land Rights within a Private Property Framework' (2006) 59 *Current Legal Problems* 319.
—— 'How Property Works: the Complex World View' (2013) 22 *Nottingham Law Journal* 143.
—— 'Land Titling and Communal Property' in W Barr (ed), *Modern Studies in Property Law: Volume 8* (Oxford, Hart Publishing, 2015) 215–233.
Clarke, G, *Pension Fund Capitalism* (Oxford, Oxford University Press, 2000).
Clarke, J, 'Dissolving the Public Realm: The Logics and Limits of Neo-liberalism' (2004) 33 *Journal of Social Policy* 27.

Çoban AR, *Protection of Property Rights within the European Convention on Human Rights* (Surrey, Ashgate, 2004).
Cohen, GA, *Self-Ownership, Freedom and Equality* (Cambridge, Cambridge University Press, 1995).
Cole, I and Furbey, R, *The Eclipse of Council Housing* (London, Routledge, 1994).
Comaroff, J and Comaroff, J, 'Alien-nation: Zombies, Immigrants and Millennial Capitalism' (2002) 101 *South Atlantic Quarterly* 779.
Communities and Local Government (CLG), *Local Choice, Local Control: Statutory Guidance on Tenant Management for Local Authorities and Local Authority Tenants* (London, CLG, 2008).
—— *Resident's Choice: Guidance on Tenant Management and Other Options Supported through the Tenant Empowerment Programme*, (London, CLG, 2008).
Connoly, C and Wall, T, 'The Impact of the Global Financial Crisis on Public-Private Partnerships: A UK Perspective' in C Greve and G Hodge (eds), *Rethinking Public Private Partnerships: Strategies for Turbulent Times* (London, Routledge, 2013) 33–56.
Coombe, RJ, 'The Properties of Culture & the Possession of Identity: Postcolonial Struggle & the Legal Imagination' in B Ziff and PV Rao (eds), *Borrowed Power: Essays on Cultural Appropriation* (New Jersey, Rutgers University Press, 1997) 74–96.
Correa, CM, *Intellectual Property Rights, the WTO, and Developing Countries: The TRIPS Agreement and Policy Options* (London, Zed Books, 2000).
—— *Trade Related Aspects of Intellectual Property Rights: A Commentary on the TRIPS Agreement* (Oxford, Oxford University Press, 2007).
Cottier, T, Pauwelyn, J and Bonanomi, EB (eds), *Human Rights and International Trade* (Oxford, Oxford University Press, 2005).
Cotula, L, *The Great African Land Grab?: Agricultural Investments and the Global Food System* (London, Zed Books, 2013).
—— and Mathieu, P (eds), *Legal Empowerment in Practice: Using Legal Tools to Secure Land Rights in Africa* (IIED and FAO, 2008).
—— and Mayers, J, *Tenure in REDD—Start-point or Afterthought?* (2009) International Institute for Environment and Development Natural Resource Issues No 15.
Cowan, D, *Housing Law and Policy* (Cambridge, Cambridge University Press, 2011).
—— and McDermont, M, *Regulating Social Housing: Governing Decline* (London, Routledge Glasshouse, 2006).
—— et al, 'Risk, Trust and Betrayal: A Social Housing Case Study' (2009) 72 *Modern Law Review* 157.
——, O'Mahony, LF and Cobb, N, *Great Debates in Property Law* (Basingstoke, Palgrave Macmillan, 2012).
Cox, M, Arnold, G and Tomás, SV, 'A Review of Design Principles for Community-based Natural Resource Management' (2010) 15 *Ecology and Society* 38.
Craig, CJ, 'Locke, Labour, and Limiting the Author's Right: A Warning Against a Lockean Approach to Copyright Law' (2002) 28 *Queen's Law Journal* 1.
Crane, A, Matten, D and Moon, J *Corporations and Citizenship* (Cambridge, Cambridge University Press, 2008).

Craven, M, 'The International Covenant on Economic, Social and Cultural Rights—A perspective on its Development' (DPhil thesis, University of Nottingham 1992).

Crook, A and Kemp, P, 'Housing Investment Trusts: A New Structure of Rental Housing Provision?' (2002) 17 *Housing Studies* 741.

Croce, R Della, 'Trends in Large Pension Fund Investment in Infrastructure' *OECD Working Papers on Finance, Insurance and Private Pensions*, No 29 (OECD Publishing, 2012).

Dagan, H, *Property: Values and Institutions* (Oxford, Oxford University Press, 2011).

—— and Heller, M, 'The Liberal Commons' (2001) 110 *Yale Law Journal* 549.

Dallmayr, F, *G WF Hegel: Modernity and Politics* (Newbury Park, SAGE Publications, 1993).

Davis, AI, 'Ecosystem Services and the Value of Land' (2010) 20 *Duke Environmental Law & Policy Forum* 339.

Davies, J and Bennett, R, 'Livelihood Adaptations at Risk: Constraints and Opportunities for Pastoral Development in Ethiopia's Afar Region' (2007) 3 *The Journal of Development Studies* 43.

Davies, P, 'Access v Contract: Competing Freedoms in the Context of Copyright Limitations and Exceptions for Libraries' (2013) 35 *European Intellectual Property Review* 402.

Defra, *Securing a Healthy Natural Environment: An Action Plan for Embedding an Ecosystems Approach* (London, Defra, 2007).

Deininger, K and Feder, G, 'Land Registration, Governance and Development: Evidence and Implications for Policy' (2009) 2 *The World Bank Research Observer* 24.

——, Ali, DA and Alemu, T, 'Impacts of Land Certification on Tenure Security, Investment and Land Market Perception: Evidence from Ethiopia' (2011) 2 *Land Economics* 87.

——, Ali, DA; Holden, S and Zevenbergen, J, 'Rural Land Certification in Ethiopia: Process, Initial Impact, and Implications for other African Countries' (2008) 1 *World Development* 36.

——, Zevenbergen, J and Ali, DA, 'Assessing the Certification Process of Ethiopia's Rural Lands' (Montpellier, Colloque International, 2006).

Demian, M, 'Land doesn't Come from your Mother, She didn't Make it with her Hands: Challenging Matriliny in Papua New Guinea' in H Lim and De Soto, H, *The Mystery of Capital: Why Capitalism Triumphs in the West and Fails Everywhere Else* (London, Black Swan, 2001).

Demsetz, H, 'Toward a Theory of Property Rights' (1967) 57 *American Economic Review* 347.

De Schutter, O, 'The Green Rush: The Global Race for Farmland and the Rights of Land Users' (2011) 52 *Harvard International Law Journal* 503.

DETR, *Quality and Choice: A Decent Home for All—The Housing Green Paper* (London, DETR/DSS, 2000).

DFID, USAID, UN and Irish Aid, 'Multi-agency 'Villagisation' Mission to *Gambella* Regional State, Ethiopia Report' (3–8 June 2012).

Dicken, P, Kelly, P, Olds, K and Yeung, H, 'Chains and Networks, Territories and Scales; towards a Relational Framework for Analysing the Global Economy' (2001) 1 *Global Networks* 89.

Dickson, B, *Human Rights and the UK Supreme Court* (Oxford, Oxford University Press, 2013).
Dickenson, D, *Property in the Body: Feminist Perspectives* (Cambridge, Cambridge University Press, 2007).
—— 'Alternatives to a Corporate Commons: Biobanks, Genetics and Property in the Body' in I Goold, J Herring, K Greasley, L Skene (eds), *Persons, Parts and Property: How Should We Regulate Human Tissue in the 21st Century?* (Oxford, Hart Publishing, 2014) 177–95.
Dierckx, S, 'After the Crisis and Beyond the New Constitutionalism? The Case of the Free Movement of Capital' (2013) 10 *Globalizations* 803.
Dietz, T et al, 'The Drama of the Commons' in E Ostrom et al (eds), *The Drama of the Commons* (Washington DC, National Academy Press, 2002) 3–36.
Díez-Picazo, L, *Fundamentos de Derecho civil patrimonial V* (Madrid, Civitas, 2012).
Dixon, R and Posner, EA, 'The Limits of Constitutional Convergence' (2010–2011) 11 *Chicago Journal of International Law* 399.
Dolzer, R and Schreuer, C, *Principles of International Investment Law* 2nd edn (Oxford, Oxford University Press, 2012).
Donnelly, J, *Universal Human Rights in Theory and Practice* (New York, Cornell University Press, 2013).
Dowell-Jones, M, 'Financial Institutions and Human Rights' (2013) 13 *Human Rights Law Review* 423.
Drassinower, A, 'Capturing Ideas: Copyright and the Law of First Possession' (2006) 54 *Cleveland State Law Review* 191.
DuBois, WEB, 'Liberia, the League and the United States' *Foreign Affairs* July 1931.
Dumas, PM, 'The Malaise of Modernity under Consumocratic Order' (2012) 5 *Economics and Sociology* 75.
—— 'Three Misunderstandings about Consumocratic Law' (2013) 35 *Comparative Labor Law and Policy Journal* 67.
—— 'Thickening Soft Law through Consumocratic Law: A Pragmatic Approach' in A Trebilcock and A Blackett (eds), *Research Handbook on Transnational Labour Law* (London, Edward Elgar, 2015 forthcoming).
Dusollier, S, 'The Commons as a Reverse Intellectual Property—from Exclusivity to Inclusivity' in HR Howe and J Griffiths (eds), *Concepts of Property in Intellectual Property Law* (Cambridge, Cambridge University Press, 2013) 258–82.
Dyal-Chand, R, 'Exporting the Ownership Society: A Case Study on the Economic Impact of Property Rights' (2007) 39 *Rutgers Law Journal* 59.
Economist, *Economist Intelligence Unit Country Report Cameroon* (London, 2008).
Endicot, TH, Getzler, J and Peel, E (eds), *Properties of Law* (Oxford, Oxford University Press, 2006).
Engelen, E, Ertürk, I and Froud, J, et al, *After the Great Complacence* (Oxford, Oxford University Press, 2011).
Epstein, RA, *Takings: Private Property and the Power of Eminent Domain* (Cambridge MA, Harvard University Press, 1985).
European Union, *Cultural Heritage: A Challenge for Europe* (JPI Cultural Heritage and Global Change—Heritage Plus Call, 2014).
Fabella, RV, 'Comprehensive Agrarian Reform Program (CARP): Time to Let Go', Discussion Paper No 2014-02, University of the Philippines School of Economics.

Falk, RA, *Human Rights and State Sovereignty* (New York, Holmes & Meier Publishers Inc, 1981).

—— 'United States Foreign Policy as an Obstacle to Realising the Rights of Peoples' (1989) 16 *Social Justice* 57.

—— 'The Making of Global Citizenship' in J Brecher, J Childs and J Cutler (eds), *Global Visions* (Boston, South End Press, 1993) 39–50.

—— *Human Rights Horizons: The Pursuit of Justice in a Globalizing World* (London, Routledge, 2000).

FAO, 'Voluntary Guidelines to Support the Progressive Realisation of the Right to Food in the Context of National Food Security' (adopted by the 127th Session of the FAO Council) (November 2004).

Farber, DA, 'Rights as Signals' (2002) 31 *Journal of Legal Study* 83.

Farrier, D, 'Conserving Biodiversity on Private Land: Incentives for Management or Compensation for Lost Expectations?' (1995) 19 *Harvard Environmental Law Review* 303.

Federal Democratic Republic of Ethiopia Ministry of Finance and Economic Development, *Ethiopia, Building on Progress: Plan for Accelerated and Sustained Development to End Poverty (PASDEP), 2005/06-2009/10.*

Felice, B, 'Rights in Theory and Practice: An Historical Perspective' (1989) 16 *Social Justice* 35.

Fernando, EM, 'An Asian Perspective on the American Constitutional Influence in Asia: Its Impact on the Philippine Legal System' (1976) 18 *Malaya Law Review* 281.

Filer, C, 'Local Custom and the Art of Land Group Boundary Maintenance in Papua New Guinea' in JF Weiner and K Glaskin (eds), *Customary Land Tenure and Registration in Australia and Papua New Guinea: Anthropological Perspectives* (Canberra, Australian National University Electronic Press, 2007) 135–73.

Financial Services Authority, *Mortgage Market Review: Feedback on CP11/31 and Final Rules* (London, FSA, 2012).

Fisher, W, 'Theories of Intellectual Property' in S Munzer (ed), *New Essays in the Legal and Political Theory of Property* (Cambridge, Cambridge University Press, 2001) 168–200.

Fisiy, CF, *Power and Privilege in the Administration of Law: Land Law Reforms and Social Differentiation in Cameroon* (Leiden, African Studies Centre, 1992).

Fitzpatrick, P and Joyce, R, 'Copying Right: Cultural Property and the Limits of (Occidental) Law' in F Macmillan (ed), *New Directions in Copyright Law: Volume 4* (Cheltenham, Edward Elgar, 2007) 169–90.

Flessas, T, 'Cultural Property Defined and Redefined as Nietzschean Aphorism' (2003) 24 *Cardozo Law Review* 1067.

—— 'The Ends of the Museum' *Law Society & Economy Working Papers* 14/2013 (London, London School of Economics, 2013).

Forde, S, 'The Charitable John Locke' (2009) 71 *The Review of Politics* 428.

Forest Trends and Katoomba Group, *Payments for Ecosystem Services—Getting Started: A Primer* (Washington DC, Forest Trends, The Katoomba Group & UNEP, 2008).

Forrest, R and Hirayama, Y, 'The Financialisation of the Social Project: Embedded Liberalism, Neoliberalism and Home Ownership' (2014) 52 *Urban Studies* 233.

Foster, G, 'Investors, States and Stakeholders: Power Asymmetries in International Investment and the Stabilizing Potential of Investment Treaties' (2013) 17 *Lewis and Clarke Law Review* 361.

Fox, L, *Enron: The Rise and Fall* (New York, Wiley, 2002).

French, S and Leyshon, A, 'Dead Pledges: Mortgaging Time and Space' in K Knorr Cetina and A Preda (eds), *The Oxford Handbook of the Sociology of Finance* (Oxford, Oxford University Press, 2012) 357–75.

French, S, Leyshon, A and Wainwright, T, 'Financializing Space, Spacing Financialization' (2011) 35 *Progress in Human Geography* 798.

Fried, BH, 'Left-Libertarianism: A Review Essay' (2004) 32 *Philosophy and Public Affairs* 66.

—— 'Left-Libertarianism Once More: A Rejoinder to Vallentyne, Steiner and Otsuka' (2005) 33 *Philosophy and Public Affairs* 206.

Friedman, B, 'From Deontology to Dialogue: The Cultural Consequences of Copyright' (1994) 13 *Cardozo Arts and Entertainment Law Journal* 157.

Friedman, M, 'The Social Responsibility of Business is to Increase its Profits', *The New York Times Magazine*, 13 September 1970.

Friedman, T, *The World Is Flat: A Brief History of the Twenty-First Century* (New York, Farrar, Straus and Giroux, 2005).

Friedmann, D and Barak-Erez, D, *Human Rights in Private Law* (Oxford, Hart Publishing, 2001).

Froud, J, 'The Private Finance Initiative: Risk, Uncertainty and the State' (2003) 28 *Accounting, Organizations and the State* 567.

Furbey, R, Wishart, B and Grayson, J, 'Training for Tenants: "Citizens" and the Enterprise Culture' (2006) 11 *Housing Studies* 251.

Gaines, SE, 'Processes and Production Methods: How to Produce Sound Policy for Environmental PPM-Based Trade Measures?' (2002) 27 *Columbia Journal of Environmental Law* 383.

Geiger, C, *Droit d'Auteur et Droit du Public à l'Information* (Paris, Litec, 2004).

—— 'Promoting Creativity through Copyright Limitations: Reflections on the Concept of Exclusivity in Copyright Law' (2009) 12 *Vanderbilt Journal of Entertainment and Technology Law* 515.

——, Gervais, DJ and Senftleben, SMF, 'The Three-Step Test Revisited: How to Use the Test's Flexibility in National Copyright Law' (2013) 29 *American University Law Review* 581.

Genugten, V, 'Protection of Indigenous Peoples on the African Continent: Concepts, Position Seeking and Interaction of Legal Systems' (2010) 1 *The American Journal of International Law* 104.

Gerber, DJ, 'Sculpting the Agenda of Comparative Law: Ernst Rabel and the Facade of Language' in A Riles (ed), *Rethinking the Masters of Comparative Law* (Oxford and Portland, Hart Publishing, 2000) 190–208.

Gereffi, G, 'Global Value Chains in a Post-Washington Consensus World' (2014) 21 *Review of International Political Economy* 9.

Gervais, DJ, 'Towards a New Core International Copyright Norm: The Reverse Three-Step Test' (2005) 9 *Marquette Intellectual Property Law Review* 1.

—— *The TRIPS Agreement: Drafting History and Analysis* 4th edn (London, Sweet & Maxwell, 2012).

——, Schmitz, I and Anell, L, *L'accord sur les ADPIC* (Brussels, Lacier, 2010).
Gewirth, A, *Human Rights: Essays on Justification and Applications* (Chicago, University of Chicago Press, 1982).
Gibson, J, 'Community and the Exhaustion of Culture. Creative Territories in Traditional Cultural Expressions' in F Macmillan and K Bowrey (eds), *New Directions in Copyright Law: Volume 3* (Cheltenham, Edward Elgar, 2006) 15–36.
Gilbert, D, Rasche, A and Waddock, S, 'Accountability in a Global Economy: the Emergence of International Accountability Standards' (2011) 21 *Business Ethics Quarterly* 23.
Gilbert, J, 'Indigenous Peoples' Human Rights in Africa: The Pragmatic Revolution of the African Commission on Human and Peoples Rights' (2011) 1 *International and Comparative Law Quarterly* 60.
—— 'Nomadic Territories: A Human Rights Approach to Nomadic Peoples' Land Rights' (2007) 7 *Human Rights Law Review* 681.
—— and Couillard, V, 'International Law and Land Rights in Africa: The Shift from States' Territorial Possessions to Indigenous Peoples' Ownership Rights' in R Home (ed), *Essays in African Land Law* (Pretoria, Pretoria University Law Press, 2011) 47–67.
Ginsburg, J, 'Copyright or "Infograb": Comment on General Report on Limitations Found Outside Copyright' in L Baulch, M Green and M Wyburn (eds), *ALAI Study Days: The Boundaries of Copyright—its Proper Limitations and Exceptions* (Australian Copyright Council, 1999) 55–57.
Golay, C and Cismas, I, 'Legal Opinion: The Right to Property from a Human Rights Perspective', SSRN Scholarly Paper, Rochester, NY, Social Science Research Network, 2010.
Goldman, L, 'Incorporating Huli: Lessons from the Hides Licence Area' in JF Weiner and K Glaskin (eds), *Customary Land Tenure and Registration in Australia and Papua New Guinea: Anthropological Perspectives* (Canberra, Australian National University Electronic Press, 2007) 97–115.
Goldman, R and Papson, S, *Landscapes of Capital* (Cambridge, Polity, 2011).
Goldstein, P and Hugenholtz, PB, *International Copyright: Principles, Law and Practice* 2nd edn (Oxford, Oxford University Press, 2010).
Gomes, C and Unger, RM, *O Próximo Passo* (Rio de Janeiro, Topbooks, 1996).
Goold, I, 'Why Does It Matter How We Regulate the Use of Human Body Parts?' (2014) 40 *Journal of Medical Ethics* 3.
——, Greasley, K, Herring, J and Skeane, L (eds), *Persons, Parts and Property. How Should We Regulate Human Tissue in the 21st Century* (Oxford, Hart Publishing, 2014).
Gordon, WJ, 'A Property Right in Self-Expression: Equality and Individualism in the Natural Law of Intellectual Property' (1992) 102 *Yale Law Journal* 1533.
Gorsuch, AM, 'To Indent Oneself: Ownership, Contracts, and Consent in Antebellum Illinois' in J Allain (ed), *The Legal Understanding of Slavery: From the Historical to the Contemporary* (Oxford, Oxford University Press, 2012) 135–51.
Graber, CB, 'The New UNESCO Convention on Cultural Diversity: A Counterbalance to the WTO?' (2006) 9 *Journal of International Economic Law* 553.
—— and Burri-Nenova, M (eds), *Intellectual Property and Traditional Cultural Expressions in a Digital Environment* (Cheltenham, Edward Elgar, 2008).

Gray, K, 'Land Law and Human Rights' in L Tee (ed), *Land Law: Issues, Debates, Policy* (Portland OR, Willan Publishing, 2002) 211–45.
—— and Gray, SF (eds), *Elements of Land Law* 5th edn (Oxford, Oxford University Press, 2009).
Grear, A, 'Challenging Corporate "Humanity": Legal Disembodiment, Embodiment and Human Rights' (2007) 7 *Human Rights Law Review* 511.
Green, L, 'Two Views of Collective Rights' (1991) 4 *Canadian Journal of Law & Jurisprudence* 329.
Greiber, T and Schiele, S (eds), *Governance of Ecosystem Services: Lessons Learned from Cameroon, China, Costa Rica, and Ecuador* (Gland, the International Union for Conservation of Nature, 2011).
Griffin, J, *On Human Rights* (Oxford, Oxford University Press, 2008).
Griffiths, A, *An Economic Perspective on Trademark Law* (Cheltenham, Edward Elgar, 2011).
Grimsey, D and Lewis, M, *Public-Private Partnerships: The Worldwide Revolution in Infrastructure Provision and Project Finance* (Cheltenham, Edward Elgar, 2004).
Grosheide, W (ed), *Intellectual Property and Human Rights: A Paradox* (Cheltenham, Edward Elgar, 2010).
Hacault, AF, 'A Primer on Expropriation: Are You Missing Elements of Compensation?' (Prepared for the Annual Conference of the Appraisal Institute of Canada, Mont-Tremblant, Quebec, 27–30 May 2009).
Handler, R, 'Who Owns the Past? History, Cultural Property and the Logic of Possessive Individualism' in B Williams (ed), *The Politics of Culture* (Washington, Smithsonian Institution Press, 1991) 63–74.
Hanstad, TM, 'Philippine Land Reform: The Just Compensation Issue' (1988) 63 *Washington Law Review* 417.
Hardcastle, R, *Law and the Human Body: Property Rights, Ownership and Control* (Oxford, Hart Publishing, 2007).
Hardin, G, 'The Tragedy of the Commons' (1968) 162 *Science* 1243.
Hardt, M and Negri, A, *Empire* (Cambridge, Harvard University Press, 2001).
Hare, D, *The Power of Yes* (London, Faber and Faber, 2009).
Harris, JW, 'The Survival Lottery' (1975) 50 *Philosophy* 81.
—— *Property and Justice* (Oxford, Oxford University Press, 2001).
Harris, N, 'Welfare Reform and the Shifting Threshold of Support for Disabled People' (2014) 77 *Modern Law Review* 888.
Harrison, JL, 'Creativity or Commons: A Comment on Professor Lessig' (2003) 55 *Florida Law Review* 795.
Harriss, J, 'Politics and Redistribution in India' in A Kohli and P Singh (eds), *Routledge Handbook of Indian Politics* (London, Routledge, 2013) 211–21.
Hart-Landsberg, M, *Capitalist Globalization* (New York, Monthly Review Press, 2013).
Harvey, D, 'Globalization and the "Spatial Fix"' (2001) 2 *Geographische Revue* 23.
Haufler, V, 'Globalization and Industry Self-regulation' in M Kahler and DA Lake (eds), *Governance in a Global Economy* (Princeton, Princeton University Press, 2003) 226–54.

Haugen HM, *Technology and Human Rights—Friends or Foes? Highlighting Innovations Applying to Natural Resources and Medicine* (vol 2, Netherlands, Dordrecht, Republic of Letters, 2012).

HCA, *Affordable Homes Programme 2011 to 2015: Guidance and Allocations* (London, HCA, 2011).

—— *Private Registered Provider Social Housing Stock in England: Statistical Data Return 2013/14* (London, HCA, 2014).

—— *Sector Risk Profile 2014* (London, HCA, 2014).

Helfer, LR, 'Human Rights and Intellectual Property: Conflict or Coexistence?' (2003) 5 *Minnesota Intellectual Property Review* 47.

—— 'Regime Shifting: The TRIPS Agreement and New Dynamics of International Intellectual Property Lawmaking' in LR Helfer (ed), *Intellectual Property and Human Rights* (Cheltenham, Edward Elgar, 2013) 553–635.

—— and Austin, GW, *Human Rights and Intellectual Property: Mapping the Global Interface* (Cambridge, Cambridge University Press, 2011).

Heller, MA, 'The Tragedy of the Anticommons: Property in the Transition from Marx to Markets' (1998) 111 *Harvard Law Review* 621.

—— and Eisenberg, RS, 'Can Patents Deter Innovation? The Anticommons in Biomedical Research' (1998) 280 *Science* 698.

——*The Gridlock Economy: How Too Much Ownership Wrecks Markets, Stops Innovation, and Costs Lives* (New York, Basic Books, 2008).

Helm, D and Hepburn, C, 'The Economic Analysis of Biodiversity: An Assessment'(2012) 28 *Oxford Review of Economic Policy* 1.

Hemmungs Wirtén, E, *Terms of Use: Negotiating the Jungle of the Intellectual Commons* (Toronto, University of Toronto Press, 2008).

Hickey, R, 'Seeking to Understand the Definition of Slavery' in J Allain (ed), *The Legal Understanding of Slavery: From the Historical to the Contemporary* (Oxford, Oxford University Press, 2012) 220–41.

Himma, K, 'The Legitimacy of Protecting Intellectual Property Rights: The Irrelevance of Two Conceptions of an Information Commons' (2007) 11 *Journal of Information, Communication and Ethics in Society* 210.

HM Government, *The Natural Choice: Securing the Value of Nature*, CM 8082 (London, The Stationery Office, June 2011).

Ho, P and Spoor, M, 'Whose Land? The Political Economy of Land Titling in Transitional Economies' (2006) *Land Policy* 23.

Hoang, D and Jones, B, 'Why do Corporate Codes of Conduct Fail? Women Workers and Clothing Supply Chains in Vietnam' (2012) 12 *Global Social Policy* 67.

Hobsbawm, E, *Fractured Times: Culture and Society in the Twentieth Century* (London, Little Brown, 2013).

Hodkinson, S, 'From Popular Capitalism to Third Way Modernisation: The Case of Leeds, England' in S Glynn (ed), *Where the Other Half Live: Lower Income Households in a Neoliberal World* (London, Pluto Press, 2009) 99–123.

—— 'The Private Finance Initiative in English Council Housing Regeneration: A Privatisation too far?' (2011) 26 *Housing Studies* 911.

—— 'Housing Regeneration and the Private Finance Initiative in England: Unstitching the Neoliberal Straitjacket' (2011) 43 *Antipode* 358.

—— and Robbins, G, 'The Return of Class War Conservatism? Housing under the UK Coalition Government' (2013) 33 *Critical Social Policy* 57.

Hoffman, D (ed), *The Impact of the UK Human Rights Act on Private Law* (Cambridge, Cambridge University Press, 2011).
Hoffmann, M, 'Why Community Ownership? Understanding Land Reform in Scotland' (2013) 31 *Land Use Policy* 289.
Hohfeld, WH, *Fundamental Legal Conceptions* (New Haven, Greenwood Press, 1964[1919]).
Holden, S and Tefera, T, *Land Registration in Ethiopia: Early Impacts on Women* (UN-HABITAT 2008).
Holden, ST, Deininger, K and Ghebru, H (2009) 'Impacts of Low-Cost Land Certification on Investment and Productivity' (2009) 2 *American Journal of Agricultural Economics* 91.
—— 'Tenure Insecurity, Gender, Low-Cost Land Certification and Land Rental Market Participation in Ethiopia' (2011) 1 *Journal of Development Studies* 47.
Holder, JB and Flessas, T, 'Emerging Commons' (2008) 17 *Social & Legal Studies* 299.
Holland, S, 'Contested Commodities at both Ends of Life: Buying and Selling Gametes, Embryos, and Body Tissues' (2001) 11 *Kennedy Institute of Ethics Journal* 3.
Home, R, 'Culturally Unsuited to Property Rights?: Colonial Land Laws and African Societies' (2013) 3 *Journal of Law and Society* 40.
Home Office, *Rights Brought Home: The Human Rights Bill*, Cm3782 (London, Home Office, 1987).
Honoré, AM, 'Ownership' in AG Guest (ed), *Oxford Essays in Jurisprudence (First Series)* (Oxford, Clarendon Press, 1961) 107–47.
Hossain, N, Fillaili, R and Lubaale, G, 'Invisible Impacts and Lost Opportunities: Evidence of the Global Recession in Developing Countries' (2010) 18 *Journal of Poverty and Social Justice* 269.
House of Commons Communities and Local Government Committee (2012), *Financing of New Housing Supply*, 11th Report of Session 2010–12, HC 1652.
House of Commons Research Paper 12/61 25 October 2012 on the Growth and Infrastructure Bill.
Howse, R and Teitel, RG, 'Beyond the Divide: The International Covenant on Economic, Social and Political Rights and the World Trade Organization' in S Joseph, D Kinley and J Waincymer (eds), *The World Trade Organization and Human Rights: Interdisciplinary Perspectives* (Cheltenham, Edward Elgar, 2009) 39–68.
Hudec, R, '"Like Product": The Differences in Meaning in GATT Articles I and III' in T Cottier and P Mavroidis (eds), *Regulatory Barriers and the Principle of Non-Discrimination in World Trade Law* (Michigan, University of Michigan Press, 2000) 101–23.
Hudson, A, *New Perspectives on Property Law, Human Rights and the Home* (London, Cavendish Publishing, 2004).
Hugenholtz, PB, 'Limits, Limitations and Exceptions to Copyright under the TRIPS Agreement' in CM Correa (ed), *Research Handbook on the Protection of Intellectual Property under WTO Rules* (Cheltenham, Edward Elgar, 2010) 319–42.
Hughes, J, 'The Philosophy of Intellectual Property' (1988) 77 *Georgetown Law Journal* 287.

—— 'Locke's 1694 Memorandum (and More Incomplete Copyright Historiographies)' (2010) 27 *Cardozo Arts and Entertainment Law Journal* 555.
Hull, G, 'Clearing the Rubbish: Locke, the Waste Proviso, and the Moral Justification of Intellectual Property' (2009) 23 *Public Affairs Quarterly* 67.
Hunt, D, 'Unintended Consequences of Land Rights reform: The Case of the 1998 Uganda Land Act' (2004) 22 *Development Policy Review* 2.
Hunt, L, *Inventing Human Rights. A History* (New York, WW Norton and Company, 2008).
Hunt, M, 'Constitutionalism and the Contractualisation of Government in the United Kingdom' in M Taggart (ed), *The Province of Administrative Law* (Oxford, Hart Publishing, 1997) 21–39.
IMF, *Cameroon: Poverty Reduction Strategy Paper*, IMF Country Report No 03/249 (Washington DC, IMF, 2003).
—— *Poverty Reduction Strategy Paper -- Growth and Employment Strategy Paper 2010/2020* (IMF Country Report No 10/257, Washington DC, IMF, 2009).
International Financial Services London, *PFI in the UK & PPP in Europe* (London, IFSL Research London, 2008).
Inwood, M, *A Hegel Dictionary* (Oxford, Blackwell, 1992).
Jacobs, K and Manzi, T, 'Investigating the New Landscapes of Welfare: Housing Policy, Politics and the Emerging Research Agenda' (2014) 31 *Housing, Theory and Society* 213.
Jeon, YD and Kim, YY, 'Land Reform, Income Redistribution, and Agricultural Production in Korea' (2000) 48 *Economic Development and Cultural Change* 253.
Johnston, C, 'Tory MP's Family Firm Pulls Out of Hoxton's New Era Estate over Rent Row', *The Guardian*, 13 November 2014.
Joint Committee on Indian Constitutional Reform, *Report of the Joint Committee on Indian Constitutional Reform* (1934).
Jones, C, 'Private Investment in Rented Housing and the Role of REITS' (2007) 7 *European Journal of Housing Policy* 383.
Kahale, Ö, 'Project Finance and the Relevant Human Rights' in S Leader and D Ong (eds) *Global Project Finance, Human Rights and Sustainable Development* (Cambridge, Cambridge University Press, 2011) 37–66.
Kant, I, *Critique of Practical Reason* in *Practical Philosophy*, trans MJ Gregor (Cambridge, Cambridge University Press, 1996).
—— *Groundwork of the Metaphysic of Morals* in *Practical Philosophy*, trans MJ Gregor (Cambridge, Cambridge University Press, 1996) .
—— *The Metaphysics of Morals*, ed M Gregor, int R J Sullivan, (Cambridge, Cambridge University Press, 1996).
Kapstein, EB, 'Land and Rebellion: Lessons for Counter-insurgency' (2014) 56 *Survival: Global Politics and Strategy* 109.
Katz, L, 'Exclusion and Exclusivity in Property Law' (2008) 58 *University of Toronto Law Journal* 275.
Kennedy, D, 'Some Caution about Property Rights as a Recipe for Economic Development' (2011) 1 (1) *Accounting, Economics, and Law* 1.
Kinderman, D, '"Free Us up so We Can Be Responsible!" The Co-Evolution of Corporate Social Responsibility and Neo-Liberalism in the UK, 1977–2010' (2012) 10 *Socio-Economic Review* 29.

King, B and Pearce, N, 'The Contentiousness of Markets: Politics, Social Movements, and Institutional Change in Markets' (2010) 36 *Annual Review of Sociology* 249.
Kisliuk, M, 'Performance and Modernity Among BaAka Pygmies: A Closer Look at the Egalitarian Foragers in The Rain Forest' in B Diamond and P Moisala (eds), *Music and Gender* (Urbana, University of Illinois Press, 2000) 25–46.
Kitson, M, Martin, R and Tyler, P, 'The Geographies of Austerity' (2011) 4 *Cambridge Journal of Regions, Economy and Society* 289.
Kitz, V, 'The New Free for Education Licence in Australia' (2005) 36 *International Review of Industrial Property and Copyright Law* 555.
Kiwanuka, RN, 'The Meaning of "People" in the African Charter on Human and Peoples' Rights'(1988) 82 *American Journal of International Law* 80.
Kleyn, D, 'The Constitutional Protection of Property: A Comparison Between the German and the South African Approach'(1996) 11 *SA Public Law* 402.
Kohli, A, 'State and Redistributive Development in India' in R Nagaraj (ed), *Growth, Inequality and Social Development in India: Is Inclusive Growth Possible?* (Basingstoke, Palgrave Macmillan, 2012) 194–226.
Koivurova, T, 'Jurisprudence of the European Court of Human Rights Regarding Indigenous Peoples: Retrospect and Prospects' (2011) 18 *International Journal on Minority and Group Rights* 1.
Koo, AYC, *The Role of Land Reform in Economic Development: A Cast Study of Taiwan* (New York, Praeger, 1968).
Krause, C and Alfreðsson, G, 'Article 17' in GS Alfreðsson and A Eide (eds), *The Universal Declaration of Human Rights: A Common Standard of Achievement* (The Hague, Martinus Nijhoff Publishers, 1999) 359–78.
Krippner, G, 'The Financialization of the American Economy' (2005) 3 *Socio-Economic Review* 173.
Künnemann, R and Suárez, S, 'International Human Rights and Governing Land Grabbing: A View from Global Civil Society' (2013) 10 *Globalizations* 123.
Krugman, P, 'Inequality and Redistribution' in N Serra and JE Stiglitz (eds), *The Washington Consensus Reconsidered: Towards a New Global Governance* (Oxford, Oxford University Press, 2008) 32–41.
Kur, A, 'Of Oceans, Islands, and Inland Water—How Much Room for Exceptions and Limitations under the Three-Step Test' (2009) 8 *Richmond Journal of Global Law & Business* 288.
Kwak, Y, Chih, Y and Ibbs, C, 'Towards a Comprehensive Understanding of Public Private Partnerships for Infrastructure' (2009) 51 *California Management Review* 51.
Kymlicka, W, 'Beyond the Indigenous/Minority Dichotomy?' in S Allen and A Xanthaki (eds), *Reflections on the UN Declaration on the Rights of Indigenous Peoples* (Oxford, Hart Publishing, 2011) 132–38.
——, *Multicultural Citizenship* (Oxford, Clarendon, 1995).
Kysar, DA, 'Preferences for Processes: The Process/Product Distinction and the Regulation of Consumer Choice' (2005) 118 *Harvard Law Review* 525.
Law, DS, 'Globalization and the Future of Constitutional Rights' (2007) 102 *Northwestern University Law Review* 1277.
—— and Versteeg, M, 'The Evolution and Ideology of Global Constitutionalism' (2011) 99 *California Law Review* 1163.

Lawson, RA and Schermers, HG, *Leading Cases of the European Court of Human Rights*, (Nijmegen, Ars Aequi Libri, 1997).
Lee, J and Garikipati, S, 'Negotiating the Non-negotiable: British Foraging Law in Theory and Practice' (2011) *Journal of Environmental Law* 415.
Lehavi, A, *The Construction of Property: Norms, Institutions, Challenges* (Cambridge, Cambridge University Press, 2013).
Lenzerini, F, *The Culturalization of Human Rights Law* (Oxford, Oxford University Press, 2014).
Leyshon, A and Thrift, N 'The Capitalization of Almost Everything: The Future of Finance and Capitalism' (2007) 24 *Theory Culture and Society* 97.
Likosky, M, 'Mitigating Human Rights Risks Under State-Financed and Privatized Infrastructure Projects' (2003) 10 *Indiana Journal of Global Legal Studies* 65.
—— *Law, Infrastructure and Human Rights* (Cambridge, Cambridge University Press, 2006).
Lim, H and Bottomley, A (eds), *Feminist Perspectives on Land Law* (Abingdon, Routledge-Cavendish, 2007).
Linarelli, J (ed), *Research Handbook on Global Justice and International Economic Law* (Cheltenham, Edward Elgar, 2013).
Lippert-Rasmussen, K, 'Against Selfownership: There Are No Fact-Insensitive Ownership Rights over One's Body' (2008) 36 *Philosophy and Public Affairs* 86.
Lipton, M, *Land Reform in Developing Countries: Property Rights and Property Wrongs* (Oxford, Routledge, 2009).
Little, PD, Behnke, R; McPeak, J and Gebru, G, *Pastoral Economic Growth and Development Policy Assessment, Ethiopia (Reports 1–4)* (Future Agricultures, 2010).
Locke, J, *Two Treatises of Government*, ed Peter Laslett (Cambridge, Cambridge University Press, 1988).
—— *Some Thoughts Concerning Education and Of the Conduct of the Understanding* (London, Hackett Publishing, 1996).
—— *Political Essays* (Cambridge, Cambridge University Press, 1997).
Low, DA, 'Congress and Mass Contacts, 1936–37: Ideology, Interests, and Conflict over the Basis of Party Representation' in R Sisson and S Wolpert (eds), *Congress and Indian Nationalism: The Pre-Independence Phase* (Berkeley, University California Press, 1988) 134–58.
Macmillan, F, 'Altering the Contours of the Public Domain' in C Waelde and H MacQueen (eds), *Intellectual Property: The Many Faces of the Public Domain* (Cheltenham, Edward Elgar, 2007) 98–117.
—— 'The UNESCO Convention as a New Incentive to Protect Cultural Diversity' in H Schneider and P van den Bossche (eds), *Protection of Cultural Diversity from a European and International Perspective* (Mortsel, Intersentia, 2008) 163–92.
—— 'Human Rights, Cultural Property and Intellectual Property: Three Concepts in Search of a Relationship' in C Graber and M Nenova (eds), *Intellectual Property and Traditional Cultural Expressions in a Digital Environment* (Cheltenham, Edward Elgar, 2008) 73–95.
—— 'Is Copyright Blind to the Visual?' (2008) 7 *Visual Communication* 97.

—— 'The World Trade Organization and the Turbulent Legacy of International Economic Law-making in the Long Twentieth Century' in J Faundez and C Tan (eds), *International Law, Economic Globalization and Developing Countries* (Cheltenham, Edward Elgar, 2010) 158–79.

—— 'Many Analogies, Some Metaphors, Little Imagination: The Public Domain in Intellectual Space' (2010) *Pòlemos* 25.

—— 'The Protection of Cultural Heritage: Common Heritage of Humankind, National Cultural "Patrimony" or Private Property?' (2013) 64 *Northern Ireland Legal Quarterly* 351.

—— 'Arts Festivals: Property, Heritage or More?' in K Bowrey and M Handler (eds), *Law & Creativity in the Age of the Entertainment Franchise* (Cambridge, Cambridge University Press, 2014) 197–215.

—— 'Arts Festivals as Cultural Heritage in a Copyright Saturated World' in H Porsdam (ed), *Copyrighting Creativity: Creative Values, Cultural Heritage Institutions and Systems of Intellectual Property* (Farnham, Ashgate, forthcoming).

Macpherson, CB, *The Political Theory of Possessive Individualism* (Oxford, Clarendon Press, 1962).

—— 'Capitalism and the Changing Concept of Property' in E Kamenka and RS Neale (eds), *Feudalism, Capitalism and Beyond* (London, Edward Arnold, 1975) 105–24.

—— *Property, Mainstream and Critical Positions* (Oxford, Basil Blackwell, 1978).

Malbon, J, Lawson, C and Davison, M, *The WTO Agreement on Trade-Related Aspects of Intellectual Property Rights* (Cheltenham, Edward Elgar, 2014).

Malloy, RP and Diamond, M (eds), *The Public Nature of Private Property* (Surrey, Ashgate Publishing, 2011).

Malpass, P, 'The Wobbly Pillar? Housing and the British Postwar Welfare State' (2003) 32 *Journal of Social Policy* 589.

Maneschi, A, 'International Trade Theory and Comparative Advantage' in J Linarelli (ed), *Research Handbook on Global Justice and International Economic Law* (Cheltenham, Edward Elgar, 2013) 278–88.

Manzi, T, 'Cultural Theory and the Dynamics of Organizational Change: The Response of Housing Association in London to the Housing Act 1988' (2006) 24 *Housing, Theory and Society* 251.

Maran, R, 'The Universal Declaration of Human Rights at 40' (1989) 16 *Social Justice* 146.

Marceau, G, 'WTO Dispute Settlement and Human Rights' (2002) 13 *Journal Européen de Droit International* 753.

Marella MR (ed), *Oltre il Pubblico e il Privato. Per un Diritto dei Beni Comuni* (Verona, Ombre Corte, 2012).

Martin, ALA, 'Philippine Land Reform Cycles: Perpetuating US Colonial Policy' (1999) 47 *Philippine Studies* 181.

Mbakogu, IA, 'Is There Really a Relationship Between Culture and Development?' (2004) 6 *Anthropologist* 37.

McCorquodale, R (2009) 'Corporate Social Responsibility and International Human Rights Law' (2009) 87 *Journal of Business Ethics* 391.

—— 'Group Rights' in D Moeckli, S Shah and S Sivakumaran (eds), *International Human Rights Law* 2nd edn (Oxford, Oxford University Press, 2014) 333–58.

McDonald, M, 'Should Communities have Rights? Reflections on Liberal Individualism' (1991) 4 *Canadian Journal of Law & Jurisprudence* 215.
McKean, MA, 'Management of Traditional Common Lands (*Iriaichi*) in Japan' in DW Bromley (ed), *Making the Commons Work: Theory, Practice, and Policy* (San Francisco, Institute for Contemporary Studies, 1992) 63–98.
McRae, D, 'Article XX and the WTO Appellate Body' in M Bronkers and R Quick (eds), *New Directions in International Economic Law: Essays in Honour of John H Jackson* (The Hague, Kluwer Law International, 2000) 217–36.
Mehta, US, 'Constitutionalism' in NG Jayal and PB Mehta (eds), *The Oxford Companion to Politics in India* (Oxford, Oxford University Press, 2010) 15–27.
Melish, T, 'Putting "Human Rights" Back into the UN Guiding Principles on Business and Human Rights: Shifting Frames and Embedding Participation Rights' in C Rodriguez-Garavito (ed), *Business and Human Rights: Beyond the End of the Beginning* (Netherlands, Brill, 2015 forthcoming).
—— and Meidinger, E, 'Protect, Respect, Remedy *and Participate*: "New Governance" Lessons for the Ruggie Framework' in Radu Mares (ed), *The UN Guiding Principles on Business and Human Rights* (Leiden: Martinus Nijhoff, 2012) 303–36.
Melone, S, *La Parenté et la Terre dans la Stratégie du Développement, l'Expérience Camerounaise: Etude Critique* (Paris, Klincksieck, 1972).
Merges, RP, *Justifying Intellectual Property* (Cambridge, Harvard University Press, 2011).
Merillat, HCL, 'The Indian Constitution: Property Rights and Social Reform' (1960) 21 *Ohio State Law Journal* 616.
—— *Land and the Constitution in India* (New York, Columbia University Press, 1970).
Merrill, T, 'The Property Prism' (2011) 8 *Economics Journal Watch* 247.
Mertens, B et al, *Interactive Forestry Atlas of Cameroon (version 2.0): An Overview* (A World Resources Institute Report Prepared in Collaboration with the Cameroon Ministry of Forestry and Wildlife Washington, DC 2007).
Meyer, K, Mudambi, R and Narula, R, 'Multinational Enterprises and Local Contexts: The Opportunities and Challenges of Multiple Embeddedness' (2011) 48 *Journal of Management Studies* 235.
Mezey, N, 'The Paradoxes of Cultural Property' (2007) 107 *Columbia Law Review* 2004.
Miles, MM, *Art as Plunder: The Ancient Origins of Debate about Cultural Property* (New York, Cambridge University Press, 2010).
Miller, DLC and Pope, A, *Land Title in South Africa* (Cape Town, Juta & Co, 2000).
MINEPAT, *Cameroon Vision 2035—Working Paper* (Yaounde, 2009).
Misiedjan, D and Gupta, J, 'Indigenous Communities: Analyzing Their Right to Water under Different International Legal Regimes' (2014) 10 *Utrecht Law Review* 77.
Montague, A, *Review of the Barriers to Institutional Investment in Private Rented Homes* (London, Department for Communities and Local Government, 2012).
Montgomerie, J, and Budenbender, M, 'Round the Houses: Homeownership and Failures of Asset-Based Welfare in the United Kingdom' (2015) 20 *New Political Economy* 386.

Moore, A, 'A Lockean Theory of Intellectual Property Revisited' (2012) 49 *San Diego Law Review* 1069.
Morris-Jones, WH, 'India Elects for Change—and Stability' (1971) 11 *Asian Survey* 719.
Mossoff, A, 'Locke's Labor Lost' (2002) 9 *University of Chicago Law School Roundtable* 155.
—— 'What Is Property? Putting the Pieces Back Together' (2003) 45 *Arizona Law Review* 371.
—— 'The Use and Abuse of IP at the Birth of the Administrative State' (2009) 157 *University of Pennsylvania Law Review* 2001.
—— 'Saving Locke from Marx: The Labor Theory of Value in Intellectual Property Theory' (2012) 29 *Social Philosophy and Policy* 283.
Mostert, H, *The Constitutional Protection and Regulation of Property and its Influence on the Reform of Private Law and Landownership in South Africa and Germany* (Berlin, Springer, 2002).
Moustafa, T, 'Law versus the State: The Judicialization of Politics in Egypt' (2003) 28 *Law & Social Inquiry* 883.
Moyn, S, *The Last Utopia: Human Rights in History,* reprint edition (Cambridge MA, Harvard University Press, 2012).
Mullins, D and Craig, L, *Testing the Climate: Mergers and Alliances in the Housing Association Sector* (Birmingham, National Housing Federation and University of Birmingham, 2005).
Munzer, S, *A Theory of Property* (Cambridge, Cambridge University Press, 1990).
—— 'An Uneasy Case Against Property Rights in Body Parts' in EF Paul, FD Miller and J Paul (eds), *Property Rights* (New York, Cambridge University Press, 1994) 267.
—— 'Property as Social Relations' in SR Munzer (ed), *New Essays in the Legal and Political Theory of Property* (Cambridge, Cambridge University Press, 2001) 36–75.
—— 'A Bundle Theorist Holds on His Collection of Sticks' (2011) 8 *Economics Journal Watch* 265.
—— 'Property and Disagreement' in J Penner and H Smith (eds), *Philosophical Foundations of Property Law* (Oxford, Oxford University Press, 2013) 289–319.
Naldi, GJ, 'Limitation of Rights under the African Charter on Human and Peoples' Rights: The Contribution of the African Commission on Human and Peoples' Rights' (2001) 17 *South African Journal on Human Rights* 109.
Nathanson, NL, 'Constitutional Adjudication in Japan' (1958) 7 *American Journal of Criminal Law* 195.
National Audit Office, *Financing PFI Projects in the Credit Crisis and the Treasury's Response* (London, NAO, 2010).
—— *PFI in Housing* (London, NAO, 2010).
—— *Lessons from PFI and Other Projects* (London, NAO, 2011).
Nesvetailova, A, 'Innovations, Fragility and Complexity: Understanding the Power of Finance' (2014) 49 *Government and Opposition* 542.
Newman, DW, *Community and Collective Rights: A Theoretical Framework for Rights Held by Groups* (Oxford, Hart Publishing, 2011).
Ngombe, LY, *Le Droit d'Auteur En Afrique* (Paris, L'Harmattan, 2004).

Ngwasiri, CN, 'The Impacts of the Present Land Tenure Reforms in Cameroon' (1984) Editions Clé *Cameroon Law Review* 73.
—— and Nje, YN, *Advocacy for Separate Land Legislation for the Rural Areas of Cameroon* (Yaounde, A PVO-NGO/NRM Cameroon, 1995).
Nickel, JW, *Making Sense of Human Rights: Philosophical Reflections on the Universal Declaration of Human Rights* (California, University of California Press, 1987).
Njoh, AJ, 'The Political Economy of Urban Land Reforms in a Post-Colonial State' (1998) 22 *International Journal of Urban and Regional Research* 408.
—— 'Indigenous Peoples and Ancestral Lands: Implications of the *Bakweri* Case in Cameroon' in R Home (ed), *Essays in African Land Law* (Pretoria, Pretoria University Law Press, 2011) 69–90.
—— 'Equity, Fairness and Justice Implications of Land Tenure Formalization in Cameroon' (2013) 37 *International Journal of Urban and Regional Research* 750.
Nozick, R, *Anarchy, State and Utopia* (Oxford, Blackwell, 1977).
Oakland Institute, *Understanding Land Transfer Deals in Africa: Country Report, Ethiopia* (2011).
O'Faircheallaigh, C, 'Resource Exploitation and Indigenous People: Towards a General Analytical Framework' in P Jull and S Roberts (eds), *The Challenge of Northern Regions* (North Australia Research Unit, Northern Territory Australian National University, 1991) 228–71.
Offer, A, *Property and Politics, 1870-1914: Landownership, Law, Ideology, and Urban Development in England* (Cambridge University Press, 1981).
Ohenjo, N et al, 'Health of Indigenous People in Africa' (2006) 367 *The Lancet* 1937.
Okediji, R, 'Toward an International Fair Use Doctrine' (2001) 39 *Columbia Journal of Transnational Law* 75.
Okin, SM, *Justice, Gender and the Family* (New York, Basic Books, 1989).
Olasunkanmi, A, 'Development in Africa: The Need for a Culture-Sensitive Approach' (2011) 2 *Journal of Sociology and Social Anthropology* 97.
Oliver, D and Fedtke, J (eds) *Human Rights and the Private Sphere: A Comparative Study* (London, Routledge, 2007).
Olivecrona, K, 'Locke's Theory of Appropriation' (1974) 24 *Philosophical Quarterly* 220.
Olsson, PH, 'Every Natural or Legal Person Is Entitled to the Peaceful Enjoyment of His or Her Possessions: Article 1, Protocol 1 to the European Convention on Human Rights' in F Dorssemont, K Lörcher, and I Schömann (eds), *European Convention on Human Rights and the Employment Relation* (Oxford, Hart Publishing, 2013) 381–416.
O'Neill, P, 'The Financialization of Infrastructure: the Role of Categorization and Property Relations' (2013) 6 *Cambridge Journal of Regions, Economy and Society* 441.
Ostrom, E, *Governing the Commons: The Evolution of Institutions for Collective Action* (Cambridge, Cambridge University Press, 1990).
——, Dietz, T, Dolšak, N, Stern, PC, Stonich, S and Weber EU (eds), *The Drama of the Commons* (Washington DC, National Academy Press, 2002).
Otsuka, M, *Libertarianism without Foundations* (Oxford, Oxford University Press, 2003).

—— 'Why Left-Libertarianism Is Not Incoherent, Indeterminate, or Irrelevant: A Reply to Fried' (2005) 33 *Philosophy and Public Affairs* 201.

Oyono, PR, 'From Diversity to Exclusion for Forest Minorities in Cameroon' in CJP Colfer (ed), *The Equitable Forest: Diversity, Community, and Resource Management* (Washington DC, RFF Press, 2005) 69–90.

Packer, I, *Lloyd George, Liberalism and the Land: The Land Issue and Party Politics in England, 1906–1914* (Royal Historical Society Studies in History New Series, 2001).

Palmer, T, 'Are Patents and Copyrights Morally Justified? The Philosophy of Property Rights and Ideal Objects' in A Mossoff (ed), *Intellectual Property and Property Rights* (Cheltenham, Edward Elgar, 2013).

Pardhan, P, 'Irrigation and Cooperation: An Empirical Analysis of 48 Irrigation Communities in South India' (2000) 48 *Economic Development and Cultural Change* 847.

Pateman, C, *The Sexual Contract* (New York, Polity Press, 1986).

Pauwelyn, J, *Conflict of Norms in Public International Law: How WTO Law Relates to Other Rules of International Law* (Cambridge, Cambridge University Press, 2003).

Pawson, H, 'Restructuring England's Social Housing Sector since 1989: Undermining or Underpinning the Fundamentals of Public Housing?' (2006) 21 *Housing Studies* 767.

—— et al, *Investigation of Rent Arrears Management Practices in the Housing Association Sector* (London, HCA, 2010).

—— and Mullins, D, *After Council Housing: Britain's New Social Landlords* (Basingstoke, Palgrave MacMillan, 2010).

—— and Milligan, V, 'New Dawn or Chimera? Can Institutional Financing Transform Rental Housing?' (2013) 13 *International Journal of Housing Policy* 335.

Peck, J and Tickell, A, 'Neoliberalising Space' (2002) 34 *Antipode* 380.

Penner, JE, 'The Bundle of Rights Picture of Property' (1995–96) 43 *UCLA Law Review* 711.

—— *The Idea of Property in the Law* (Oxford, Oxford University Press, 1997).

—— 'The Concept of Property and the Concept of Slavery' in J Allain (ed), *The Legal Understanding of Slavery: From the Historical to the Contemporary* (Oxford, Oxford University Press, 2012) 242–52.

—— and Smith, HE (eds), *Philosophical Foundations of Property Law* (Oxford, Oxford University Press, 2013).

Phillips, A, *Our Bodies, Whose Property* (New York, Princeton University Press, 2013).

Picciotto, S, 'Copyright Licensing: The Case of Higher Education Photocopying in the United Kingdom' (2002) 24 *European Intellectual Property Review* 438.

Platt, RH, *Land Use and Society: Geography, Law, and Public Policy* (Washington DC, Island Press, 2004).

Pollitt, C, 'Cuts and Reforms—Public Services as We Move into a New Era' (2010) 32 *Society and Economy* 17.

Posner, EA, 'The International Protection of Cultural Property: Some Skeptical Observations' (2007) 8 *Chicago Journal of International Law* 213.

Posner, RA, 'When Is Parody Fair Use?' (1992) 21 *Journal of Legal Studies* 67.

Pottage, A and Mundy, M (eds), *Law, Anthropology, and the Constitution of the Social: Making Persons and Things* (Cambridge, New York, Cambridge University Press, 2004).

Pritchard, R, 'Privatisation and Private Provision of Infrastructure' in R Pritchard (ed) *Economic Development, Foreign Investment and the Law* (London, Kluwer Law and International Bar Association, 1996) 76–92.

—— (ed), *Economic Development, Foreign Investment and the Law* (London, Kluwer Law and International Bar Association, 1996).

Prott, LV and O'Keefe, PJ, '"Cultural Heritage" or "Cultural Property"' (1992) 1 *International Journal of Cultural Property* 307.

Prouzet, M, 'L'Expropriation Pour le Cause d'Utilisé Publique au Cameroun' (1972) 1 *Cameroon Law Review* 27.

Putzel, J, *A Captive Land: The Politics of Agrarian Reform in the Philippines* (London, Catholic Institute for International Relations, 1992).

Quimpo, NG, 'The Limits of Post-Plunder Reform in the Philippines' Oligarchic Democracy' in ESK Fung and S Drakeley (eds), *Democracy in Eastern Asia: Issues, Problems and Challenges in a Region of Diversity* (Abingdon, Routledge, 2013) 119–37.

Rabel, E, 'A Draft of an International Law of Sales' (1937–38) 5 *University of Chicago Law Review* 543.

—— 'The Hague Conference on the Unification of Sales Law' (1952) 1 *American Journal of Criminal Law* 58.

Radcliffe, SA (ed), *Culture and Development in a Globalising World: Geographies, Actors, and Paradigms* (London, Routledge, 2006).

—— and Laurie, N, 'Culture and Development: Taking Culture Seriously in Development for Andean Indigenous People' (2006) 24 *Environment and Planning D: Society and Space* 231.

Radin, MJ, 'Property & Personhood' (1982) 34 *Stanford Law Review* 957.

—— *Contested Commodities* (Cambridge MA, Harvard University Press, 1996).

Rafat, A, 'Compensation for Expropriated Property in Recent International Law' (1969) 14 *Villanova Law Review* 1.

Rahmato, D, 'Land Rights and Tenure Security: Rural Land Registration in Ethiopia' in JM Ubink, AJ Hoekema and WJ Assies (eds), *Legalising Land Rights: Local Practices, State Responses and Tenure Security in Africa, Asia and Latin America* (Leiden, Leiden University Press, 2009) 59–95.

Rawls, J, *A Theory of Justice* (Cambridge MA, Harvard University Press, 1999).

Réaume, D, 'Individuals, Groups, and Rights to Public Goods' (1988) 38 *University of Toronto Law Journal* 1.

Redford, KH and Adams, WM, 'Payment for Ecosystem Services and the Challenge of Saving Nature' (2009) 23 *Conservation Biology* 785.

Reid, CT, 'Between Priceless and Worthless: Challenges in Using Market Mechanisms for Conserving Biodiversity' (2013) 2 *Transnational Environmental Law* 217.

Report of the UN Special Rapporteur on the Right to Food, J Ziegler, A/56/210, 23 July 2001.

Rhodes, R, *Understanding Governance: Policy Networks, Governance, Reflexivity and Accountability* (Buckingham, Open University Press, 1997).

Ricardo, D, *Principles of Political Economy* (London, John Murray, 1817).

Rich, R, 'The Right to Development: A Right of Peoples' in J Crawford (ed), *The Rights of Peoples* (Oxford, University of Oxford Press, 1988) 39–55.
Riedinger, JM, *Agrarian Reform in the Philippines: Democratic Transitions and Redistributive Reform* (Stanford, Stanford University Press, 1995).
Rifkin, J, *The Age of Access: The New Culture of Hypercapitalism, Where All of Life is a Paid-for Experience* (New York, JP Tarcher/Putnam, 2000).
Ritter, J, 'Personne et propieté selon Hegel' (1968) 31 *Archives de Philosophie* 179.
Rogowski, R, *Reflexive Labour Law in the World* (Cheltenham, Edward Elgar, 2013).
Rook, D, *Property Law and Human Rights* (London, Blackstone, 2001).
Rosas, A, 'Property Rights' in A Rosas, J E Helgesen and D Goodman (eds), *The Strength of Diversity: Human Rights and Pluralist Democracy* (Dordrecht, Martinus Nijhoff, 1992) 133–58.
Rousseau, JJ, *Emile or on Education*, ed, trans and notes A Bloom(New York, Basic Books, 1979).
Skoot, R, *The Immortal Life of Henrietta Lacks* (New York, Crown Publishers, 2010).
Rowan-Robinson, J and Ross, A, 'Compensation for Environmental Protection in Britain: The Legislative Lottery' (1993) 5 *Journal of Environmental Law* 245.
Rugg, J and Rhodes, D, *The Private Rented Sector: Its Contribution and Potential* (York, Centre for Housing Policy, 2008).
Ruggie, J, 'Global Governance and "New Governance Theory": Lessons from Business and Human Rights' (2014) 20 *Global Governance* 5.
Rugman, A, 'How Global are TNCs from Emerging Markets' in K Sauvant (ed), *The Rise of Transnational Corporations from Emerging Markets* (Cheltenham, Edward Elgar, 2008) 86–106.
Ruhl, JB, Kraft, SE and Lant, CL, *Law and Policy of Ecosystem Services* (Washington DC, Island Press, 2007).
Salzman, J, 'Creating Markets for Ecosystem Services: Notes from the Field' (2005) 80 *NYU Law Review* 870.
Sassen, S, 'Global Finance and its Institutional Spaces' in K Knorr Cetina and A Preda (eds), *The Oxford Handbook of the Sociology of Finance* (Oxford, Oxford University Press, 2013) 13–32.
Sawchenko, A, 'Choosing a Mechanism for Land Redistribution in the Philippines' (2000) 9 *Pacific Rim Law & Policy Journal* 681.
Scanlon, K and Whitehead, C, *The Profile and Intentions of Buy-to-Let Investors* (London, CML, 2005).
Schefer, KN, *International Investment Law: Text, Cases and Materials* (Oxford, Hart Publishing, 2013).
Scolnicov, A, 'Lifelike and Lifeless in Law: Do Corporations Have Human Rights?' *University of Cambridge Legal Studies Research Paper No 13*, 2013.
Scott, RJ, 'Under Color of Law: *Siliadin v France* and the Dynamics of Enslavement in Historical Perspective' in J Allain (ed), *The Legal Understanding of Slavery: From the Historical to the Contemporary* (Oxford, Oxford University Press, 2012) 152–64.
Sen, AK, *Development as Freedom* (Oxford, Oxford University Press, 1999).
Senftleben, MRF, *Copyright, Limitations, and the Three-Step Test: An Analysis of the Three-Step Test in International and EC Copyright Law* (The Hague, Kluwer Law International, 2004).

Serino, G, *The Bilateral Disputes between Museums & States of Origin for the Recovery of Cultural Objects, Artistic Creations & Indigenous Heritage* (PhD thesis, Università Roma Tre, 2014).
Seuba, X, 'Mainstreaming the TRIPS and Human Rights Interactions', in CM Correa (ed) *Research Handbook on the Protection of Intellectual Property under WTO rules* (Cheltenham, Edward Elgar, 2010) 192–215.
Shabalala, D, 'Knowledge and Education: Pro-Access Implications of New Technologies', in T Wong and G Dutfield (eds), *Intellectual Property and Human Development: Current Trends and Future Scenarios* (Cambridge, Cambridge University Press, 2010) 250–78.
Shamir, R, 'The Age of Responibilization: on Market-Embedded Morality' (2008) 37 *Economy and Society* 1.
Sheehan, J, 'Towards Compensation for the Compulsory Acquisition of Native Title Rights and Interests in Australia' (Paper presented at the FAO/USP/RICS Foundation South Pacific Land Tenure Conflict Symposium, University of the South Pacific, Suva, Fiji 10–12 April 2002).
—— and Small, G, 'Biota and the Problem of Property' (2005) 22 *Environmental and Planning Law Journal* 158.
Sheffer, M, 'Bilateral Investment Treaties: A Friend or Foe to Human Rights' (2011) 39 *Denver Journal of International Law and Policy* 483.
Shvidenko, A, Barber, CV and Per, R, 'Forest and Woodland Systems' in R Hassan, R Scholes and N Ash (eds), *Ecosystems and Human Well-Being: Current State and Trends: Findings of the Condition and Trends Working Group*, vol 1 (Washington, DC, Island Press, 2005) 587–621.
Simpson, MD, *Making Representations: Museums in the Post-Colonial Era* (London, Routledge, 2001).
Singer, NJ, 'Islamic Law and the Development of the Ethiopian Legal System' (1971) *Howard Law Journal* 17.
Singer, JW, *Entitlement: The Paradoxes of Property* (New Haven, Yale University Press, 2000).
Smith, A, *The Wealth of Nations* (London, W Strahan and T Cadell, 1776).
Smith, AM, 'Making Itself a Home—Understanding Foreign Law in Domestic Jurisprudence: The Indian Case' (2006) 24 *Berkeley Journal of International Law* 218.
Snider, L, 'Interrogating the Algorithm: Debt, Derivatives and the Social Reconstruction of Stock Market Trading' (2014) 40 *Critical Sociology* 747.
Snyder, F, *Global Economic Networks and Global Legal Pluralism* (Florence, European University Institute, 1999).
—— *The EU, the WTO and China: Legal Pluralism and International Trade Regulation* (Oxford, Hart Publishing, 2010).
Soederberg, S, 'Taming Corporations or Buttressing Market-Led Development? A Critical Assessment of the Global Compact' (2007) 4 *Globalizations* 500.
Sprankling, JG, *The International Law of Property* (Oxford, Oxford University Press, 2014).
Sténs, A and Sandström, C, 'Divergent Interests and Ideas around Property Rights: The Case of Berry Harvesting in Sweden' (2012) *Forest Policy and Economics* 56.
Stevenson, GG, *Common Property Economics: A General Theory and Land Use Applications* (Cambridge, Cambridge University Press 1991).

Stothart, C, 'Landlord's PRS Subsidiary to Manage Manchester Homes' *Inside Housing*, 11 December 2013.
Strathern, M, *Property, Substance* and *Effect: Anthropological Essays on Persons* and *Things* (London, Athlone Press, 1999).
Strauss, K, 'Financialisation and Gendered Risk in Occupational Pensions' in G Clark, A Dixon and A Monk (eds), *Managing Financial Risks: from Global to Local* (Oxford, Oxford University Press, 2009) 258–79.
Suzuki, T, 'Custom and Legal Theory of *Iriai* in Japan' in T Murota and K Takeshita (eds), *Local Commons and Democratic Environmental Governance* (Tokyo, United Nations University Press, 2013) 69–86.
Tai, HC, *Land Reform and Politics: A Comparative Analysis* (London, University of California Press, 1974).
Tavani, H, 'Locke, Intellectual Property Rights, and the Information Commons' (2005) 7 *Ethics and Information Technology* 87.
Taylor C, *Sources of the Self: The Making of Modern Identity* (Cambridge, Cambridge University Press, 1989).
Terblanche, NS, 'The Challenges to Valuers with Regard to Compensation for Expropriation and Restitution in South African Statutes' (PRRES Tenth Annual Conference, Bangkok, Thailand, 25–28 January 2004).
The Economics of Ecosystems and Biodiversity (TEEB), *The Economics of Ecosystems and Biodiversity: Mainstreaming the Economics of Nature: A Synthesis of the Approach, Conclusions and Recommendations of TEEB* (2010).
The Law Commission, 'Towards a Compulsory Purchase Code: (1) Compensation, An Overview', Consultation Paper (2004), No 165 (Overview).
The Scottish Government, *Applying an Ecosystems Approach to Land Use: Information Note* (Edinburgh, The Scottish Government, 2011).
The World Bank and International Food Policy Research Institute, *Gender and Governance in Rural Services: Insights from India, Ghana and Ethiopia* (Washington, World Bank, 2010).
The World Bank, *Federal Democratic Republic of Ethiopia-Options for Strengthening Land Administration* (Washington, World Bank, 2012).
—— *World Development Report 2012: Gender equality and development* (Washington, World Bank, 2012).
Thornberry, F and Viljoen, F, *Overview Report on the Constitutional and Legislative Protection of the Rights of Indigenous Peoples in 24 African Countries* (International Labour Organisation and the African Commission on Human and Peoples Rights, 2009).
Tjouen, AD, *Droits Domaniaux et Techniques Foncières en Droit Camerounais: étude D'une Réforme Législative* (Paris, Economica, 1982).
Tomuschat, C, *Human Rights: Between Idealism and Realism 2nd edn* (Oxford, Oxford University Press, 2008).
Torrance, M, 'The Rise of a Global Infrastructure Market through Relational Investing' (2009) 85 *Economic Geography* 75.
HM Treasury, *Partnerships for Prosperity: the Private Finance Initiative* (London, Treasury Taskforce Private Finance Policy Team, 1997).
Trebilcock, MJ, *The Limits of Freedom of Contract* (Cambridge, Harvard University Press, 1997).

Tully, J, *A Discourse on Property. John Locke and His Adversaries* (New York, Cambridge University Press, 1980).
Tushnet, M, 'The Inevitable Globalization of Constitutional Law' (2009) 49 *Virginia Journal of International Law* 985.
UK National Ecosystem Assessment, *The UK National Ecosystem Assessment: Synthesis of the Key Findings* (Cambridge, UNEP-WCMC, 2011).
Unger, RM, *Democracy Realized: The Progressive Alternative* (London, New York, Verso, 1998).
Valcke, C, 'Locke on Property: A Deontological Interpretation' (1989) 12 *Harvard Journal of Law and Public Policy* 941.
Vallentyne, P, Steiner, H and Otsuka, M, 'Why Left- Libertarianism' (2005) 33 *Philosophy and Public Affairs* 201.
van Banning, TRG, *The Human Right to Property* (Oxford, Intersentia, 2002).
van Boven, T (1989) 'Can Human Rights Have a Separate Existence from Peoples' Rights?' 16 *Social Justice* 12.
—— 'Categories of Rights' in D Moeckli, S Shah and S Sivakumaran (eds), *International Human Rights Law* 2nd edn (Oxford, Oxford University Press, 2014) 143–56.
van Gils, H, Siegl, G and Bennett, RM, 'The Living Commons of West Tyrol, Austria: Lessons for Land Policy and Land Administration' (2014) 38 *Land Use Policy* 16.
Vogel, D, 'Private Global Business Regulation' (2008) 11 *The Annual Review of Political Science* 261.
Vrdoljak, AF, *International Law, Museums and the Return of Cultural Objects* (Cambridge, Cambridge University Press, 2008).
Wagner, RP, 'Information Wants to Be Free: Intellectual Property and the Mythologies of Control' (2003) 103 *Columbia Law Review* 995.
Wainwright, T, 'Laying the Foundations for a Crisis: Mapping the Historic-Geographical Construction of Residential Mortgage Backed Securitization in the UK' (2009) 33 *International Journal of Urban and Regional Research* 372.
Waldron, J, *The Right to Private Property* (Oxford, Clarendon Press, 1988).
—— 'From Authors to Copiers: Individual Rights and Social Values in Intellectual Property' (1992) 68 *Chicago-Kent Law Review* 841.
—— 'Can Communal Goods be Human Rights?' in *Liberal Rights: Collected Papers 1981–1991* (Cambridge, Cambridge University Press, 1993) 339–60.
—— *God, Locke and Equality, Christian Foundations in Locke's Political Thought* (Cambridge, Cambridge University Press, 2002).
Watson, EE, 'Culture and Conservation in Post-Conflict Africa: Changing Attitudes and Challenges' in SA Radcliffe (ed), *Culture and Development in a Globalising World: Geographies, Actors, and Paradigms* (London, Routledge, 2006) 58–82.
Weber, M, *The Theory of Social and Economic Organization* (New York, Free Press, 1964).
Weissbrodt, D and Schoff, K, 'The Sub-Commission's Initiative on Human Rights and Intellectual Property' (2004) 22 *Netherlands Quarterly of Human Rights* 181.
Wettstein, F, 'CSR and the Debate on Business and Human Rights: Bridging the Great Divide' (2012) 22 *Business Ethics Quarterly* 739.
Wheeler, s, 'Global Production, CSR and Human Rights: the Courts of Public Opinion and the Social License to Operate' (2015, forthcoming) *The International Journal of Human Rights*.

Williams, J, Martin, P and Stone, C, *Using Ecosystem Services as a Means to Diffuse Political Land Use Decisions in Peri-Urban Regions*, CRC for Irrigation Futures (Armidale, University of New England, 2010).

Williamson, J, 'From Reform Agenda to Damaged Brand Name' (2003) 40 *Finance and Development* 10.

Winkler, IT, *The Human Right to Water: Significance, Legal Status and Implications for Water Allocation* (Oxford, Hart Publishing, 2012).

Wolters, WG, 'The Development of Property Rights to Land in the Philippines, 1850–1930' in T van Meijl and F von Benda-Beckmann (eds), *Property Rights and Economic Development: Land and Resources in Southeast Asia and Oceania* (London and New York, Kegan Paul International, 1999) 110–38.

Wright, G, 'Indigenous People and Customary Land Ownership under Domestic REDD+ Frameworks: A Case Study of Indonesia' (2011) *Law, Environment and Development Journal* 117.

Xu, T, 'Hidden Expropriation in Globalisation and Soft Law Protection of Communal Property Rights' in B Hoops, E Marais, L Verstappen, H Mostert and J Sluysmans (eds), *Context, Criteria and Consequences of Expropriation Law* (The Hague, Boom/Eleven Law Publishers; Cape Town, Juta Law Publishers, 2015 forthcoming).

Yen, ACC, 'Restoring the Natural Law: Copyright as Labor and Possession' (1990) 51 *Ohio State Law Journal* 517.

You, JS, 'Inequality and Corruption: The Role of Land Reform in Korea, Taiwan, and the Philippines' *Annual Conference of the Association for Asian Studies*, Atlanta, Georgia, 3–6 April, 2008.

Yu, PK, 'Cultural Relics, Intellectual Property and Intangible Heritage' (2008) 81 *Temple Law Review* 433.

—— 'EU Economic Partnership Agreements and International Human Rights', in J Drexl, H Ruse-Khan and S Nadde-Phlix (eds), *EU Bilateral Trade Agreements and Intellectual Property: For Better or Worse?* (Berlin, Springer, 2014) 109–32.

Zaloom, C, 'Trading on Numbers' in M Fisher and G Downey (eds), *Frontiers of Capital: Ethnographic Reflections in the New Economy* (Durham, Duke University Press, 2006) 58–85.

Zamir, D, 'Consumer Preferences, Citizen Preferences, and the Provision of Public Goods' (1998) 108 *Yale Law Journal* 377.

Zemer L, 'The Making of a New Copyright Lockean' (2005) 29 *Harvard Journal of Law and Public Policy* 891.

Index

www.ingramcontent.com/pod-product-compliance
Ingram Content Group UK Ltd.
Pitfield, Milton Keynes, MK11 3LW, UK
UKHW020133290926
15471UKWH00003B/462

9 781509 921157